Young Voices

*British Children Remember the
Second World War*

LYN SMITH

In Association with the Imperial War Museum

VIKING
an imprint of
PENGUIN BOOKS

VIKING BOOKS

Published by the Penguin Group
Penguin Books Ltd, 80 Strand, London WC2R ORL, England
Penguin Group (USA) Inc., 375 Hudson Street, New York, New York 10014, USA
Penguin Group (Canada), 90 Eglinton Avenue East, Suite 700, Toronto, Ontario, Canada M4P 2Y3
(a division of Pearson Penguin Canada Inc.)
Penguin Ireland, 25 St Stephen's Green, Dublin 2, Ireland (a division of Penguin Books Ltd)
Penguin Group (Australia), 250 Camberwell Road, Camberwell, Victoria 3124, Australia
(a division of Pearson Australia Group Pty Ltd)
Penguin Books India Pvt Ltd, 11 Community Centre, Panchsheel Park, New Delhi – 110 017, India
Penguin Group (NZ), 67 Apollo Drive, Rosedale, North Shore 0632, New Zealand
(a division of Pearson New Zealand Ltd)
Penguin Books (South Africa) (Pty) Ltd, 24 Sturdee Avenue, Rosebank, Johannesburg 2196, South Africa

Penguin Books Ltd, Registered Offices: 80 Strand, London WC2R ORL, England

www.penguin.com

First published 2007
I

Set in 12/14.75pt Monotype Bembo
by Palimpsest Book Production Limited, Grangemouth, Stirlingshire
Printed in England by Clays Ltd, St Ives plc

A CIP catalogue record for this book is available from the British Library

ISBN: 978-0-670-91593-4

For my dear grand-girls Martha and Iris, with love,
wishing them a more peaceful world

'The whole of the warring nations are engaged,
not only soldiers but the entire population,
men, women and children. The fronts are everywhere.'

Winston Churchill, House of Commons, 20 August 1940

Contents

List of Illustrations

1. Gas drill: a baby is fitted with a specially designed gas mask (D651)
2. Off to safety: the evacuation of East End schoolchildren, 2 September 1939 (HU87925)
3. Evacuees ready for departure from a London railway terminus: for many, the holiday mood soon wore off (FX3129A)
4. Victoria station, London, 2 September 1939: mothers with their babies and young children were among the first evacuees (HU36237)
5. Children try out the newly erected Anderson shelter in their back garden (D778)
6. Dennis Hayden (*right*) with his mother and younger brother (© Dennis Hayden)
7. Evacuee John Starling with his host, Mr Penton, Winchester, Hampshire (© John Starling)
8. Young evacuees from Rotherhithe, all carrying their gas masks, enjoy a walk in Reading, Berkshire (D824)
9. East End children tuck into their meal at an improvised feeding centre in the Gloucestershire village of Chipping Campden (HU 63760/FX14760)
10. Reg Baker (*right*) with his blacksmith host, Mr Dorling, and pal Ronbo (© Reg Baker)
11. Molly Bihet (Finigan), who lived through the German occupation of Guernsey (© Molly Bihet)
12. Parents and friends wave off youngsters during the second wave of evacuation in the summer of 1940 (CP7095)
13. Thurle Folliott Vaughan's (Laver Eriksen) 'official' identity card. These were provided by the Danish authorities throughout the German occupation (© Lady Thurle Folliott Vaughan)

14. Ann Thornton (Helps) lived in Denmark under the German occupation before escaping by sea to Sweden in 1943 (© Ann Thornton)

15. June Knowles (Watkins), the youngest WAAF serving in the Middle East, cuts her birthday cake with the help of the commanding officer (© June Knowles)

16. The Douglas family pose by a shot down Heinkel bomber in Hayes, Middlesex, 1940. The downed plane was used to promote an RAF appeal fund for Battle of Britain widows and their children (MH24171)

17. London carries on: repair squads get to work as auxiliary firemen dowse the flames, September 1940 (D1475)

18. A friendly engine driver greets a group of evacuees at a London station before they travel to safety, April 1941 (PL5137A)

19. Lifeboat No. 12 from SS *City of Benares*, which was picked up by HMS *Anthony* (© Derek Bech)

20. The rescued children on the deck of HMS *Anthony* (© HU54058)

21. The surviving members of the Bech family, with Colin Ryder Richardson, after their return to Glasgow where they were kitted out with new clothes. *Left to right*, Barbara, Marguerite Bech (mother) clutching Derek, Colin Ryder Richardson, Sonia (© Derek Bech)

22. Rodney Giesler and brother Neville ready for their four-mile cycle ride to school, 1943 (© Rodney Giesler)

23. An Oxfordshire village schoolboy displays his National Savings poster to the rest of the class (D3665)

24. London evacuees from Streatham enjoying a very different walk to school in the lovely village of Caio, Carmarthenshire (D1053)

25. A flooded north London air-raid shelter. This mother has tied her two children to the bench to prevent them falling into the water (D1550)

26. The Morrison indoor shelter was available to householders from February 1941. It not only provided shelter for families, but could also be used as a table (D2055)

27. A south-east London air-raid shelter underneath the railway arches. Nine of a family of thirteen share a covering while the four older children rest nearby (D1614)
28. Undaunted, a young Londoner hangs out the flag over his bombed home (D1303)
29. Children enjoy their games among the ruined homes (HU90296)
30. Evacuee Freddie King of Fulham makes friends with a hen (D2224)
31. Three boys in a boat: Rodney Giesler *(left)*, with his friend and brother on the river Tone, near Taunton, 1945 (© Rodney Giesler)
32. Evacuee John Carter helping out on the farm (© John Carter)
33. Pamela Leopard (Brownfield), the proud owner of a new, home-made dolls' pram (© Pamela Leopard)
34. London evacuees searching for trout at Farmers, Carmarthenshire (D1051)
35. Helping the war effort in Balderton, Nottinghamshire. Boy Scouts do their bit by collecting salvage (D21562)
36. Evacuees from Greenwich give the smith a helping hand in Llandissilio, Pembrokeshire (D997)
37. Children at Moorside Road School, Bromley, in south-east London, survey bomb damage to the school premises (D3171)
38. An open-air sewing class in Pembrokeshire for evacuees from Battersea, London (D989)
39. Women's Land Army girls clean a cattle fodder mangel, on a farm at Cannington, Somerset (D208)
40. Jill Monk (Holman), ready for her auxiliary messenger job, on Merry Monarch (© Jill Monk)
41. Donald Swann sunning himself in Greece while on humanitarian service in 1945 with the Friends' Ambulance Unit (© Alison Smith)
42. Ready to tackle that bull! Land Girl Iris Hobby (Cutbush), Farnham, Surrey (© Iris Hobby)
43. Conscientious objector Tony Parker, experiencing the life of a coal miner, Lancashire, 1942 (© Tony Parker)

Unless otherwise credited, all images come from the Imperial War Museum. Image library reference numbers are given in brackets.

Drawings and Documents in the Text

During the war, two schoolboys who lived in Brighton, Guy Barnett and Derek Tongs, produced *The War Weekly*, a series of illustrated newsletters covering war events. These drawings on pages 15, 22, 56, 78, 86, 172, 237, 331 are reproduced by kind permission of the Imperial War Museum (61/19/1) and donor Chris Armstrong. Letters in the text are also reproduced by permission of the Imperial War Museum: on page 53 letter from John Carter (KM14524) courtesy of John Carter; on page 255 letter from Graham Willmott (05/15/1) courtesy of donor Lorna Rhodes; on page 105 letter from Lord Beaverbrook (MISC 257/3524) courtesy of donor Mrs K. Faro Wood.

Acknowledgements

I am very pleased to acknowledge and thank those who have helped to make this book possible. Within the Imperial War Museum, I should like to thank the Director General, Robert Crawford, for allowing the use of the Museum's resources. The Sound Archive has provided the bulk of services and material. My thanks to Margaret Brooks, the Keeper, and Peter Hart, Richard McDonough, John Stopford-Pickering, and Richard Hughes. Roderick Suddaby, the Keeper of the Documents Department, has been most generous in allowing me access to the vast collection held by his department, as well as providing work space and use of departmental facilities. My thanks to Rod, and his staff members Kate Martin and Ellen Parton who have helped so much with the task of selection. I thank the staff of the Photographic Department for their assistance, particularly Rose Gerrard for her advice and help. Terry Charman, the Museum's historian, read the script with a sharp eye for error; I am very grateful for his valuable criticisms and suggestions. Elizabeth Bowers, the Publications Manager, ably assisted by Gemma Maclagan and Kay Trew, has proved a wonderful support and has guided the book through all stages to publication with great enthusiasm. My thanks to them all.

Eleo Gordon, my editor and publisher, has proved an encouraging, patient and most discerning critic from whom I have learned a great deal. Thank you, Eleo, for an enjoyable and rewarding working partnership. I also wish to pay tribute to Hazel Orme for her copy-editing skills, and Debbie Hatfield for the extra assistance. A considerable debt of thanks is owed to my agent, Barbara Levy, who has given her usual encouragement and support at key points throughout. I am very grateful for the help Debbie Locke has given in dealing with my computer's gremlins.

The interest my husband, Peter, has taken in this project is much appreciated, as is the encouragement of my son Nicholas, daughters Alison and Kate and son-in-law, Nicholas Tromans – so, thanks to the family.

Without the co-operation of those who were children during the Second World War, this book would not have been possible, and my greatest debt is to them. I have very great pleasure in thanking all those who have given so generously of their time over the past thirty years for interviews, and for those who have donated memoirs, photographs, letters and diaries pertaining to their wartime childhood years. I am also very grateful to copyright holders for granting permission for use of recordings, documents and photographs. My apologies to any copyright holder that I have failed to trace.

Preface

The story of British children growing up in the Second World War is one of rich diversity. Each child lived the war and reacted to it in their own particular way. Gathered together, their memories provide a unique insight into the nature of childhood during this momentous time, and capture the human reality and emotion behind the abstract statistics of death, injury and destruction. More than a hundred testimonies are included in this book, primarily of those who were children at the time, but also of adults who have a story to tell. In the main they have been selected from the vast range of in-depth interviews I and others have recorded for the Sound Archive of the Imperial War Museum over the past thirty years. A selection of original documents – memoirs, letters and diaries – written during the war or in its aftermath, complements them.

Uprooting is a major part of the story. On the home front, evacuation took place in three main waves between 1 September 1939 and the end of 1944. Experiences of evacuation are as varied as the social range, personalities and number of children involved, and depended on whether a child went on the government scheme, having to fit into a stranger's home, or was sent privately to family or friends. Many, like May Moore, were lucky in being welcomed with open arms; others, like Joan Reed, had a succession of foster-homes, good and bad. Some, like Gwendoline Stewart, were exploited to the point of desperation. Whatever the system, government or private, all children suffered the loss of home and community, and had to adapt to a different area, new friends and crowded, disorganized schools.

When invasion threatened in June 1940, many children were evacuated to the Dominions or the United States. Generally their experiences mirrored those of children on the home front, with the important difference of distance. The 'seavacuees' were cut off from home and family for years, and mail services were intermittent at best. Not only were they faced with huge culture clashes on arrival in new countries but, at the end of the war, had the challenge of reverse adjustment to a drab austerity Britain, reunited with parents and siblings who were now strangers.

Not all British children were resident in the home country when the war started. Some, like Michael Hart, were trapped in Nazi Germany while others came under German occupation in places like Denmark or the Channel Islands after the blitzkrieg of 1940. It is often overlooked that when Britain 'stood alone' in 1940, she was supported by a huge empire and had many citizens serving overseas. With the spread of war, after Pearl Harbor in December 1941, many British children who had been living in far-flung places with their parents were stranded. Some, like Jacqueline Towell, came under Japanese control and suffered the harshest physical conditions of any British children in wartime. Ann Thornton, in Denmark, found a total lack of understanding among those in Britain of what living in a European war situation was like. Unlike the majority at home, the moral complexities of war were conveyed to these children when they found that the evil enemies of Allied propaganda often turned out to be ordinary human beings caught up in extraordinary circumstances. They could see beyond crude stereotypes and judge for themselves. This sometimes happened, too, when British children came into close contact with enemy prisoners-of-war in Britain.

The age range of children was a major factor in how they experienced and perceived wartime events. Those who were teenagers in 1939 grew up during the early war years and were old enough to take jobs or, like John Wheeler, enter the services. They had clear pre-war memories as a standard by which to measure wartime life. For them, war became a watershed: it divided their lives into 'before the war', 'the duration' and 'after the war' – phrases that were often repeated in interviews. Yet, as youngsters, they were adaptable, excited by a new turn of events; they took great interest in the course of war and many gained a sense of responsibility, wanting to contribute to the war effort – perhaps volunteering as a Civil Defence messenger, like Peter Izard, or, like Peter Smith with his Scout group, erecting Morrison shelters. As they grew into adolescence, they fell in love, and many got married in their teens, some like Joyce Reeves to American GIs. These older children's experiences are in sharp contrast with those who were babies at the start of war or, like Maggie Lanning, were born during the war years.

Between the two extremes there was the great mass of children to whom growing up in wartime was normal childhood. To many it was an exciting time, a 'bit of a game'. These children, born in the thirties, remembered less of peacetime and had a different sense of danger from older children or adults. Those in target zones or beneath flight paths in rural areas became used to the threatening drone of enemy aircraft, the shriek of sirens, the blackout, the endless nights in shelters, the bangs and crashes, shattered homes and communities, and reacted with a wide range of emotions. Many were psychologically disturbed, but others marvelled at the sight of buildings on fire and competed to recognize the awesome sounds of particular bombs, even, like Thomas Houlton, making jokes, 'Number seven is ours!', to tease his terrified neighbour in the shelter. They'd play on bombsites, entering condemned buildings to collect trophies of war or see what could be salvaged.

Some children felt they were out of the war altogether. Dennis Hayden, living in the Hampshire countryside, explained, 'We were tucked up in an environment where we were quite safe. It [war] didn't bother us.' But everyone, even those in peaceful areas, accepted that their fathers, like most men and many women, wore a uniform, and thousands accepted single-parent care as the norm during their formative years. The scarcity of sweets and absence of ice-cream was unremarkable: they knew nothing but war. As John Leopard, a war orphan, put it, 'My childhood *was* war.'

The war also impacted on children at different stages. Janet Shipton's chronology of it began before it had started with the sinking of the submarine *Thetis* and the loss of her crew, in June 1939. For many, it became real on 1 September 1939 when they were wrenched from their families, or during a later wave of evacuation when they fled the blitz. Derek Bech's 'real war' started when he saw a dead pilot in a crashed plane during the Battle of Britain. Patricia Fitzgerald had endured the Plymouth blitz and much else, yet it was only with her brother's death in 1944 that she realized, 'That was wrong. War had *come*.'

Many had been born into pacifist families, who took a strong stand against war. The children of Quakers or Jehovah's Witnesses, for example, adopted pacifism almost by osmosis. Others, influenced by their knowledge of the carnage and waste of the First World War, were appalled by the suffering and futility of war and wanted no part in it. When these children reached conscription age – eighteen at the outbreak of war – many signed on as conscientious objectors, refusing to bear arms and fight, although many, like Donald Swann, undertook humanitarian work to mitigate suffering (they would bind, rather than cause, wounds) and often went into the thick of fighting zones. Although there was nothing like the degree of hostility towards conscientious objectors as had been shown to them during the First World War, they were often treated with contempt, and their children, unless linked to groups like the Quakers, whose position was more accepted, often suffered abuse and hardship from friends and neighbours. Sylvia Taylor describes how they were known locally as 'that family', and were ostracized throughout the war, even at their street's party on VE Day.

As with all major historical events, myths about the Second World War abound – the undaunted defiance, 'Business as usual' against all odds, heroism, endurance, stoicism and cheerfulness – but there are elements of truth in them that many of the voices in this book support. Despite John Tatum's anti-war stance today, he felt that 'People pulled together a lot and shared hardships.' Many speak of how, with the fair-shares ethos of rationing and the mixing of social classes, they felt part of a more egalitarian society, which drove the post-war social reforms and worked to the benefit of the next young post-war generation. Children like Reg Baker and Margaret Woodhead relished the freedom of wide-open spaces and country life. But others, like Jack Keeley, remind us of another side of the story – 'It wasn't exactly like that' – with the less than welcoming reception many evacuees experienced, the stereotyping of 'vaccies' as 'dirty and nitty', especially during the first wave, the lasting misery caused by severing of family bonds with separation, divorce or death, the break-up of close communities, like Millicent Morgan's, the disruption of education from which many never recovered, and the looting of vacated or bombed property. On top of this, instead of the longed-for peace when war ended, many were sent to conflict zones, such as Malaya, Korea and Cyprus, as soon as they entered national service.

Given the enormous diversity of British children's wartime experience, it is impossible to generalize about its nature. What can be said is that the Second World War was a most powerful experience for those children who lived through it and many, even those who suffered great loss and hardship, insist that they wouldn't have missed it. It is by listening to their voices that we gain some understanding of what it was like to be a child of that time.

Lyn Smith, May 2007

1. The Road to War: 1930s

During the 1930s British children grew up in the difficult circumstances of W. H. Auden's 'low, dishonest decade'. Although they had no direct experience of the First World War, it was still fresh in people's minds, and most families had lost at least one relative or friend. Stories and images of war were the norm for most children, and many speak of a haunting sense of sorrow and loss. The majority also lived through difficult economic times, with the post-war recession and the depression of the mid-1930s, which affected the opportunities and lives of most. Although the economic situation improved later in the decade, with a rise in living standards and the subsequent expansion of the middle classes, Britain was still a hierarchical, unequal society, with vast areas of slums in major cities, 1,710,000 unemployed in 1938, and little social welfare to cushion the hard times.

It was the memory of the First World War, and particularly the use of air power between 1914 and 1918, that in 1924 preoccupied those planning for the defence of Britain: by the end of 1918, German bombers and zeppelins had made more than a hundred raids on Britain, causing 1,400 deaths and thousands of casualties. It was realized that the country could no longer depend on the Royal Navy for protection, that 'the bomber would always get through'. London was identified as the most likely target of any air attack, and children became top priority in the evacuation plans that were developed in the early inter-war years.

From 1933, with the rise of Adolf Hitler, the planning was stepped up as the threat from Nazi Germany became clear, and the first circular on air-raid precautions was sent to Britain's local authorities. Air-raid committees were formed, and wild predictions made of the tonnage of explosives that would be dropped on the capital, and the number of likely deaths and casualties. Since poison gas had been used in the First World War, and by the Italians during their invasion of Abyssinia, it, too, was expected, so gas masks were manufactured and distributed for civilian use. Although Britain, like France, kept out of the Spanish Civil War, German and Italian forces had the perfect location for testing their new aerial weapons – in support of General Franco. The reports and pictures that reached Britain of the devastating bombings of Barcelona, Madrid and particularly Guernica, on 26 April 1937, caused alarm and even more pessimistic estimates of what this might mean for British cities. At this point, paid full-time as well as part-time Air Raid Precautions (ARP) volunteers enrolled for training in dealing with raids.

In May 1938, the first Committee on Evacuation meeting took place under Sir John Anderson. By its third meeting, in the summer, Germany had annexed Austria, and Nazi agitation in the Sudetenland, the German-speaking area of Czechoslovakia, made it clear that Hitler intended further expansion. On 15 September, the British Prime Minister, Neville Chamberlain, flew to Berchtesgaden, Hitler's summer retreat, where he was assured that Germany had no wish to include Czechs within the German Reich; the British and the French capitulated over the separation of the Sudetenland from Czechoslovakia. On 30 September the Munich Pact was signed, which, in effect, 'sold the Czechs down the river'. On returning to London after his third visit to Hitler, Chamberlain announced, to rejoicing crowds, that it was 'peace in our time'.

Although some opposed Chamberlain's appeasement policy, most notably Winston Churchill, they were in a minority. After the First World War, a vibrant anti-war movement had gathered momentum and even non-pacifists, albeit with unease, supported the Munich Agreement. Peace was certainly more attractive than a war that was bound to be even more calamitous than the one that had ended just twenty years earlier. But the German occupation of the remainder of Czechoslovakia, on 15 March 1939, dashed such hopes and was a significant factor in the change of the public mind towards Germany. On 21 July 1939, the Committee on Evacuation decided that war was inevitable and the need urgent to finalize the evacuation plans.

By this time, Britain had accepted thousands of child refugees from abroad and, in the process, learnt a few lessons about billeting. Nearly four thousand Basque children, refugees from Nationalist bombings during the Spanish Civil War, had arrived in Southampton on 23 May 1937 on the SS *Habana*. In November 1938, the shock of Kristallnacht – the Night of the Broken Glass – in Nazi Germany, when more than 7,500 Jewish shops were wrecked, synagogues desecrated or destroyed, and some thirty thousand German Jews imprisoned in concentration camps impelled Britain to take ten thousand Jewish children. In the event just over nine thousand arrived, the last group on the eve of war.

In October 1938, Sir John Anderson became Lord Privy Seal and was put in charge of the ARP, which by now had forged ahead with its preparations. It had issued streams of advice to the public and distributed millions of boxed gas masks, with those for babies and small children to follow, while expenditure on civil defence had risen from £9 million in 1937, to £51 million in 1938. As instructed, civilians were making blackout curtains, and criss-crossing windows with sticky tape, to prevent glass shattering in bomb blasts – a task often undertaken by children.

During these years, British children of Italian origin were seeing the effects of the rise of Fascism in Italy and Mussolini's expansionist foreign policy. Those living in, or visiting, Germany saw at first hand the nature of Hitler's Nazi regime. In the Far East, in 1931, the Japanese had begun to expand into north China, with the occupation of Manchuria. The League of Nations' feeble response encouraged further encroachments southward and, in July 1937, the Sino-Japanese war broke out. Although this seemed far away to most in Britain, British families were living and working in China, so their children were caught up in the war, and experienced modern bombing well before their contemporaries at home.

Jacqueline Towell (Honnor)
British child, Chungking, China

I was born in 1933 in a small town up the Yangtze river called Wuhu. My father was working for Standard Vacuum Oil as an engineer, running their big oil depot. When we returned to China after a six-month break in Britain, he was posted to Chungking and we went up the Yangtze on a riverboat through the gorges. My father was running a very important oil installation there – this would be about 1935 and it wasn't long after that when the Chinese-Japanese war started. We were very heavily bombed in Chungking. We lived within the compound of the oil installation – the depot was probably the safest place as the Japanese didn't want to destroy that: they wanted it themselves ...

My mother had been a primary-school teacher before her marriage and she taught my brother and me. We had definite school hours, and the rest of the day we were free. We spoke fluent Mandarin and our biggest treat was to be invited to have dinner with the Chinese staff, but when we went through our own front door we spoke English because our parents didn't speak Chinese the way we did. We had the most wonderful, happy childhood there.

James Maas
Schoolboy, Shanghai, China

My father worked as an engineer for the Chinese, on the authority that kept the Wong Pu river clear. We arrived in 1937. All our friends were either British or American. I went to a pre-prep school. Then, when I was about seven, I went to the cathedral prep school for boys, which Ballard [J. G., author of *Empire of the Sun*] went to. At this time we heard the bombing during that phase of the Chinese-Japanese war . . . We just lived our own lives, went to school and naturally grew up as kids do. Servants were taken for granted.

Carmin Sidonio
Schoolboy, Invergordon, Scotland

I was born in 1926, the first in my family born in Invergordon; four more followed me. When my older brothers, Tom and Luigi, grew up, they got cars and began to build up the business, starting mobile ice-cream rounds . . . We also had a big fish-and-chip range in the back of the shop. Invergordon was a naval base and when the sailors had shore leave, we were busy with fish and chips, and in the spring manoeuvres with ice-cream, so things were very, very good.

We were very Scottish. My parents would often speak Italian, but always talked to us in English with a few odd Italian words. I felt like all the other Scottish children, didn't feel different. But in 1935, when Mussolini was at his powerful peak, and Italy invaded Abyssinia, I went into school one morning and was surrounded by all my classmates, who were jeering at me and dancing around, saying, 'Eyetye, Eyetye, Mussolini Eyetye.' I was so upset that I started hitting and punching the boys until the teachers rescued me. That was the first time I realized there was a difference.

In early 1938, Tom and Luigi had gone to London and were well settled, and the family followed. The new shop was in Black-heath Hill, with good accommodation for us all. We were used to an even smaller space, so when we found we could have just two to a bed, rather than three, we were excited. I was twelve and Tom took me to the senior school in Lewisham Road, and introduced me to the headmaster. I was asked my details. When I gave him all the names on my birth certificate, Carminio Antonio Sidonio, he was rather tickled.

Jean Greaves (Catchpool)
Schoolgirl, Nazi Germany

Hitler didn't come to power until we'd been there for two years. I remember that election, and the rest all followed from that. My father wrote personally to Hitler for an amnesty for political prisoners – not so many Jewish people then – saying, 'By this time the Reich is secure enough for you to make a gesture.' Father had many contacts with all groups in Germany. I used to say, in a rather pompous way, that my parents went to Germany to try to prevent another war coming, that was their bottom line, but their actual remit was to support and encourage German people working for peace and to be friends of the German people, hence our going to German schools.

I went to kindergarten almost immediately, and so did my sister, Pleasaunce. My teacher was in the Brown Shirts – I remember a column of Brown Shirts going along and he was among them. But if you think of the conditions that prevailed at the time: the unemployment, the hunger, the deprivation ... Hitler offered them hope. He built *Autobahns*, he had work schemes, he had soup kitchens and welfare provisions of all kinds ... By the time we left in 1936, the Hitler influence was being felt in the schools. I did my '*Heil Hitler*', to my eternal regret. I find it very hard to think I did that, but it wasn't very meaningful. I very much wanted to join the BDM – the Bund Deutscher Mädel, the girls' movement. It is hard for me to say this to you but there were some good aspects. It was very innocent at first – like the Girl Guides – and the Hitler Jugend [Hitler Youth] were like the Scouts. In primary school, my sister and I were the only English girls. I remember my teacher taking me out in front of the class. He said, 'You have the same blood in your veins as we have.' It was obviously important to him that it was Saxon blood – blood became so important to the Germans in Nazi times. We had to listen to Hitler and I remember feeling extremely bored sitting in the gallery at school, listening to this poor wireless broadcast of what he was saying, and standing a long time in the street and cheering as he was passing in his motorcade.

Rodney Giesler
Anglo-German schoolboy, Ashford, Kent

My father had a house near Cologne, the old Schloss Falkenlust, which was a family monument. In the thirties Hitler had frozen the Reichsmark mainly to stop fleeing Jewish families taking their assets with them, so the income from my father's property in Germany was frozen. My mother said, 'Let's go over and spend it.' So we had skiing holidays, spending a night or so at the *Schloss*, then moving on south . . . I was very much aware of Nazi Germany then because no one ever said '*Guten Morgen*', or '*Guten Tag*', it was always '*Heil Hitler*' everywhere. They'd pick up the telephone and say, '*Heil Hitler*,' and do the salute holding the phone. You went into the hotel in the evening to collect your key, and even before you approached the desk, the porter said, '*Heil Hitler*.' Neville and I used to get the giggles, and my father was terrified that we'd be arrested. But the whole thing about Nazism was so ludicrous – the goosestepping, the *Heil Hitler*ing – they looked like automatons.

Bess Cummings (Walder)
Schoolgirl, Kentish Town, London

I had a very happy life in a close family. My brother came five years after me. My father was in the cigar trade, and when I was eight years old, he had an accident with his hand and had to find another job. Now, this was the 1930s and the worst time to find another job because of the unemployment during the depression. The poor were really poor in those days, but because of our extended family and our neighbours, we had a lot of support. That was one of the things about living in the East End then. East-Enders had a great affection for one another. There was a real community spirit and my father and mother were part of it. Poverty then was very different to today: the degree of deprivation went into all levels of society. Even what we would now call 'middle class' people lost their jobs and were without any form of financial support, just the absolutely paltry allowance of those

7

who were 'on the dole', as it was called – it was considered a disgrace to be on the dole ... My father was fortunate because he found a job as a school caretaker with the old LCC [London County Council]. It wasn't well paid, but we had a new house in Kentish Town where our family life went on.

My father was of Dutch origin and, with his foreign connections, used to travel abroad quite freely to visit his relatives. As the years went by, into the later 1930s, he came back looking very preoccupied because he had seen at first hand just what was going on with the National Socialist movement. He prophesied that we should be at war with Nazi Germany very shortly. Now this was during the Spanish Civil War in which he and my mother took a great interest. I can remember quite clearly going to bed knowing that there had been bombing in the main cities of Spain. So I was quite aware of the dangers. I wouldn't say that they kept me awake at night, but I thought about them when I went to bed and said my prayers.

Jesus 'Cai' Martinez
Spanish schoolboy, Barakaldo, Spain

In the beginning of the Civil War we didn't really know what it was all about until we heard the German aeroplanes coming over, the Junkers 52s; they had this terrible rolling noise – *rroom rrroooom, rrrooooom*. They seemed to fill the whole sky, not only with their noise but with their presence, like big crows. They could come at any height because at the beginning of the war there were no anti-aircraft guns or other defence. It was very easy for them. They were after the petrol places – they would come and bomb them every morning. The Basque government didn't have any aeroplanes until six or seven Russian fighters came over, but they were shot down by the Germans with their more advanced warfare. We had a bomb fall near our house that killed my mother's chickens ... Our food supply was affected to such an extent that I remember my father coming home to lunch at two o'clock and all my mother had was a saucepan of water with nothing to put in it ... Eventually there was nothing – the butchers, the bakers, *nothing.* You had to wait for the meagre ration to come and at the end of the week it was gone ... By the time I left Spain in '37 the hunger had reached many homes.

For us to come to England was fantastic. It was like going to Eldorado. We arrived in Southampton. We knew two English words, 'okay' and 'all right', which we'd picked up from the British sailors that used to come ashore. This was 23 May, soon after the Coronation of King George VI [12 May 1937] and we thought the streets were garlanded for us. Apparently the mayor of Southampton, knowing we were coming, had stopped the decorations being taken down. A good gesture ...

The people who met us now had their hands full, wondering what they were going to do with these four thousand children. We were taken to Eastleigh, where a farmer had lent some fields. They had hired tents and arranged them in sections, like an army camp. We were divided into three encampments: the Basque Nationalist Party, the Republicans, and those who were socialist and Communists – I suppose during our medical they must have asked our parents which group we belonged to. A little surprise for us was when they started serving little triangles of bread, two pieces of bread, with something in between. They also gave us cups of tea. In Spain we only had tea if we had a tummy-ache, and then it would be prescribed by the chemist, but here everyone was given some. We were treated very well. People used to come to throw chocolate, a fantastic thing to have, and unfortunately Woodbines [cigarettes] in little packets of five. They used to stand there and try to take photographs of us ... Before autumn they had to disperse us everywhere: we had the Salvation Army, the Quakers, the Catholic Church and other religious people there, and some of the children were fostered all over England. I went to a place in Diss, Norfolk, a beautiful place where we were flooded out ...

Paul Eddington
Schoolboy, Sibford Quaker School, Banbury, Oxfordshire

I was about nine, ten maybe, when I first went to Sibford, rather young to go to boarding-school, really. I was a very weepy child, always clinging to Mummy's skirts, but I was very proud of myself in that I never wrote a weepy letter home from school. I took to it straight away. I didn't like the headmaster, but the school I loved. I wasn't an academic high-flyer by any means, but I enjoyed the atmosphere. One of the attractive things about the school was that it didn't conform, it didn't share the views about war and other things of those around it. I knew that my mother's [pacifist] views – she was the strongest influence on me in that respect – were contrary to the majority. So it was a very congenial feeling of coming home in a way to be at this particular school.

It was at boarding-school that I experienced the first of several waves of refugees; this would be from 1937. The first who stopped at our school, only for a night or two, were about two busloads of Spanish children. As war approached, we got more and more refugees. There were Austrians and Czechs, but many, many Germans, almost all of them Jews. In fact, there was a considerable number in school and, of course, we got to know them very well ... The Quakers did quite a lot of work in getting children out. All this was a strong influence on us, and you might have thought that it would lead us to feelings of such extreme hostility towards Germany, and the Nazis in particular, that no thought of pacifism would enter our heads. Our opposition towards Nazism was as keen as anyone's, but we felt it ought to be expressed in a different way, even after that close contact with its victims ... that no matter how extreme the circumstances, a way other than war has to be found. As early as I can remember, certainly before the war, I knew I was a pacifist.

Janet Shipton (Attlee)
Schoolgirl, Stanmore, Greater London

I was very much a child of the First World War because my contemporaries didn't exist. There were so few of us, only five in a class where there should have been fifteen. There were very few parents of my parents' generation because so many had been killed in that war. The First World War had a devastating effect on England that you didn't see after the Second World War – there were always people sitting with no legs selling combs and such, and there was a man with a wooden leg, known to us as the 'man with the bonky leg'. Later, when we moved to Stanmore, there was a place for people they couldn't repair; they were put into homes and pretty much forgotten. We never visited it but we knew that was the place that had the disasters – the living, not the war dead. Awful, *awful*. That was utterly awful, and it was so stupid. It made the futility of that war very terrible.

I had begun to realize the problems with Hitler earlier. At my school, for instance, we had Hilde Weiss, whose father was the deputy police president of Berlin. Hitler threw him out because he was Jewish. They were one of the earlier families who decided they had to leave. We had two children in our village. One was Hans Paul who was eleven ... He was sent to the local boys' private school and Mother was horrified because all he came back with were swear words. He stayed with us in our home for six or seven months and then went to somewhere safer in the country. His little brother stayed somewhere else. But with Hilde Weiss and Hans Paul, this was the beginning of my understanding of the troubles in Berlin. To me it's very important that we had a German-Jewish refugee who came over with the *Kindertransports*. That's how Hans Paul came.

Countess Mountbatten of Burma, Lady Brabourne (Patricia Mountbatten)
Schoolgirl, London

The treatment of the Jews was certainly something that horrified people. Nothing was known of the concentration camps then, but the way they were treated in daily life upset people very much ... We had two fairly distant cousins from the Cassel family in Germany. My mother's grandfather, Sir Ernest Cassel, was Jewish – and these two girls arrived right at the beginning of the war. They didn't stay very long, but it gave a very personal sort of feeling of what it must have been like to be thrown out of your own country, or obliged to escape.

Vera Schaufeld (Löwyová)
Czech Jewish schoolgirl, Klatovy, Czechoslovakia

We lived in a small town near Pilsen called Klatovy. I was an only child, very wanted and maybe very spoilt. I had a nurse who looked after me and I was very fond of her. In 1933, after Hitler came to power, my grandmother left Germany and came to live with us. My father was the head of the Jewish community in Klatovy, but it wasn't an Orthodox community and we only had a kosher home when my grandmother, who was very Orthodox, came to live with us. In 1936 my mother, who had qualified as a doctor in 1935, set up as a paediatrician in Klatovy in the upper floor of my father's law offices in the main square. I was then six and had started school. I remember my childhood as exceptionally happy. I was a very loved child. It's very difficult to be objective about these things – when you lose something, perhaps you give it a more golden glow. I travelled with my parents – we went on a wonderful cruise to see the midnight sun in Norway, and we went to Lapland. We went skiing in the Tatra mountains and I can remember skating with my friends. I had a lot of friends, some Jewish, some not. I think of it as a very happy childhood. I don't remember any anti-Semitism until Munich ...

The first time I was aware of trouble brewing was when we were all sitting around the radio and we heard that Czechoslovakia had been invaded by the Germans. I remember my nurse saying that England had betrayed Czechoslovakia, and almost immediately my father was arrested because he had made speeches against Hitler. I was kept away from school for a couple of days, and when I returned my friends told me that the teacher had said I wasn't there because the Jews were always the first to run away. When I heard this I was very upset because I liked my teacher. That was my first experience of anti-Semitism.

One day when I was alone with my grandmother, there was a banging on the door and German soldiers came, demanding our radio. I pretended I couldn't understand them, but I was very frightened and they took it away. My nurse wasn't allowed to work for us any more. I don't think my parents were allowed to work. I remember my mother coming to meet me one day after school, which was very unusual, and taking me to a small park. She told me they had decided to send me to England on a *Kindertransport*. I thought it was exciting then ...

I left from Prague. I can remember there was a barrier. My parents weren't allowed on to the platform and I remember them behind the barrier. I got on to the train and into a compartment with some older boys, I was nine years old. Later on I remember a boy saying to me, 'A few minutes ago you were crying and now you want the window seat!' That's the only reason I know that I cried when I said goodbye to my parents ... I can see my parents waving large white handkerchiefs as the train drew out of the station ...

I can remember being on Liverpool Street station and sitting on a bench. There were rows of benches and lots and lots of children being collected, and I remember thinking that nobody was ever going to collect me ... Then, when there were very few children left, a lady came. Her name was Mrs Lee and she worked for the Czech Refugee Trust Fund in Bury St Edmunds. She took me and two other children in her car and she started driving us to Suffolk.

Peter Smith
Schoolboy, Petts Wood, Kent

My father was a bus driver and we were living in suburbia with neighbours who were, shall I say?, of a superior economic class to us. And, of course, we had an allotment and Father was usually in rough working clothes. Basically, I think a lot of the neighbours didn't really have much to do with us and my mother always felt we were rather looked down upon – 'Oh, he's only a busman ...' However, it soon became apparent that when things got a bit hot with the bombing raids, and tiles on the roofs were lifted, they were only too pleased to come round – 'Oh, Mr Smith, could you come and bring your ladders and help put them back?' Then, it seemed, they wanted to know us, and a lot of these reservations tended to break down. But this was typical, I think, of pre-war

Britain: everyone in their own social stratum and I think we were probably living a little bit above our station, being just a busman's family.

But my memories of life pre-war are very happy. I made good friends at Crofton Lane School and we were in a new house with modern conveniences. I can remember things such as Empire Day when we used to have parades at school. I can also remember seeing the Crystal Palace fire, standing in our garden and seeing this great glow in the sky – very reminiscent of when the Surrey docks were on fire during the Blitz. So it was a settled life. We were a very happy family in those days and it seemed that life ought to go on like that . . .

We would have heard things on the wireless and in the newspapers and, of course, my parents were discussing things. I can remember saying to my father once when Mussolini had tended to intervene [in negotiations], 'Oh, Dad, perhaps he's going to sort it out, and there won't be a war.' And he said, 'No, son, there is definitely going to be a war. He is not the one to sort *this* out.' It's difficult to pinpoint the actual timing of preparations: I think there were surface shelters being built. A big container with the initials EWS – my father's initials, Ernest William Smith – on it, Emergency Water Supplies, was down the road. They were digging trenches in some of the parks and I know a barrage balloon was erected in front of my grandmother's enclave of little cottages in Peckham. The air-raid wardens, with their black helmets with ARP on them in white, were being organized and, of course, preparations went ahead for black-out. We were issued with gas masks and identity cards. One of our neighbours, who had been an officer in the First World War, dug a trench in his back garden with wooden supports – we thought this was getting a *bit* serious. I suppose, in a child's eye, it was difficult to see all this being a threat. It was a bit of a game, in some respects. There were searchlights and anti-aircraft batteries set up, and the populace were supplied with Anderson shelters; these were corrugated, a half-hoop-shape, and bolted together. We dug a foundation in the garden down about three feet, and then covered it with soil and

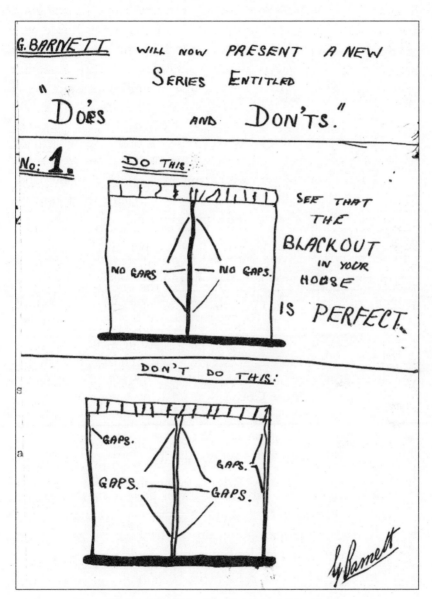

From *The War Weekly* by Guy Barnett and Derek Tongs

turf – most people tended to grow vegetables on top of them. A kind of wooden platform was put in, but later on they had to be completely cemented because of the water collecting in the base.

John Hammon
Schoolboy, Stowting, Kent

We were very simple people living in this little village of Stowting, and certainly not very wealthy. There were three important people in the village: the village squire, the headmistress of the village school and, of course, the parson. Other than that we were small farmers and farmworkers earning our living mostly on the land. My father had a smallholding of thirty-eight acres and from that he earned a living – not of the standard we expect today because farming was in terrible trouble before the war and it was very difficult to make a living. Stowting is on the North Downs and lots of land wasn't productive at all, and we used to range over these hills, which were full of wild flowers and wild strawberries – so different from now. Really, I think we had a wonderful life and there was no fear for boys and girls being up on the downs: we all went wherever we wanted to go and, of course, we knew everybody around. My father bought our first wireless, either for the Silver Jubilee or the Coronation [of King George VI]. Before this, I can remember going to one of the neighbours to hear the King's speech on Christmas Day. We all sat around it, listening to this wonderful thing that gave us the King's speech as it was actually happening . . .

Prior to the war we had one night of pretending there was a war on and we had to black out everywhere – I mean, no lights were shown. I remember going up the bank at the back of the house with my father. He looked out and said, 'I hope this never happens.' We couldn't see a light anywhere.

Barbara Partridge (Bech)
Schoolgirl, London

We really had an idyllic pre-war childhood in our big mansion flat in the Marylebone Road, with weekends down in our summer place at Aldwick Bay, Sussex, because we had that combination of much more freedom and security than children have now ... We were lucky, of course, because we were only a small section of British children who had this comfort and security. In London we lived on the edge of a poor area, and we'd see children shuffling around in cut-down adult clothes, and at St Paul's School we ran a centre down in Stepney in the East End – so we were conscious that we were lucky ...

I remember in 1938, with the Munich crisis, we all went down to Aldwick because we expected that if war did come they would bomb the living daylights out of London the moment it was declared. I kept a diary that year and had written, 'This man Hitler has been very bad and there may be a war, so we have gone down to Aldwick ...'

Peter Biglin
Schoolboy, Hull, Yorkshire

I can remember the air-raid warden coming round and issuing gas masks. Everyone had these black ones with a clear visor and this canister in front, and my sister at that time was quite small and she had one of these large baby's things where she was fitted inside and it was tied round the waist. Later on in the war, she got one of these peculiar pink or orange ones with a nosepiece on the front with two little eyes and I think they were called Mickey Mouse gas masks for small children, and my brother had a Mickey Mouse one, too, to start with.

Reg Baker
Schoolboy, Bethnal Green, London

Stories used to go round, 'It's going to be a war.' But you're only a child, I mean you're only eight or nine. Although you played games with guns – '*Bang*, you're dead!' – it still didn't register. War, it seemed, would happen over the other side, it wasn't going to come to *us*. Hitler wasn't going to drop his 'pineapples' on us – as my father used to say . . . Putting the gas mask on was *terrible*. I can smell the rubber now. I don't like being closed in like that for a start and I think I would rather have been gassed than wear it. But at the time you had to practise, you had to try it on in school. They'd say, 'Right, put your gas masks on!' *Terrible*.

Doreen Hartley (Saunders)
Schoolgirl, India

My father was an officer in the Indian Army. He was in the Dogra Regiment. I was born in Lahore; I had an elder brother and a younger sister. My father was posted to the North West Frontier district, so he came and went. My mother was often left alone with us, but there were lots of other women about. They were lovely times: we would ride out, shooting peacocks and partridges and coming back with loads of them. We loved the army life: the parades, the polo and the children's parties. At the age of seven, children were sent back 'home', as they called it. I went to Battle Abbey [school] and was there for seven years. I remember my mother leaving me there, walking away, and I couldn't bear it! But there were lots of children and I grew to love it. She would come back every year and a half, then go back to my father, so really she was always on a ship, being separated in some way. My father came back every three years and we'd all be together for the summer holidays. We didn't see much of him. Really, this was the pattern of life for people like us then . . .

During the crisis of 1938, my parents were on leave in England and they said, 'You're coming back [to India] with us, you're not going to stay in England.' They thought there was going to be a war so they took us out. My sister and I got on a ship and were thrilled to be going back to India. But then the crisis died down and back we came.

Jean Greaves (Catchpool)
Schoolgirl, Nazi Germany

I was nine when my father was arrested. There was a great deal of tension at the time, with people coming and going to our house, and our Nazi neighbours had got suspicious. From very early on my father had started helping people who were suffering because of their beliefs and were in distress; he actually got state recognition for Jews to leave legitimately early on, although later this was shut down . . . We had Nazi police standing outside our gate, and the policeman had a big coat, which my brother, sister and I hid beneath. My parents were undergoing a most dreadful time. They were separated into different rooms, and my father was tormented because documents he had held for safe-keeping from journalists, from Jewish people, from political opponents, were taken. Then he was taken to Alexanderplatz prison, but was released after twenty-four hours due to the intervention of a Nazi woman who told them, 'You've got this all wrong. This man is a friend of Germany . . .'

At the time of Munich, I think there was more or less a universal sense of relief that there wasn't a war. I think people nowadays, especially those who weren't there, don't realize that we genuinely felt, 'Thank God, another war has been averted.' The pacifists get blamed for that, don't they? [Canon] Dick Sheppard and others were trying to persuade people not to fight, and the Oxford Resolution was passed – 'This House will not fight for king or country.'

Rodney Giesler
Anglo-German schoolboy, Ashford, Kent

What I was aware of in those days was the approach of war. My father, who was once German and who understood German fluently, used to have the radio tuned to the various German stations. And, of course, I can remember hearing Hitler's voice echoing through the house. And then this massive crowd. I used to think they were shouting, 'Ha-hee, ha-hee', but it was '*Sieg*

Heil!' To hear this bestial voice, like a wolf howling in the woods, yes, it was strange. The physical power was there although I couldn't understand a word of it . . . We took the *Illustrated London News*. It was about the time of Munich and I can remember the vivid description of what war might be like. It was all sketched: how to make your house gas-proof, how to dig an air-raid shelter, and I was terrified at that time – the same dry-mouthed fear I felt years later during the Cuban missile crisis. When my parents told me that Chamberlain had come back and that there'd be no war – God, I was *so* relieved!

During our last time in Germany, I remember the train journey back from Munich to Cologne. In our compartment there were two SS officers in their black uniforms and red swastika armbands – good 'Aryan' specimens: crew-cut blond hair and blue eyes, impeccable manners and good English. There had obviously been an edict from Hitler: 'Be Polite to Foreigners'. Everyone was polite and helpful. We never came across any anti-Britishness: they didn't want to fight us, they wanted accommodation. And these two SS officers were charming to us kids. When the train stopped at Stuttgart, they got out and bought us the most enormous chocolate bars. They had swastika tiepins, which they gave us. You see, all the brutality was carefully screened. Nobody knew about the concentration camps or what went on in them. When I tell you that I burst into tears when the war started, it wasn't from fear of the Germans as soldiers. Those SS soldiers didn't frighten me. It was the fact of war and what could happen . . .

Janet Shipton (Attlee)
Schoolgirl, Stanmore, Greater London

People think that we [the children of Clement Attlee] would hear about political events, but I did not get that sort of political education. What I remember vividly was the *Thetis* – the submarine that sank in the 1930s [1 June 1939]. They couldn't get it up and all those men died. Hour after hour we waited, but they couldn't get them up. For me the Second World War began when the *Thetis* sank. The crisis in Czechoslovakia I knew a lot about – we had a political programme every week in my boarding-school and I was in a debate with a French teacher about the situation.

John Gibson
Schoolboy, Belfast, Northern Ireland

We lived in the very working-class, Loyalist area of Sandy Row. My father was a coal heaver, taking coal off the ships from England, and my mother was a linen worker in a factory. There were three daughters, then two boys were adopted – my brother and me – and then my parents fostered another little brother. Times were very hard in the 1930s. We had one room downstairs and the scullery, and my mother asked my father to build a counter and some shelves and a window display area in the room, and that's where she opened her little sweets and grocery shop. The fireplace was in the shop and she used to sell hot peas, which she cooked on the hearth. That went on until the war came.

Myra Collyer (Murden)
Schoolgirl, Reigate, Surrey

My father used to sit and argue with a man from the Co-op insurance and he'd say, 'There's going to be a war.' And this chap would say, 'Oh, no, no, *no*, you don't know what you're talking about.' My father used to talk to me a lot about the First World War in which he served, and he said that it would take one year for every man who was killed in that war to walk past our gate . . . We were on holiday in Falmouth during the summer holidays, and my father felt sure there was going to be a war soon, so we came trundling home in an old Ford 8, with the dog and deck-chairs and goodness knows what, and the car got stuck in first gear on Salisbury Plain. But I remember, at each village we went through, my mother got out at the village shop and bought sugar because she knew there would be a shortage, and we came home with sixty pounds [27 kg], which lasted us through the war.

From *The War Weekly* by Guy Barnett and Derek Tongs

Elisabeth Small (Fabri, née Hadfield)
Schoolgirl, Stalybridge, Cheshire

In August 1939 we went on a cruise to the Baltic countries calling at Finland where we were to meet relatives who were living there ... In Finland it was good hot weather and we had a beautiful meal, out of doors. After the meal drinks were served and one of the Finns got up and said, 'We are for Hitler, we'll drink to Hitler because he's the only one to stop the Russians' – they were so terrified of the Russians. Well, everyone sat in silence. Then my father said, 'I will not drink.' Down with his glass. That rather spoilt the atmosphere. Then we got a telegram from our aunt: 'Come back as soon as possible.'

We were returning via Danzig and Hamburg. The ship had to go down the Kiel Canal. It was the end of August and the canal was lined with troops. Then the announcement was given, 'The trip to Hamburg is cancelled, we are going straight back. If you wish to go into Danzig, you will be able, otherwise stay on board.' So we went by a little boat into Danzig. Nazi flags were every-where, we were open-mouthed. The German soldiers were all over the place and they were not in uniform but in shorts and shirts. My father told my brother, George, to take photographs and he promptly did so and, of course, a German officer came up and whipped the film out. We went to this church, which had a wonderful organ, decorated with angels that lifted up their trumpets at the high notes. They played the *Valkyrie* by Wagner, and when it got to the top note all the angels raised their trum-pets high and two Germans nearby raised their hands, '*Heil Hitler!*' My father said, 'I *must* complain.' My mother hissed, 'Be quiet, Arnold, you'll have us all in a camp' – she was well ahead of the time. We trooped back to the boat and were off as soon as possible.

By the time we reached Southampton, about 28 August, there were searchlights out and we were in no doubt that war was imminent.

In March 1939, after the Nazis had occupied the rest of Czechoslovakia, Britain and France guaranteed that they would go to the aid of Poland should Hitler threaten her independence. In April 1939, the British government announced military conscription for men aged twenty to twenty-one years. During the summer of 1939, the Nazis continued to menace Poland, with demands for the Free City of Danzig and the Polish Corridor. On 23 August 1939, Hitler signed a non-aggression pact with Stalin, which gave him the green light to invade Poland.

In the glorious summer of 1939 many Britons were enjoying their holidays when those involved in mass-evacuation plans were recalled for duty. Those who lived in the wealthier areas of London and other cities were leaving in their cars, hoping to be out of harm's way before the first anticipated air raid. By 26 August special trains were carrying staff from London offices to 'safe' areas. Almost two million people made their own arrangements to evacuate to the countryside. Some five thousand who could afford it, took passage for North America in the first two days of the war. The huge majority, mainly children evacuated with their schools but also mothers with small babies and infants, were bound for designated 'reception' areas in the safety of the British countryside. This was a daunting task for those arranging transport, which consisted of trains, coaches and even boats. Rumour abounded as to the date and time of evacuations, but this was where the radio – many homes had one – came into its own, providing information and urging parents to prepare.

On Friday, 1 September 1939, German forces launched a blitzkrieg – lightning war – on Poland. From that date, over four days, four thousand trains transported more than 1.3 million evacuees from immediate danger. At the same time, orders were issued for Britain's armed forces to mobilize, the conscription of men aged eighteen to forty-one, and black-out measures were enforced. The country waited.

Margaret Woodhead (Butler)
Schoolgirl, Portsmouth, Hampshire

The well-known image of evacuees is a child with a carrier-bag, but most of us had little suitcases and we had gas masks and labels. I remember my mother coming to the school with other mothers and they saw us on to the coaches. I don't remember being upset. I don't think we really knew what was happening, it was like a day's outing. We all thought it was a big adventure – you were going to the country, that was it, you were *off*. The fact that we had our clothes with us didn't strike us. It was exciting because you were going on a train and you were with all your friends, so you didn't feel strange at first, and even for the first couple of nights it was a novelty. It was only after a week or so that I realized I wasn't going to be taken home again. You were there and there was nothing anybody was going to do about it.

John Starling
Schoolboy, Portsmouth, Hampshire

By the time war started I had been at the grammar school for a year. This was the Northern Secondary School, James Callaghan's [British prime minister 1976–9] old school. Mr Hancock was the headmaster just prior to the school being evacuated to Winchester. My parents were very apprehensive about evacuation as I was their only child, and they were distressed at the thought of losing me at the age of eleven for heaven knows how long. I said that I didn't particularly want to go, but if the school was going then I didn't want to be left behind and lose out on my schooling, as I would have done if I had stayed at home. I'd have had to cope with a very disrupted situation.

We left by train for Winchester on 1 September. We all had labels giving our ages and the form we were in, and when we arrived they had lists of various billets. Some were sent to hostels and others to private billets. I was down for a private billet. I remember trudging around in crocodile fashion with about fifty boys to be allocated to billets. I was about last on the list and it was dark when we arrived at 29 Paul's Hill where I was billeted along with another boy called Peter Grundy.

Our foster mother appeared to be formidable, and so it turned out to be. She was a strict disciplinarian with very little love to show to children. It was a terraced house. Now, I came from a terraced house but ours was a very nice house; this was a very old stone and flint house, which was rented from a local milkman, Mr Clay. Instead of electric light, they had gas. The first problem was that when we were taken up to bed, there were no lights at all, just a candle. And Peter Grundy and I had to share this double feather bed and we were absolutely enveloped in this thing. And sharing a bed with a stranger was something I didn't like at all. That first night I didn't get much sleep.

Dorothy Lester
Primary-school teacher, East End, London

We had a trainload, nearly nine hundred children. We eventually ended up in Swindon about six o'clock. The children were tired and grubby, but they were very good. They took us off in buses and we were landed up in a church hall somewhere and we were given lemonade or tea and buns ... Eventually, as time went on, we were shut out into the street in this first night of complete black-out, and by then it was really dark. Some ladies came along with torches and sheets of paper and said, 'Mrs So-and-so says she'll take one ...' So that child would go off with a helper. Then the next one, 'Mrs So-and-so says she'll take two,' and two more would go off, chosen because they looked nice and had fair hair and blue eyes. 'Mrs So-and-so says she can't have any evacuees because she's got her niece with her.' It went on and on, and by that time we were worn out, all sitting on the pavement in the street. It was just like a slave market. They would look around and say, 'I'll have that one,' and off would go that child. We didn't know where they were going or who they were with or anything. On the whole girls went before boys.

Eventually we were left with only two children, a little girl from my class and her six-year-old brother. The boy had his arm in plaster. People said, 'Oh, we can't have anyone with their arm in a sling, we'll have the girl.' The girl cried and said, 'Mummy said I'm not to leave him.' I said, 'You stick to it, dear.' Eventually, a St John's Ambulance man took them and off they went. I could have *kissed* him! I was taken in by a nice woman for one night, sleeping in her son's bed. I had to get up early and wash in the sink before he came home. We had told the children to meet us in the church hall where we asked them about their billets. They all had a postcard to send home to Mum with the names and addresses of their foster-parents on it. Two little girls had been made to sleep on the bathroom floor. The little girl told me, 'My auntie told me I was too dirty to go in the bed.' I thought, This *won't do*. They took me to this house. They were two maiden ladies who had never had anything to do with children. I said to them, 'These children were clean and tidy before they left London. It's only the train journey, travelling all day, that made them dirty. I'll get them moved.' Well, they were *devastated*. They didn't want the neighbours to know they'd treated evacuees badly, so they said they had a bed and the children could sleep in it. So I gave them another chance and the story ended happily. About a week after that I met one of the children in the town with a shopping basket. She was as bright and cheerful as a sandboy and told me, 'I'm buying a loaf of bread for my auntie.' And that little girl stayed there and they treated her like a daughter.

Sylvia Townson (Limburg)
Jewish infant, Marylebone, London

The first thing I remember is walking through the streets with my mother in a crowd. This would be unusual: I wouldn't usually be walking in the middle of the road with a lot of people. At Marylebone station they put labels on us. As I travelled with my mother, I didn't have any worry at that time. I remember getting off the train at High Wycombe and being pushed into some kind of crocodile and walking, in the middle of the road again, to a reception centre. People were standing on the pavements and my mother told me afterwards that they were shouting quite a lot of abuse and calling us foreigners and refugees, they obviously didn't want a great influx of Londoners at somewhere as suburban and select as High Wycombe was in those days.

I remember the little house my mother and I were taken to. They bred rabbits and I fell in love with the beautiful white chinchilla rabbits there. I don't think we were very happy with them – they were older people and we were home a lot because we had nothing to do with ourselves, and I wasn't old enough to go to school. We were there for six or eight weeks. Looking back it seems an eternity . . . My mother was very sad at this time. I remember her sitting in our room and crying so much, and she was so much happier when my father came at weekends. She obviously felt her place was back in London with my father and we had to go before a committee to get permission for her to leave me as I was under five years old. They found a family willing to take me, a young family with children of my age. She went home and I was left behind with this new family, who couldn't have been nicer. For the first time in my life I was living in a house with other children, and it was nice to have someone to play with.

Joanna Lawrence (Rogers)
Schoolgirl, West Wickham, Kent

My twin sister and I were at the Grey Coat School, a private school, which meant it wasn't clear whether we'd be evacuated privately or under the state system. We both longed to be away on our own because Mother was extremely strict. She would often not allow the children who went to the local school home because she considered them not good enough for us . . . We were evacuated on 1 September, and my mother was very upset, but to us it was an adventure – we were terribly keen to go. Victoria station was *full* of evacuees and I remember being marshalled to keep together – my sister and I had on our very distinctive grey uniform – and we knew exactly where we were going because we were put on the *Brighton Belle* . . . We ended up at an athletics centre in Preston Park, Brighton. It wasn't as much fun then. We were a rather forlorn lot. We were then allocated to people – I think it was done socio-economically and, by and large, the children at our school got fairly good houses. Being twins we were kept together. We went with a quiet little lady, called Mrs Winton, who lived in the Varndean school area.

Millicent Morgan (Miller)
Schoolgirl, Hackney, London

I've lived in Hackney all my life. Our house was a small one, just four rooms and a scullery, with an outside toilet in a tiny yard. And all the yards backed on to one another. It was a little cul-de-sac street we lived in. The doors were always open. We just used to go into one another's houses. But they were really poor houses, all bug-infested. And it's amazing how clean they used to keep them, they were very proud of them, you know. We were lucky, we had electric light. Some places still had gas light ...

[Sir Oswald] Mosley [leader of the British Union of Fascists] was in the East End at that time, and Florfield Road, where I lived, was just behind Hackney town hall where he used to have his meetings. When he was about to hold one, the people of Hackney would get to know about it and we were all told to keep the doors and windows closed. But when they started fighting, they used to run down Florfield Road thinking they were going to get into Richmond Road, but it was a cul-de-sac. And it got rather nasty with all this fighting going on. And we used to open the door and let one in if he got knocked about ... All the children were kept off the streets when the Black Shirts came down.

All I knew about evacuation was that my mother told us we'd got to go away because there was likely to be a war. We must have had a list of things to take but obviously if we didn't have them there was no way you could get them – I mean, there wasn't any social services where you could go to get them. If you had a pair of shoes and a coat you counted your blessings. The whole street went but we didn't all go to the same place. I don't think there was any hesitation whatsoever that all the children should be evacuated. But it was entirely different when we left the school and got into the coaches, and we went off not knowing where we were going. The parents and the children became very frightened at being parted, because clinging together was probably all we had. Yes, it was a big wrench. I was then eleven and my little brother was five.

We must have all gone on the train together because the whole school was evacuated to Norfolk. It did take many hours and we were looking at the country – country, *country*, that's all we saw. I remember we were singing – 'Sing a Song of Sunbeams'. It was a Bing Crosby one. We were picked up by a coach at the other end, but I went in a car with the rector because my brother had hurt his ankle. We went to Oxborough, with the rector leading the way and the coach following. My brother and I went to the rectory. It was very late when we got there and we were taken up into this massive room with a lovely great big bed and all fresh sheets in it ... But we didn't stay there – probably when they saw the state of us we were transferred to the servants' quarters, where we stayed. Their education and upbringing were so different and no way would we have expected to eat with them because it's like the doctor or your Sunday-school teacher – you held them on that pedestal.

Evelyn Fee (Moss)
Mother of four, East Dulwich, London

We had to get the clothes together for the two older girls who were being evacuated: two or three sets of clothes, and nightgowns, facecloths, soaps – all that sort of stuff, ready for them to go. And the gas mask, of course, they carried, and the label that was pinned on them the morning they went. It was a bit of extra expense but you tried to get them everything as nice as you could afford for them to go with. We had to be at the school at nine o'clock. I can remember that morning: we had no idea where they were going. I think the children more or less thought they were going on a picnic. The mothers and fathers felt it most – well, I know I did. In fact, I didn't stay to see them off. I said to my husband,

'Oh, come on, let's go!' We heard from the school that they had arrived and everything was all right. Also, I heard from the lady and gentleman they were evacuated with, very nice people. I was naturally upset when they left, I mean we'd never been parted – it was a big wrench for them to go away. We had filled in this form asking that they be placed together, they were not to be separated.

I left later with the two little ones ... We arrived in Bury, Sussex. We were taken to the village hall and there we sat until we were picked out. I think that was the awful part of it – the worst part of the war for me. I was all right once I was picked or, rather, I picked myself, really. The ladies of the village were sort of looking you over, but I was very fortunate – it must have been my lucky day. I went home with this Mrs Hennessy. I thought I was going to one of the cottages but we went into this big house and, oh, it was *beautiful*! I'll never forget it. We went into this kitchen – and the size of it! And, oh dear, oh *dear*, I nearly had a heart-attack when I saw our bedroom. It was a massive room with mullion windows and window-seats over-looking beautiful grounds and an orchard. Well, I was absolutely *petrified*. I can see the beds now with the beautiful shot-taffeta covers and eiderdowns and cushions. I thought, I'll never be able to put the kiddies in that. I stripped the covers off and packed them all up on the window-seat. And Mrs Hennessy came in to say good night to the children and she said, 'Oh, look at them, don't they look lovely there?' And they did, they were both fast asleep. Then she said, 'What have you done with the eiderdowns?' and I told her of my worries and she said, 'Mrs Fee, this is your home for a week and you must treat it as your *own home*.'

Vera Bullman (Tipson)
Schoolgirl, West Ham, London

I was very lucky when this sweet lady said, 'You come with me, darling. I'll ring for my chauffeur.' And I thought, Golly! The house was very, *very* beautiful, quite a lot of bedrooms, spiral staircases, beautiful study, lovely drawing room, and they gave me everything they possibly could to make me happy. My bedroom could have been one of the servants' but it was very nice and they would never go to bed without coming up and saying goodnight to me. The husband went away during the war, took his chauffeur with him, and they both got killed. The servants were fine. The only one who didn't like me very much was the lady's maid: she could be hurtful, she criticized me from time to time about my dress, and it made me feel quite bad. But the others were really quite nice. I wasn't overawed at all. The only thing that overawed me was when the lady said, 'Stay here, darling, I'll just ring for my chauffeur.' And I thought, My *God*! When my father first came down to Sherston [Wiltshire] to see me, I told him to wear his bowler hat and his black coat to look really smart.

Dennis Hayden
Schoolboy, Portsmouth, Hampshire

I had no idea that a war was imminent, all I knew was that it was in our own interests that we should go away. What these 'interests' were, I don't know ... The family my younger brother and I went to I recall were very, very young and they had a three- or four-month-old child. This was in a place called Sway, on the edge of the New Forest. There were a lot of tears on both sides when we left, and I don't think my younger brother had stopped crying even after we had arrived at the house. I was upset, too, not knowing how to comfort him and having all this responsibility thrust upon me. I was then seven and a half and my brother was five years old ... I wasn't very happy having that label on me either. It seemed like you were a parcel being bundled off somewhere, but you didn't know where you were going. All it said was where you came from – you could have finished up in the 'dead-letter office' even!

We arrived and they reacted as if we were intruders into their family life, and it was our fault that we had come there – as if we had something wrong with us that we'd been sent away from our own homes and we'd been put with them. I recall that my brother cried most of the night. I can remember them tying him to the banister at the bottom of the stairs with a long woollen scarf to stop him crying. And, of course, he cried even more shut down there in the dark – he made more noise than ever. We were there not more than two months. Those two months seemed like two years.

May Moore (George)
Schoolgirl, Chorlton-cum-Hardy, Manchester, Lancashire

I didn't have a clue as to what war would mean, and when war came – or, rather, when evacuation came – it was just a complete adventure, exciting when you didn't quite know what it was all about. My youngest sister, Myra, she was eight and a half and it couldn't have meant a thing to her. Enid was ten and I was twelve then.

We got to Eyam, and I should think the whole village had turned out at the school. The people were absolutely *fantastic*. It didn't matter who you were, what size, age, anything, they'd come. We stood there with Mother, who had accompanied us down. Enid was in tears, and we were looking quite limp by then. All the children were going: 'And Mrs So-and-so will have a boy, and she will have a girl . . .' I think we were the last ones standing at that school. Mother had said, 'They're not to be split up.' So this woman called Lucy said, 'Now, I wonder if Mrs Sharples will have you. Come on, we'll go up to see her.' So we walked right up the top of the village from the school. She knocked on the door, 'Mrs Sharples, I've brought your evacuees.' 'Come in, come in.' Oh, from then it was absolute kindness itself. 'Come *in*.' The three of us were put into one big bed at night. Mother stayed for that first night. Mrs Sharples was absolutely fantastic, *marvellous*. This was 1 September 1939.

Kathleen Korybut (Daly)
British schoolgirl, Dunkirk, France, from her journal of 1945

We had arrived in Dunkirk at the end of 1936 from Mauritius. Daddy had been appointed chaplain for the Missions to Seamen there, and we lived in the beautiful war memorial that formed the Institute.

1939 came – spring, then summer with its rumours of war. Kitty [Kathleen's sister] and I became tremendously excited. To us war brought no thoughts of death and destruction. Instead we thought vaguely of rations, and I was amazed when I was told people had to pay for rations. I thought they were handed out to you! But at the sight of the serious faces around us, we thought of other things too. I remembered the charabanc excursions to Vimy Ridge, its tall white monument rising sheer from the flat landscape, startling, incredibly handsome; the thousands of names inscribed on the Menin Gate – the names of those who had died in the last war; the muddy trenches of Ypres, the exciting voyages in the underground tunnels where there were pathetic inscriptions made by the Canadian soldiers who had sheltered there twenty years ago. At Poperinghe we had peered curiously at slides showing scenes from the last war – soldiers in old-fashioned uniforms, splattered with mud in the desolate fields of Flanders; smoke clouds billowing from heavy cannon; and we became a little uneasy, but in the end, there was the tingling feeling that something exciting was going to happen to us, predetermined . . .

2. War: 3 September 1939

On Sunday, 3 September 1939, after Hitler had refused to withdraw his troops from Poland, Britain and France honoured their guarantee to the Poles and declared war on Germany. It was at 11.15 that morning, not 11 a.m., as is often recalled, that Neville Chamberlain, the Prime Minister, made the announcement to the British people, who resigned themselves to the inevitable. The news was received sombrely. In contrast to the First World War, there was little enthusiasm for conflict and no rejoicing.

Countess Mountbatten of Burma, Lady Brabourne
(Patricia Mountbatten)
Schoolgirl, Sussex

We used to go down to Sussex for the weekends to this lovely rented country house about six miles from Chichester, just under the downs. The downs were a magical place and, like most young girls, I was mad on riding and would explore the downs on horseback. I remember 3 September 1939 most vividly. We all knew that war would be declared at eleven o'clock on that day, because Chamberlain had said that, unless we heard from the Germans that they agreed the terms, we would be at war. And so I decided that I would get on my horse and go up to the downs. I rode to the top of one of the tumuli – the ancient burial grounds – and stood there and looked all around at the view. I thought: How *extraordinary* that from now on, and who knows for *how* long?, we are going to be at war, with all that that means . . .

Evelyn Fee (Moss)
Evacuee mother of four, Bury, Sussex

We got up on the Sunday morning. And I remember sitting in this beautiful orchard with the children and they brought the wireless down and we listened to war being declared. And it really hit me then that we were at war. Before, it hadn't, even with the upheaval and the coming away from home. I thought it was all going to pass over. And I can remember the children – there were low trees in the orchard and they were picking the apples up from underneath and taking a bite out of them. And Jeannie, the little girl, was having a bite and throwing it away, and I was going to tell them that they mustn't do it and Mrs Hennessy said, 'Oh, leave them alone, they're thoroughly enjoying themselves. Let them carry on. There's nobody here to eat them.' Later I was taken all over the house, which was going to be turned into a nursing-home for the troops. John Galsworthy, the author, had lived there before and Sir Hugh Walpole, another writer, she told me, had stayed there.

Meanwhile a billet had been found for me at a place called Upper Lodge in the nearby hamlet of West Burton. The first day there, I had nothing to cook on and had to go over to the big house for water to make tea. And I remember the lady who worked there showed me how to make a fire out in the garden to cook a pot of potatoes on, but later I got an oil stove which I soon got used to.

Kathleen Schaller
Schoolgirl, Lack, Northern Ireland

In 1939 we went back to Northern Ireland for a holiday, but I think my parents knew the war was coming and that's why. we went. We were in a village called Lack – very well named: it had *nothing*. It was a miserable little place wedged between two mountains. My uncle was the village policeman and my brothers and I were there. I remember hearing on the radio that war had been declared. I was eleven and not fully aware of what it meant, of course, but I can remember the effect on my mother, the sort of hush and shock. I didn't realize what it would mean to us then.

Peter Cox
Schoolboy, Coventry, Warwickshire, from his war memoir

I was an eight-year-old child living in Coventry when war was declared on Germany in 1939. I had heard about Germans from my teacher at my council school in Coundon Road, when we children were asked to bring whatever cast-offs and spare toys we had into school. It was to help the children of Spain, who had been bombed by them and had lost all their own toys and clothes because they had been destroyed when their houses were blown up. I remember thinking how wicked that was and the next day, as I proudly clutched my offering on my way to school, I was trying to imagine what it was like to be bombed, and what sort of people would want to do such a thing to children. One thing was clear: I was very lucky to be living in England, safe from anything those naughty people could do ...

It therefore came as a terrifying shock to find that the reason for the cries of 'Extra!' 'Extra!' from the newsboy in the street heralded the declaration that now England was at war with Germany. All the images of those poor children flooded back, coloured now by the fear that we were next. I can remember the empty atmosphere of those early days ... It was as if some strange spell had been cast over the whole neighbourhood. We children now gave the Indians [in their games] a well-earned rest ... Hitler, though, was great fun and we goosestepped up and down our street, with our left index finger stuck under our noses and our right arms rigid at the slope in front of us, hooting with laughter as we convinced ourselves that anyone who looked so stupid and made his soldiers march in such a ridiculous fashion could not be a serious threat to anyone.

Peter Biglin
Schoolboy, Hull, Yorkshire

I can remember Chamberlain's announcement of war, the instant when he said that no reply had been received and that we were now at war with Germany. My reaction would have been one of uncertainty. I can vaguely remember the First World War because my father had a lot of books about it – you know, *The Great War* and *I Was There*, and things like that. I knew from looking at some of the pictures about all the damage and casualties and people killed on battlefields, but I had no idea at that time what it would be like living in this country at war, no. Just a little bit apprehensive, I suppose.

Noel Dumbrell
Schoolboy, Ashurst, Sussex

In those days I used to go to church three times a Sunday, and at matins that morning we were interrupted by the sound of the first siren I'd heard. There was no panic: everyone just went out of the church and walked through the lychgate and was talking to the soldiers – the army camp had moved from King's Barn, where it had earlier set up, to opposite the church. A lot of the boys in the searchlight battery were there, and the congregation was talking to the troops, asking what was going on. Eventually we all went home. There had been no raid: it was just sounded to let us know that war had started. But I can remember later, when things became really serious, being told that church bells mustn't be rung any more, only for an invasion alarm.

Peter Smith
Schoolboy, Petts Wood, Kent

It was Sunday morning. I remember it vividly, I had gone to the cub mistress's house with some others for a meeting, and then Chamberlain broadcast at eleven o'clock and we heard that war had been declared on Germany. We thought we'd better go, and I was cycling home and there was this very officious ARP man out in the road, blowing his whistle. 'Get under cover!' So I was pedalling like mad to get home and everyone was very apprehensive, and I think the sirens went shortly afterwards. The thought was that Hitler had not waited for Chamberlain and had already got the bombers on their way . . . There was no official evacuation from our school. I think there may have been some on a private basis where families made their own arrangements.

Iris Hobby (Cutbush)
Teenager, North Cheam, Surrey

I was then sixteen and working in a confectioner's and tobacconist's as a manageress with two juniors under me. At that time it was the fashion to wash your hair and roll it up in pipe-cleaners and when you combed it out it was all lovely and frizzy. I had just washed my hair and it was all up in pipe-cleaners. My father was out in the garden mowing the lawn, my little brother was there and my sister was out with one of her many boyfriends. After Neville Chamberlain told us we were at war, the siren went off immediately and I was quite sure we were going to be gassed. So I put this gas mask on over all these pipe-cleaners and was sitting there. My father came in – he had been in the 1914 war and badly wounded, twice in the head, and he said, 'What do you think you're doing? You're not going to be gassed. Take it off.' Well, I couldn't *get* it off, I had to pull it and I tore all the rubber so it wouldn't have been any good in a gas attack after that.

Rodney Giesler
Anglo-German schoolboy, Ashford, Kent

Hearing Chamberlain's broadcast on 3 September, I was absolutely inconsolable. The air-raid sirens started. Oh, my God, I thought, they're *coming*. We had a cellar in the house, so we went down there and waited, but nothing happened and we came up again and the all-clear went. My half-sister had been in Berlin, learning German, and she had to be fetched back in a bit of a hurry in

August. Then the war started, then it didn't, we went through the winter of the Phoney War period ... Our gardener, Pearce, was called up with the Territorials, and I remember the big anti-aircraft guns in the car park in Ashford.

Carmin Sidonio
Evacuee schoolboy, Northiam, Sussex

The Standens – the couple my brother Dan and I were billeted with – always waited for a certain programme or news before the wireless was turned on, but this morning it was on and there was a lot of talk. Mrs Standen said to us, 'The news is very serious. The Prime Minister is going to speak at eleven o'clock, something to do with the German invasion of Poland.' So it was a very sombre, quiet mood. They gave us some breakfast and we just sat there. When eleven o'clock came – I can still remember Mr Chamberlain's pronouncement: '. . . and consequently this country is at war with Germany' – I remember looking at Mr and Mrs Standen, and they were just looking at each other and at us ... That was etched on my memory.

Vera Schaufeld (Löwyová)
Refugee Czech Jewish schoolgirl, Bury St Edmunds, Suffolk

It was dreadful when war started. I remember my guardian, Mrs Faires, saying that I wouldn't be hearing from my parents so much – they had been sending daily letters – and I can remember crying and Mrs Faires saying that I mustn't be a selfish little girl because other people were going to suffer much worse. But I did get a few letters from Holland, and then from Switzerland, letters that were full of hope that they were coming. I remember feeling very guilty because I was forgetting my Czech and German and in the end had to write in English. The last letter I have came from Switzerland, in November 1941. My father had written it entirely in English. It was a very sad letter saying they hadn't heard from me ...

Their daughter said to me very unkindly once that the reason they took me was because they didn't want any dirty evacuees from London, that Mrs Faires preferred to have somebody from a good home abroad. I don't think so. I think they took me from the photos of me and the synopsis of my family.

Dorothy Lester
Evacuee primary-school teacher, Swindon, Wiltshire

All I could think of was my poor mother and father in London with everyone expecting bombs to start dropping at once.

Joanna Lawrence (née Rogers)
Evacuee schoolgirl, Brighton, Sussex

On Sunday, 3 September, Mrs Winton said that we could go down by bus to the front. We were only ten. She gave us half a crown [13p] each and we went on the pier – never been on a pier in our lives – and we did all the things we'd never been allowed to do, like What the Butler Saw. We went on all these machines and used all our money. Then, suddenly, the siren went. We'd heard practice sirens before, but we were instantly terrified and didn't have any money to get back. We saw a policeman and asked for the fare, 'My daddy is a policeman', that sort of thing. We got on the bus and eventually got to our destination and when we arrived poor Mrs Winton was in the street in her gas mask, waving ours. We went in and heard Neville Chamberlain on the radio saying that war had been declared, and we felt that the bombers were going to start there and then. We listened to the King in the evening, and I remember being very worried that he stuttered so much. The next day we started school, sharing the premises with Varndean grammar school – just afternoon school as the local children had the mornings.

Peter Bennett
Schoolboy, Godalming, Surrey

We'd gone down to Hove as a family. We stayed in a boarding-house and we'd gone out to Beachy Head for the day. And I suppose it was about tea-time we saw somebody reading an evening paper that had a banner headline: 'War Declared.' We took one or two photographs on Beachy Head on that particular day as a sort of memento for the days that were to come ... I wasn't worried about the war at all. It was a new experience, I suppose, because one was growing up. I remember things like the *Daily Telegraph*, the paper my parents had, always used to have a map on the front page of the areas of warfare. We used to talk things over, but I wasn't worried, no.

Bess Cummings (Walder)
Schoolgirl, Kentish Town, London

I felt exhilarated and I think quite a lot of children did. For us peacetime children, it seemed that war might provide a chance to do something really splendid. I was fourteen in 1939, a lot of girls in my form had actually left school. I felt, with the outbreak of war, 'Here's my chance.' So one morning, instead of going to school, I went to the local labour exchange dressed in my school uniform, and asked if I could see someone as I wanted to have a job. I was told to sit down and wait, They rang up my school and my father came down and wafted me straight back to school – the lecture I got!

Janet Shipton (Attlee)
Schoolgirl, Stanmore, Greater London

When war broke out we were on vacation in Wales. It was a strange vacation because the crisis was on and Father [leader of the Labour Opposition] often had to go back on an all-night train to London, and Mother had to drive fifty miles to take him to the train. In a day he'd be back and she'd have to do it all again. She did that a few times, and he was with us in the farm-house in Wales on the day war broke out. He left immediately. I remember we expected something to happen, and alarms went off in London, but nothing happened for a long time.

The outbreak of war was decision time for men of call-up age who opposed war on principle. Under the National Service Act of 1 September 1939, they could be placed on the Register of Conscientious Objectors rather than the Military Service Register. They would then, in due course, be called before a tribunal to explain their objection and be categorized by a panel according to its nature and their sincerity. Category A granted unconditional exemption from military service; B directed objectors to civilian work; C meant non-combatant duties in the services; and D ruled that a man's name should be removed from the Register of Conscientious Objectors, making him liable for military service. Many who had an anti-war stance, were children at the outbreak of war but reached call-up age, eighteen, before it ended and had to face a tribunal. Others were the children of conscientious objectors.

Sylvia Taylor (Bell)
Schoolgirl, Hook, Surrey

There were unpleasant incidents because my father was a conscientious objector and this had repercussions on the whole family. We were called names – like 'Jerry lover' – by other children, and the teachers at school were a little frosty. A lot of the neighbours in our road wouldn't speak to my mother. And as a very small child of four, being aware of atmosphere, I think I noticed a lot of things.

Before the war my father had a good job in a bank in the City, earning a very good salary. Then along came the war, and he had decided he wasn't going to fight because he didn't believe in war. He had to go before a tribunal. I can always remember my mother saying that what hurt her most was when my father was asked, if the Germans invaded – actually came to England – and his family were threatened, would he fight to protect us? And he said, no, he wouldn't. I don't think my mother could ever forgive him for that. He was offered the choice of going to prison or working on the land and was sent to various farms to work ...

earning to begin with something like thirty shillings [£1.50] a week, going up to about three pounds towards the end of the war. Our rent was twenty-seven shillings [£1.35] a week so I really don't know how my mother managed. I've got an idea that she had to sell various possessions in order to pay the rent and buy us food ... I know my father had principles and I admire him for that, and he obviously had courage, but I think when he had a family of young children he should have put them first.

Donald Swann
Schoolboy, Westminster School, London

When the announcement of war came, in September '39, all this turmoil I had felt about my pacifist feelings had more or less established itself. I just loathed the whole idea of being a soldier. I think I must have changed from being very intellectual about it to being rather practical. I was wondering what was going to happen. I do remember from now on definitely going around with a pacifist demeanour: was I going to wear a gas mask? How would I react to the talk about going into the shelters? I was always drawing back. There was always a reserve. Somewhere along the line I knew I would personally get more unpopular. There was no persecution of such people in the school, but I knew I was driven into a corner.

Tony Parker
Schoolboy, Manchester, Lancashire

I was at school when the war broke out and my father's business had gone bust. Eventually, in an attempt to make money, he started a second-hand-book shop, the stock of which consisted almost entirely of his own library. I was very keen on that and wanted to leave school and join him in the shop, which I did. A lot of his books were from the mass of material that came out of the First World War – Siegfried Sassoon, Robert Graves, Wilfred Owen and other anti-war writers – and these profoundly affected me and I became very anti-war. It was the complete waste of life, the nonsensical way of trying to solve international problems in that way. Anyway, I knew that I would eventually be called up and in the book shop I was meeting a wide range of people and they were finding out that I was a pacifist, and I was finding out that they were pacifists or Quakers, which I'd never heard of before. I'd thought it was only *me*, that I was the only person in Manchester who was against the war. That was when I first began to realize there was a wide range of opposition, on all sorts of different grounds, to war and to fighting.

Early in the war, the War Office in London considered that a German attack on the Channel Islands was a remote possibility, but the authorities in London and on the Channel Islands were complacent: the islands continued to be promoted as ideal holiday resorts, ships plied between them and the mainland, and life went on very much as it had in peacetime.

The outbreak of war also had repercussions on the lives of British children living in other countries.

Marion Tostevin (Letissier)
Schoolgirl, Guernsey

I had a very happy childhood, living in the north of the island. My father was a cobbler and my mother used to pack tomatoes – a very big industry, in those days. I remember the outbreak of war in 1939: my father had *Picture Post* and other magazines, and I would look at them, so I was very much aware of what was happening. People were still coming on holiday after the war had started, and some of them just made it back in time before the Germans arrived.

Ann Thornton (Helps)
British schoolgirl, Rungsted, Denmark

We lived in Denmark where my father worked in a big rubber factory. I had two brothers who were at public school in England.

My elder sister, my parents and I really took to Danish life as Denmark was an idyllic society in those days ... I don't know what my parents thought about the coming war – we were too young to worry about *that*. But I remember we were in a cake shop on our way to a picnic on a glorious beach north of Elsinore, when the man in the cake shop said, 'I think you will be interested that England has declared war.' We just bought the cakes and went out, and my parents started talking about what to do with the boys – they were sixteen and seventeen. My father knew he was going back to do political work, being a German expert, but the picnic carried on. There was no panic. When we got home they started organizing for my father and brothers to get back to England. This was very difficult as everyone was trying to do it ... There was no question of the rest of us getting a passage, and as we so loved our school we said, 'All right, we'll stay.' My mother had heard that there was all sorts of fuss in England with children being evacuated, so she thought that another reason for not moving. We must wait until things settled down. We were very comfortable in Denmark, no getting away from it.

June Knowles (Watkins)
Schoolgirl, en route to Kenya

I went out to Kenya when I was about three months old from England, and I was brought up there until I was nine years old when my father, a very senior administrator, retired from colonial service, and I went to school in England ...

In late August we travelled home to Kenya via South Africa. War was declared, on the day we arrived in Durban to rejoin our ship only to find that she had been turned back to become a trooper. And then it was a case of all the passengers floating around Durban, looking for passages up-country. At that time the South Africans were very undecided which side to join, or whether they'd join at all. They didn't like us, and I always remember them throwing our passports in our faces ... We eventually ended up staying in a place that turned out to be a brothel. We were given a double room and my mother locked the door and wouldn't let me out. The ladies were parading themselves outside and the customers started coming in. This was just past my sixteenth birthday. Eventually we got a passage on a terrible old coastal boat. I can remember my mother being asked at a party what kind of trip she had. She replied, 'Excellent, I'm still scratching!'

Jacqueline Towell (Honnor)
British child, Chungking, China

We were due for another home leave to Britain, but we couldn't return to Europe because the war had started so we flew to Hong Kong. We had to fly at night in a blacked-out Dakota because of the Japanese fighters [active in the Sino-Japanese war] and we landed in Hong Kong in the dark. Our intention was to go to Canada, but the night before we were due to get on the ship, it was requisitioned by the army. Meanwhile, all the women and children had been evacuated from Hong Kong as the British government wanted us out of there. The only other ship was going to Sydney, Australia, so we went to Sydney. I was then six or seven. We found Australia very strange. We couldn't believe it when we docked and saw that the dockyard people and men working as stevedores were white and – this sounds terrible now – I said to Mother, 'Oh, look, foreigners doing *coolie* work!' because we were always 'foreigners' in China ... My brother and I had one year of schooling in Australia, from 1939 to 1940.

Joseph Stagno
British schoolboy, Catalan Bay, Gibraltar

When war started we were incorporated into the ARP and my particular job was to go into the dockyard, where my father worked, as a messenger. We were a religious Catholic family, British subjects, although we had no connections at all with Britain. You just knew you were British and were aware that you lived in a colony – the older people were very proud that they were British. I had seen some of the effects of the Spanish Civil War in Gibraltar

– we all had. I happened to live close to the frontier at the time and saw a lot of refugees coming over from Spain, and we heard the gunfire and so on, and we did have a stray bomb one day. It hit the racecourse during a game of polo … Border restrictions were also tight and for a time the border was closed.

Really, the war with Germany had little effect on Gibraltar at first, apart from the ARP activities. Civilians weren't allowed to go into the defences on the Rock, and new gun emplacements were erected, but as a young boy I didn't see much of that. I knew about the clash between Germany and Britain over Poland; also, people had been against Mussolini's invasion of Abyssinia. There was no ill-feeling with Spain in 1939 and workers came to work in the dockyard as usual.

Michael Hart
Anglo-German schoolboy, Berlin, Germany

I was born in Wimbledon, a British subject but of mixed Anglo-German parentage. I spent quite a few years in England. My [German] father then worked in Germany, and because my parents entirely misread the political situation, I found myself in Germany at the outbreak of war. As a dual-national, this was rather complicated and the local German secondary school that I attended threw me out almost immediately after we refused to renounce my British nationality. The way out of this was to attend a well-known international school in Berlin – the *Lycée Français*.

On the day war was declared many children were still awaiting evacuation, but by the end of September, 825,000 schoolchildren, 624,000 mothers with children under school age, 13,000 pregnant women and 113,000 schoolteachers had moved and were now adjusting to their new surroundings.

For those evacuees who had left earlier and seen their journey as a holiday, things were suddenly different, and those who had taken the children into their homes were

now faced with the daunting prospect of an indefinite stay.

John Wheeler
Schoolboy, Purton, Wiltshire

That Sunday my father went off after Chamberlain's broadcast at eleven and worried my mother to death. He came back late in the afternoon or early evening, having been to a meeting with senior members of the council, to tell us that he had been appointed billeting officer for this area and that they had to make some preparations ... There were a number of meetings in our home and I know they drank copious amounts of cider, so their meetings were both friendly and, presumably, productive because eventually they arranged to accommodate six hundred unaccompanied children. The legislation that had been passed meant that no one had any option. They had to declare on a form, which I helped my father to sort out, the number of people in their house and the number of rooms, and then the billeting team went through the record and said, 'Well, there's only three people in that house, and they've got three bedrooms. So they can double up and we can put two children in there.'

But my clearest memory of that time is that my mother was very worried because I was sixteen, and if the war went on too long I would join up as all her friends and relations had twenty years earlier. I think that probably worried her more than anything else. But, like most lads of sixteen, I was mad on football and chasing girls, and war was an unknown factor that happened in France in my uncle's picture books. One didn't really envisage that it was going to affect us in the village of Purton.

As a lad of sixteen, I was pressed in to be my father's messenger. There were a number of us in that category, all the young lads of the village. And the thing I recall quite clearly, as the coaches arrived and the passengers debussed and came into the school, they weren't unaccompanied children at all. They were, in fact, three hundred mothers with children and one or two elderly men

... So other helpers were called in and I think in some sense we did a blackmailing job on the villagers for them to take them in, telling them that the next evacuation would be chronically sick and mentally ill people ...

Amongst all this milling throng were a boy and a girl who turned out to be William and Kathleen Milcoy. Bill – as we knew him – was eight and a half and his sister was six. And they were sitting side by side, holding hands, and had a label on each of them which said, 'These two must not be separated.' My father sought me out and said, 'John, look after these two.' When the dust had settled and everybody had gone, my father said, 'Right, take these two home to Mum and tell her to give them a jolly good bath.' So I took Billy and Kathleen home and they very quickly became part of our family.

Mary Whiteman (Walker)
Wife of billeting officer, Saffron Walden, Essex

Saffron Walden was untouched by the world at that time, a sleepy little market town where people from outside were considered 'foreigners'. My husband's concern was with evacuation, and in 1940 he became chief billeting officer ... When it started, we all gave a hand and went to a meeting in the town hall, and it does credit to the town that on the first night everyone had somewhere to go. People were warm-hearted, 'Oh, yes, we'll have a little boy,' and 'We'll take a little girl.' The billeting officers were often teachers on their summer holiday. They knew the town and the people, each had a zone and they managed to find somewhere for everybody. There was a bit of resistance from some, but mostly the smaller houses were ready to go. Really, I think this town showed as good a spirit as was possible.

Noel Dumbrell
Schoolboy, Ashurst, Sussex

That evening at evensong we were interrupted by knocks on the door and the vicar went outside. Charabancs had come down from the London area and evacuees were at the church. The service stopped and, of course, they had to be housed and bedded down for the night. The church, the school and the village hall were used. There were one or two mothers, and the children were crying and we tried to comfort them as best as we could. That was the day when the war started. I remember it vividly. The thought of war didn't mean much at the time. I didn't realize the dangers then. It was something new, and for a choirboy to have a service interrupted was something completely different. From one point of view it was a bit exciting, but a bit worrying when you saw all the children. At one time we had about a dozen evacuees in our house to sleep. People were very, *very* good and helpful and took them in; there were no problems whatsoever in housing these evacuees.

Charles Kemp
Secondary-school teacher, Gravesend, Kent

I understand we were the only people evacuated by boat, and on the Sunday when war was declared, later than the rest. It was a paddle-steamer with the usual accommodation below and on deck. Our deputy head organized things so that each master had one hour on duty supervising the children. I wasn't on until five o'clock and I realized we'd be there by then so I volunteered for anything required. I did nothing until about half past two. By then many of the children had eaten everything they'd been given, especially the sweets, and had become seasick. So I spent from two thirty until we reached Yarmouth dashing down below, finding a child about to be sick, dashing it up the stairs and holding it over the rail. I managed not to be sick myself, and one or two of the teachers needed assistance too.

At eleven o'clock that morning, we had been informed by the skipper that war had been declared. This caused hysteria in one or two of the women who were acting as helpers, but they soon overcame this. We were told then that it was Yarmouth we were going to, and that a destroyer escort was with us. Once the children settled down they quite enjoyed it. Having left Mum upset some, but once on the boat they had a good time. The journey lasted seven or eight hours.

At East Dereham, the billeting officer had made complete arrangements. He knew who was coming, which parents would take certain children. Unfortunately, many ladies came to the school and immediately grabbed one or two children, usually good-looking girls, 'I'll have this one', and 'I'll have these two', and took them off, so within ten minutes the billeting officer's plan was gone for nothing. He then took over and did as best he could ... We finished up with two dozen children at about seven at night with no billets, so some of the staff, I was one of them, accompanied the billeting officer in a procession round the streets with the unwanted children, mainly the scruffs and the poorest ones. We had one family of eight, and the procedure was, the billeting officer would find a house on his list, knock on the door and say, 'Will you take one or two of these children?' And by half past eight it was getting dark and we were left with only the family of eight. After much more door-knocking, the officer finally got them into two separate houses. It was obvious that they were outcasts, even to them, and it must have been a great blow because in Gravesend, although they were amongst the poorest and scruffiest, they lived in an area where there were others like them.

Ena Kemp (Drinkwater)
Wife of Charles Kemp, evacuee helper, East Dereham, Norfolk

East Dereham was a great contrast to Gravesend, it was a little market town, with a market day when all the stalls came out, and all around was lovely countryside, which many of the children had never seen. They lived down by the river in Gravesend and in pretty squalid places for some. Those who got into the right homes settled well, but one of the big troubles I heard from foster-parents, apart from food, was bedwetting. This happened when they were mismatched with higher-class homes. The foster-mothers would be annoyed because they didn't have the facilities to dry the mattresses, but it was the emotional strain of the upheaval of going away and problems of readjustment that did it. Bedwetting seemed pretty general; even those who seemed quite happy wet their beds. But the unhappy children soon went home and those who stayed adjusted, so it solved itself.

John Carter
Evacuee schoolboy, Langham, Rutland, from his war memoir

I soon realized that here was a rather different way of life from the one I had known in Walthamstow. For example, I had my first introduction to middle-class table manners where serviettes had to be used (and carefully folded in a ring after use), where elbows had to be tucked in when eating and mouths shut during mastication, where you asked for an item across the table instead of reaching. Gradually we lost our Cockney accents with

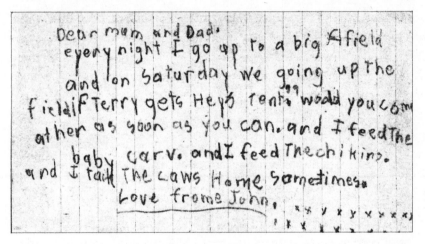

Young evacuee John Carter writes home to his parents about life on the farm

Mrs Smith expressly forbidding the word 'ain't'. What impression my parents and Mrs Smith made on each other when they first met I cannot say, but judging matters later, it cannot have been happy. There was none of the social ease I soon noticed between the Smiths and Terry's [the other evacuee] parents ...

Joan Reed (Chantrelle)
Evacuee schoolgirl, Ongar, Essex

I was so happy in the first home we went to in Ongar, but we were only there a fortnight because the old man who lived with them died ... The next place was with a younger couple with a baby and also a grandmother. I had this feeling that we were a bit of a nuisance and wasn't happy there ... But then we came to this lady who had a very poor council house with five children, the eldest a boy of sixteen, and the youngest a baby. But she was absolute kindness itself. I don't know where the husband was, but she was *very* poor. She was great. We slept four in bed, sideways on, the bed pushed against the wall, Naomi and I and two of hers. She was such an outgoing person in her old bedroom slippers and hair in curlers, but she was so *nice*, she loved us. It was a very poor home, very overcrowded, it was dirty – Naomi got scabies there. But she was *so* kind. Every Friday she bought us a sixpenny [3p] savings stamp to stick in our little books, and every Friday we had cheese and Spanish onions for supper, and it was lovely. I was so happy there because she was nice to us and so genuine, and that was all that mattered.

My mother came down and saw Naomi covered in sores and I got the brunt of it because I was supposed to be looking after her, wasn't I? I remember she was quite short and sharp with this dear lady. Quite a battle of words went on. Obviously she was dirty, but that didn't matter to me. And so we were promptly moved from there to the worst place of the lot. That broke my heart, because she was so lovely ...

Thomas Houlton
Evacuee schoolboy, Algarkirk, Lincolnshire

The thing that upset me most was the method by which they allocated people to houses: they lined everybody up. At that time I had a birthmark on my left cheek, and I was the last one, nobody seemed to want me, and I felt quite derelict as everybody went, one by one. Finally the teachers persuaded a farm labourer's wife to take me on board. That's the only upsetting thing I can remember about evacuation, otherwise I enjoyed life in the country ...

Reg Baker
Evacuee schoolboy, Weston-on-the-Green, Oxfordshire

It was another sort of adventure, but you was still frightened – you were going into the unknown, really. On the whole the people didn't have a lot of time for you. You were Londoners. We weren't really accepted, you know, we were scruffy because our environment was that way ... But it was the picking out that was so embarrassing, but you're a kiddie and you have to stand things like that.

Eventually I was evacuated with the village blacksmith family. Grandma Dorling was the mother and Ted and Fred were the sons. I can recall the first night. She gave us a wash first and she gave us pyjamas. I'd never had pyjamas before – which I only thought you had in case of fire – a little joke! It was still frightening, really, because we expected to switch on the electric light but they didn't have it: they had these dark, eerie places. See, in the East End at least you had street-lights but not here, and then we'd been travelling all day, so we went to bed.

I don't think the local people were keen on us. I'd say their attitude was indifferent. Some had their own children anyway. And, as I say, you were still from London. The way we spoke was right coarse, you know, but then again they'd say, 'How be?', 'I be all right, how be 'ee?' We couldn't understand it at first, and sometimes if they used their local dialect that threw us out. They definitely lived better than we did. Well, they've got all their own produce, haven't they?

Derek Bech
Schoolboy, Aldwick Bay, Sussex

With the outbreak of war we had to think what to do. My mother had read all these reports of the bombing of Warsaw and felt that London would be next on the list so, in her wisdom, she took us out of London to our summer house in Aldwick Bay, my father

From *The War Weekly* by Guy Barnett and Derek Tongs

keeping the London flat because of his business ... We had a beach hut there and would go down and spend the day there with our Danish nanny, Meta. There was a club and the adults would play tennis and go dancing, and they had beach parties in the summer and midnight bathing, and the teenagers and young adults would have a whale of a time. But now things were happening and it wasn't so carefree. They started to close the beach because of possible invasion and our lovely sand dunes were dug up to make sandbags, and there were more aeroplanes flying around. We lived fairly near Tangmere aerodrome and a lot of fighter planes were there, much to my excitement. I used to cycle over and watch these planes taking off and landing.

Patricia Fitzgerald (Stringer)
Schoolgirl, Sidcup, Kent

When war came, my brother Wilf joined the Territorials. He used to draw and I remember he drew a picture, which I still have. It was of a bomb exploding and on it he had put the caption, 'The war to end wars?' Note the question mark! He was killed in September 1944, towards the end ... At the start of the war, my father went down to Plymouth, then considered a 'safe area', with his work for Shell Petroleum. I was ten, really a spoilt child with a good and happy life – ice-creams, every day seemed like summer. It was lovely. But in September we had to have the dog and cat put to sleep. The main fear was that, with the expected gas and bombing attacks, they'd go crackers, so it would be better if they were out of the way. Everything seemed to go: my brother, Dad, the cat and the dog too ... Then, in November, Mum and I went down to Plymouth to join Dad.

Countess Mountbatten of Burma, Lady Brabourne (Patricia Mountbatten)
Schoolgirl, Sussex

One thing I remember about those early September days: the army remount people came around to look at the horses. *Incredible* to think of it! Our horses weren't the sort they wanted, but I was absolutely *terrified* that they were going to take my favourite horse. But luckily the groom pointed out that one foot was smaller than the other three – something I hadn't noticed – and he was saved. But that's a thought: that your horse would go off to war! It's extraordinary now to think that the cavalry was still a very important part of the army in those days.

Evelyn Fee (Moss)
Evacuee mother of four, West Burton, Sussex

After a few weeks I had got a bit browned off and I said to this old lady, also an evacuee, that I had made friends with, 'Well, I think I'm going home.' And she said, 'Well, I don't think I can stick much more. If you go, I'll go.' But then my husband, who was in Scotland with the navy, put in for a few days' leave to see if we'd settled all right. I told him I wasn't going to have no more of it, I was going back home. He was a bit upset and said, 'Look, I'm going away, I know where I'm going and I won't be back for a long time, so I'd far rather know you're still here.' So I said, 'Well, what's the good? There's the two girls [evacuated] on the other side of the country and me here.' Well, Mrs Wilson, the lady in the big house, came over and said, 'Well, Mrs Fee, supposing we went and got your two daughters back and you can stay in the cottage on your own, with no one else billeted on you? The cottage is yours.' So I thought, Well, that's different altogether, because apart from all that I'm quite happy in the village, and if I stay, the old dear will stay with me and I'll have a bit of company. So I said, 'All right, then, I'll stay.' And on that Sunday morning her husband went with my husband and got them. They were home in time for Sunday dinner and it was lovely . . .

In the end I was the only one that stayed. In about a fortnight, nearly thirty or more had gone. We all used to meet at the river in Bury of an afternoon, it was the only place we had, and gradually just a few of us were left and then just me . . . I think really and truly Bury was glad to see the back of their evacuees. A lot of the villagers were very old country people and primitive in the way they lived, and those coming from Peckham Rye, as a lot of them did, found it hard to get on with the village people – as hard for the takers as the givers. But when we met up at the river, you'd sit and listen to them, the different things that had happened and about the people they were evacuated with, and I can quite understand why some of them went back. Even that dear old lady I palled up with, she was very unhappy yet she was a dear old soul. I would have thought that anybody could have got on with her. But village people – the proper country ones – are very narrow, and we were different.

Joanna Lawrence (Rogers)
Evacuee schoolgirl, Brighton, Sussex

Some time in the autumn our parents had to start paying for us and they considered whether it was worth it financially, keeping the two of us down there. I think Mother was also bothered about the schooling. They decided that we might go home as nothing was happening, and in December my father brought the car down and took us home – this was the last time it was used because petrol rationing had started. We helped to put bricks under it and take the wheels off.

Rodney Giesler
Anglo–German schoolboy, Ashford, Kent

A family from the East End came down, and to us they could have been from Mars. We were pretty haughty middle-class people. We saw the working class only when we needed them, like the bus-conductor or the street-sweeper or the maid. I can't remember this family very well. There was a mother and three or four kids and my mother found them a bit of a pain. They were put well out of the way. I think they were put in a big loft above the garage. It was a culture shock for both sides. It didn't last very long because the authorities realized that the cities weren't going to be flattened overnight. The Phoney War had started, and a lot of people went back.

3. Phoney War: September 1939–May 1940

After the first wave of evacuation in September 1939, it was soon clear to town and city authorities that more children had remained at home than expected, also that large numbers were drifting back. In London alone, estimates suggested that almost six thousand were returning weekly. As well as homesickness, culture shock and sheer misery on the part of many, this was also due to the stalemate on the land front.

At sea, things were different. On the first day of the war, the passenger liner *Athenia* was torpedoed by a U-boat, thus marking the start of what Churchill called the Battle of the Atlantic. But the country was more shocked when another U-boat sneaked into Scapa Flow, in the Orkneys, and sank the battleship *Royal Oak*. The terrible news coming from occupied Poland, not least the bombing of Warsaw, reminded everyone of the nature of modern warfare. But despite this, it was considered the 'strangest of wars', as Neville Chamberlain put it, and the questions on most people's lips were 'Where is the action?' and 'Should we bring the kids home?'

The trickle back, which had started in the early autumn of 1939, soon gathered enough momentum to cause concern to the city authorities. Schools had been closed or commandeered by the military, or ARP, which meant that numbers of children were idle and many got into mischief. The government tried to encourage evacuees to stay put, but by now foster-parents' reluctance to co-operate and the difficulty in finding new billets had created severe problems for billeting officers. The latter were urged to exert pressure on those – often the wealthy – who had so far evaded their responsibility. Meanwhile, the War Cabinet's Civil Defence Committee continued with its plans for a further wave of evacuation after air attacks had started.

John Starling
Evacuee schoolboy, Winchester, Hampshire

But this was the Phoney War, of course – that's what it was called, from 3 September 1939 until May 1940, when the Germans invaded the Low Countries and spread into France. We had a false sense of security at that time. In fact, a lot of the parents said, 'Well, there's nothing happening in Portsmouth. I'm going to bring you home.' And the school authorities had great difficulty in persuading them that they would have to keep their children in Winchester because they wouldn't get much education at home. If this hadn't happened, there would have been a wholesale movement by parents to get their children back. We children resented it. We felt we were there under false pretences.

Richard Hancock
Evacuee headmaster, Portsmouth Northern Secondary School, Winchester, Hampshire

I think I shocked my colleagues at the first staff meeting I had by saying, 'We've got to plan for being here five years.' One couldn't see the possibility of winning a war short of that time, and I was about right, unfortunately. But, clearly, one couldn't improvise from day to day. One had to plan long-term and get regular work done ...

Some boys were in private homes and, of course, there was stress for the householders. What isn't always realized is that there was stress for the youngsters too, and oddly enough for older boys. They felt they were being sent to safety whereas Mother and the little kids were staying in danger. This could gnaw at your mind if you were a fifteen-, sixteen-, seventeen-year-old. I don't want to exaggerate this, but one had odd difficulties. Looking back on it, though, the astonishing thing is how few the difficulties were and how resilient and capable of coping were these youngsters. The boys had very wide contacts: father may have served in the navy – Bermuda and Hong Kong – but an astonishing number of them had not been north of Portsdown Hill under their own steam and Winchester was a foreign country, twenty-odd miles away from Portsmouth. It was a strange land. It was new.

Margaret Woodhead (Butler)
Evacuee schoolgirl, Zeals, Wiltshire

After my first billet with Mrs Carter, I was with a couple from the end of October 1939 until January 1940. He was a cowman for the very big farm in the area; they had one daughter. There was an air of poverty there and, looking back at it now, I realize they were quite poor people. I couldn't compare their home with my own because it was the country, which we had never come across before. The fact that you had to go out in the yard to the toilet, which was bitterly cold, and they had no tap or hot water – in the mornings you had a washbasin and jug, and I can remember breaking the ice on top of this jug to have a wash. I was really unhappy there. There was no conversation with the woman. The other evacuee and I were kept clean but the food was really dreadful. We didn't have meat at all. Every day we would come home to masses of potato, mashed swede and watery gravy. And every single day she would make an apple batter pudding. So that was our dinner every day – mashed potato and mashed swede and apple batter. I was often very hungry there, and cold. Going to bed was *awful*. We took a candle upstairs and got undressed into a cold bed and woke up in the morning really cold to a cold-water wash and a plateful of porridge . . . I remember writing to my parents saying, 'Please let me come home!' But my mother said I couldn't. I can remember sitting outside in the toilet and reading her letters and crying. Eventually I couldn't eat any more swede and mashed potato. I was so unhappy that my mother wrote and asked for me to be removed. I was taken to another house in the village, with the Virgo family, where I stayed for a while and was very happy there. But in the spring of 1940, my mother decided that I was going home.

Ena Kemp (Drinkwater)
Evacuee helper, East Dereham, Norfolk

My day would be going round the billets and asking if they had any problems. How were the children adjusting? Were they settling down nicely? Were their parents coming to see them? And some did. Some of the women invited you in and made you very welcome and gave you a cup of tea, and some kept you waiting on the doorstep – so there was great variation in the way I was received, too. But all along I think that the evacuees had been thrust upon them and they'd got to put up with it. That was the attitude. It was my job to listen to the complaints. I don't remember the children complaining or criticizing their homes, but I did feel at times that they weren't happy. Then they would say, 'Oh, we're going home next week.' And it would sort itself out. We were there from September 1939 until early 1940. When we returned there were just about twenty left with only one master; as the children drifted back, so did the teachers and helpers. I wanted to get on with my life again. It seemed that it had stagnated a bit over the past few months. I wanted to go home.

Charmian Sutton (Willmot)
Evacuee schoolgirl, letter to her father, late 1939, Sudbury, Suffolk

We have no news of coming except that we can come home, no one can stop us doing so, and I would like to come home and after all I am just as safe at home as here, and though I shall be happy here it is not the same as being home ... Darling don't think I am complaining but I can't help feeling homesick occasionally ...

Joan Reed (Chantrelle)
Evacuee schoolgirl, Ongar, Essex

The next home was with a woman who had a husband and son, Cyril, who seemed a bit sickly, presumably not fit enough for the army. We arrived there one evening. She was a very tough nut, biggish, homely on the face of it, but not at all. Once again we had a bedroom with a double bed and we were taken straight upstairs to bed. Naomi woke up, of course, and wanted to go to the lavatory. I came out of the bedroom, pitch dark on the landing, two or three doors there, didn't know what to do. So I came back and whispered, 'I don't know where the lavatory is.' 'I *must* go to the lavatory,' she said, and she was beginning to cry. I said, 'Get out of bed, put on your knickers, sit on the carpet here and spend a penny.' I thought if she had her knickers on, it would spread through the rug and be absorbed. She squatted on the rug and went. That was never discovered. Nobody said a word. I never slept that night, I was so frightened . . . I remember going down the next day and looking up expecting that it had come through the ceiling, but probably there wasn't sufficient for that. That is so *vivid* still. I expected to be battered around because of this.

She was the most unfriendly woman. We came down, sat at this table. Nothing was said to us. Naomi started crying and she started wetting, and she had her face rubbed in it, her wet knickers wiped around her face and, oh, it was awful . . . the worst of the worst. I didn't like being an evacuee. I thought, Why are we being evacuated? It seemed that you were being punished. It was a long time before anything happened, and here we were, going through all these traumas, when we could have been home with Mother, like most of our schoolmates who weren't evacuated then. I think I would have felt happier if they'd been dropping bombs because I would have felt it was all worthwhile.

Evelyn Fee (Moss)
Evacuee mother of four, West Burton, Sussex

I went back to London for a day to pick up my wireless and my pram and some odds and ends from the house. But when I got there it was all boarded up. It had been looted. I lost such a lot of stuff, but fortunately my wireless and pram were still there. But it was shocking, really. My husband was in the navy and he'd done a lot of time on the China station, and he'd brought me home some very, *very* nice tea-sets and all that, which I'd put in this lovely ebony cabinet. And he had some big pot-bellied Buddhas and one of them he'd touch for luck if he'd done a horse. And he also had four silver Chinese dollars that we'd had made into ashtrays. *Every bit* was gone. And we had bought all new carpet for the hall and stairs, a new bedroom, and the house really looked lovely. But I never even bothered to go upstairs to see that. When I went into the sitting room and the back room and saw all that I just thought, Bugger the lot! That's my exact feeling. When I told Mrs Wilson she said, 'Oh, Mrs Fee, you must be heartbroken!' I said, 'Well, funnily enough, I'm not. The only thing I'm thankful for is that I'm away from it all, and the children are safe.' Because going from Dog Kennel Hill to East Dulwich where we lived was *awful* – everything was boarded up, there were barrage balloons over there. And I thought: The sooner I'm out of here the better ...

Very soon after that we moved to a much better house in Byworth ... We did feel different from the village people in Byworth and, yes, they didn't like evacuees. I mean, they used to, well, not exactly poke fun, but throw out to the children about the 'vaccies' from London. But, thank God, the children didn't *have* to play with them. We were the other end of the village and the people in the big houses near us were lovely – the Gatehouses, the Bebbs, they absolutely adored the children.

Vera Bullman (Tipson)
Evacuee schoolgirl, Sherston, Wiltshire

The village people had fixed ideas about East-Enders. I had to go somewhere else to live and I was very unhappy there: the woman was horrible. When my mother discovered that, she insisted that I would change [billets] and this woman said, 'Oh, you're just like all the other dirty East-Enders!' My mother said, 'I've never been called that before. We have a very good family and my home is very clean ...' But obviously there was some truth in it. We came from a poor area. There were problems with the children's heads, even mine – I had nits as well. I don't think you can mix without catching them. It worried me because I never had such a thing before. We had checks on our heads, and if we had fleas or nits they put stuff on and used a small-toothed comb ... The local gentry were kinder than the ordinary village people. They'd take us to the cinema, arrange treasure hunts with lovely little parcels. They did such a lot for us: lovely Christmas parties and Easter-egg hunts. How did they *get* them?

Millicent Morgan (Miller)
Evacuee schoolgirl, Oxborough, Norfolk

Eventually me and my brother were the only evacuees left in Oxborough. The main reason was that the others just couldn't bear being parted from their families ... Oxborough had a community of about two hundred and fifty then, and they all knew one another. There was nothing else in the village except church, either the Protestant or the Catholic. That was *it*. And some of them were a little bit ... well, mealy-minded, like, you know. They just didn't accept the Cockney kids for what we were. I suppose we were tearaways and probably a bit scrawny, compared with the robust country children, so perhaps they found us a little bit difficult to accept. Probably about three families were very lucky and got good foster-parents, but I do remember that some weren't very happy. They didn't have the warmth that they so sadly needed. Those people were doing society a favour by taking us in – you know, there was a war on and they'd got to do their bit. I mean, if they had a spare bedroom they *had* to take you and that was that. Some took it with good grace and others with bad grace so you were just lucky if you got with someone who wanted you.

Peter Bennett
Schoolboy, Godalming, Surrey

We had the London evacuees come down to Godalming. There were evacuee officers who used to trail the children around looking for places for them to live. And there was this one particular girl with impetigo nobody would take. She was the last to go – must have felt rotten to be the last, I think. We had one teacher who lived with us as an evacuee, and sometimes we had two. They used to have the front room and one bedroom, and we lived in the back. But I don't remember making friends with any evacuees. They were kept to themselves. But I do remember seeing individual evacuees looking terribly lonely and lost, and just sort of looking out on everybody else playing. Must have been dreadful, really, but you don't think of that when you're a boy. It's only looking back over the years . . . I think that we were still a small community and not used to mixing. I remember there was an Indian man who lived there. He was the 'black man', the only black man, and he wasn't even black, but we were all a bit afraid of him because he was *different* . . . There was never any talk of our being evacuated as we were supposed to be a 'safe' area, although we weren't at all safe.

Irene Mead (Weller)
Evacuee schoolgirl, Stratford-on-Avon, Warwickshire

We were always swapping tales – 'What did you have for breakfast this morning?' and 'What time does she get you up in the morning?' and 'Is she kind? Does she come and kiss you good-night?' And some of them would like it. But some not – my cousin, for instance, he walked all the way home to Birmingham, every step of the way, from Stratford to Birmingham. He just walked in and said, 'I've come home, Mum. I don't want to go back.' He walked all the way, twenty-odd miles …

I'd always have my two brothers with me, they never left my side, never. If we were asked anywhere I would always say, 'Well, I've got to bring my young brothers.' And when I used to come to the gate to go in my billet, the younger brother used to always cling on to me and there were always tears in his eyes and he'd always kiss me. And the other brother would say, 'Come along, come along, we've got to go in.' But the little one, he'd cling on to the very last minute.

Thomas Houlton
Evacuee schoolboy, Algarkirk, Lincolnshire

The Hull children fitted in well. There didn't seem to be much friction. The town children seemed to enjoy country life and the Lincolnshire children seemed to enjoy our presence. The thing I do remember is that we took our glass marbles with us and the country children had these little clay ones, and we turned our noses up in disgust at these, I think the rate of exchange was five to one. They had a much slower way of life and a slower way of speaking, quite broad Lincolnshire. They were constantly asking, 'Speak more slowly, please.' This wasn't helped by the Hull accent … We were there for eighteen months and then Dad decided that things didn't seem too bad in Hull so we came back in March 1941, just in time for the May blitz.

Noel Dumbrell
Schoolboy, Ashurst, Sussex

We only had three bedrooms in our house and I can remember people coming with palliasses, and we filled those with straw, clean oat straw, from the farms, because the barley straw would have been too prickly. And these were their little beds, and I can picture loads of blankets around, don't know who brought them because Mum and Dad didn't have them. Later we used them to black out the windows. We only had oil lamps and the wardens would come round, and if there was a chink of light there was trouble.

We got on with the evacuees very well. I can still picture them with their caps and their gas-mask boxes strung round their necks. We all mixed in together. We were just children and played together all the time, there were no problems. Those I can remember came from the East End, and I can picture the little shavers when they came in: they didn't talk our way, but I realized later that their speech was pretty similar to Sussex, not in accent but in the actual words they used. I can't remember the girls much. Those that came to the school disappeared, I can't remember when they went: most of them just went back to their mums and dads. One family stayed; the boy worked on the farm, and his dad came back from the war and they stayed in the village. I can't think of anything nasty to say about our evacuees – they were such lovely people.

John Wheeler
Schoolboy, Purton, Wiltshire

Most of the evacuees were verminous, which caused enormous problems in most of the homes to which they were taken. But it wasn't just their bodily state, it was also their lifestyle. For example, Mrs Kennett, who ran the family sweets and grocery shop in the village, took pity on a woman and three children. She had prepared a cooked meal for them, a leg of lamb and fresh vegetables from the garden – a typical lamb roast. When the children and the lady came, Mrs Kennett immediately became aware of the fact that they weren't very clean. Nevertheless, in the dining room she began to serve the meal. And, to her aston- ishment, they had their plates of food handed to them and all of them sat on the floor. Also, they wouldn't use knives and forks, refused to eat the vegetables because they didn't know what they were and picked up the meat with their fingers and covered themselves and – as she recalls – the carpet with gravy. And nothing she could do would persuade them to do other than

what they were doing. And she said, really, they were like animals
... And to Mrs Kennett's dismay, they all went into the garden
and performed their bodily functions – and the garden backed
on to the school so they were in full view of people who were
still in the school ...

It is, of course, an understatement to say that the village took
years to recover from that experience. And during that first week
of the war, there was the most unusual phenomenon when the
village pub, the Angel Hotel, was besieged at about half past nine
in the morning by all the ladies who queued up and sat around
in the street waiting for the pub to open ... Such was the resilience of the villagers that they were able eventually to come to
terms with the initial evacuation and I think probably – happily
for them – most of the mothers got so disenchanted with country
life, and the fact that there was nothing to do, that in a matter
of two or three weeks just about all the women had gone back
to London. But most of the children remained in the village, and
stayed for the whole of the war.

Bill, our evacuee boy, was quite irrepressible. He was a
gorblimey Cockney, but he was a most amusing lad. At that
time, September, Dad was digging potatoes for our lunch and
Billy was watching him. 'What's that, then?' he said, and my
father said, 'These are potatoes, Bill.' He said, 'What's potatoes?'
'Well, spuds.' 'No, they ain't spuds, they comes in nets.' And my
father fell apart at this. Billy didn't know that potatoes came
out of the ground. He only knew potatoes in bags or nets,
presumably in the markets he went to in London. And his
education in country ways went on constantly, and the fact that
milk came from a cow was a source of wonderment to him ...
Equally, the sort of sophistication that he had as a youngster left
us lagging, I mean, he was wily in many ways. He was a townie
and was very slick and much quicker than any of us in the
village ... Like the other evacuees, Billy used to swear – it
seemed part of his natural language. My mother used to say,
'Billy, you shouldn't say that, it's naughty,' but when he wasn't
looking she used to chuckle like anything. And my father often

had to leave the room when Bill had let some pearl drop – he'd go into the garden and have a jolly good laugh.

Mary Whiteman (Walker)
Wife of chief billeting officer, Saffron Walden, Essex

One of the problems in those days of settling unaccompanied children was the parents at weekends. They wanted to see how their children were, so often Mother and Father would come down, and when it came to every weekend, a lot of the households found it very hard going. So a train was put on once a month for evacuee parents, and the town hall was taken over and you could get food and drinks and there was a general social gathering, and the parents could take their children out, and that worked very well. And we had occasional socials and even a Christmas entertainment for them – this was in the winter of 1939–40 before the drift back started.

There was a boys' school evacuated here. The headmaster was a fine man, very good in his evacuation work, and he told the story of two families: one where the parents came down and said, 'Oh, we can't *bear* life without these boys, I know we'll be all right,' and they took them back and they were all killed. Then the other parents came down and wanted to take their boy back, and he said, 'No, leave him. Do leave him a bit longer if you can.' And they went back and they were killed, but the little boy settled and stayed on the farm for the rest of the war. So it was a question of advising people, but on the other hand trying to understand the parents' feelings. But nothing was happening in this Phoney War, and by 1940 the town had settled into a pattern of losing its evacuees. They drifted back but a residue stayed.

Carmin Sidonio
Evacuee schoolboy, Northiam, Sussex

Schooling wasn't worked out for a couple of weeks but Mr and Mrs Standen took us to a hop farm where they went hop-picking for extra money. I was fascinated. I could see the big oast-houses and the hopfields and all the people with their bins, and then a man would come, pull up a pole of hops and put atop a bin, and they would quickly pick the hops off, and they were paid for a binload. I started helping them, and eventually my brother and I got a bin of our own. I thought it was marvellous and we'd have breaks with tea out of a flask or water from a bottle and some sandwiches. It was *idyllic*. I'd never experienced anything like it. After that, we started a bit of schooling. But as there was no panic in the air, and we heard that a lot of children were going back to London, we wrote to Mum and Dad, 'Can we come back home?' 'Why not?' they replied, and we all went home, had Christmas at home, and next year we went back to school in London. Tom was called up into the army – he had served as a Territorial in Scotland. George was a very sensitive person: he was called up but didn't want to know anything about the services and he became a conscientious objector and went to do land work in Jersey. Things were hard to get for the shop, and the ice-cream side of it had been shelved, so it was only trade with the local people.

That was occupying us until June 1940 when the war, which had been a Phoney War up until then, suddenly took off.

Signs that the so-called Phoney War was ending came with the invasion of Denmark in April 1940, and with the evacuation of most British forces from Norway in early May. The situation deteriorated further as Allied forces were swept back to coastal areas against the fast-advancing German blitzkrieg. When Chamberlain stepped down, Winston Churchill became prime minister. On 13 May he made the first of his inspirational speeches in the House of Commons in which he warned Britons that they faced 'one of the greatest battles in history', and went on to say, 'I have nothing to offer but blood, toil, tears and sweat.'

Lady Thurle Folliott Vaughan (Laver Eriksen)
British schoolgirl, Copenhagen, Denmark

After my father died, my mother married a Dane based in Denmark and we went to live there ... The night before the Germans arrived, my mother woke my stepfather up, saying, 'Oh, darling, isn't it lovely to hear that the Danes have got plenty of aircraft?' And went to sleep. Going to school the next morning, I was aware that people on the train were extremely tense and worried, and I couldn't understand why grown-ups were like this. As I walked up the steps towards the school, the headmistress came down with her arms out and said, 'Thurle, Thurle, your enemy has occupied us!' Of course I didn't know what she was talking about, but a little while later my stepfather came and took me home.

Everyone was very shocked, the Danes had always thought that the Germans wouldn't bother with them because they were such a little country; they had no army or anything, and didn't think they were any sort of threat. At first the Germans wanted to demonstrate how friendly they could be to an occupied country. Well, this didn't work very well because the Danes wouldn't co-operate. Among my stepfather's friends, for instance, there was only one young man who wasn't active in the patriot movement and that was because his parents insisted he pass his exams.

Ann Thornton (Helps)
British schoolgirl, Copenhagen, Denmark

After the Germans had invaded, my mother tried to ring the British Legation; some of them she knew quite well. But they had cleared out, just disappeared, got on a special train. Only one person managed to ring to say goodbye. She was told, 'You're in the charge of the Americans. They will look after you.' Mother said, 'That's that!' So we got into our little car and drove into the centre of Copenhagen to see what was happening – typical of my mother not to be frightened of anything! And we found ourselves at the head of this German column gorgeously singing some German song and marching very beautifully into Copenhagen. When we got there, we went to see *The Wizard of Oz* because we thought it was our last chance to see anything. The whole thing was frightfully silly and frivolous, but she'd done what she could and thought, Well, we'll just have to take it easy and see what happens.

We got rid of the rented house and moved to a house in an idyllic part of Copenhagen which the owner, who lived in America, let furnished for a very low rent. And we found an extraordinary Dutchman to be our lodger, so that worked well. He kept us very cheerful and was a calm and excellent companion for us and he knew lots of Danes. And, of course, the money helped as we were then fairly poor. My mother had lots of rich friends whom she borrowed from and she ended the war with huge debts, which she paid off. Everyone was very kind to us. We registered with the Danish police: we had to give our passports to them and go to the local police station weekly to show we were still there. They were extremely sympathetic, very nice and helpful. After we led that column into Copenhagen, we hardly noticed the Germans.

Janet Shipton (Attlee)
Schoolgirl, Stanmore, Greater London

Our school had been evacuated when Holland was invaded. When they threw out Chamberlain, I knew about that because I was home from school with chicken-pox. I remember my father [Clement Attlee] coming and talking to me, saying there were two choices, either Lord Halifax or Winston Churchill would become prime minister, and wondering whether he would bring the Labour Party into a coalition government. I remember that very clearly.

Iris Hobby (Cutbush)
Teenager, East Cheam, Surrey

One day in the cinema there was a film of land girls marching along – they were saying, 'Come and join the Land Army.' I rather liked the look of their uniform and thought, *Yes*. I was only sixteen and was told I was too young, but when I was seventeen, in March 1940, I applied again. The lady who interviewed me didn't have a clue. She said, 'What kind of farming do you want to do?' I said I wanted to work on arable land and drive a tractor. 'Oh, no, *no*, you must belong to a dairy farm, with all those lovely cows. You'll be able to skim the cream off the milk and make butter . . .' She made it sound so romantic – in fact, you weren't allowed to do any of that! When I told my mother, she threw up her hands and said, 'Good heavens! The cows will be milked at midnight!' I had to get a certificate from my doctor. He didn't know me or anything about my past knee history. I told him I had had a bovine tuberculosis knee and had worn a calliper for years, and he said, 'How did you get here?' I said I had cycled. He said, 'Oh, if you do all these things, then grade A.' I didn't even have a medical and I could only bend my knee half-way when I became a land girl.

Peter Smith
Schoolboy, Petts Wood, Kent

Petts Wood lay about six miles north-east of Biggin Hill, which was later a Battle of Britain aerodrome, so we were really in quite a vulnerable area. We were only about twelve miles south of central London and during the period between autumn 1939 and spring 1940 we had some disturbed nights because one of the two air-raid sirens would sound, and off we would have to troop down into the Anderson shelter. At this time my grandmother, Nan Smith, was living with us. Now, she was rather a portly lady, and we also had a little Sealyham dog, called Bonzo. He used to get very frightened and would shake at the high-pitched sound of the sirens. The drill was: when the sirens went, out of bed, down the stairs, take your gas mask, troop out and down into the shelter. It was always a race to see who was first in – the dog or my younger sister, Jean, arms flailing! There was one amusing incident that happened in daylight: we were just coming out into the back garden, my grandmother following, and this Spitfire shot across at literally roof-top height and *roared*.

My grandmother was frightened out of her life and grabbed the nearest thing, which was a broom, to hide behind. We children fell about laughing to see this portly lady trying to hide behind a broom handle!

It turned out to be a brilliant summer, and then the raids gradually intensified, and I can recall in those summer days aerial dog-fights going on and the big vapour trails. And one day there was a huge circle of vapour, and people were saying that the German fighters form these big circles, then the bombers come and drop their bombs through the middle of them! There was a lot of ack-ack at night and, of course, in the mornings we children used to rush out and pick up the shrapnel, and if you got a nose cone of an AA shell, that was a great prize and you'd go to school and swap these, and boast of what you'd found ... I believe the first six to ten months of the war subsequently became known as the Phoney War. But at this time I think I was aware of the rape of Poland, and a certain number of terrible bombing events and the fall of Warsaw. And later, in the spring of 1940, we would have seen on the newsreels in the cinema the German invasion of the Low Countries and the terrible bombing of Rotterdam and roads clogged with refugees ... Like most families, we had a big map provided by one of the national newspapers and were sticking little flags with the British, French and German positions on them as we followed events on the wireless.

Living just twenty miles off the Cherbourg peninsula, and with Germany's rapid advance through the Low Countries and France, the Channel Islanders suddenly felt very vulnerable. From the outbreak of war until the spring of 1940, the tourist industry was still advertising with slogans such as 'Jersey – Ideal Wartime Resort', and the islanders believed that their home would be defended. But their confidence was shattered with the news of the blitzkrieg and they were confronted with a choice: to stay or evacuate.

Marion Tostevin (Letissier)
Schoolgirl, Guernsey

Evacuation took place before June 1940. It wasn't compulsory. At first my mother was thinking of sending me, but as I was an only child she changed her mind in the end. Most of my friends went – I think two-thirds of the children did. I was one of the thousands who stayed. It was a terrible time. I remember the mothers going around in tears, wondering what to do. The atmosphere was *awful*. I didn't mind being left behind and to this day I don't regret that I stayed, although I did regret it a little bit when the others came back because they were full of tales of what they'd seen in England and we'd been stuck here.

Molly Bihet (Finigan)
Schoolgirl, Guernsey

I can remember the children and the queues on the quayside. People didn't know what to do. There were some saying, 'You go,' and others saying, 'Stay, don't be yellow.' It was proper chaos down there and bewildering to us children, who didn't realize the importance of it at all. In those days, an important day out would be to go to the other end of the island for a day, so I can imagine that leaving the island was a big thing for the majority of the grown-ups.

Ron Hurford
Teenager, Guernsey

I had left school when I was fourteen and was too old to go with the children, but not old enough to go on my own. So my mum and dad and two of my brothers went down to the harbour to catch the boat going to England, but we were too late. The last boat had gone. My sisters and two of my brothers went; we were a divided family in the war.

From *The War Weekly* by Guy Barnett and Derek Tongs

As the Wehrmacht poured through Holland and Belgium into France, the Allied forces were forced to retreat to Dunkirk and other northern French ports where they scrambled on to any vessel that could carry them to safety.

Rodney Giesler
Anglo-German schoolboy, Ashford, Kent

The first meaningful time came in April 1940. Suddenly troops appeared everywhere – in the fields and orchards, digging trenches. It was very exciting for us kids. They were drilling and setting up gun emplacements. Bren-gun carriers were clattering up and down the roads and we had rides on them. The officers came in for hot baths. I can remember the Somerset Light Infantry and the Queen Victoria Rifles. Then, when we woke up one morning, there was silence: they'd all gone – Dunkirk was happening. We heard they'd gone to Calais to hold the port while other troops were evacuated from there. All the QVRs ended up as prisoners. There was a Major Albert in the SLI who had a house in Chewton Mendip, Somerset. My mother was worried that Ashford was getting vulnerable. Being middle class, we didn't join the hordes of evacuees getting on trains with labels tied on. We did it privately. My mother rented the major's house, and at the beginning of May 1940 we drove down to Somerset.

Kathleen Korybut (Daly)
British schoolgirl, Dunkirk, France, from her 1945 journal remebering the war

The twentieth of May. A day of hot, hazy blue sky and sun-bathed streets and the heavy scent of lilacs. In the morning refugees began pouring into Dunkerque, from Belgium and Holland. Dusty, tired little groups of old women in shawls, men smoking old clay pipes as they rested in the cool shadows of the cloisters, and squalling babies. The streets were crammed with them as they lay on the pavement, too exhausted to move ... Later that day, looking out of our window at home, suddenly Kitty pointed to the sky and we all saw a lurid red glow, which could have been nothing but a fire. Immediately there were many explosions, and simultaneously the air-raid warning went and there was a shriek and bellow of gun fire ... Daddy came and told us 'We'd better go down to the cellar ...' For a moment we stood at the window, thrilled. Caught in the long beam of a search-light was a silver shape – now two silver shapes, both spitting fire at each other, while the guns below sent up beautiful globes of red and orange, and tongues of yellow. 'Come on Spitfire!' I yelled. At that moment a thunderous explosion rent the air, making the windows rattle. 'Ooh! Come on Kathleen,' cried Kitty. 'OK,' I replied gaily. Down in the cellar, occasionally, the very cellar would rock with the force of an explosion, and we could hear the drone of planes above the booming and whining of the guns ... When at last we went upstairs to bed, I had the same feeling I have after a long-looked-forward-to dance: the feeling that all the fun was over, and when will the next one be?

Peter Smith
Schoolboy, Petts Wood, Kent

In the early summer of 1940, I was becoming aware of the setbacks in France, and as June approached the retreat of the British Expeditionary Force, the BEF, towards the coast and, of course, eventually the evacuation through Dunkirk. The main railway line from the coast through Orpington to London ran at the bottom of our school playing-field. I can recall a lot of us going and standing by the railings and watching these trains going through, filled with troops. Some of the blinds were partly down, but we did realize these were our chaps having to come back from France. I think we thought of it as a bad setback, but I don't think we were ever given the impression that we would lose the war – no way: somehow we would come through this. Invasion scares were being put about, but I don't think we ever felt terribly anxious about that.

David Morrish
Schoolboy, Plymouth, Devon

I think the wartime period can be broken down into a number of phases. The first phase was before the bombing and that would be the evacuation of France. Plymouth was flooded out with refugees who came by boat. You suddenly became aware of displaced people: some servicemen in uniform, some civilian refugee families. I remember going down to see the boats coming in and people in all sorts of conditions getting off, and feeling that whatever was happening was beginning to get a bit close. But still a bit of excitement. I had an autograph book and one of the sports for kids was going on the Hoe and seeing how many autographs we could get from servicemen – the exiled Poles and Dutch and everybody else. Suddenly it was all becoming very near.

Bess Cummings (Walder)
Evacuee schoolgirl, St Albans, Hertfordshire

During the Phoney War people in Britain had hardly been affected and were lulled into a false sense of security. We knew nothing of the tribulations of the Jewish people in Europe, the pogroms and the terrible way they were being treated ... But, of course, after the fall of France, and having to evacuate all our soldiers from there, the war became quite unphoney ... Dunkirk came home very vividly to me: we had connections in Kent and my mother's family saw these poor men who came back. Some of her relatives actually sent out the ships across the Channel from Margate and Dover. Some people said it was shaming to the nation. I don't think so. I think it was seminal in the way the war progressed after that. It brought the war home to the ordinary Briton and I think that was necessary.

Kathleen Korybut (Daly)
British schoolgirl, Dunkirk, from her 1945 journal

We arrived at the docks. We also heard a terrific explosion very close by and the deadly whine of more than one bomb before it exploded with a fearful roar. The next thing I remember is being in the lighthouse, almost suffocated by the press of human bodies around me. The noise was terrific: French voices jabbering, crying, raised in command, the drone of dive bombers, followed by the 'crump' of explosion and, above all, the sound of the departing ship that was to have carried us to England. As we stood, blinking, in the smoke-laden sunlight once more, dreadful fear gripped my heart: the last ferry to Dover had left the docks of Dunkirk, and we were still here. The Germans would come and torture us before they finally shot us . . . Now, it seemed that our doom was certain . . .

Accustomed as we were to the noise of the bombing, we knew that it had never been more fearsome than that night after our return from the docks. Closer and closer they fell . . . Then, down in the cellar, we heard the steady clump of marching feet above us, I only thought dazedly, Here it is. Kitty clutched my hand tensely. There was nothing we could do . . . The heavy feet reached the top of the stairs and I could only think, Oh God, oh God. In staggered 50 of our men – our own British Tommies and a handful of Raff [sic, RAF] boys . . . Here they were, the boys we knew, dazed with exhaustion and horror at the sights they had seen. And here were we, still alive, and absurdly cheerful. The next afternoon we went to the docks and we did not return to the mission.

By the time I had got over the first excitement of being on a boat again – a boat hardly visible for the mass of people cramming its decks – and made my way to the deck rail, the coast of France was nothing but a bank of smoke and flame. A stretch of silken blue water lay between us and the shore. I gasped to see the impenetrable black smoke stretching for miles. A friendly, red-faced soldier beside me stopped rolling his cigarette and said, 'That's the oil at Saint Pol.' Another soldier with bitterness in his voice said, 'That's the last we'll see of France.' Dunkirk fell on June 4th 1940. It took the Wehrmacht only 5 weeks to humble their historic foe.

4. The Great Awakening: June–September 1940

As the troops were evacuating from France, children were moved from coastal towns to new homes in South Wales and the Midlands. A ten-mile zone along the coast from Norfolk to Sussex was cleared of all non-essential personnel in preparation for the now serious prospect of an invasion. Until the German blitzkrieg and the capitulation of France on 22 June 1940, minds had been concentrated on air attacks rather than land assaults, and the idea of invasion had not been taken seriously. But now, with the Wehrmacht poised on the beaches of northern France, the threat was apparent.

On 14 May, Anthony Eden, the Secretary of State for War, broadcast an appeal for British civilian men between the ages of seventeen and sixty-five, to come forward to defend their communities with the Local Defence Volunteers (LDV). In rural areas as well as towns and cities, men of all ages responded, their numbers reaching nearly a million and a half by the end of June. Subsequently the LDV changed its name to the Home Guard, or, as it was affectionately known, given the average age and amateurish image of its members, 'Dad's Army'.

The LDV was not the only civilian-defence organization set up during the Dunkirk crisis. Far less well-known today is the top-secret underground resistance network known as the Auxiliary Units. Many members belonged to the Home Guard, which provided excellent cover for their work. 'Auxiliers', as they were called, were specially selected civilians, trained in the art of sabotage; they worked underground in their localities with no knowledge of their counterparts in any of the twenty operational areas around the coast of

Britain. In the case of invasion, they would emerge in their local patrol areas to carry out guerrilla operations on German forces behind the line. If caught, they knew they would be shot as spies. The units were well supplied with the best equipment possible, guns, knives, hand grenades, explosives and bomb-making materials, to be kept in hideouts, which were usually dug in woods. Although those trained in guerrilla and sabotage activity were usually men, women played an important role, especially in communications. The Auxiliary Units remained in place from the summer of 1940 to November 1944, long after the threat of invasion had passed.

On 10 May, a lone aircraft made an attack on English soil near the villages of Petham and Chilham in Kent. It caused little damage and no casualties, but it marked the start of German reconnoitring flights. By early June and July, enemy aircraft over British skies became a more familiar sight, raids more frequent and widespread as the Luftwaffe took advantage of its new bases in France and Belgium.

On 28 June, just before the Germans landed on 1 July, the Channel Islands were bombed in a daylight raid, killing thirty-nine civilians and injuring many others.

In July 1940, the first bombs dropped on Greater London fell in Croydon.

John Starling
Evacuee schoolboy, Winchester, Hampshire

The masters, particularly the geography and history teachers, updated us on the war events. We had maps put around the walls of the school, which indicated with arrows the advances of the German forces into the Low Countries and France, and by the time of Dunkirk, we all felt that the war was going to be right on our doorstep. I remember going to Winchester station and seeing a batch of Belgian and French troops who'd returned from France, and a lot of British troops arrived and went into barracks in Winchester. We all felt that what little resistance we could put

84

up would only be a token resistance, and were pretty certain that we'd go the way of the French and Belgians, irrespective of how resolute we were and how stirred by Winston Churchill's speeches. I don't know what we would have done without Churchill at this time. There was no better leader to inspire the country. They had started to form the Home Guard. It was a 'Dad's Army', there's no doubt about that. They had no proper equipment to try to fight off the German invaders – just broom handles, sticks and shovels. And I do think we felt a bit pessimistic then. We kept hearing rumours of bodies and barges being washed ashore on the south coast of England, and I believe there were one or two commando attempts by the Germans to infiltrate some areas – lots of rumours buzzing around.

I remember some tragic naval cases. The *Royal Oak*, for instance: several children lost their fathers when she went down in October 1939. And later when the *Hood* was blown up [24 May 1941], more children lost fathers. We were told to be as sympathetic as possible and help them at this difficult time. Very often the mothers would come up and take lodgings in Winchester so that they could be near their children.

Margaret Woodhead (Butler)
Evacuee schoolgirl, Winchester, Hampshire

I was in Winchester at the time of Dunkirk. A couple of girls I knew lost their fathers there. One was killed in the navy and the other had one of these small boats which rescued the troops and it was sunk. I can remember walking home with this girl. She was telling me about it, but she accepted it. Having lived apart from your family, you couldn't take in that it had happened: you were so absorbed into the families you were living with that your own family seemed to recede into the background. It was some-thing unreal . . . When the ships went down in Portsmouth, they used to have these big bulletin boards at the naval dockyard, and you'd see crowds of people going there. They used to post up ships that had gone and lists of those who had been lost on them. That was really traumatic, seeing those people who were hoping

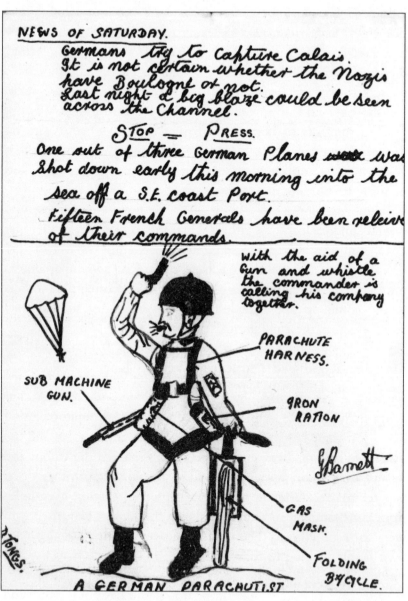

From *The War Weekly* by Guy Barnett and Derek Tongs

86

that their loved one wasn't on that list. And when it really did hit them ... that used to be pretty dreadful.

Elisabeth Small (Fabri, née Hadfield)
Schoolgirl, Stalybridge, Cheshire

In July 1940, I was to take my School Certificate. In May everybody expected that we were going to be invaded. My parents rang the boarding-school and told them to put me on the first train with my trunk. I arrived home at the time of Dunkirk. I remember in June, my mother ringing up the colonel of Ashton-under-Lyne barracks saying, 'We have a lot of lovely strawberries. I want to give our boys a strawberry tea. Will that be all right?' The colonel said, 'Of course, but you must realize that some of them are not in their proper uniforms.' We had a cook and a maid, and Mother told them, 'No uniforms, put on your pretty dresses.' We had a long table, and the soldiers came and had this strawberry tea and home-made scones. The atmosphere was *amazing*, because not only my parents but all their friends who had been so worried said, 'All is well, the boys are back!' And the boys *were* back, but without any ammunition, guns or whatever. The atmosphere just *turned* and I can hear Churchill's voice now, 'We shall fight on the beaches ... we shall fight in the fields and in the streets ... We shall never surrender.' Everybody was cheering, quite *extraordinary*.

John Leopard
Infant, Dagenham, Essex

I was only two years old when war started. My first memory of it would be in 1940, travelling with Mum and my baby sister from Dagenham to the family home in Deptford ... My father was in the Rifle Brigade and one of the last thirty of his regiment to get away from Calais. I have a vague recollection of seeing him. He came in and apparently put a .303 rifle across my shoulder and I landed up on the floor – my *only* recollection of my father ... He was then transferred to Devon before being sent off for North Africa. We lost contact with him and it was some two years before we found out what had happened to him. He was captured in Tobruk and sent across the Med in an Italian ship, which was sunk by Allied action. Unfortunately they never found his body. I do remember walking down the high street with my mother and asking her why there were no lights when it got dark, and she used to say, 'John, those lights can only come on when Daddy comes home from war.' I repeated that a few months later and she said, 'Sorry, John, Daddy isn't coming home.' That was the first time I knew ... Later on in the war, my mother died of heart failure, which meant us three children being split up between relatives. I went to live with my aunt Sophie Fitzgerald and her husband.

Peter Bennett
Schoolboy, Godalming, Surrey

My father was in the Home Guard. One day he was showing us how to present arms, not with his rifle but with a music stand, and he shot it through the window and broke the glass. Glass wasn't easy to get in those days either. I think he probably enjoyed himself in it. Everybody seemed to work evenings as well as days, and he had very, *very* little time off. They took it quite seriously. We thought the Home Guard was better than the air-raid wardens. At least they were defending our country and willing to fight.

Myra Collyer (Murden)
Schoolgirl, Reigate, Surrey

I didn't think about invasion at all, but my papa once said, 'There's a gun on that wall. If the Germans invade, your mother and you are for the chop.' I thought, You won't get *me*! But he'd been through the First World War, you see ...

One day I heard a little old lady saying, 'We need a new secretary for the Home Guard, thirty shillings [£1.50] a week.' I thought, That's me! I got the job. I interviewed what to me were old men, and I also typed up reports. Captain Osborne, the adjutant, was my boss. He ran the shop for the blind. The local doctor joined, the man who ran the hardware store – a lot of elderly men all trying to do the Captain Mainwaring thing, all trying to be boss, all showing their authority. It used to amuse me, bless their hearts – 'We must do this, we must do that ...' There was a huge pit in Reigate, which they used for their shooting practice. They had this red balloon in a bucket to aim at. Who was the person to replace the balloon when it was shot? Me! So I was backed against the pit with all this shooting going on and I'd run across and put another in and rush back, hoping to God they didn't hit *me*! ... I can remember going home to my mother and telling her, 'Gee, I've interviewed an old man today, he's got a bald head and he's not allowed to join up because his mother's German.' I found out later that he was only twenty-eight – that shattered me a little bit.

John Hammon
Schoolboy, Stowting, Kent

The army came and dug huge trenches and took poles from the trees in the wood, stood these up at an angle and put camouflage netting over it all, and that did look as if there was a whole line of guns through the woods to deceive the enemy. But, of course, we went to play in it, and when I think about it, it was the silliest place to play, but no one worried. Then they started putting gun emplacements on the hills to try to give us a proper line of defence. We were right in line – Calais, Folkestone – right up the line to London, which was why they called Kent 'Hellfire Corner'.

As for 'Dad's Army', I know people laugh at them, but many of those men had fought twenty years before in the previous war and they were skilled and they'd got a whole line of medals. The Captain Mainwarings were about. There were two officers who had never served in a war at all, they were just senior people in the village, but when you saw the old soldiers ...

Brian Ryland

Schoolboy, Sidcup, Kent, taken from his memoir

One particular exercise had been arranged when my father's group was to attack an anti-aircraft gun site that had been positioned on a local golf course. The agreed plan was that the raid would take place early on Sunday morning – in daylight, as it was summer. Because of all the ridicule and jokes they received from all and sundry, the men were determined to show what they were capable of, which in this case meant trying to capture the gun site from the regular troops.

The Home Guard decided to attack before dawn, and they were specially supplied for the occasion with thunder flashes, while each man had a rifle and bayonet. The regular servicemen were still asleep as dawn broke, not expecting the exercise to start until after breakfast ... The Home Guard platoon went in, determined to show what they could do. Tempers snapped when the regulars realized they had been caught with their trousers down. Fists, rifle butts and anything to hand were used in the fight that followed, but the Home Guard soon mopped them up, rounding up the 'prisoners' at the business end of their bayonets. There were a few bruised heads and other injuries at the end.

A day or so later, a strong letter of protest was received from the commanding officer of the regulars, saying that they were not expected until 9 a.m. The captain of the Home Guard replied, telling the army CO that the Germans would not send a telegram before invading, and that his guards had not been vigilant. He thought the exercise had been a complete success ... Members of the Home Guard platoon continued to tell the story over pub bars with much glee for a long time ... There is no doubt that if Hitler had invaded this country the Home Guard would have given a good account of themselves, alongside the regular army, regardless of the jokes.

John Wheeler
Schoolboy, Purton, Wiltshire

One night a pal and I – both under age – went to the local police sergeant and enlisted in the LDV. My mother was worried to death because our duty began that very night. My friend, Nelson, and I were put on a farm cart, which was pulled across the road in the village, with Mrs Lloyd, then the maths teacher at school. The three of us were stuck there for a night's duty waiting for the Germans. Now this was the most incongruous thing you could think of, looking back. But when it got daylight – the first dawn I ever saw in my life – shortly before we packed up and pulled the farm cart off the road, Billy, our evacuee, arrived with my breakfast and thought he was playing an enormous part in fighting the Germans. It seems so ridiculous now – what we could have done with a farm cart and no weapons if the Germans had come, I don't know! But it was the spirit of the time.

Jill Monk (Holman)
Schoolgirl, Aylsham, Norfolk

Dad's Home Guard uniform was just a cover for his work with the Auxiliaries. Being a GP, he was in a very good position should there be an invasion, because he would obviously be given a permit to visit his patients and could keep his eye open for troop movements, or targets to bomb and put out of action. The next thing was that we had a radio transmitter, which was eventually concealed in the coal cellar. They blocked off the chute where the coal went down from outside, and in the place where the coal was they fitted the transmitter. In front of the transmitter and receiver they fitted an asbestos sheet with an electric stove on it. On the right-hand side was a little space where you could fit a thin knife, which would release a catch. This would release the asbestos sheet so that we could get to the transmitter. The aerial was very cleverly led up a nearby chimney where it looked like a lightning conductor. The Signals men would come and change the batteries, and it became impossible for my mother and me not to know what was happening. So we both had to sign the Official Secrets Act. I was fourteen, still at Cheltenham [Ladies' College] when I first started. This would have been 1940, just after Dunkirk.

The messages were sent in code, and these were frequently changed. They were rather like a text message now, sort of shortened words, and the code would be part of the letters. I transmitted messages myself. It was just a question of knowing the right buttons, quite a simple thing, which seemed to come naturally to me. We had this wonderful refectory table, which Dad had designed, and we used to spread the codes out on this. The sheets were kept in one of the drawers of Mum's bureau.

I left Cheltenham when I was sixteen and went to work on local farms. I was also breaking in horses for people because there was nobody else to do it. Getting about doing that, I was able to keep my eye on troop movements and anything else worth bombing – who would suspect a young girl riding around on a horse? I could get into the woods and over the fields where the troops were camouflaged, and that information would be sent through by Mum or Dad in the code of the day. We never knew where it went, we never knew anybody else who was functioning on this. It was all very hush-hush, because if we didn't know anything, they could torture us as long as they liked, but there was nothing we *could* tell. If the Germans invaded and found our [radio] set, we would have been treated as spies.

Janet Shipton (Attlee)
Schoolgirl, Tintagel, Cornwall

When the invasion seemed imminent and the school was evacuated to Tintagel, I remember very well planning to drop our wardrobes out to kill the enemy if they came, which, of course, was *totally* impracticable. But in those days we had so little to defend ourselves with. Things were so desperate that schoolgirls were going to tip their wardrobes on the enemy!

John Hammon
Schoolboy, Stowting, Kent

We would often have to go into the shelters at school when these intermittent raids started and we carried our gas masks all the time. Then they brought in something like a furniture-removal van, and they filled it with gas, and we all had to pass through wearing our gas masks in blocks of ten or twenty boys, and we were in it for about five minutes and then came out the other end. This was to prove whether our gas masks worked or not. It must have been something like tear gas, not very lethal, but anyone afterwards who had tears in their eyes had their gas masks readjusted so that they fitted better ... Being just thirty miles away from the enemy now in France, we must have been aware that the Germans could invade. But we thought we would win. I don't think it ever entered our heads that we wouldn't win.

After the fall of France, invasion became a real prospect, and fears of a German 'fifth column' prompted Churchill's government to round up so-called 'enemy aliens' who, although restricted in their movements since the outbreak of war, had not been arrested and incarcerated – although individuals categorized as high-risk had been imprisoned at the outset. Most were Jewish refugees who had come to Britain to escape Nazi persecution. When Italy entered the war, on 10 June 1940, it was the turn of the Italians: four thousand men, from seventeen to seventy, were arrested in London alone. Of these, it was estimated that six hundred had been born in Britain. Italy's entry into the war, treated mockingly by Churchill and others, had serious repercussions for the Allies, particularly in Malta and North Africa.

Carmin Sidonio
Schoolboy, Blackheath, London

After the Germans swept through France, the next big event for us that year, of course, was when Italy entered the war. We realized then that this was a new development. My father didn't say a lot about it, but I think it worried him ...

Then I remember one morning from upstairs hearing my mother crying and loud shouting from my father, Luigi and others. I quickly dressed and went downstairs and there was my father, Luigi, my mother, sister Angelica and two tall men in raincoats and trilby hats. They were policemen and had these papers in their hands. I said, 'What's going on?' My mother said, 'They've come to take Dad and Luigi away because Italy's come into the war.' 'What's that got to do with them?' And the men said, 'That's what we've got orders for. You're Italian nationals and we have to intern you because you're not naturalized subjects.' My father said, 'For goodness' *sake*, I've been here since 1910. That's *thirty years*. My son Luigi was *three months* when he came here. He can't even speak Italian!' 'Sorry, but that's what we've got orders to do.' My mother said, 'You're breaking up my family, my older son's in the army already and now you're taking the others away.' They were a bit discomforted because they moved to one side and were looking and talking, then one of them said, 'I'll tell you what, *one* of you will have to come. We don't care which one but one will have to come.' Luigi said, 'Well, I'll go.' Father wasn't in the best of health and Luigi insisted, and went upstairs to pack some things, and they took him away. We were all shattered by it, absolutely. That's when I realized how involved I had become in the war from a personal family point of view.

David Gray
Evacuee schoolboy, Bransbury, Yorkshire

My father was headmaster of Bootham Quaker School in York. I remember his grief and anxiety when the government issued an order that all 'enemy aliens' should be interned in Britain and the police took away Jewish sixth-formers and they were interned. It was a very dark period at the beginning of the war. No one really knew what the war was going to be like, did they? The theory was that we were all going to be gassed out of existence in the opening months of the war. Also, two of the Bootham boys, Peter Hume and Tom Tanner, who went into the Friends' Ambulance Unit as conscientious objectors, were torpedoed and drowned. I can remember my father grieving over them, killed so young in the war. I'm sure he was reliving the First World War and the death of so many of his contemporaries.

Madge Howell
Mother of four, with her Service husband in Valetta, Malta, extract from her memoir

On 10 June 1940, Italy had declared war. We wondered how this would affect us. We were soon to know. At 7 a.m. the next morning, the screaming of the sirens, soon followed by the Italian aeroplanes coming over and bombs being dropped, awakened us. Eight times that day they came. We tried to carry on as usual for the children's sakes, playing tennis and so on, but it was quite a job. The nearest bombs were across the creek ... Our house was outside the barrack gates, and we were promised room in the Officers' Mess tunnel, but we decided to stick it out in our own house, rather than let the children get 'shelteritis' – the feeling that they must get down a shelter quickly ...

A ship went off taking wives and children back to England. Once more we decided to keep together, but many of our friends left. Maltese friends asked both Adrian and me anxiously if we were going home to England. They were very relieved when they heard that we had resolved to stay with them. They told us they felt that if all the United Kingdom families left the island, it would be obvious that there was little hope that we should be able to hold Malta. Some seven hundred United Kingdom women and children remained in Malta throughout its siege ...

On 29 July 1941, our son, Peter, was born during the night. It was the first raid-free night for three weeks. The King George V

Seamen's Hospital was on the very edge of the Grand Harbour. The front entrance was in ruins. There was a deep shelter but no way down for bedridden patients. Our beds were wheeled into the 'strong room' (so-called) but it did not feel at all strong when bombs whistled down on ships being unloaded just below us.

The day after France's capitulation, on 22 June, the Channel Islanders were appalled to learn that their islands were not to be defended: they were on their own. It was then only a matter of waiting for occupation, and worrying about what kind of rule it would be.

In Gibraltar, after the fall of France and the establishment of the Vichy government, the situation had deteriorated drastically for Gibraltarian evacuees, who had been sent to Morocco in early 1940. It meant their repatriation to Gibraltar and a second evacuation, this time to Britain, to clear the Rock of non-essential personnel and prevent pressure on precious resources in the case of a blockade.

Joseph Stagno
Gibraltarian evacuee, London

We came back from Marrakesh where we had been sent in February 1940. After the surrender of Dunkirk in June, we became more or less hostages ... It meant we had to get out ... We tried to settle back in Gibraltar again – there were feelings of relief, we were glad to get home – but not for long as the second evacuation soon took place. With this second evacuation after the fall of France, we *all* had to go and most people came to England. Gibraltar, in those days, was very vulnerable to blockade as it had to rely on importing all its food and water, so by evacuating the civilian population, they were cutting down on the need, so really it was sensible to evacuate ...

I was very excited to be going to England. The older people felt depressed and sad. I had a terrific impression of Glasgow the morning we landed. Unlike the usual Scottish weather, it was a beautiful morning. The place seemed *huge* and there were all these barrage balloons up in the air – terrific, massive! Everything seemed so big compared with our little rock. I'd never seen a train or a bus, and all this added to the excitement of the arrival . . . There was an organized welcome, probably from the WVS [Women's Voluntary Service] and other voluntary bodies. Language was no problem: we all spoke English, except the very old people. The problems came with food and climate. We were then sent by train to London. In our case we went to the Royal Palace Hotel, received again by the WVS and given meals. That first morning in London – looking out of our window on the sixth floor to see such a massive area, houses, tall buildings and barrage balloons floating overhead – made quite an impression. When people in Gib talked of England, it was all centred around London, and to be there was to be in the right place, regardless of what was happening.

Molly Bihet (Finigan)
Schoolgirl, Guernsey

We'd just been to a shop and were looking over a wall by the side of our house, and we saw these three planes coming over the harbour. I was waving a cucumber because we thought they were British planes, and then they started machine-gunning and my mother grabbed us and we ran down a little corridor of a house opposite and stayed there the whole time. We were very close to the harbour and it must have lasted about an hour. There were quite a few people there and when it had quietened down, we all came up and we could see the commotion down there and see the lorries alight, and hear the terrible things that had happened. That was the first we knew that the Germans were so close and were going to land.

Ron Hurford
Teenager, Guernsey

There were quite a few killed down at the harbour. It was a devastating sight: there were horse-drawn carriages loaded with tomatoes, and lorries too, and they were queued right back to the weighbridge, and everybody was running around and it seemed chaotic to me, as a young lad. My first wife's brother was killed on the lifeboat. It was a terrible shock, frightening. Some of the islanders had put cows on the airstrip to stop the Germans landing, and the Germans said if they didn't move them, they would bomb them, so they moved them. We had a Royal Guernsey Militia, but as far as I can remember that had left for the mainland and there were only a few students with guns. But there was no resistance when they came. What could you do? You couldn't fight them with your hands.

My first sight of them was outside the Channel Hotel, which is along the little promenade. I remember thinking, Coo, crummy! They don't look much different to us. That was my first encounter with them. They were very dictatorial, oh, *yes*, you didn't have to look at them sideways! There were a few SS and a few black uniforms, but mainly Wehrmacht, the ordinary soldiers.

Marion Tostevin (Letissier)
Schoolgirl, Guernsey

My grandmother was thinning grapes at the vinery down the road, and when the bombing started my mother panicked and ran to fetch her home. My father – I'll never forget it – he had his two arms on a chair, and as he looked out of the window he could see the bombers coming, and his arms were trembling and he said, 'I think we ought to go into the cupboard under the stairs.' ... Then I remember my mother came into my room on that Monday morning and she sat on my bed and said, 'The Germans have landed.' And that very day I saw one pass on a motorbike, which was really very, very frightening. Even though we didn't know a lot about them, I knew they were our enemies in the war, but I didn't know all the horrific things yet.

Throughout the summer, enemy air activity intensified until on 13 August, 'Eagle Day', around 1,485 German aircraft

attacked Britain. The RAF's Spitfires and Hurricanes took to the air to defend their airfields as they had done since 10 July. They engaged with the Luftwaffe in 'dog-fights' over the skies of southern England. These proved particularly thrilling for children, and those living in the south at this time have vivid memories of them, the skies etched with vapour trails, and of crashed planes which fell into their areas from 10 July to 31 October 1940 during the Battle of Britain.

Although Hurricanes outnumbered Spitfires in the battle, and pilots still argue about their relative merits, the Spitfire has become an icon of the Battle of Britain. The Minister for Aircraft Production, Lord Beaverbrook, had run a series of public-relations campaigns or 'stunts', as they were sometimes called, designed to boost output of the planes. The 'Saucepans for Spitfires' appeal was intended to coax housewives into handing in anything made of aluminium to help build the desperately needed planes. The response was enthusiastic, and practically every town in Britain launched its own Spitfire Fund, which attracted many contributions from children, who handed over their pocket money.

Between mid-August and early September there were fifty-three major raids on airfields. RAF losses were devastating, the casualty rate running to 22 per cent. On 7 September, the Luftwaffe's attention turned to London. This did not mean the fight was over, just a switch of the battle area. However, it gave Fighter Command a much-needed, albeit brief, respite and a chance to repair airfields and regroup.

Derek Bech
Schoolboy, Aldwick Bay, Sussex

We used to laugh when the siren went and say, 'They've got it wrong again!' But in 1940, things did change drastically. We had German planes coming over and dog-fights overhead. Being a nine-year-old boy, I was in my element. As soon as I saw a plane coming down, I was on my bike and often was first at one of those sites. I must say I saw some horrible sights. The worst one was in the marshes behind Pagham harbour. You couldn't get to it by road – we used to go across the Pagham dyke, and I went on my bicycle with my friend. It was a Dornier bomber, which was on fire when we got there. They were all dead, I think, but we saw the bodies of airmen on fire as well. I was told that when I got home that day I was very quiet . . . It had been an awakening for me – far more than just games . . . But one of the nastiest things I witnessed was when I was standing in my back garden and heard planes. I looked up and saw an English Beaufighter flying along under some low clouds, and immediately three Spitfires came out of the clouds on top of it. They realized they were going to crash into it, and two of the Spitfires broke formation and cut each other in half. Again, we were very quickly on the scene. Somebody else had got there first – one of the pilots had tried to bale out and was decapitated, I was told. They were both killed. So I did experience a bit of the real war at quite an early age.

Noel Dumbrell
Schoolboy, Ashurst, Sussex

Well, the height of the Battle of Britain! If you could look up to the sky – I can see it to this day – the *trails*, the vapour trails! The Jerries came over, dozens and dozens of them, and our boys would come from Tangmere and all over the place and they would dive on them. I've seen as many as seven falling out of the sky at one time, on fire, crashing. Unfortunately on one occasion two were ours – Spits. These two planes had had a good day and were so excited that they did a 'victory roll' and hit each other. One pilot got out, the other didn't. We knew all the different planes and could tell them by the noise: the German bombers were a deep *drroww rrroww rrrowww*, whereas our boys were *whowwisssh* and they were gone. Even our bombers when they went over didn't make the same noise as the Germans . . .

We certainly didn't know it as the Battle of Britain then, it was just a daily occurrence, every day, every night. I started to get a bit more worried then about an invasion . . . And they altered the clocks, which upset country life. The kids used to come to school all at different times, and 'We couldn't milk our cows – we couldn't put clocks back on our cows!' This was done to get more daylight hours.

Doreen Hartley (Saunders)
Schoolgirl, Battle Abbey, Sussex

We used to see the dog-fights overhead. There were these young men fighting for their lives, and we would be looking up as we played tennis saying, 'That one's ours, that one's theirs . . .' It was a lovely summer, very clear . . .

Eileen Woods (Cox)
Schoolgirl, Spelding, Kent, extract from her memoir

On one occasion Canon Mallison called us and asked my mother to attend the funeral of a young German airman who had been killed when his plane crashed near our village. She was a little reluctant as this man was the enemy. Canon Mallison pointed out that he had also been some mother's son, perhaps a husband and a father too, and it was a Christian duty to give him a decent funeral. She agreed, and so did many of the villagers. The funeral was well attended and there were many flowers. I remember that there was a simple white cross on his grave and I used to put wild flowers on it from time to time.

Myra Collyer (Murden)
Secretary to Home Guard, Reigate, Surrey

We lived on Reigate Common. The Germans were attacking our planes from Redhill aerodrome and this chap baled out of his plane, and the German flew round and round him in his plane and shot him in his parachute. This infuriated my mother. We could see it and hear the gunfire – and, of course, he went limp and came down. That really horrified me, how people could be so cruel.

Peter Izard
Schoolboy, Beckenham, Kent

We all watched the Battle of Britain from the back garden. And I remember walking one day across a field with my aunt in Tunbridge Wells, when this Messerschmitt came down very low and machine-gunned us. That was followed by a Spitfire trying to shoot him down. Everywhere around this area of Kent was involved, I mean, you'd look up and couldn't really tell whether it was one of our chaps being shot down or a German. It was only if he landed close to you. I was then twelve – it was all very exciting for a small boy, the whole war was. I still look back on it as *the* experience of my life ...

John Hammon
Schoolboy, Stowting, Kent

It wasn't until what we now know as the Battle of Britain that suddenly the Germans started coming in great formations into Kent – they looked like lots of flies coming and, of course, they went for Lympne airfield. We watched that being bombed by German dive-bombers: a whole line of them just dived down. It was a complete fireball in a matter of three or four minutes – they wiped out all the main buildings and the hangars. And then we looked the other way and could see the same thing happening on Hawkinge airfield – a great fireball there. And other planes were going and bombing inland. At that time we saw far more German than British planes.

Really, it was pathetic to see a squadron of twelve Spitfires or Hurricanes going up to tackle maybe forty bombers and a whole host of German fighters. 'Dog-fights', they were called: the bombers would come leaving their condensation trails – 'con trails', we called them – the British planes would go up into them and for a few minutes there would be machine-gun fire everywhere, and then suddenly it was all over and you'd get a lull of two or three hours. They came about nine in the morning, then at eleven, and again in late afternoon. We stood out and watched and it wasn't until we heard the whiz of machine-gun bullets and shrapnel coming down that we thought we'd better go under some sort of shelter. We often saw a plane smoking and down it would come. We were then quickly on our bikes to get there and watch. But if the plane was alight, you didn't want to be within fifty yards of it because ammunition was exploding, and within no time that plane would be just a burnt-out wreck. The tails and tips of the wings wouldn't burn, but the rest would be a great pile of rubble. I did see one pilot burnt to nothing. We just stood there. I don't know my feelings then . . . I think a kind of fright, really, that this could happen to people. But very often the pilot would bale out. Even then they were often injured – it was quite a sad time, these young boys of eighteen or twenty, German and British.

Audrey Hammon (Cobb)
Schoolgirl, Romney Marshes, Kent

Our farm was about half a mile from the end of one of the runways of Newchurch airfield, so when things started we experienced a lot of what was happening. I can remember a plane crash in one of our fields – for a child this was something out of the ordinary and exciting. This field was surrounded by ditches filled with water. By the time we got there, the pilot was climbing out of the aeroplane. As Mother, Father and I neared, I remember him standing by the plane and saying, 'Don't need you this time, but might do next!'

Eileen Woods (Cox)
Schoolgirl, Spelding, Kent, extract from her memoir

About once a week my mother and I would go to the Ritz cinema in Tunbridge Wells. During these trips we saw many of Sir Archibald McIndoe's – the famous World War Two plastic surgeon – 'Guinea pigs' – walking wounded. Some had dreadfully burnt faces. I remember that I was often very frightened at the sight of them and tried hard not to show it as I knew they were all brave men. They were always allowed to go to the front of the cinema queues and rightly so ...

Rodney Giesler
Anglo-German schoolboy, Chewton Mendip, Somerset

Even in Chewton Mendip we saw air battles. They were coming over in daylight to bomb Bristol and straight over us to bomb Cardiff docks. You heard the sirens: the wailing made you heavy-hearted. You heard the characteristic drone of their engines. We'd run out and see these formations and we watched the fighters ducking and diving among them. My mother was frightened because there was anti-aircraft fire, and what goes up comes down, and shrapnel was falling around. So we saw dog-fights even though we weren't in the Battle of Britain area. There was a lot of aerial activity. Summer 1940 happened there as well as in Kent and Sussex ... There were the Women's Institute aluminium drives – 'Saucepans for Spitfires', which was nonsense because the grade of aluminium in saucepans was totally unsuitable for aircraft ...

David Gray
Schoolboy, Bransbury, Yorkshire

I think I remember Battle of Britain news on the radio and in the newspapers while we were at Bransbury, and feeling that it all happened far away down in Kent and, being a Yorkshire boy, Kent seemed *miles* away and I couldn't really believe those stories of Spitfires and German planes in the sky over Kent. But it was obviously important to my parents and very worrying.

Tony Parker
Teenage pacifist, Manchester, Lancashire

I remember at the time of Dunkirk and the Battle of Britain a clergyman who used to come into the shop asked me to go out

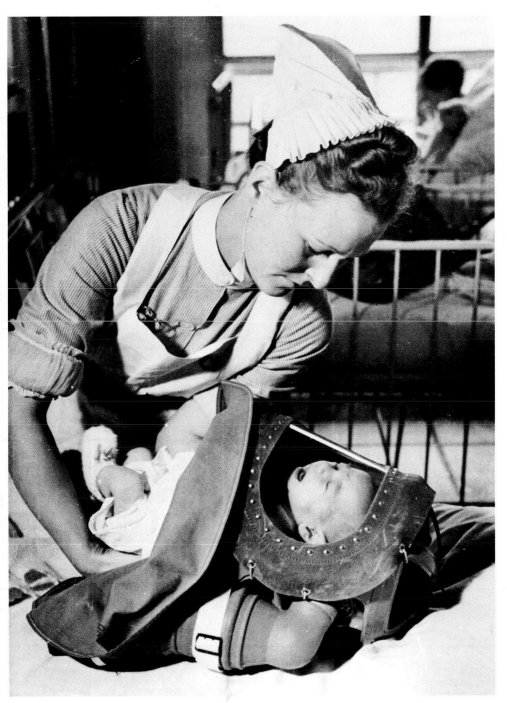

1. Gas drills: a baby is fitted with a specially designed gas mask.

2. Off to safety: the evacuation of East End schoolchildren, 2 September 1939.

3. Evacuees ready for departure from a London railway terminus: for many the holiday mood soon wore off.

4. Victoria station, London, 2 September 1939: mothers with their babies and young children were among the first evacuees.

5. Children try out the newly erected Anderson shelter in their back garden.

6. Dennis Hayden (*right*) with his mother and younger brother.

7. Evacuee John Starling with his host, Mr Penton, Winchester.

8. Young evacuees from Rotherhithe, all carrying their gas masks, enjoy a walk in Reading, Berkshire.

9. East End children tuck into their meal at an improvised feeding centre in the Gloucestershire village of Chipping Campden.

10. Reg Baker (*right*) with his blacksmith host, Mr Dorling, and pal Ronbo.

11. Molly Bihet (Finigan), who lived through the German occupation of Guernsey.

12. Parents and friends wave off youngsters during the second wave of evacuation in the summer of 1940.

13. The 'official' identity card that belonged to Thurle Folliott Vaughan (Laver Eriksen). These were provided by the Danish authorities throughout the German occupation.

14. Ann Thornton (Helps) lived in Denmark under the German occupation before escaping by sea to Sweden in 1943.

15. June Knowles (Watkins), the youngest WAAF serving in the Middle East, cuts her birthday cake with the help of the commanding officer.

16. The Douglas family pose by a shot down Heinkel bomber in Hayes, Middlesex, 1940. The downed plane was used to promote an RAF appeal fund for Battle of Britain widows and their children.

17. London carries on: repair squads get to work as auxiliary firemen douse the flames, September 1940.

MINISTRY OF AIRCRAFT
PRODUCTION,

MILLBANK,

S.W.1.

5th September 1940

Dear Roger,

Lord Beaverbrook has asked me to thank
you very much indeed for sending him your
threepenny pieces to help buy a Spitfire.

He is very grateful to you.

Yours faithfully,

Personal Secretary.

Master R. Wood,
Lydney View,
Bradley Road,
Wotton-under-Edge,
Glos.

No. 6597   **AIR MINISTRY.**   A.M. Form 1096.

ADASTRAL HOUSE, KINGSWAY,
LONDON, W.C.2.

MINISTRY OF

RECEIVED 3/9/40 ...in respect of *gift for aircraft*
the sum of:

..........pounds *nine* shillings *Four* pence

£ — : 9 : 4

from:— *Master R. Woody*
Lydney View,
Bradley Road,
Wotton-under-Edge,
Glos.

NOTE.—Under 54 & 55 Vic. c. 39 no stamp is necessary on a
receipt given by an officer of a Public Department of
the State for money paid in adjustment of an account
where he derives no personal benefit therefrom.

(3239—1392) Wt. 22344—1677 80 Bks. 8/39 T.S. 700

G a Coe

for the Director of Accounts.

Roger Wood's generous contribution (47p) to the Spitfire Appeal Fund. This
would have been a considerable sum for a six-year-old child in 1940

walking on the fells with him, which I did one Sunday. It was a beautiful day, and we stood and looked at the countryside, and then he suddenly turned to me and he said, 'Don't you think this is worth defending?' And it's a common mistake that people make with pacifists, that they think we don't believe in defending things. It's really a matter of method. It's not a matter of not resisting, it's just a matter of a *different way* of resisting. I've always been a very obstinate, truculent sort of person, and I felt that passive resistance was the most difficult thing to deal with. And I said to him, 'Yes, I *do* feel this is worth defending, but I certainly do not agree that killing or attacking people is the right way to defend it.' I think I did feel patriotic but as a different thing from jingoistic or nationalistic, in the sense that one has a liking for one's own country and one's own people ... The patriots, I think, were people who said, 'It's outrageous that my country should do this.'

Colin Perry
Junior City clerk, Upper Tooting, London, diary, 15 August 1940

Overhead a hum of aircraft became audible, and I looked upwards into the slowly setting sun, thinking to see a 'Security Patrol'. Then I saw three whirling planes and brother Allan yelled, 'Look! See them? It's a German!' and by God it was ... Yes, thunder alive, there over Croydon were a pack of planes so tiny and practically invisible in the haze and – by God! The Hun was bombing Croydon airport ... At last the war was here! At last I was seeing some excitement. Anti-aircraft guns threw a dark ring around the darting planes, Spitfires and Hurricanes roared into battle ... Boy, this was IT!

Peter Smith
Schoolboy, Petts Wood, Kent

As 1940 went on, we were witnessing daily air battles as the Germans stepped up their attacks on Britain and, of course, Biggin Hill would have been one of their main targets. I don't think we were conscious that they were going for the airfields initially until 7 September, when they switched their blitz to London.

'Black Saturday,' 7 September, saw the start of what is now known as the Blitz, Hitler's revenge attack for ten Berliners who had been killed during an RAF attack on that city on the night of 25/6 August. This lengthy and intensive raid on London's dockland was the most awesome, apocalyptic spectacle that many who were children at the time recall vividly. The raid lasted from 4.43 p.m. until 4.30 a.m., with just a two-hour respite between 6 p.m. and 8 p.m. The Royal Victoria Docks and the Surrey Docks were at the centre of the conflagration, which raged along the banks of the Thames for a thousand yards downstream, covering Silvertown, Bermondsey, West Ham, Stepney, Poplar, Bow and Shoreditch. The Docklands then consisted of densely packed streets of small houses, built mainly for dock-workers, and housed some of the poorest people in London. That night many homes were destroyed, along with factories and warehouses containing highly inflammable materials, causing the glow that could be seen from as far away as the South Downs in Sussex and acted as a marker for the returning waves of bombers. Other parts of London were also attacked during that first raid. On 7 September, 430 people were killed and 1,600 were seriously injured, presenting the first major challenge to hard-pressed hospitals and medical personnel in the East End.

Raids on London continued throughout September, and by the end of the month 5,730 people had been killed and nearly ten thousand seriously injured, with massive damage to the capital's infrastructure, industry, public buildings, railways, offices and homes. London was not the sole target of the Luftwaffe: many other towns and cities, including Hull, Warrington, Merseyside, Avonmouth, Cardiff, Swansea, Plymouth, Portsmouth and Hastings, also suffered.

On 15 September, the crucial daylight battle took place

between RAF Fighter Command and the Luftwaffe, and confirmed the RAF's mastery of British skies. It is now commemorated as Battle of Britain Day, when the 'Few', as Churchill called them, thwarted Goering's plan to wipe out the RAF in preparation for Operation 'Sealion', the invasion of Britain. On 17 September, Hitler postponed the invasion indefinitely.

John Hammon
Schoolboy, Stowting, Kent

I remember standing out on the bank in our garden on 7 September 1940 and seeing this great mass of planes come in straight over Folkestone, and over us, towards London. I remember there were two four-engine bombers among them, painted black. They always said there weren't any four-engine bombers, but I *saw* them. When they bombed London, we stood out in our garden and we could see the sky lighting up and dying down, and we were something like seventy miles away.

Brian Ryland
Schoolboy, Sidcup, Kent, extract from his memoir

It all really started on 7 September, a fine clear day. The sirens sounded and I heard aircraft approaching. Looking up, I could see the largest number of aircraft I had ever seen. In fact it turned out to be over 400 German bombers, plus a large fighter escort. What really stuck in my memory of that moment was seeing one solitary Lysander spotter plane of the RAF flying at right angles to the enemy bombers but at a lower height. There was no sign of the RAF and not a gun to be heard. The German squadrons were in perfect formation, and nothing was being done to stop them, and by now the sky seemed to be filled with them. That night, the London docks were set ablaze and we could see the fires very clearly from our home in Sidcup. All next day, clouds of black smoke billowed high into the sky. The raids continued night after night, with 100 to 250 bombers each time. As we went into October, the raids intensified still more and the defences became more organized. At around six o'clock each night, our ginger cat would suddenly dive under the solid oak sideboard at the back of the room, so we knew the bombers were on their way.

Carmin Sidonio
Schoolboy, Blackheath, London

I remember the first air raid on London – I think it was 7 September 1940. It was Saturday and the first daylight blitz on London. I was in the shop and we could hear the warning sound. It was a lovely day and our neighbour, Mrs O'Flynn, was in the shop talking with my mother. We heard the guns going off and went out into the big yard at the back. This faced Lewisham and we could hear the drone of planes. I remember looking up and to the right, and going across the west part of London was this big mass of planes, with another mass going east towards Woolwich. Then this noise was getting louder and I looked due south and I suddenly saw this huge mass of planes coming closer and guns going off. The next thing was my brother George rushing in, 'Quick, quick, they're dropping bombs, get downstairs!'

We turned and ran in. We had always said the cellar would be a good place if we were bombed and we raced to the top of the cellar stairs. My mother went down, followed by Mrs O'Flynn. I was just about to go down with George when there was this terrific explosion and suddenly there was dirt, dust, noise everywhere, and I heard the smashing of glass. We carried on down to the cellar and just crouched there with all the noise going on ... Through the grille in the cellar we could see a huge crater in the garden of the opposite house. This house was the only one set back from the road and towards the bottom of the garden was their air-raid shelter, and we saw their faces looking out about ten yards from the crater. It damaged the house to the right of the garden but didn't demolish it. The street outside was full of earth, rocks and bits of railings but at least we were safe ... That night there was another raid and we realized that we had to make the cellar habitable, so we cleaned it up and laid down some mattresses and blankets so that we could sleep there. And that became a way of life. It also meant that Dad and Tom were working all different shifts with their ARP work, and we didn't go to school because everything was so disorganized, and that continued through that winter of the Blitz.

Peter Bennett
Schoolboy, Godalming, Surrey

My father had a certain amount of petrol for his business commitments and we were taking somebody home one evening and we saw what we thought at first was the sunset and realized that it was in the wrong position for the sunset. It was the London docks on fire. And the whole sky was red. It was something that I would never forget: the fire of London.

Colin Perry
Junior City clerk, Upper Tooting, London, diary, 9 September 1940

London, my London, is wounded and bloody.

5. Evacuation: Second Wave, Home and Abroad

Black Saturday, and the heavy raids that continued throughout 1940 on London and other cities triggered the next big wave of evacuation. This time, the evacuees were welcomed more sympathetically: lessons had been learnt about billeting procedures, and the majority of hosts, knowing of the terrible ordeals their charges had endured, willingly opened their homes. By now the reception areas had been expanded, which meant that children leaving London and other cities were distributed over a far greater area, and even to Scotland, Northern Ireland and neutral Eire. Although 20,500 children left London after 7 September, in October 1940 250,000 still remained. As well as enduring the raids, many experienced disrupted education and, for those whose homes had been damaged or destroyed, very poor living conditions.

Peter Smith
Schoolboy, Petts Wood, Kent

The first damage to our home happened one night in September 1940. There had been incendiary raids. I can remember my father putting out fires with one or two neighbours. Then it was in the early hours of the morning when this parachute mine floated down and fell into the next street to ours. It demolished or badly damaged 130 houses. I believe there was one fatality. Anyway, when we crawled out in the grey dawn we found that our house had been very badly damaged. We had leaded lights in our windows: all the glass had gone and the lead had twisted. The interior walls were cracked, the stairs were badly damaged and half the roof was off.

Amazing things had happened: cupboards had been blown open, the contents thrown out, and then the doors shut again. It was quite extraordinary to see this. Of course, the ceilings were down so everything was covered with plaster dust, and there was broken crockery and glass everywhere. I think my father gingerly climbed the stairs, but we children weren't allowed to because they were too rickety. So we camped out in our garage – we didn't have a car – and a lot of neighbours came, and we set up chairs and made tea and congregated there until it became fully light. The immediate effect was that a lot of the families seemed to disappear. But we remained, living in the shelter in the evening. Subsequently some officials came round and they were somewhat aghast to find that we were still living there – 'What are you doing? These properties have been condemned. You must get out at once.'

After we had been evacuated, my father got lodgings in Bromley, and used to cycle over to the house to see what was happening; one day he found it had been broken into and he caught a young chap coming out with some of our stuff. He tackled an ARP officer there, a young man with a high, feminine voice. Dad mimicked him well: 'Oh, you mustn't do this, it's very *naughty*.' Dad said, 'Bugger that, I've got a gun inside and the next bugger I catch coming out, I'll shoot the sod!' And he meant it. He was absolutely furious.

I can't say that I was ever frightened as such. I'm not trying to make out that I was very stoic, but it was all such an adventure in some ways. It probably seems terrible in retrospect, but there we are, this was going on, and we just carried on with life . . . I think the school must have closed at that time, and I don't think we ever went back.

Mary Whiteman (Walker)
Wife of chief billeting officer, Saffron Walden, Essex

The Blitz came on my birthday. This was when they raided Silvertown, right down in the East End, and of course that brought people out in *hundreds*, and they came out any way they could. Families were separated. They came on buses, on bicycles, and we weren't prepared at all. We were indulging in the feeling that the threat of invasion was going. But the Blitz came very suddenly on 7 September and you could see the red glow over London all through the autumn from here and it was a horrible sight. That's when I felt that evacuees became refugees and they were a very sad lot. Every town had them, but we only got those who managed to come further still. I think a number went back when it eased off a bit, but most of them did stay. During the war there were two thousand evacuees in this town. Several hundred could come out in a day, all separated. The great problem for the billeting officers was to unite families – 'Can you find my wife? I know she came out with the children this morning, I had to go to work . . .' My job was collecting things for furnishing from a wonderful man called Neville Cox who ran a junk-yard. You could buy anything you wanted for a shilling. Our one fried-fish shop was very good for feeding them. The owner fried all day and they were dealing it out, all so rudimentary.

The earlier influx of 1939 had helped people to understand, and this brought back the original warmth of the town . . . There was a great feeling of anxiety and compassion for people who were in distress . . . I happened to be in a billeting office when two military police came in with a soldier and a young woman in tears, with a baby. He had gone absent without leave to find his wife when the Blitz started. He was mad with anxiety so he'd gone to London to bring her out and he was arrested. He was saying, 'I'm going to fight a war, I can't be safe and have my wife and child in danger, I couldn't *bear* it.' And my husband said to the Military Police, 'You must show compassion, you really must. This is not desertion: we'll find a billet at once and the husband will know where they are and that they're all right.' That's how it ended.

Sylvia Townson (Limburg)
Evacuee Jewish schoolgirl, Great Tew, Oxfordshire

I went home in the spring of 1940, just in time for some bad bombing. Back in London, I was eligible for school. I went to a sweet little school behind the church in Marylebone Road. I was in the baby class and I was very happy there. I learnt to read and tell the time. At the end of the summer term, because of the Blitz, we were evacuated from this school.

This was a general evacuation and I wasn't too upset as I was with the children from my school this time. At Oxford station, we were put into coaches and travelled to Great Tew. I was taken to a little cottage on the village green with two other evacuees for a couple of nights and I know I was certainly sad to leave that house when my billet was ready for me with a farming family, my third foster-home. Unfortunately my relationship with them was very difficult and I wasn't happy there. It could have been that I was difficult, but it was also their mistrust and ignorance of how to deal with a child other than their own. I found the house rather frightening. It was a large cottage with a thatched roof that came down low, and the upstairs rooms were very dark and it was noisy when the wind came. I slept in a little room with a door in the corner, which led into a storage space in the roof. I remember hearing someone remark that the 'potatoes were shooting', I hadn't got the faintest idea what they were talking about and it terrified me, and when I lay in bed at night with the wind blowing through the eaves, I could only imagine that something awful was happening in that room, with potatoes jumping about and shooting each other. Also, they had no lighting and I used to take a candle to bed and this cast creepy shadows. I can't remember much about the husband but his wife was a much more formidable person, very narrow-minded. Her body was a motherly shape and she only ever wore an enormous overall, but she had a hard, unsmiling face, not a happy face at all, and I think that's what upset me a lot, the hardness of her expression. I didn't like her, I didn't find any love in her. Thinking back, she probably had a hard life: the eldest boy had his legs in callipers. I played with the little girl, but the baby turned out to be retarded. They were poor, living hand to mouth as farm labourers would then ...

I remember at that time London was suffering quite badly and letters would come from my mother, and she would read them to me, saying, 'Your mother's been bombed,' in her usual blunt way. I found out later that it was a blasting and not a serious bombing, but it upset me. I thought I wouldn't see my parents again. I think my father realized that I didn't fit into the family, or I might have been causing them problems, because he decided that I should go back home. This would be early March 1941.

Michael Nicholson
Evacuee schoolboy, Romford, Essex

I can remember being evacuated vividly. I remember being put on a train in Paddington with other kids and my mother in a raincoat fussing around me. And I can remember being upset at the time because kids wore shorts then and I had a pair of long underpants longer than my trousers. I remember being terribly embarrassed by this – it concerned me more than saying goodbye to my mother. And I do remember, as the train pulled out, her turning round very suddenly, very fast, and walking quickly away. She'd lost her husband, who was a Royal Engineer serving in Scotland, my two older brothers had been evacuated, and all she had left was my sister Jacqueline, who was also to be evacuated later. So there she was, left on her own. Like all mothers, in order to save their children they had to *lose* them, and she lost her entire family during the duration of the war ...

It was an idyllic existence for a boy from Essex to be suddenly dumped into the middle of the countryside, in the village of Theale, between Wells and Cheddar, in this wonderful old farmhouse, surrounded by toy animals, as they seemed to be. It was a village of farmhouses, a small shop, and a wooden hut where Bill Kick, the cobbler, lived. He was a polio victim, with a huge top half, and he wore a leather apron. His nose was always running, but he was a fabulous guy and taught me so much about the countryside.

Peter Smith
Evacuee schoolboy, Penton, Cumberland

After we were bombed out, my mother, my grandmother and my sister Jean and I went to relatives in Cumberland – this was the beginning of November 1940 ...

It was pitch dark when we arrived at this rather gaunt-looking house – stone and brick with a slated roof – and we piled out of the taxi which had brought us from Carlisle station and, of course, we children were somewhat sleepy and met by the family there. 'Ah, twa bairns as well,' was what we heard. We went in, had a quick wash and straight to bed. The next morning, when we started to get our bearings, it was quite a culture shock. Having come from a modern house with all indoor facilities – that is, gas, electricity, bathroom, toilet – this house, it seemed to me, was fifty years behind the times. No electricity: it was either oil lamps or candles. There was a cold-water tap, and a coal-fired range to get hot water. The toilet was an earth-closet across a muddy yard out the back – very nice at night in winter! Aunt Tamer was the matriarch who ruled the roost there. Her husband, Josh, a dear man, was away working on the farm of one of his sons. There was his sister Hannah, a frail, bent crone of a woman. Both women were dressed from head to toe in black, and to us they looked like something out of the Victorian era. I think the greatest shock was to my grandmother, who had fond memories of going there just prior to the First World War when they were gentleman farmers and lived in good style, and she was absolutely aghast at how their position in life had deteriorated. The farming up there during our stay was small mixed farms, quite a lot of sheep-rearing, and most of them kept between one and six cows, a little bit of general farming and chickens, of course.

The first thing was to get the children fitted with clogs. This was quite a novelty to us. There was a local maker and these were wooden-soled with a metal ring around them – the 'corkers'. They were very warm and quite practical and hard-wearing. We arranged our meals separately. The first problem my mother encountered was when she wished to cook a Sunday roast for us, so she got the vegetables and I remember the joint was put in the oven and we're sitting back expectantly, and all of a sudden she found that the whole thing had been shut down. So she turned, rather surprised, to Aunt Tamer and asked what was going on. 'Oh, it's Sunday, we don't cook on Sunday, it's the Sabbath.' Well, of course, this was nonsense – a more irreligious lot I don't think I've come across! So that was the first upset. You can imagine things weren't particularly happy for my mother or grandmother, but we children took it in our stride.

One event that occurred up there of great importance was when Rudolf Hess from Germany crash-landed up in Scotland. That caused quite a gerbumble. There was probably a lot of wild talk about it, but I don't think anyone knew any more than what was told in the media.

Leslie Alexander
Evacuee schoolboy, Mursley, Buckinghamshire, extract from his memoir

After being introduced to an elderly couple, Mr and Mrs Fred North, and their son Charles and given something to eat, we had our first bath for many months, and were put to bed in our own bedroom. It had a small window overhung with thatch ... The next morning we were told to write a letter to our parents and tell them where we were. Naturally by this time we were feeling very 'homesick' and the only words I could write was 'Please Mum come and get me I want to come home.' To post our letters we had to go to the post office at the top of the village. This meant that we had to walk up the road past some cows behind a fence in a field. I was terrified and refused to go because I had never seen a real cow before, only the pictures, and to me the cows were very big and the fence so small they could easily get out ... A few days after our arrival it was discovered that we were lousy with fleas. This was because of the conditions we had been living in during the last few months [of the Blitz] in London.

Aunt Dolly, as we called Mrs North, disinfected our clothes, our hair was soaked in paraffin and we stood in the warm sun whilst the fleas crawled from our hair and were destroyed . . .

Lorna Rhodes (Willmot)
Evacuee schoolgirl, Exmouth, Devon, extract from her letter to her parents

I hope you are well and happy. Did you hear that some bombs were dropped in Exmouth? If you were wondering about us we are all right . . . This sentence will sound as if I'm telling you of [*sic*]. Mummy darling please take your gas mask with you where ever [*sic*] you go because you never no [*sic*] what might happen . . . Thank you very much for the chocolate and sweets. I was overjoyed to have them because we have not seen them for such a long time . . .

Mrs Greenwood
Foster-mother to evacuees Charmian Sutton (Willmot) and Lorna Rhodes (Willmot), Exmouth, Devon, extract from her letter to their parents

Dear Mrs Willmot, I do want to thank you for your kind letter. It has made me feel that I know you already! . . . Most certainly Lorna and Charmian have taken to us like ducks to water and I can truthfully say that my husband and I feel the same about them. They are delightful children (as though you don't know!) and it seems incredible we have only known them for about ten days. Theirs is the credit, I may add . . . We are not slow to realize our good fortune in having Lorna and Charmian to care for instead of some of the little urchins from Lambeth Walk of whom there are several hundreds in the town . . . The word billet is never used by them now – it's a hateful word at the best of times and comes in the same category as 'evacuees' to my mind . . .

Joseph Stagno
Gibraltarian schoolboy, London

The biggest part of the population of Gib came to London and they must have taken over a lot of the hotels in Kensington. There was very little contact with the rest of the London population. It didn't enter my mind, but it did the older people's, that it was odd that we had been evacuated into a city that had itself evacuated its own children. This came home to me when the Blitz started and we were right in the middle of it.

'Hotel' was really only relevant to the location of the place. Basically they became evacuee centres, their facilities not open to us, all the trimmings taken away. Our food was catered for by Joe Lyons: you went to the dining hall for breakfast and dinner and ate at long tables. Eventually things like concerts and religious services were organized. There were lounges where you could go and sit, but with children running all over the place, we tended to stick to our own room or go out in the park.

My mother seemed to adapt to it: she helped in the sick bay and then took a job in a nearby hospital. In general, the Gibraltarians felt the cold that first winter: we'd never seen snow or ice and it would have been twice as bitter for us. The younger people seemed to integrate more easily than the older ones, especially those of Spanish stock who had never been out of Gib; coming to a strange land, they found it impossible to settle to this way of life. But the young people got into the swing of things. The scale of things was important – the size of the streets and houses made a great impact.

We became acclimatized to the English way of life. We were never treated as foreigners, but we resented the term 'refugee' very strongly, even to the extent that it appeared in the national press. We felt we had no wish to be here, and to be classed with people who had run away from something we found annoying. So we insisted on being called 'evacuees'.

Meg Oliver (Adams)
Evacuee schoolgirl, Kennington, Oxford

My aunt had a daughter at Brixton Central School and they were looking for helpers to go and be with the school, and she got one of the posts and spoke up for my mother, who got a job as well. So we all went down to Kennington, Oxford, to this big house where we lived in the servants' quarters with the cook and the maid. The house belonged to the retired vicar of Kennington who was then in his eighties, Father Trevelyan, and his daughter Elizabeth ... We were definitely not part of the Trevelyans' lives, we were part of what they had to do because the war was on ...

Several of us little girls went to the music master, and he had wandering hands, and none of us said anything. I don't know why you don't say anything, but you don't when you're seven, eight, nine. Oh, yes, I had his wandering hands. You just pretend it's not happening. He would put his hands *in* my knickers! He would be teaching, 'Now, play this ...' and then I sort of switched off. I just went along. I liked him. He was a *brilliant* music teacher and I was progressing so well with him. I certainly didn't say anything to my mother. But one of the ten-year-olds mentioned it and there was a great deal of annoyance. The lady of the house asked them not to say anything because he would lose his job at the leading girls' school. So after that a relative would interrupt the lesson by walking through. I remember I used to get very annoyed that my concentration was interrupted by this wandering-through!

Dennis Hayden
Schoolboy, Highclere, Hampshire

Our next evacuation happened just after the first bombs had been dropped on Portsmouth. The rush was on again – we must get the children away! We understood this time why we were going, and again I remember the resentment of having this big label tied on me, same situation ... One or two bombs had dropped on Portsmouth and they got rid of us again. As if to say, 'Let's get rid of them.' Yes, we did feel rejected ... And with being left until last to be billeted, a growing resentment came as if to say, 'Why doesn't anybody love us?'

Eventually they found a new place for us. And I remember going into a car and off up a country lane and there at the end of this lane was this monstrous – to us – castle. The house was completely round and there were battlements over the top of the kitchen area, and to us it was a castle ... rather frightening, but exciting – this was something we'd read about and seen on film! We were met by 'Aunt Daisy' – and her husband was 'Uncle George'. She always wore shapeless clothes, and I don't suppose one could ever determine her age. To compare her with anyone, she reminded one of Olive Oyl out of *Popeye*. She seemed all arms and legs. She wore tortoiseshell glasses and always a blue beret on her head. And she would hang on to this like Old Mother Riley, running around. Her husband was the gamekeeper on the estate of Lord Caernarvon – the lord who financed the opening of King Tutankhamun's tomb in the 1920s. She had seven children. The youngest was Pamela between the ages of my brother and myself. And, of course, wherever we went, Pam came along ...

Then, having come into the main room, immediately alongside the fireplace, with her foot resting on the fender was – to my brother and I – an old witch. Very Victorian in her dress, clothes right down to her ankles, grey hair, smoking a pipe. The tobacco was called Black Beauty Shag, and it smelt to high heaven. She puffed away merrily at her pipe there all day. I think she was just about blind and her hearing wasn't good. This was Uncle George's mother, 'Granny Baker'. Some say she was of Romany origin. We were treated very warmly there. I can always remember a cuddle and a kiss before going off to school. We felt as one ...

Millicent Morgan (Miller)
Evacuee child, Oxborough, Norfolk

At this vicarage we had been taken to, well, they wanted Sunday clothes, Sunday shoes, school shoes, wellies, all this, and it used to worry the life out of me: 'Write home to your mother and ask her for this, say you need that ...' And I couldn't bear to do it because I knew she didn't have the money. We had little single iron beds but my little brother used to come in my bed because he was frightened. And he used to wet the bed and I used to get in trouble because they knew he'd been over to my bed.

I was always writing home and my mother used to always be writing to us. And my dad came down once for a week, and that was the only time we saw my father in the war because he died in September 1940. I think he missed us because we had a lovely time with him. He came to the rectory, and even though they knew he was ill, he wasn't allowed to stop with us: they made him walk to the village to stay. But I remember those few days were very happy. We all kind of clung together and he said how lucky we were to be in the country and all that ... My mum came down a few times, but though the rectory was so big and so far away from the village, she was never allowed to stay there. So when seven o'clock came and we had to go to bed, she'd have to go in the dark and walk all the way back to the village, which was hard to find, really ... I was very homesick. I was so fond of my mother, I couldn't bear to be parted from her, really. And my brother, he used to cry, he wanted to go home, and I'd just have to try and console him. And obviously my mum missed us so it was all a charade, really: she's making out she's not missing us and we're making out we're having a lovely time ...

We were sent home for my father's funeral on our own from Thetford where the rector put us on the train. Mum had to rig us out from the pawnshop and we had black clothes. She was working as a barmaid and we had to be in the shelter with a neighbour to look after us. The first night we were in a brick shelter and I couldn't stand that because the guns were going up and down the railway, which was just behind, plus the fact that it was right outside our front-room window where my dad was laying, so I was more petrified that it was going to blow him on the floor or something ...

Margaret Woodhead (Butler)
Evacuee schoolgirl, Zeals, Wiltshire

Life with the Rabbitz family was completely different from life at my earlier billet ... I called Mr and Mrs Rabbitz 'Aunty' and 'Uncle' right from the start. The family life there was absolutely fantastic. It was a lovely little cottage, again no water laid on or electricity. But coming home from school I'd get, 'How be thee then, girl? Had a good day? Good.' Mr Rabbitz was just as interested in me as he was in his own family. The children loved their parents, who would be firm with them but kindly at the same time ... With the Rabbitz family, every day was so full and you packed so much in that you just remembered having a wonderful time and being completely happy. The local people were very kind to us; we were just accepted into the village community. The children taught us how to go scrumping, how to roast potatoes in a bonfire, how to catch rabbits, we were really integrated into their lifestyle. I don't think there was much to remind us that there was a war on. We knew that the local farmers' sons went into the Dorset Yeomanry and other sons were away, but nothing to make an impact on you. You felt very secure, that nothing could happen to you there. You didn't even see aircraft flying over, it was just so completely another world.

Joan Reed (Chantrelle)
Evacuee schoolgirl, school camp, Itchingfield, Sussex

From the moment I arrived at my new place, the camp, it was absolutely bliss. There were several hundred of us and it was co-ed, which I liked. It was like going to boarding-school and that was *tremendous*. The whole point of evacuation was completely changed. I wasn't worried about leaving Naomi, I was relieved at getting rid of her at last! It really was freedom, and I soon forgot about the guilt I felt, because I was going to have *fun*. Our teachers were there and everybody was happy. There I was, on my own: no worries about my sister crying or being miserable, no responsibilities. It was called Coopers Farm and was in the Barnes Green area, near Horsham.

Diana Owen (Houston-Boswald)
Schoolgirl, Lewes, Sussex

I was in Southover Manor School, which had been evacuated from Lewes to Firle Place, because the school was right by the

Brighton railway lines and it was thought that enemy aircraft followed railway lines. Then I left that school to go out to South Africa, not because of the bombing but because we were trying to join my father, who was in the diplomatic service and had been posted to Japan ... In South Africa we had a telegram to say that my father was very ill with a kidney infection and was not expected to live. There were no planes going to Japan and my mother just packed up everything at very short notice and we got on to a Dutch cargo-passenger ship.

When we got to the Philippines it was to find telegrams had been sent, trying to stop this mad English woman and her daughter going in when everyone else wanted to get away. But my mother had the bit between her teeth. We hadn't seen my father for nearly three years, so she was frantic to get there if only to a deathbed. But by this time we knew he was much better and out of hospital, which the Foreign Office used as ammunition to try to make us retrace our steps. We were told we were a nuisance – I mean, a forty-five-year-old woman and a sixteen-year-old girl turn up, the last thing they wanted as they were about to be invaded! But then we caught a Japanese ship at Manila – an enormously luxurious liner – and at Kobe my father met us. He'd had a miraculous recovery and was so thrilled to see us. We arrived at the beginning of November 1941.

I was very excited to be in that part of the world. My first impression was that the house was filled with the biggest chrysanthemums I'd ever seen – absolutely enormous and with this bitter-sweet, smoke smell. It was a very nice modern house in the embassy compound in Tokyo. The ambassador's residence was a huge and palatial house. The ambassador was Sir Robert Craigie, and he and his wife lived in great splendour with masses of servants. There were other buildings for diplomatic and consular staff and their secretaries. Everyone lived inside the embassy compound, which was guarded by Japanese police, just as embassies in London are guarded by British police.

After the shock of Dunkirk, the growing threat of invasion and the start of the Blitz, offers to take British children poured in from the Dominions and the USA. It seemed particularly urgent for Jewish parents, most of whom knew what lay in store for them and their families should Britain fall under Nazi rule. Various private arrangements and schemes were set in motion: professors from Yale University took in Oxford dons' children and the children of Hoover workers – the so-called 'Hoover children' – went to North Canton, Ohio. Eventually, and reluctantly, due to the shortage of shipping and Churchill's feeling that this was 'defeatist', the government set up the Children's Overseas Reception Board (CORB). It proposed to send abroad a number of children of all social classes, between the ages of five and sixteen, with the proviso that the majority should come from state schools. Parents of privately educated children who travelled under the scheme had to foot the bill.

During June 1940, 2,345 children had sailed privately to the Dominions. On 20 July, the first group of CORB children was despatched to Canada. By then 211,448 children had applied to go – half of those eligible in the entire country – an indication, perhaps, of their parents' pessimism, which countered the upbeat propaganda.

Countess Mountbatten of Burma, Lady Brabourne (Patricia Mountbatten)
Evacuee schoolgirl, Dorset

After the catalyst of Dunkirk in early June, it was quite obvious that France was lost, and the Germans were sitting there, twenty miles across the Channel. Everybody thought, quite rightly, that an invasion was imminent ... My father, who was in the navy, said to my mother, 'Well, look, you're certainly not going to leave your job [with the Red Cross and St John's Ambulance], it's very important; and I'm at sea, being mined and torpedoed.' (Because of my mother's Jewish grandfather, she and we would have been in great danger if the Germans had landed – we would have landed up in the ovens because we were an eighth Jewish; it went down that far.) So he said, 'You must send the girls away with the other evacuees.' A lot of children were being evacuated. Apart from saving lives, it was very important that you didn't have more mouths to feed than was absolutely necessary, as every item that wasn't home-grown had to be brought across the sea, and ships were frequently torpedoed ... When we left on the American ship *Washington*, I was fifteen and my sister Pamela only ten. How did we feel about it? Fairly desperate in a sense. You see, it wasn't really a question of *when* we were going to come back but whether we were ever going to be *able* to come back. And would there be anything to come back to if the invasion went ahead? We had this awful dread of what the future held.

Jack Keeley
Schoolboy, Brixton, London

With my father's experience of the First World War, I think he expected the Germans to get across to England and I assume that's why he sent us to Canada. My sister was only six when we went, so it must have been a very difficult decision ... I don't think we ever realized that we were going three thousand miles and to another continent. We had a medical examination, and we had to take all the clothes we were going with – a sort of kit inspection. A lot of the children in those days, due to the poverty and unemployment, wouldn't have had much to take. And the people who inspected us were there to make sure we were provided for. We didn't need anything; my mother somehow got it together.

Barbara Partridge (Bech)
Schoolgirl, Aldwick Bay, Sussex

I don't think I realized the full import of it [going to Canada] at first. It seemed an adventure as much as anything else. I think what really brought it home was when we went to say goodbye to my aunt and her family. Her eldest son was in the RAF and was home on leave. I remember him looking at us and saying, 'Rats leaving the sinking ship.' That was the first indication of how people might look at us: running away. Because it *was* running away. I mean, we had just been listening to Churchill telling us that we would fight on the beaches and in the towns and we would *never* give in! I could see that Mummy had a great responsibility with the younger ones and there were those who said, 'Well, the less young people there are to worry about, the easier it will be to get on with the war.' So it was a bit of a balance, but I was just old enough at fourteen to feel that I wanted to be part of the party.

Beth Cummings (Walder)
Schoolgirl, Kentish Town, London

Eventually, the decision was made and all the arrangements put in place. My brother and I were examined physically and given some intelligence tests to make sure Canada was getting the right stuff. We were to go to my mother's sister who lived in Canada. Without the government scheme, our parents couldn't have afforded to send us . . .

When my father actually saw this letter telling us that we could go, he said, 'Right, that's it!' And he gave me a list of instructions, including to look after my brother. My mother said to me, 'You've got to grow up to be a very good woman.' I couldn't understand why they were so sad. You see, what they knew, and what I *didn't* know, was that they thought they would probably never see us again. When I think of it now, I think how brave they were, as were all the parents of children who were sent away . . . So, that morning, they were all there on the station platform at Euston. It was like a scene from a highly charged opera. There were parents hugging and kissing their children, there were children crying, the station was full of noises of distress – except for my parents, who were very cool, they hugged and kissed us, but they didn't cry and neither did we. They repeated their instructions and left. I found out later that my mother, a teetotaller, asked my father to take her to the Euston Hotel and buy her a drink . . .

Frank Bower
Evacuee schoolboy, Napanee, Canada, extract from his memoir

On what do you base such a momentous decision at the age of thirteen years? 'The Germans had my first family,' said my father. 'They're not going to have my second.' ... All I can remember is that it [Canada] seemed to offer the opportunity of a grand adventure and the chance to escape from a rather dull school. The agony for our parents of making the decision to let us go did not really dawn on me until I had children of my own. The reality facing them, that they might never see us again, never crossed my horizon of thought ...

Derek Diamond
Evacuee schoolboy, New Zealand

By the time the war came the proposal in the family was that our mother plus we three children would go and stay with distant cousins in the North Island of New Zealand in a town called Hamilton. And this is what happened. My family paid for the passages − it was a private rather than a public evacuation.

We left England as part of a convoy from Clydebank to sail across the Atlantic to the Panama Canal and then across the Pacific to Wellington, New Zealand. The ship was a fairly large passenger liner and it was just *full* of women and children. I remember very vividly being on deck and looking at the sea, as a small boy of seven. It seemed as if the sea was just *full* of ships because in every direction, almost uniformly spaced apart, were ships, ships and more ships. And it was on an evening, almost at dusk as the light was going, I remember my mother saying, 'Come on, now, time to go to bed,' when there was a very large *bang*, almost an explosion. And the ship a little bit in front of us simply stood up vertically and disappeared in what I recall now as being a few seconds. This was just a few days out of Clydebank, somewhere off the coast of Northern Ireland. I remember the approach of what must have been a destroyer coming very rapidly past the ship I was on, and there were enormous spouts of water, which shot into the sky, which I now realize were the depth charges going off as it was trying to sink the German submarine. Subsequently, another convoy a little bit later than ours had a much more disastrous occurrence when a large passenger ship [*City of Benares*] taking evacuees to Canada was in fact sunk and there was a large loss of life . . .

I remember as a small boy what an extraordinary thing going through the Panama Canal was: how these ships were taken through these locks, and then we sailed through lakes and then another set of locks, then the water went down and eventually we reached the Pacific Ocean. At this point it was thought that we were out of the war zone, and it was time to relax, therefore a big children's party was held. So, after six weeks we reached Wellington from where we took a train and went to Hamilton and stayed some weeks with our cousins until we found a house to rent. This was to be my home for the next five years.

Marjory Mingo (Ursell)
Evacuee schoolgirl, Western Australia, extract from her memoir

At the age of eleven I set sail with 480 Boys and Girls between the ages of 5 and 15 from all over the country, from every home background, every size and shape! We embarked at Liverpool, after four nights in a school, the classrooms being dormitories, and the only experience I had of air raids. We had been gathered together by train, and really we could have had no knowledge of the adventure that was about to begin. Our ship was Polish with a Polish crew and Polish food! *Batory*. She acted as our house for eleven weeks! . . . We were spoiled by the 'Tommys' on board. We travelled to Capetown, Bombay, to Colombo and to Singapore. Everywhere we were fêted and spoilt . . . And always a reception at Government House and oranges and presents and such hospitality. Our soldiers left at Singapore. We missed them and the ship was quiet.

Doreen Hartley (Saunders)
Schoolgirl, en route to India

Our return to India was organized by Lady Linlithgow, the vice-roy's wife. There were five hundred of us under the age of sixteen, many unaccompanied. A whole battalion of the Argyll and Sutherland Highlanders was on the ship so, really, it was a troopship and the captain was unhappy to have so many children on board. We went half-way to Canada by convoy, then turned south with one little merchant ship and zigzagged all the way to Freetown and Cape Town. We had one or two alarms, but nothing happened. I can remember arriving at Cape Town, and everyone standing and looking in wonder because the glow of lights lit up the sky – we couldn't believe it because we had come from blackout. Then we were off to India, sailing straight for Bombay. I then had a two-day journey up north to Jalanda in the Punjab where my father was commanding a battalion. He was thrilled because he felt we were safe in India. This was October 1940, before the Japs came in. A lot of young officers were coming out then. I was too young to leave school, but started to learn shorthand and typing. I was sent to school in Delhi and that's where I met some of the girls who later, like me, joined the Wasbies [Women's Auxiliary Service (Burma)].

Elizabeth 'Bussie' Grice (Hearn)
Evacuee schoolgirl, en route to Nova Scotia, extracts from her letters to her parents

25 June 1940, aboard SS Scythia, *Liverpool*

I am sorry to say I have been crying all day, I can't help it, just crying quietly like I was at the station. Writing this letter has started me crying again, it is nearly killing me writing to you and knowing I won't see you for ages and ages. I am dreading tonight because I can't stop crying . . . We all have to go to bed with our clothes on. I have my lifebelt by my side now. I managed my papers O.K. and only have my money and passport left on me. I must stop now because you make me use too many handkerchiefs while I write this ... Bussie. P.S. I want to come back so badly, bring me back soon.

2 July 1940, at sea

I have never seen such mixed company before. The ship holds Siamese, American, Canadian, Chinese, Irish, French, Portuguese, Danish and German Jews. In fact I seem to be the only English one ... I have now got several boy friends, it is great fun ... Last night Mrs Price said we could stay up as it was my last night. We had horse racing, a gambling game, and I threw the dice. Then we danced. I danced mostly with a young man who we call 'Cad No. 1' ... I have enjoyed this trip more than I can say, it has been wizard.

Lady Beatrice Wright (Rathbone, née Clough)
Wife of John Rathbone MP, who was killed in action

There was a scheme set up to offer hospitality to English children by the *Boston Union Transcript*, a newspaper that I was well acquainted with. A committee was set up in this country, which I was on, to make it possible for people of all means to go, whether they could afford the sea fare or not. There was an enormous demand from families wanting their children to go and who'd had invitations separate from this set-up. There was an enormous spate of offers of hospitality, and we used to meet in the ballroom of the Grosvenor House [Hotel, London] once a week to interview the parents and the children and get the necessary paperwork, and when this was all accumulated and there was a ship going, under convoy, of course, we then would have them gathered there and send them off – the parents were not encouraged to go. The children were in groups and we said our goodbyes in the Grosvenor House ballroom. My son and daughter went. They knew the house and people in America who were taking them, so it was a very different proposition for them compared with others.

Countess Mountbatten of Burma, Lady Brabourne
(Patricia Mountbatten)
Evacuee schoolgirl, New York, USA

We landed in New York into a totally different world – I mean a world really overflowing with milk and honey – which one rather resented. We came from blackouts and rationing and clothing coupons and no petrol and life being really very unpleasant ... You could take hardly any money with you – something like fifty pounds. The only people my parents knew and felt could afford to look after us were the Vanderbilts, and Mrs Cornelius Vander-bilt, already eighty, very kindly took us in.

I think the most frightening experience I had was arriving at this house and entering the vast hall and being greeted by a very smart young woman: makeup, high heels, beautifully dressed, who I thought must be at least thirty – and you know thirty to a fifteen-year-old is very over the hill. So I was appalled to discover that she was three months younger than me! I thought, Oh, my goodness, what am I going to *do*? On leaving England, my mother had thrust one of those little orange lip salves into my hand and said, 'Darling, you'd better use this, because you'll find that all the girls over there use makeup. Also, remember to shake hands a lot, because Americans like to shake hands.' Basically, the only advice I got!

Molly Atkey Walford
*Evacuee escort, SS **Antonia**, extract from her memoir*

The day came early in September. There were 250 children attached to our boat, 15 girls and boys to each escort. We arrived at Liver-pool as the light was going and were finally taken to an empty school for the night where we bedded them on fresh straw in clean cellars. Raids were constant on the port, so we were told it was unwise to embark for another 24 hrs; we had to provide distraction. Later in the day there was a bizarre incident. A plump, youngish man in clergyman's rig came into the big classroom where we were having a sing-song and offered to entertain with songs at the piano. This he proceeded to do with great confidence and gusto, with such titles as 'Old Joe Somebody', etc., which were well received. So I took a welcome break and learnt that the visitor was the Padre to the Bermuda Prison, on leave and wishing to help. Perhaps he was, and did, but later I had an unwelcome surprise as we were bedding them down for another night on the straw, to find the same person, or parson, embracing the prettiest girl on the floor, full length, saying that she needed comfort and missed her daddy! I didn't doubt it, but I managed to yank him up forcibly by the arm and eject him, to his astonishment, and the child stopped snivelling – that was the only whimpering that we had on the whole trip – after that we kept them busy without outside help . . .

Finally we headed westwards again and word went round the ship that the *Benares* ahead of us had been lost with a similar cargo of children. This accounted for our altered course, which took us almost to Iceland and finally decided our splendid organizers to send no more. At that time, invasion was more than a possibility, and we could understand the agonizing choice the parents had to make when this offer presented itself to them. The organizers, largely American, saw the exodus of a few thousand children to their safe country [this was before Pearl Harbor] as a possible remnant of Israel, just a random few who could be saved if England, overrun, collapsed. This was a view that I, and other service wives, never envisaged for one moment . . . If I had had children, I should never have taken that decision . . .

After about ten days out, I put my head in my hands on the table and wept . . . One of the Canadian boys comforted me and I just explained that I was exhausted, all in, that was all. So they sent for the purser, who kindly led me to his cabin to 'talk'. Talk was the last thing I wanted, only sleep, but he plied me with questions and suggestions – viz., he thought it was hard work but we were nearly there and once ashore we would have a good time together. Did I like high spots? He knew a place where you could get anything you wanted, and so forth. Dazed tho' I was, I realized he thought I was a drug addict! Someone (the

woman in my cabin?) must have told him I was taking white
pills daily ...

Geoffrey Habesch
Teenage British officer, Merchant Navy

One trip we did on the *Settler* which was quite interesting was
when we carried kids, evacuees. We were very worried when we
heard about this – we were going to have something like a
hundred children and their escorts, to take them to Halifax. The
City of Benares had been torpedoed in the North Atlantic, with
very heavy loss of children's lives. We said, 'My God! I hope we
don't get torpedoed.' But after this tribe had been on board for
about two days, we were hoping we *would* be. They were the
most *awful* crowd, honestly, *uncontrollable* – talk about young people
today, you should have seen this lot! Oh, crikey! The way they
were running around! I was on the bridge one day with the chief
officer and he suddenly went puce in the face: 'Go over and stop
that so-and-so ...' And there was a small boy of about eight or
nine, and he was actually hanging outside the ship on a piece of
rope. As soon as he saw me coming, he did a sort of Tarzan act
and ran away, disappeared into the accommodation. I remember
one was armed with a large knife. The officers' cabins had doors
of solid teak, nice polished wood, and he carved his initials in
one. We took the knife away. I would think this was the worst
trip we ever made ... I'm sure some of them suffered a few thick
ears from members of the crew at various times or a kick up the
backside, but that was all. We were certainly glad to see the last
of them when they got off at Halifax.

Pamela Winfield (Witcher, née Phillips)
Schoolgirl, Wimbledon, Greater London

I wanted to be evacuated. My father wouldn't allow it. And then
later, when they were going to evacuate children to America, I
begged to go and he wouldn't allow it then. He felt strongly that
if we were going to go, we were going to go together. And of

course that ship [*City of Benares*] went down with all the children. And my father said, 'You see? You see what would have happened to you?' And that was the end of me having any say on being evacuated.

6. Disaster at Sea

On 30 August 1940, the Dutch liner, SS *Volendam*, was torpedoed, but all passengers, including more than three hundred evacuee children, were saved, and only one crew member lost. The *City of Benares*, which sailed from Liverpool on 13 September 1940, was not so lucky. It was the commodore (lead) ship of a convoy bound for Canada, and the passengers included ninety children being evacuated under the Children's Overseas Reception Board (CORB) scheme and ten who went privately.

Shiela Grimsdale (MacKay)
Evacuee schoolgirl, SS Volendam, *extract from her memoir*

I fell sound asleep as soon as my head hit the pillow. It was about half past ten that same night that I woke to find someone shaking me violently. Then I heard the alarm ringing. I got up [and dressed] and I just drifted along the crowded passage the way the rest were going. Then a big black sailor came up to me and asked me my boat station. I told him and I can remember he just hoisted me over his shoulders and took me safely there. By this time I was wide awake ... Then we had to climb into the lifeboats. I realized with a shiver it was no practice. I've never seen the sea as rough as it was that night. It was also pitch black ...

We were rocking up and down in the very stormy seas. Then I discerned a man coming down the rope-ladder into our boat. The iron thing that had held the rope was swinging about. It went towards the man and crashed against his head. He was knocked unconscious and fell into the water and got drowned. I didn't realize how horrible it was at the time. I was just wondering if I would go the same way as him. Wondering if I would ever see dry land again. Wondering if I would ever come out alive. We were all squashed on top of one another. And, what was worse, I was sitting near the edge. I kept looking at the deep water and shivering, thinking how cold it would be to be in there ... We could see our ship going down-down-down, down. But it never went right down ... [Later] Suddenly we saw a black shape looming up in front of us; we suddenly crashed into it and nearly got jerked into the water. It was an oil tanker. I was nearest the railings and I had to put my hands out and catch a hold of the railings and try to keep the boat in, then it wouldn't slide away again. I was nearly in tears. But at last the captain just took hold of me and lifted me right out of the lifeboat on to the tanker ... It was when I was talking to a nice cheery man with a smiling face that I suddenly felt terribly homesick. I longed to get back home again quickly ...

Sheila Cooley (Westcott)
Evacuee schoolgirl, Montréal, extract from her memoir

There was some difficulty in getting a passage across the Atlantic at that time and Father went round all his friends in shipping trying to get one ... As he was with Ellermans, no one could understand his reluctance to book me on the *City of Benares*, which would have been easy. However, his Cornish 'second sight' made him so uneasy about her that he refused to consider it. This was justified when the *City of Benares*, full of children, was torpedoed in September 1940.

Fred Steels
Evacuee schoolboy, **City of Benares**

I was all for going, it was going to be a great adventure, and it was! My parents had lost four children, I was the only one left and they must have thought quite a bit of me ... The ship was out of this world. If I hadn't been on this scheme, I would never have seen anything like it, she was beautiful. One of the main things I remember was the smell of curry, because she had a

Lascar [Indian seamen] crew. There were three of us to a cabin, myself, Paul Shearing and another lad, whose name I can't remember. Once you put to sea and you saw all the ships in the convoy forming up, it was very exciting. Our ship was the commodore, and we were right in the front of the middle line ... Life on board was *beautiful* – we had the run of the ship virtually. The food was more than we would have got at home. It was like a first-class hotel. We had games on board, shuffleboard, quizzes, musical sessions, virtually everything you could think of for a kid.

Jack Keeley
Evacuee schoolboy, **City of Benares**

My mother told me to look after my sister. It made things awkward because, on the train and in the school where we stayed overnight, the boys and girls were separated. We had no experience of travel, no experience of liners, hotels or anything, so when we saw this liner, to me it was *gigantic*, especially when you walked up the steep gangplank. Again, the separation – girls on one side, boys on the other. We were all on the same deck but it was only during playtimes that I saw my sister. But the thing that sticks in my mind was not only the size of it but the *luxury* of it. When we went to dinner you could have two or three helpings of ice-cream if you felt like it. It was a totally different world. We sailed on Friday the thirteenth – when you think of it, a bad omen to start with ...

The white officers spoke to us occasionally, but the Lascars were total foreigners to us. It wasn't that we were frightened of them being black, but we had never seen this before, not like today ... The lifejackets had to be on all the time, they were like a sort of waistcoat, but on the morning of the 17th, they relaxed this order ... The weather was never brilliant and the waves were always choppy; on the morning of the 17th it was getting worse ...

Colin Ryder Richardson
Evacuee schoolboy, private passenger, **City of Benares**

My mother had given me this red kapok lifejacket to wear and I got the nickname of 'Will Scarlet' because I was always wearing it and it was bit unusual, very noticeable . . . When I wasn't playing with Derek, Sonia and Barbara Bech, I'd be in the cocktail lounge because I remember some ladies having cocktails and giving me their cherries . . . I was amazed to be told that our escorts had gone and that we'd be unaccompanied until we were picked up by the Canadians on the other side. It struck me as not beyond the bounds of possibility that submarines could get out there. I realized that the Germans had probably got very fine machines, and I wasn't at all surprised when we were torpedoed.

At 10.30 p.m. on 17 September, a torpedo fired from a German U-boat struck the ship just below the cabins where the CORB children slept. Two were killed instantly. Almost immediately the order was given to abandon ship, and just half an hour after the attack the *City of Benares* sank. It was a bitterly cold night, with a force-eight gale blowing.

Fred Steels
Evacuee schoolboy, **City of Benares**

We were in bed, about ten o'clock at night. I was in a bottom bunk with this empty bunk above me, and Paul was with this other lad. We heard this terrific *thump,* and the alarm bells started going. What woke me up was not so much the thump, but the top bunk fell on me and I was soaking wet because the explosion had burst all the waterpipes and I was getting the lot. I managed to get out of there, and got Paul and shook the other lad. We got out and started heading for the upper deck with these alarm bells going like the very devil. Up there I wouldn't say there was panic but there was a lot of running around; some of the children were crying. The next thing I remember was that a member of the white crew picked me up and just flung me into the lifeboat, just threw me in. They filled it up, there were about forty or fifty in the boat, the biggest percentage were the Lascars; there were just six children, Mary Cornish, Father O'Sullivan and a Polish count, another couple of people and a white seaman, who took charge of the boat. We got down to the water and could see the damage – the torpedo had blown a hole in her and, without a lie, you could have put two double-decker buses in it.

Bess Cummings (Walder)
Evacuee schoolgirl, City of Benares

Having got ourselves geared to go out of the cabin, we found we were blocked. So we hammered on the wardrobe doors hanging across the cabin door and, by a stroke of good fortune, one of the crew came along with a hatchet and made a hole big enough for us to scramble through. In scrambling through, two of the girls injured themselves and were taken away by two escorts. I was led away. The staircase up which we should have gone had by now disappeared. Huge gaps were appearing in the decks. I was pushed up some very narrow steps on to the boat deck and this crew member said, 'Go!' and I was literally picked up and flung into a lifeboat that was being lowered. The scene was one of total confusion because the lifeboats were not being lowered properly. There were people waiting to get into lifeboats that never came, there were people jumping on rafts, there were some just jumping straight into the sea – children and adults alike. It wasn't so much a scene of panic as of confusion and bewilderment. I didn't know what had happened to my brother. My father's injunction for me to look after him was impossible to obey. The lifeboat was not lowered straight, but was tipping at one end with the result that one end hit the ocean and the lifeboat filled with water and the thirty to forty-five people inside sat in water. It was obviously very unstable, added to which was our difficulty in getting away from the sinking ship because some of the gear was fouled up. So, everything was combining to multiply the problems of the disaster: the weather, the difficulty in safely lowering the lifeboats, the difficulty of getting into them, and getting anywhere near the boat deck. So it was no wonder that loss of life had started even before people reached the sea. Many of the children never left the *City of Benares*. Only the very fortunate few did, and even then their lives depended on whether they had been successfully lowered into their lifeboats and the boats had been steady.

Derek Bech
Evacuee schoolboy, private passenger, **City of Benares**

My mother was awake in an instant. She said, 'Get up.' I got up and got dressed – I put on my school trousers and blazer and raincoat and even my school cap and my gym shoes, and we went through to Barbara and Sonia and they both started to dress. Then we heard the alarm bells ringing, which meant we had to go to our muster station. We all went up the main stairwell to the lounge on the upper deck. There was certainly no panic. People were standing around smoking and drinking, playing cards and joking. I do believe there were even people dancing – it was as casual as that! We went to a corner, sat around a table and nothing happened. There were rumours that we might have been hit by another boat and that the officers were investigating the damage and then we could all go back to bed. Then, after about ten minutes, the door from the deck burst open. It was blowing a force-eight gale and the ship was pitching up and down, and this sailor came in aghast. 'What the hell are you all doing here? The ship is sinking fast! You must all go to your boats.' And that was the first we knew about the danger. There wasn't a panic, we knew that we had to go to where the lifeboats were. We went to our number-four lifeboat, only to find it had been launched and was in the sea bobbing up and down, and no way could we get into it. Then one of the crew said, 'Can anyone climb a rope?' Barbara said, 'Yes, I used to do this in the gym.' So he said, 'Right, down you go.' And here was this fourteen-year-old girl going out on to one of the davits over the sea, with the boat going up and down, and down she went, and landed safely in the boat. That left my mother and us . . .

We started to walk back to the bows. By this time the ship was settling by the stern so it was like walking uphill. We met another man and he saw my mother with two children and said, 'Follow me. I know where there are some rafts.' We did follow him, and as we were going past the main part of the ship, there was an explosion, but he went through all this. How he did it, I don't know, but he floated two rafts round the corner, big rafts. Then he told my mother, 'Quick, jump!' And she quickly jumped and we were put on these rafts. There were five people on that raft: my mother, Sonia and myself, Doris Walker, an Australian lady, and the ship's engineer.

When we were first in the water, we could hear a lot of crying, and screaming of the children because they suffered far more than we did. The torpedo had hit their part of the ship and many had been injured or entombed in their cabins and they couldn't get out. And those that got on to lifeboats, well, they were badly launched. They had the Indian crew and instead of lowering the lifeboat gradually, they came down one end first and then the other end and they were all pitched into the water, and we're talking of children as young as four years old . . . So there was an awful loss of life amongst these children, who didn't have much of a chance. The ship sank literally in front of our eyes. We were very close to it, and it heeled right up in the air, then fell slightly sideways to where we were, and slid away from us backwards, going down stern first. It had all its lights on, it was a blaze of light, and then it went. Our first reaction – Sonia and I – was, 'What a waste of ice-cream!' Because we'd lived with all this ice-cream, which we loved.

Fred Steels
Evacuee schoolboy, **City of Benares**

I always remember a light going round the ship and one of the crew said it was the captain going around with a torch, making sure everyone was off. And then she nosedived and away she went.

There was a massive amount of logs and debris floating past us and people in the water too.

Colin Ryder Richardson
Evacuee schoolboy, private passenger, **City of Benares**

My main concern in our waterlogged boat was looking after the elderly nurse who was beginning to slip down into the boat. Really, I was hanging on to her clothes rather than her. I usually looked to her for help and, at a time like that, it seemed our roles were reversed. I could see people being swept out of the boat. Sitting next to me on the other side of the nurse was an elderly man from a Canadian university, and he was gently suggesting to me that I should release the nurse as in his view she was dead. I was so cold, I couldn't move my arms and legs, and I was holding on to her for my life. But then it became apparent to me that she was dead, but I just *couldn't* let go of her. I felt that at any moment we would be rescued and there might be a possibility of life within her, and it seemed cruel to let her go even though she was patently dead, her mouth was open, and everything else ... And they said, 'Come on, Colin, let go of her, let go of her.' I just couldn't do it. Eventually the storm solved the problem and she was swept away ... There was a young English student who said he wanted something to eat and drink, and he started to drink seawater although others were telling him not to, but he was insistent on it and the next moment he jumped – if 'jumped' is the right word – from the relative safety of the lifeboat into the sea. By now there were fewer and fewer people and the sea was running high. We really just sat there watching people dying slowly – dying left, right and centre ... I think there were only three or four of us left by the time we were picked up by HMS *Hurricane*, three or four out of forty or fifty people. I was waterlogged up to my chest until I was rescued.

Derek Bech
Evacuee schoolboy, private passenger, **City of Benares**

The raft was a wooden construction, probably like those diving platforms you see by the seaside today, a series of wooden duck-boarding and in between the buoyancy cylinders – ours were old forty-five-gallon kerosene drums – held together with nails and rope. Being in a very rough sea, we were like a little cork going up and down these huge twenty-foot-high waves. We would go to the top of the wave and come down to the bottom and the next wave would hit these cylinders, boom! *Bang!* We were hanging on with our fingers and every time these cylinders came up they pinched our fingers, and not only that, they were slowly knocking the nails out of the raft, which was beginning to break up because you weren't supposed to have five people on a raft in rough seas. Sonia, bless her soul, was washed off twice and drifted away from the raft. And my mother called, 'Sonia, swim! Swim, like you've never swum in your life.' And she somehow came back and the Scottish engineer pulled her aboard. So the going on our big dipper, as we called it, was extremely rough. I do remember a fairly full moon. I could look up and see this, and then the clouds would rush over it and it would become pitch dark and we'd get these hailstones. We were terribly cold, numb with the cold. There was nothing you could hold on to, just your fingers round the planks. My mother said her fingers were red with blood and, apart from looking after herself, she had her arms around me, holding on to me, because I kept dozing off. She told me that more than once I was completely asleep. 'Wake up! *Wake up!*' she'd say, and I had to wake up.

Bess Cummings (Walder)
Evacuee schoolgirl, **City of Benares**

Some of the children had been lowered on to a raft, and the raft, as soon as it reached the sea, collapsed because of the weight ... I had to stop thinking of my brother because I had to look after myself ... At the point of the sinking of this lovely ship, suddenly all the lights worked and it sank illuminated. And as it sank, it made the most terrible, *terrible* noise. It sounded like a gigantic groan. Many years later, a sailor said to me, 'When you saw the ship go down, Bess, did it cry?' I said, 'Yes, yes, it did.' He said, 'They always do.' We fortunately had managed to draw away from the sinking ship, but the boat was so badly loaded with water – I was sitting in water up to my chest, some of the adults had water up to their thighs. The little ones had *no* chance. They were drowned in the lifeboat in which I was sitting. Then the inevitable happened: the whole thing turned upside-down and everybody was flung out.

I was fortunate because my father taught me to swim in the sea and I was a strong swimmer, same with my brother ... and so I heard my father say to me, 'When you are in difficulties, remember you are like a cork, when human beings go down, they come up and it's when you come up that's when you have to work.' And I did, having gone down what seemed to be a long green tunnel, I came up, stretched my arms out to do a stroke and touched the side of the upturned lifeboat. It had edges that I could get hold of and I literally scrambled my way up and hung on to the keel, which was now at the top. So my body was lying along the rounded side of the boat, now uppermost, my hands clinging to the keel. My feet were actually in the water and the waves were breaking over me, but not over my head ... There was a row of hands along the keel to one side, some adults, some children. Also, there was a girl hanging on opposite to me whose name was Beth. Next to Beth there was an elderly lady hanging on, and she had the most exquisite rings on, and by and by, like most of them, these hands slipped away.

The ocean was covered with debris from the *City of Benares*. Basket chairs would float by, lovely chairs that had been on the open decks, where people had their drinks, and the beautiful rocking-horse, which I had illegally climbed on in the nursery, was rocking up and down in the ocean – a surreal object ... Finally, only four of us were left on that upturned lifeboat: Beth, myself and two of the Indian seamen. We were being flung up

145

and down. Our bodies were being lifted by the force of the waves, then banged down back on to the hull again. The fact that Beth and I could look at one another and nod and very briefly speak was important. I said to Beth, 'We'll hang on.' And she said, 'Yes.' One of the Indians drowned because he had tied himself on, so couldn't raise his head when a big wave came. The other one was delirious. So there we were: two girls, one fourteen, one fifteen, one delirious Indian and one dead one, in the middle of the Atlantic six hundred miles from anywhere . . .

Barbara Partridge (Bech)
Evacuee schoolgirl, private passenger, **City of Benares**

Gradually, as we began to drift away, we got separated from everything and in the end you couldn't hear anything. We seemed to be alone in the Atlantic. When dawn broke we could see one craft, which we tried to approach. It turned out to be an overturned lifeboat with two girls crouched on it, holding on to the keel, and the body of an Indian sort of slung over the far side. The two girls were Beth and Bess, although I didn't know their names then. We did try to get near them, but as we got nearer, our boat began to rock and in the end one of the men said, 'We can't do it.' And we had to leave them . . . I can remember thinking how awful it was to leave them, that all the grown-ups ought to be able to do *something* even if it was throwing them a rope . . .

Fred Steels
Evacuee schoolboy, **City of Benares**

I had on just a pair of pyjamas and a short black coat and my lifebelt, of course, nothing on my feet. We were right in the middle of the September gales and we had three storms during that period in the lifeboat, and it did get very cold. We boys were all stuffed up into the bows of the lifeboat, that was the most protected part, and one of the escorts, Mary Cornish, was up there with us. She was massaging our limbs and telling us stories and goodness knows what, trying to keep our spirits up. I don't think any of the lads broke down and gave in to it. We all believed we were going to be picked up . . . There was very little food on board. As regards the water situation, we boys used to get two little drinks a day until it started running down and then they reduced it. And hard-tack biscuits about half an inch thick, the sort of thing you could break your jaw on quite easily. We had a little bit of fruit and some condensed milk, but as the days went by it all started going down and down. At the end there was virtually nothing left at all. I think we were getting half a small beaker of water and the food had virtually gone.

Bess Cummings (Walder)
Evacuee schoolgirl, **City of Benares**

Physically, it was very difficult because our tongues began to swell and our lips and jaws also. Our eyes were beginning to close and we were encrusted with salt. Beth recalls seeing these sea creatures like glow worms on her clothes. The two big lifejackets that we wore had swollen to enormous proportions and cuffed us under our chins – I had a red-raw chin. Our fronts were like jelly from being flung up and down so many times, but we were past pain. We were barely alive.

Jack Keeley
Evacuee schoolboy, **City of Benares**

We hung on there like grim death. There was a storm. The worst thing was the hailstones, they were hitting you on the back. It was *so* cold, I couldn't stop my teeth chattering. The other chap didn't say a word, he just lay there. We devised a system of tying ourselves so that we could stop on the thing. We went up one wave and down the next one. It was later estimated that the waves were over twenty feet in height. But the *cold*, it was *so* cold – they say the Atlantic is always cold even in the middle of the summer. I was in pyjama bottoms, a vest, a pyjama top and my little life-jacket and bare feet, and cold, all the time freezing cold, cold. We were like a little speck on the water, not three inches out of the water on this raft. This was about a foot deep and six feet square ... When daylight came, we expected to find people around us, all in the same boat. But not a soul. All we saw was an occasional seagull, nothing ...

HMS *Hurricane* had been alerted at the time of the attack, but she was two hundred miles away and could not reach the survivors until the early afternoon of the following day. As they reached the area, terrible sights greeted the crew: in one boat, twenty-one children lay dead; in others they found a few survivors, barely alive, with the dead clustered around them. The *City of Benares* had gone down nineteen hours before. One lifeboat, number twelve, had drifted some distance off. *The Hurricane* did not find it, and gave it up for lost.

Bess Cummings (Walder)
Evacuee schoolgirl, City of Benares

As the skies began to darken on the afternoon of the sinking, I saw a small black dot on the horizon, and as I stared at it, it grew larger. Now, this was unusual because by then we were on a vast watery desert. We were having delusions. I had seen trays of food coming towards me, which I knew was impossible. So when this dot became larger I tried to grab Beth's attention, saying as loudly as I could, 'Ship!' She shook her head. 'No.' I went on watching as it got larger, larger, larger still, until it had the shape of a ship. I could see a great big H106 on its hull – this was HMS *Hurricane* and from it came a noise that sounded like a rugby crowd. This was the crew shouting words of encouragement, 'Hold on, *hold on*, we're coming!' We found out later they had been picking up dead children all day, and seeing two girls and one adult on an upturned lifeboat at that time in the Atlantic, in the evening, was nothing short of a miracle. So it was. They let down a whaler with a crew of young, strong men, who rowed towards us. I was lifted into it by Albert Gorman, a seaman of tremendous skill, saying, 'Come on, darling, let go, let go.' But Darling couldn't let go because my hands were stuck tight, so Albert lifted my fingers away from the keel and bent them back and back, finally releasing me, then wrapping me in a big blanket, placing me in the whaler and telling one of his mates to throw something down my throat, which I now know to have been rum. He did the same for Beth. And there we were, rescued in the nick of time. Yes, the nick of time.

Beth and I were cared for like princesses on HMS *Hurricane* ... Beth recovered very well, but I took a bit longer because I had problems about how I was going to explain to my parents about the death of my brother. It weighed heavily. But one day on our way back to Scotland, the captain of the destroyer came, and said, 'Sit up, miss, I have a present for you.' And from behind his back he produced my brother. Well, it was overwhelming. But I said to him, just like a cross mother, 'Where have you *been*?' And he said to me, 'What are *you* doing lying there?' And then, of course, we kissed and hugged. There we were, safe and sound together ... There were so few survivors. We were the only brother and sister of all the CORB evacuee children to survive. Whole families had disappeared, including the five Grimmonds; they had all gone. The wreckage of lives also meant the wreckage of the lives of mothers and fathers when they heard ...

Sonia Williams (Bech)
Evacuee schoolgirl, private passenger, **City of Benares**

All that night I was hanging on, but twice I fell off. I must have lost consciousness. Although I have said that I fought for my life, there were two moments when I didn't. The first I shall never forget. I was absolutely certain that I had drowned – it's rather a peaceful feeling, you see white when you open your eyes and it must be the foam, I suppose, but it seems as if it's heaven. It did to me, and I remember distinctly thinking, I wonder what God is going to be like. Any rate, I was pulled back and I hung on again ... When dawn came, I felt quite different: it was light and something was going to happen, I felt. It was about eleven o'clock in the morning. I said, 'Look, there's a red sail on the horizon!' Mummy said, 'Don't be silly, of course there isn't.' But I said, 'You wait. When we're on the next high wave, everybody look in *that* direction.' And they did, and there *was* a sail . . . This was the lifeboat of another ship, which had been torpedoed at the same time as us – the SS *Marina*. Her skipper, Mr Lewis, managed to get to us in a very rough sea and he hauled us aboard and told us, 'Don't worry, we know we're going to be saved because our sparks [signaller] sent a message to Land's End, which was picked up, and they're on their way.' Well, after four or five hours, at sunset, we saw HMS *Hurricane* looming in sight. She was beautiful, silver. And we screamed and shouted, and he [Mr Lewis] had a flare so we sent that up and it got to us. I always remember the ship's side was laid with netting. The sailor entangled his legs in the rope so that his two arms were free and he took me up like a sack. Then I was put on the deck. They said, 'Can you walk?' I said, 'Of course I can walk.' And I promptly fell down . . .

Jack Keeley
Evacuee schoolboy, City of Benares

The funny thing was that when rescue came, we were so cramped and it was so cold, we couldn't get off the raft. The only way was to roll off and fall in the water. They flung a net down the side of the destroyer and sort of scooped us out and on to the destroyer and took us straight down in the engine room. It was like walking out of an iceberg into a boiler. They took our clothes off and gave us a drop of rum, and then we were wrapped in blankets and put in the wardroom. The first people I saw in this place were the two I had seen standing on the deck, the Bechs. Then we slept on the floor in sleeping-bags and rolled from side to side with the movement of the ship . . . The ship's crew of HMS *Hurricane* clothed us – they gave us everything they could. The destroyer landed at Gourock in Scotland . . .

Barbara Partridge (Bech)
Evacuee schoolgirl, private passenger, **City of Benares**

Our boat was one of the last to be fished out because we were so obviously seaworthy. Eventually the destroyer came alongside and one or two sailors jumped in and handed us up, and they stuffed us into an enclosure around the funnel. And almost immediately, a head popped round the door: 'Is there a girl here called Barbara Bech?' Then, 'Thank goodness, because your mother's been so worried.' So apparently he rushed out and said, 'It's all right, Barbara's here.' We were the only family that got out whole.

Sonia Williams (Bech)
Evacuee schoolgirl, private passenger, **City of Benares**

In Gourock there was a large building where the WVS had put a whole lot of clothes for us to wear. Mummy had forty pounds and she said, 'I don't want you to have other people's clothes, I'm going shopping.' And off she went and she bought for Colin [Ryder Richardson] and Derek grey flannels, and we had beautiful Scottish kilts, and we all had gabardine mackintoshes and grey felt hats. We were smart, very smart ... This is when Sonia Bech enjoyed herself, little beast! 'Would you like to hear my story?' So I told my story of sitting on a raft, but the *News Chronicle* did something very naughty: I had mentioned our London address, and this reporter called on my father that very night and the next of kin hadn't yet been told. He met my father and said, 'I've just met your daughter. She's wonderful and alive.' And my father said, 'What about my wife and other two children?' and he said, 'I can't tell you about them.' You can imagine, he was absolutely shattered ...

Jack Keeley
Evacuee schoolboy, **City of Benares**

We were taken to Glasgow, rekitted out with brand new clothes, and stayed for about a week when we were taken out on various trips and a tram ride around Glasgow. We had film crews up there and we were on the newsreels some weeks later. We came back overnight from Glasgow to London. My mother met me at the station where she questioned me about my sister: was she in the lifeboat? Did I ever see her? I didn't – the girls went one way, the boys the other. I hadn't seen her and, knowing what the conditions were and the cold, you couldn't expect a little girl aged six to survive. My mother was very upset, and then we went home. My father, to the best of my memory, never mentioned the incident. The Blitz was starting when I arrived back. The Germans seemed to be following me about!

Meanwhile the ordeal continued for those in lifeboat twelve. For nine days, the forty-six passengers, including six CORB boys and two escorts, rowed as hard as they could in the direction of what they, mistakenly, thought was the coast of Ireland, suffering terrible privation. Their water had practically run out by the time they were sighted by a Sunderland flying-boat. It alerted HMS _Anthony_, which dashed to their rescue. The children's parents, certain they had drowned, were planning memorial services as they were rescued. The death toll of the sinking was 256: 122 crew and 134 passengers, 81 of whom were children, including 77 from CORB.

Fred Steels
Evacuee schoolboy, City of Benares

It was a very calm sea the day we were rescued, and all of a sudden, one of the lads – I think it was Ken – spotted this speck in the sky, and we watched it getting closer and closer and it turned out to be a Sunderland flying-boat ...

I was born in Hull, which was then _the_ fish place. Mum used to tell me that I was born with a cowl – a skin – over my face. Any seaman thought that if they possessed it, they would never drown ... We were on that boat from 10.30 p.m. Wednesday night the seventeenth, and we were picked up at 3.30 p.m. on the twenty-sixth, nine days later.

Kenneth Sparks
Evacuee schoolboy, City of Benares

I have since seen the picture that one of those on the plane took of us, and we were a minute little dot in the great big wide expanse of ocean. But, of course, we waved. I stood up, so I am told, and signalled – hand signals that I'd learnt in the Cadets – that we were from the *City of Benares*, and eventually they came along. Oh dear, wasn't it lovely? *Saved!* They tried to land but it was far too rough, so they signalled to George Purvis, who was in charge, that they were going to get help and they found this destroyer and brought that up to us the next day.

The aeroplane didn't leave us until the boat actually got to us. We could see the boat in the distance, just a little dot, and then it came *belting* up and pulled alongside us. But most of us were too weak to climb up the netting, so some of the sailors came down and lifted us up on to the deck. We were treated like royalty. I shall never forget it. It was the destroyer, HMS *Anthony*, grey, with H40 on the side. Oh dear, it was *lovely*! We must have been on the ship for about four days. We were taken to the lower mess decks, rubbed down and given fresh clothing. Then the doctor saw us and decided that we could drink but couldn't eat. Then we were looked after by the crew in different cabins, and we *were* looked after! There was nothing they didn't do for us. And when we could eat! I've never had sandwiches so thick – a tin of salmon between two slices of bread an inch wide! *Gorgeous*. And hot sweet tea to revive us … We were taken everywhere on the destroyer – it didn't half go! It went at terrific speed to get us back to civilization. Even when we got to Gourock, the sailors wouldn't let us walk, but carried us to the waiting coach …

Safe at last! It didn't matter about bombs falling, we were no longer *cold*. We didn't stop long in Gourock but were taken to this hotel in Glasgow, and that first night about four of us were put in this enormous great bed, but I don't think we slept at all. You see, it wasn't comfortable, was it? It wasn't *hard*! But it was really nice there, and they did everything they could for us. We even met the Provost of Glasgow. I think they classed us as heroes, but we were *survivors*, not heroes. We were kitted out in Scottish clothing, kilts, and we could choose our clans. I was Hunting Gordon. So a great fuss up there.

The Polish millionaire was met by General Sikorski [the head of the Polish government-in-exile] and his aide-de-camp as soon as he landed. I saw that myself, although I didn't know it was General Sikorski at the time. Before they left, this Polish man ensured that we were no worse off for our troubles and gave us all the money we had lost on the boat.

Mary was exceptional: without her we would not have survived. She was decorated by King George VI with the MBE, I think, then she reverted back to her old role as a music teacher. We never saw the other evacuees; we didn't know who had been saved and who hadn't. When we were at the hotel, somebody told us that a boat had been picked up but they were all dead, and then we heard that, out of all the children, just thirteen had been saved. I was reported as 'Missing, believed killed by enemy action' . . . The chap who ran the CORB scheme went round to all the parents about five days after the sinking and said there was no hope for us. Must have been a rotten job for him . . . Mother came up and brought me back to Wembley. When I got back home, the neighbours made a collection and bought me a most marvellous watch, all inscribed . . . Luckily I had an aunt in Winchester where I could recuperate for a little while. I had to go into hospital there for a time, then it was back to school, back to normal again – more like a ten-minute than a five-minute wonder!

Fred Steels
Evacuee schoolboy, **City of Benares**

People had given me up, but not my mum. They used to spend their nights in a big air-raid shelter under a factory, and this particular night, the air-raid warden went down and shook my mum and said, 'Hey, he's been picked up.' And my mum said, 'Yes, I know, I saw him.' She had a dream that she saw me coming home. The day after we were picked up, they were going to hold a memorial service because my mother had given my toys and everything away to the school ...

When I got back to Eastney, oh, I had a heyday! I had a free pass to the cinema, and everywhere I went nobody would let me pay for a thing. Not that I could go very far because I couldn't walk any distance. I was like that for about a month – my feet hurt a lot. There's nothing worse than frostbite, I'm not kidding you. I can remember being in bed and waking up *screaming* with the pain in my feet.

Sonia Williams (Bech)
Evacuee schoolgirl, private passenger, **City of Benares**

When we got back to the railway station in Bognor, they got to know we were there, and they cheered us when we got in. And when we got into the taxi, it was the same driver who had taken us, and when Mummy went to pay, he said, 'No, it has been an honour, madam.' We got home again and my grandmother was there. Everything was normal, including my dog, and Meta came back too ... We went straight back to school, a boys' school that took sisters, and I had the time of my life there. We were treated royally and were known as 'Survivors of the *City of Benares*'.

Bess Cummings (Walder)
Evacuee schoolgirl, **City of Benares**

Afterwards my own mental state was pretty good. I think it was because I was brought up by very sensible, sane people who didn't make too much fuss of me. Even if professional help had been in existence, I wouldn't have seen the need, and neither would they. My father said, 'Now look, young woman, you've been through a very trying time, but this is wartime and don't forget there are others having even a worse time than you.' Which was very good for me because I was being spoilt by all the attention.

Mr and Mrs Thomas Myatt

Letter to their daughter Beryl, to await her expected arrival in Winnipeg, Canada. Beryl drowned when the City of Benares *went down.*

Our dearest Beryl, This is our second letter to you since you set sail on your big adventure Dear, and we suppose you were very surprised when you arrived at Auntie Emmies to find a letter and your *Dandy* and *Sunny Stories* waiting there for you. We will send them each week.

We expect you enjoyed your voyage on the boat across the wide Atlantic Ocean, and your long journey on the train to Winnipeg. We don't suppose you saw any icebergs during your voyage across, as it would hardly be quite cold enough at this time of the year. How would you like to be a nurse on a big Ocean Liner when you grow up, Dear?

Now sweetheart, don't forget what we told you. We want you to let auntie and uncle see that you can be a great help to them about the house by helping to the best of your ability, such as running errands, and helping auntie with her housework and her baking, and above all dear, keep your bedroom tidy and always hang your clothes up in their right place, and this will show auntie and uncle that you really appreciate the opportunity they have given you to have a grand holiday in one of the most interesting countries in the World – CANADA – the home of the Maple Leaf for Canada, the Rose for England, the Leek for Wales, the Thistle for Scotland and the Shamrock for Ireland ... The weather here is still fairly nice – What kind of weather are you having? Well Dear, please give our love to auntie and uncle, and when you write you must tell us all about what you are doing. Everybody at home sends their love. Must close now with Tons of Love and Heaps of Kisses. God Bless You. Mummy and Daddy XXXXXX XXXXXXXXXXXXXXXXXXXXXXXXXX

7. In the Front Line: Blitz 1940–41

In September 1940, London bore the brunt of the Blitz, but two months later the Luftwaffe was dropping its bombs on towns and cities all over England, Wales, Scotland and Northern Ireland, concentrating on ports and industrial centres. Coventry, a prime industrial target, had already endured air attacks, but the huge raid that took place on 14 November 1940 became a yardstick against which other cities would measure their suffering from then until May 1941. On a brilliant moonlit night, in Operation 'Moonlight Sonata', the city centre was obliterated. The cathedral and vast areas surrounding it were gutted by fire, 2,294 buildings were destroyed and thousands damaged. All utilities were put out of action, 554 people were killed and hundreds were seriously injured. The raid lasted from 7.20 p.m. until 6 a.m., with no respite. Lacking suburbs to flee into, people trekked out to shelter in the nearby countryside, many sleeping in the fields.

The severity of the raid on Coventry shocked the country, but the Luftwaffe continued 'coventration' throughout Great Britain. Most cities had experienced previous raids, but nothing of the scale and intensity that occurred in late 1940 and early 1941. On 10 January, a raid on Portsmouth practically wiped out old maritime 'Pompey': the dockyard suffered massive damage and its Guildhall was set ablaze. From then on, the city almost emptied at night, with citizens making their way by whatever means they could to the large shelters that had been tunnelled into the chalk on Portsdown Hill.

Plymouth underwent a severe hammering throughout 1940–41, and a series of raids in April 1941 brought the total number killed to more than a thousand out of a population of 200,000 – and this in a city designated 'safe' in 1939. Terrified people fled from the target areas of the harbour and docks to seek shelter in the surrounding woods and fields.

Merseyside and Clydeside also suffered intensive and prolonged bombing in the spring of 1941, Merseyside holding the record for the longest unbroken series of raids of any provincial centre during the war. As in London and other cities, the first wave of evacuees had returned home before the Blitz started, but by July 1941, 142,000 had been moved out again to safer Scottish areas.

Comparisons have been made between the drawn-out ordeal experienced by Londoners and the raids that citizens of provincial towns endured. Generally, although London casualties accounted for half of the total deaths and serious injuries, the briefer raids on smaller cities and towns were of a particular intensity that caused an understandable lowering of morale. As the raids were so concentrated, city and town centres were levelled at a stroke, with loss of shops, administration, major amenities and central infrastructure overnight. Citizens of places like Portsmouth and Plymouth would stagger out when the all-clear sounded to find the heart of their historic town or city, the familiar and beloved landmarks, gone. Also, the suddenness and thoroughness of the destruction gave them no opportunity to get used to it, as Londoners had after their endless nights of terror.

As for the evacuees, those mothers and children who had left for the countryside once the Blitz started now knew why they had gone, unlike those who had left in early September 1939 and returned during the Phoney War. Now far more vigorous efforts were made to encourage evacuees to stay in their new homes, whatever the conditions. Hostels were opened and nurseries provided for war orphans or children whose mothers were doing essential war work. Rest centres were improved, while recuperation and convalescent hostels were set up for the elderly, mothers and child victims of air raids.

The last major attack of the Blitz, on 10 May 1941, was also the worst, with a bomber force of 550 planes. Like the first, it was on London. That night more than two thousand fires raged from Shadwell and Whitechapel in the east to Southwark and Westminster. Fifteen hundred people were killed and nearly two thousand seriously injured. Westminster Abbey and St Paul's Cathedral were hit and the debating chamber of the House of Commons was destroyed. During that raid five thousand houses were destroyed, leaving twelve thousand homeless.

In May 1941, when Hitler ordered his bombers east in readiness for the planned attack on the Soviet Union in June, the Blitz on London and other cities all but ceased. Hull – a prime target since early 1941 – was the exception, and continued to attract heavy raids well into June and July.

In the nine months of the Blitz, 43,000 civilians nationwide were killed, many more seriously injured, and vast swathes of industry, infrastructure and homes destroyed. Buckingham Palace had been hit three times and it was from his damaged home, on 23 September 1940, that the King announced in a broadcast the instigation of the George Medal for valour on the home front. By the end of 1941 it had been awarded to more than five hundred people.

In September 1940, George Orwell and others had predicted that the country's morale might be broken within three months. This was not so. 'London can take it!' was the message Ed Murrow, the American radio correspondent, despatched to the USA. Londoners did, and so did the men, women and children of many other places throughout the nation. The Blitz had ended, but there was a great deal more bombing to come, including the 'Little Blitz' of 1944 and the V1 flying bomb and V2 rocket attacks on London and the south in 1944–5.

Colin Perry
Junior City clerk, Upper Tooting, London, diary, 14 September 1940

I always admired the Duke of Windsor and wished him our King. I have changed my mind; our King and Queen are contending with the war magnificently, carrying on here in their capital when they could be miles away in safety. They visit bombed and devastated areas seeking to relieve worry. They shelter with commoners whilst the bombers roar overhead. This is the King and Queen of whom we are so proud.

John Leopard
Schoolboy, Deptford, Greater London

I went to school in Evelyn Street and I do remember the occasion when the playground was shot up by a dive-bomber and a number of children were killed and injured. Evidently this dive-bomber had shot up three schools and Lewisham hospital. I remember the guns going off and the shouting and the screaming and the plane coming over, just skimming the roofs of the houses. I saw some bodies but wasn't allowed to go near them. It did affect me a little bit, future events even more – my initiation really into the war, the first time I'd seen people injured or killed ... One day, coming out of school, there had been a bomb dropped not far away. I managed to get through the cordon with my pals. We were all excited, and one of my mates suddenly said, 'Oh, look, it's Tommy's head!' That was a shock. We were ushered out. I was struck dumb. Right up to the age of twelve I was still having nightmares, and teachers thought I was rather quiet and used to go into a shell ...

Sylvia Townson (Limburg)
Jewish schoolgirl, Marylebone, London

I can remember coming out of the shelter when our house was actually bombed and then we knew we would never be able to live in it again, and standing there watching the firemen playing their hoses on it. *That* didn't frighten me, it was just something that was happening. As long as my parents were with me standing on the pavement, it didn't matter. The only thing that concerned me was that my budgie was in the house and my father went in with the wardens and found a few belongings and my budgie ...

Paul Eddington
Schoolboy, Chelsea, London

The night raids, I think they used to start at eight o'clock, not five minutes to or five minutes after, but eight o'clock – the Germans were always very punctual ... We weren't very far from Sloane Square. I remember the huge department store there, Peter Jones, had a glass front and I used to think every night that that glass front had been demolished. I was told that the Germans put whistling sirens on the bombs' fins, and there was this most horrifying screaming noise as the bombs came down. You felt like the heroine tied to the rails as the express rushed at you – it was a noise such as you couldn't believe! And every morning I used to go out in order to inspect the ruins of Peter Jones and was astounded to find it still standing. I don't remember being particularly frightened. I remember sitting under the stairs one night with an Indo-French family, sharing this little bit of shelter with them. And I was thinking during this raid how interesting it would be to be dead, what an exciting experience. It didn't occur to me that I might have a foot blown off or something like that. It was either death or nothing. Death was quite a romantic thing for a young person. The old aunt said, '*Il a une figure très calme*' [He looks very composed]. That was translated for me and I was rather pleased.

Peter Izard
Schoolboy, Beckenham, Kent

I succumbed to an abscess on the brain, which the doctor thought was because I kept banging my head as I dived under the table for shelter. I was very frightened and consumed lots of bottles of sarsaparilla, a drink to steady the nerves ...

The problem was solved for me by a friend who said, 'Hey, the Civil Defence want messengers on bicycles, let's go!' They told us, 'You're too young.' We said, 'No, we're not, we made a mistake about our age.' So they took us, and now that I was part of it, it didn't worry me at all. We were just old men and boys, and quite often we found that we were out doing a patrol instead of a warden – at fifteen that was quite something . . . I was always up seven or eight minutes before the air-raid siren went, day or night . . . We were basically responsible for cycling round and passing messages if there was a break in telephone lines – no mobile phones or emails then! For example, cycling to the fire station, if necessary, saying, 'Can you come . . . ?'

Peter Cox
Schoolboy, Coventry, Warwickshire, extract from his memoir

Many from Coventry took to driving out into the country to sleep in their cars. Night after night the roads were packed with streams of people looking for anywhere flat at the roadside on which to park for the night. We would take flasks of hot tea – we didn't drink coffee! – and sandwiches, have a picnic supper and settle down as best we could in our 1935 Hillman Minx: Bessie, my mother, Fred, my father, my aunt Pat and me. Sometimes, just before we settled down for the night, we would look into the sky above Coventry and our sister city, Birmingham, to see which of them was burning brightest. This was no competition: we had to know where our prayers were needed most.

Then the people in the country saw a way to help and offers of accommodation began to appear in the paper. To be fair, many of these people were motivated by genuine concern, but others saw it as a means of making money by charging large sums for space and a bed with a mattress on it, nothing else . . . Our own neighbourhood remained untouched throughout but there was plenty of damage from which we children derived some obscure delight as we viewed other people's shattered houses. This curiosity led to a number of children being killed or severely injured as they clambered over the ruins and were crushed under falling masonry ... Sometimes it was not children playing their adventure games, but adults with an entirely different purpose. We all learnt a new word: *looting*!

Maggie Hantken (Edwards)
Schoolgirl, Hounslow, Middlesex, extract from her memoir

We returned to our bombed home every day to light the fire and make sure everything was secure ... The repairs were taking time, for which at least one villain was grateful. On one of our visits, we noticed the front door was slightly ajar. Furious, and without thinking, Mum flung it wide, marched down the hall and into the cupboard under the stairs. As she'd guessed, the gas and electricity slot meters had been cracked open and the money gone. On the floor, near the cupboard door, was a hefty lead truncheon. Obviously the burglar had intended using it if we'd returned too early and caught him in the act. Sadly, such looting of bombed houses was commonplace, but made us all the angrier because we had to reimburse the Gas and Electricity Boards ourselves.

John Starling
Schoolboy evacuee, Winchester, Hampshire

The first major night raid on Portsmouth was when I was on holiday there, 10 January 1941, and this was the big fire blitz on Portsmouth when the Guildhall was gutted and the whole of the central shopping area was flattened, together with a lot of the old parts of Portsea. Tremendous casualties resulted from that ... My old dad was on very exacting war work and he needed his sleep and he couldn't sleep in the shelter, so we improvised a bunk under the stairs and we all slept there – when you were bombed very often the staircase would remain intact and the rest of the house collapsed around it. But to hear these bombs whistling all around was very frightening, we were all shaking. I was longing to get back to Winchester for some peace and quiet from the raids, although I didn't want to leave my parents. How they put up with it, I don't know ...

Marjorie Bond (Cranshaw)
Schoolgirl, Hull, Yorkshire

The air raids on Hull started in the autumn of 1940, but the main raids were a big series in the first half of 1941 especially March and May ... The siren would go and then in a little while the guns would go and you'd hear the planes. It could go on for hours: we tended to have very long alerts in Hull. We also got long alerts when other major cities were bombed because very often the planes went over Hull to get to Sheffield, Coventry, Liverpool and Birmingham, and we wouldn't get the all-clear until they had left these cities. I think the people of Hull were rather upset that places like Coventry and other cities got a mention of having been raided, whereas Hull was never named. They only talked about 'a north-east town'. In fact, we had a number of very major air raids and there was a bit of feeling that we weren't getting credit for standing up to the bombing. I shared that feeling.

Thomas Houlton
Schoolboy, Hull, Yorkshire

The biggest raids were on the nights of 7 and 8 May 1941, when the May blitz occurred. We were within a mile of King George Dock so there was lots of damage around us. An Anderson shelter about a hundred yards away had a direct hit and everybody was killed. I particularly remember an earlier raid of 18 March. There was a searchlight two hundred yards down Preston Road, and after the raid a man came dashing up: 'Help my friends! Help my friends!' A dive-bomber had gone straight down the beam and dropped a bomb, which killed four men. That stuck in my memory quite vividly because his hands were all red. He'd obviously been trying to help his friends who'd been killed or injured.

Morale was outstandingly good. There was just a little feeling of panic after the second night of the blitz in so far as people were desperate to get out. I remember seeing people trekking down the roads to get into the country to escape the bombing

...There were still buses managing to get going, and a little red bus running a shuttle service – it was packed out: people were literally holding on with one foot on the running-board. People were trekking with suitcases, bicycles, little handcarts, prams. In our case my father managed to find us a place on a farm for a while ... But the main attitude was one of defiance. The city became festooned almost overnight with V signs on the tiles and slates of the houses, some of which can still be seen today ...

Kathleen Stephenson (McManus)
Teenager, Hull, Yorkshire

I had just started earning some money, and I bought myself some lime green cami-knickers and one or two delicate things, which my mum didn't want me to buy. And they'd got dusty with soot falling when our windows were blasted out during the first night of the blitz. I'd washed them very carefully and put them on the line in the kitchen. The second night I went to sleep under the stairs with my baby brother. During the night the air-raid warden came down and told us that the sawmill next door had been bombed and we had to leave our home. I was in my nightgown. I put my coat on and my slippers, then my mum and dad, myself and Michael ran across the road to White Sugar Mills. There was a great big air-raid shelter there. I remember going in, and I remember my mother had all her important papers in this attaché case. They kept dropping the bombs ... We had to move a couple of times and we finished up in a big air-raid shelter in a railway goods siding. Opposite the road were stables with horses, all crying. Oh, it was an awful sound, listening to them.

There was a lull for a long time. I got a bit impatient so I said to my mum, 'I'm going to see if the house is all right.' I picked my way along in my slippers and saw the house, which was just burning. The front door was blown absolutely flat. There was an air-raid warden there and I asked him to come in with me. He said, 'I'm not going in and you're not going in either.' It didn't stop me. I ran over the front door and when I looked up the stairs – we had lino, not carpet – there were little blobs of light all the way up. I went into the front room. Mum had brought the beds down and when I looked there were little blobs of fire everywhere and I couldn't get to anything. I went to the kitchen to save my green cami-knickers. I opened the door but it was all just a blaze – my cami-knickers had gone. I had to gingerly make my way back and had to tell my mum. She was in a state. The next morning, we walked past the house and I can remember my mum being in tears.

Peter Biglin
Schoolboy, Hull, Yorkshire

My father was a structural engineer. On the wall of his office there used to be a plan cupboard with a lock on. Inside there was a plan showing where all the bombs had dropped in Hull. And I can remember a bomb list with one of the most terrible bombs the Germans had, they nicknamed it 'Big Bastard Schickel-gruber' – that used to tickle me a lot . . . It must have been a terrible bomb, that one.

Ronnie Huzzard
Pacifist hospital stretcher–bearer, Hull, extract of letter, 11 May 1941, to his evacuee sister, Dorothy, Pickering, Yorkshire

The Germans have bombed almost all factories, big shops, docks, warehouses and other such objectives likely to smash the economic life of Hull . . . of course there have been a large number of casualties. It was my duty at the hospital on Friday and from 8 till 10 we were carrying the injured from the different wards into the ambulance buses. The hospital was being emptied in case we had another attack on Friday night . . . All Prospect St, Jameson St, Carr Lane, Waterworks St, Paragon St and King Edward St are in ruins. All East Hull and Hedon Road are badly damaged and in fact there are very few things left worth bombing . . . On Wednesday night a German bomber, hit by gunfire, crashed on the bus station and destroyed forty buses. I cannot however tell you much more in a letter and when you come back to Hull you will see for yourself the effects of modern war, which will take years and years to rebuild ... When I see both the human casualties and the material destruction I thank God I am a pacifist and have never supported for one minute the waging of this war ...

Sylvia Taylor (Bell)
Schoolgirl, Hook, Surrey

I can remember going to school and saying goodbye to my mother and not knowing if I was going to see her when I came home, whether she'd still be there. The sirens went while I was on my way and we always had to go straight to the nearest shelter if that happened, we had been told. I didn't much care for school, but I wanted to get there because I felt I'd be safer at school than I would be in the shelter.

John Gibson
Teenager, boarding-house worker, Belfast, Northern Ireland

There was quite a lot of bombing in 1941. Belfast centre was virtually destroyed because they were going after Short & Harland, and Harland & Woolf, the big shipyards and an aircraft factory, where they employed thousands and thousands of men. And the only thing they had for protection was an aircraft-carrier in the Belfast lock. The Germans came over at Easter time, and there were anti-aircraft guns going around on lorries in the street. They had brick air-raid shelters built in the streets as well and everybody went in these when the sirens went, and hundreds and thousands of people made for the hills that surround Belfast to get out of the way. My sister was bombed out by incendiary bombs. But after 1942 the bombing had virtually finished.

Richard Hancock
Evacuee headmaster, Winchester, Hampshire

We had a couple of the big fire blitzes in Portsmouth and some youngsters, when the news came of the attacks, got on their bicycles to go home because they were worried about their parents. Well, who can blame them? All these things happened ... These were abnormal conditions and in those circumstances the degree of abnormality that was shown in behaviour was remarkably small.

John Starling
Evacuee schoolboy, Winchester, Hampshire

Just after I got back from a holiday at home in 1941, rumours went round the school that Portsmouth had experienced a big bombing raid. Everybody was waiting to hear what had happened. Some of the children were billeted with families with a telephone so their parents could telephone them to reassure them, but we had no such facilities and I was very anxious about mine. I told Mrs Penton, 'I'm very worried about my parents. There's been a lot of damage around North End, I'm going down to Portsmouth.' This was against school rules, but I got on my bike and proceeded to cycle the twenty-five miles to Portsmouth. I got there and there was an awful lot of bomb damage, I had to wheel my bike over a lot of debris, but fortunately when I rounded the corner I saw the house was intact. I knocked on the door, but no reply. Then the next-door neighbour came out and said, 'Hello, John, what are you doing here? Your parents have gone up to Winchester to reassure you and see that you're all right.' Oh dear! You can imagine my feelings at the time ... I arrived back after a fifty-mile trip, exhausted. I was only thirteen. But we had a couple of hours together before they returned. Lack of communication with your parents in such situations was a big problem. I was very anxious about them always. I was their only child. I had no relatives in Portsmouth at all. The nearest were in Edinburgh and I didn't know them terribly well, and that's what was flashing through my mind: if I lose my parents, what is going to happen to me?

Dorothy Lester
Primary-school teacher, Peckham Rye, London

My parents slept in armchairs in the little hall and we had a mattress for my sister and me at the foot of the stairs. About three one morning, my father said, 'I'm going up to bed.' I said, 'Wait, Dad, I'll get a cup of tea.' Well, that saved our lives. Before I could get the tea the bomb fell and it was a direct hit just outside in the back garden. The house was, of course, demolished. I thought I'd had it! I was buried in rubble with my head on a pillow, and my first thought was, I can't move my legs. I was trying to pull the pillow down to smother myself – I'd finish it off. Then I thought, I must get out of this. And I started throwing the rubble off and found that I could move my hands. My sister said I screamed and then she knew I was alive. She was less injured and helped me out. She found my mother. We couldn't see a thing. I had a wound on my head and on my leg. She said, 'Find Dad.' So there I was groping about to find my father and I found him still in his chair. I said to him, 'Come on, Dad, we've got to get out.' He was over eighty then, and he said, 'I must have my hat!' – funny now, but it wasn't at the time. My parents weren't physically hurt at all. They were in the safest place, farther away from the back garden. But psychologically they were *very* hurt ...

After that and some other Blitz experiences, I got in a bad state. I was asked if I would like to be evacuated again. I said, 'Yes, please.' I was then sent to Corbis Bay, in Cornwall, with a hundred mentally retarded children and three other teachers. Most of the children had been in special schools before the war. I took the little ones: they were so mentally retarded that they were like babies. These children had been such a nuisance when evacuated in their billets, and their parents didn't want them back in London. I was still there at the end of the war.

Peter Izard
Schoolboy, Civil Defence messenger, Beckenham, Kent

One night when I was on duty, six hundred incendiary bombs had been dropped in our area, I had gone into the courtyard of our headquarters and lying there in the middle was this large object, it was what they called a Molotov Bread-basket, which was a container with about fifty incendiary bombs, which should have exploded at two hundred feet and showered them everywhere. As I went out, it went off in my face and it blew me straight back. I remember going past everybody about two feet off the ground and slamming against the wall at the end. I was all right. About sixty-two houses were on fire, something incredible. Two sailors coming home on leave dashed into one to rescue a woman and her baby. There were no communications at all, all gone. The first warden turned to me, but I couldn't hear what he was saying, my ears had gone, so he wrote down that I had to go to the town hall and report what was happening, and off I went. Half-way down the road, these firemen were waving at me, so I waved back. What they wanted to tell me was that I was about to fall into a bomb crater, which I did. I extricated myself, a bit like Norman Wisdom, mud all over my face, went down to the town hall and reported there. This was much to the chagrin of my classmates whose fathers, local councillors, had been appointed to Headquarters but never even got their uniforms dirty! I got a pension for it after the war.

Colin Perry
Junior City clerk, Upper Tooting, London, diary, 18 October 1940

Churchill promised us 'blood, sweat and toil' – how true he was. I have already sampled sweat and toil. Last night I sampled blood.

Just gone 8 last evening, Dad, Miller, Judd and myself were sitting in the dining room, comfortable in front of a roaring fire ... Suddenly there was a roar like an express train, a hurtling, a tearing, all-powerful, overwhelming rush. Together we sprang to our feet. We got no further. The earth seemed to split into a thousand fragments. A wrenching jar I thought signified the splitting of our outside wall. The subsiding rush of materials took, it seemed, all off the back ... I knew then that death had nearly come to us ... I pelted headlong under a barrage of bursting shells along the Upper Tooting Road, into Fishponds Road, which, as the crow flies, lies not fifty yards at the back of us. Two demolition squads and rescue parties roared up. I quickly entered the centre of the crowd, a crowd only of nurses, wardens, firemen. And there, amidst the dark suburban street, standing on charred debris of every description, I found a new Perry. I confronted war in all its most brutal savagery. I beheld blood, wounded, dying. I stood transfixed ... I stood by the side of a little boy, his head a cake of blood, his arms – I knew not where they were. A small, plump, efficient voluntary nurse put her arms round him. He cried, every so often, very sobbingly, for his Mummy. His Mummy was not to be seen ... Sitting on a chair, sobbing, convulsing, making distant moans was a stout old lady; I judged that by her red and yellow spotted dress. By her side stood a silent girl, holding her arm, as if the contact would assure this wounded, bloody carcase that she was in the hands of God. Her face I could not see. It was covered with a huge piece of cloth, slitted for the nose to breathe. Underneath seeped streams of blood, and as I watched the blood clotted itself into little mounds ... The wardens formed a protective barrier around this slowly heaving woman ... I walked across to a young, it seemed, and slim woman. She was sitting so patiently on a chair, drinking water. I saw only the back of her head – it was enough. Blood, blood, blood, it oozed from her scalp, formed cakes on her skin. Oh, God ...

Many children who stayed in London and other cities under attack explained how the Blitz became a way of life. They would return home from those schools that were still open, or from work, down a hasty tea and go off to the shelter for the night. The big question was, though, which to use? Those with Anderson shelters found them damp and

GMBarrett

WHAT do I do...

WHEN I HEAR GUNS,
EXPLOSIONS,
AIR—RAID WARNINGS. .?

I keep a cool head. I take cover. I gather my family, with gas masks, and go quietly to my shelter or refuge room. I do not look up if I am out of door, because my face shines. I do not try "to have look". I do not rush about alarming people. I remember that a lot of noise is good noise — our guns firing at the enemy. And I remember that the odds are thousands to one against my being hurt.

4062

Issued by THE MINISTRY OF INFOR...

From *The War Weekly* by Guy Barnett and Derek Tongs

unhealthy, so instead they went to the cellars and basements of houses or blocks of flats, or entire families squeezed together under the stairs in their own home. There were public shelters beneath town halls or in requisitioned basements, the vaults and crypts of churches, caves, some natural, as in Chislehurst, or man-made, as in Dover and Portsdown Hill. Some department stores opened their basements to customers. In some streets communal brick shelters were designed to serve nearby houses. They were poorly equipped, without sanitation other than a bucket, and many were regarded as vermin-infested health hazards. No shelter guaranteed safety in the event of a direct hit.

The lasting image of shelters and their occupants is that depicted by Henry Moore in his sketches of Underground stations. East-Enders wanted something deeper and more substantial than the street shelters, but nothing was available. Until Black Saturday, only travellers were allowed into the Underground, but on 7 September 1940, a large group of East-Enders pushed their way down. It wasn't until October 1940 that Herbert Morrison, the Home Secretary, sanctioned the use of stations as shelters. By March 1941, bunks had been provided in most of the seventy-six that were used by nearly twenty-three thousand people.

There were rules: no one was allowed to shelter underground until 4 p.m., and after that, shelterers were ordered to stay in designated areas to enable workers to take the trains home. After 7.30 p.m. the public areas were extended so that shelterers could occupy the passages and staircases. Safety was by no means guaranteed, and many were killed when bombs fell on stations such as Bank, Balham and Bounds Green. But for the 177,000 who took to them nightly, the inconveniences, discomfort and danger were balanced by a sense of security. Soon routines and little communities developed, and places were allocated. Eventually chemical toilets were installed. Throughout the country local councils were authorized to put lighting, seating and bunks into their surface shelters. But during the Blitz improvements were slow and many people were still enduring sordid and tiring conditions, having to stand or sit on the floor all night in damp, public shelters.

Sylvia Townson (Limburg)
Jewish schoolgirl, Paddington, London

We had brick shelters in the road. I don't ever remember people using them. People gradually used the basements of their houses and eventually we were all squashed up together in the coal-hole in the basement. I do remember a couple of occasions when the buzz-bombs started and the families living in our house all trudged up to Queen's Park Station and got on a train to Warwick Avenue, a very deep place in the bowels of the earth where people had started sleeping. They put up with it for a couple of nights, but the trains were running until two in the morning and started again at five so they didn't have much sleep and they realized they might as well stay at home. But I remember seeing rows of bunks that regulars could use as I travelled through the tube.

Colin Perry
Junior City clerk, Upper Tooting, London, diary, 23–24 September

Last night I was surprised, disgusted and horrified as I came home by Tube . . . All the Bank underground station was crawling with fat old women, filthy kids, louts of men, all with packs of food, dirty-looking blankets . . . They lined the Central Line platforms, the subway to the Northern Line and the Northern Line to the District platforms. I squeezed my way on to the train at last and was jammed in – by God, it stank like hell, of sweating bodies and body odour. Every single station all the way down the line was filled with these 'refugees' from the Luftwaffe.

Reg Baker
Schoolboy, Bethnal Green, London

There were shelters in roads, they built them in our buildings, but the tube was the safest place, you know. They built bunk-beds down there. As I go through the tube now, I can still see the cables where I used to tuck my shoes in at night. And they had bunk-beds either side three high: A, B, C, D, E, F, alphabetical order right down. We were C 71, 72, 73. So I slept on the top, my dad in the middle, my mother on the bottom. And there were toilets there, chemical – and that's another smell you always remember. It was always warm air and lights all along it. People were very friendly. But I'll give you one incident: my dad, he got drunk one night, and he's come down the tube and walks down so far and then starts to get in a middle bunk. All of a sudden, someone shouts out – I won't describe the language – 'Get out, you dirty so-and-so, what're you up to?' He was in the wrong bunk and there was a woman in there!

The Bethnal Green tube disaster happened later, on 3 March 1943. Evidently the siren went and everybody started rushing for the tube. Although we had local shelters, the tube was still the safest place to go. At the local park they had these new rocket guns and these started up and people were terrified and they all started running – normally people walked to the tube. At the entrance, there were fourteen steps down then a little landing, then another five steps into the booking hall. There have been various reports of what happened but the point is that everybody panicked and once some fell, the others pushing in just kept pushing and pushing, and people were crushed to death. My sister was fortunate because she was on top of all the bodies so they had to pull her out. She had a bad stomach for months afterwards.

Some of the sights the wardens saw were unbelievable. Most men wore boots then so there were hobnail bootmarks on children's faces – unbelievable! There were whole families wiped out. There was a family called Mead where I lived. The mum, dad, the two sisters and the boy Mead, who was in my class, all got killed there. A frightening aspect was that sons and husbands abroad weren't given compassionate leave to come home because it was wartime and it was all hushed up. I was there on the night it happened. My dad and I had gone to another shelter and when we came out we stood with a schoolfriend of mine and all the ambulances were coming up and going away, and we thought it was about fifteen killed. It wasn't until later, when people had died in hospital, that it came out that 178 had died.

Evelyn Fee (Moss)
Evacuee mother of five, Byworth, Sussex

We used to have to get up every night at one time. My hubby had put a mattress under the stairs and said that it was best if anything did happen – not that he thought it would – to get the children down and put them under the stairs. I didn't worry too much about things until we had the sirens. Before that we used to get the planes over but didn't have a siren. And when they started I used to get all the kiddies and the baby up. We always used to leave Jeannie behind. All the children under the stairs and 'Where's Jeannie?' Up in bed still and off we'd fly to get her. Oh, we had some laughs and no mistake . . . But they used to go over every night, regular as clockwork. I mean, once you've heard one of those . . . anyone who went through the war will know that *awful* noise. I never used to get into bed any night till they'd gone back again. I couldn't. I couldn't rest.

Thomas Houlton
Schoolboy, Hull, Yorkshire

My father was quite a good psychologist in that he bought a very heavily reinforced concrete shelter with an integral roof meshed into the walls and they were eight inches thick, and they had a blast wall as well. And he always impressed on us that we were perfectly safe unless we had a direct hit, so even if the houses were hit and anything fell on us, we'd be perfectly all right, so we felt reasonably safe in there. But the thing I *do* remember is the tremendous noise: the *banging* of aircraft batteries, the *falling* of bombs, the *shrieking* of sirens ... We used the public shelters very, *very* occasionally: if walking to and from school I would dive into one if an air raid happened. We spent quite a lot of time at school in similar shelters – long, rectangular things with a heavy concrete flat roof, brick walls and a blast wall at each end. A lot of Hull folk think they were not terribly well built: the foundations were very weak, the roof was not bound into the brick walls, and consequently when they did go down they caused an awful lot of death and injury, especially the heavy concrete roof. People tended to avoid them and most went under the stairs, which were considered the safest place. Probably the worst disaster was the Ellis Terrace public shelter, which was a brick construction. A land mine drifted in on the wind and directly hit the shelter and there were, at the very least, fifty people killed. That was April 1941.

Patricia Fitzgerald (Stringer)
Schoolgirl, Plymouth, Devon

The main raids came at night. They started early in the evening and then went on. We went to a public shelter in the nearby park. It had a big pump to pump water out. Lots of people from the surrounding houses came there and we all got to know each other. The seats were narrow and hard; eventually bunks were built down one side, two tiers, and we'd take our cushions, rugs and suchlike down with us. The all-clear would go about four or five in the morning. This meant we could go home and maybe go to bed properly. I had my siren suit: this was like a boiler suit, with trousers and top all in one, with a hood and a big zip up the front. With boots on my feet, it meant I was covered and would be warm and comfortable. Winston Churchill had one too. We had our regular places. Courting would go on there. The toilets were dustbins, with a curtain in front. When you went in and spent a penny, everyone could hear this tinkling noise going down the dustbin, and people would roar with laughter outside – people did laugh a lot then. I used to knit and we would all sing . . . I can remember Mum saying, 'Fancy sending us to a place like this for *safety*!'

The raids got into a rhythm and pattern, and when we heard they'd bombed Coventry, we'd say, 'It'll be us tonight!' and you'd get an extra heavy one. They seemed to be doing it in rotation. I remember Winston Churchill coming down in a terrible old car. He sat in the big dickey seat and went through the city, crying at the devastation. And he was shouted at to go. We called, 'The Germans will know you've been here, they'll be after you, *go!*' He'd hardly gone, and the raids started. He wasn't welcomed there. We were frightened for our sakes, not his.

When we walked into the city, about ten minutes away, we could see that it had all gone, it was just rubble. We used to walk along a little lane to the Hoe, and I remember going there one morning and it was all down, just smouldering, it was dreadful . . . We used to go down to the Hoe and the convoys would be going out with all the sailors lining the decks, and we'd wave to them. And you'd see the ships coming in – in early 1940, the *Ajax* and *Exeter*, from the Battle of the Plate, they hobbled in, and you'd see them shipping off the injured people.

David Morrish
Schoolboy, Plymouth, Devon

The house we lived in didn't have a direct hit, but it was sufficiently damaged that we couldn't live in it. My parents put what was left of their home in store and we went and lived in various evacuee billets in Plymouth until later I was evacuated to Cornwall for a while. I came back just in time for the second-wave blitz on Plymouth. More devastation took place then. I was thirteen or fourteen. The headmaster later told me that the youngsters he thought were under the greatest pressure were the lower half of the school, old enough to know what was going on, but not old enough to do anything useful . . . My memory of grammar school at that time is sitting up all night in air-raid shelters and going to school the next day without having any sleep, and feeling the worse for it.

A number of my schoolfriends were killed. You went to school in the morning and saw an empty desk, and you knew why it was empty. We lived near an old empty, nineteenth-century workhouse, which had become a home for elderly people suffering from senile decay. This was hit by fire bombs and gutted. I can still remember the screams of those inside ... So all this was happening and I felt a terribly patriotic young Britisher who hated the Germans who were killing my schoolfriends. There wasn't anyone more patriotic or more anxious to take part in the National Savings scheme or anything else that was going on.

Sylvia Taylor (Bell)
Schoolgirl, Hook, Surrey

I can remember my mother telling me that when a bomb fell close by and we lost all the tiles off our roof and went to see the landlord about getting the roof fixed – everyone else in the street had theirs fixed and we hadn't – he said, 'Oh, I'm not going to repair your house. Your husband's a conscientious objector. He won't fight.' And I'm afraid it always seemed my mother who suffered. And I can remember having no windows, they were all blown in, and of course the roof was leaking and it always seemed to be very cold ... and I can remember going to stand-pipes in the street because the water supply had been affected.

Margaret Woodhead (Butler)
Evacuee schoolgirl, Winchester, Hampshire

You didn't know where your relatives who were in the war were. Letters came two or three together. I remember when I was in Winchester with my mother, who had joined me because of the blitz, my grandfather, who was in the Merchant Navy, appeared one Christmas morning. Apparently he'd come into Liverpool, and when they docked, the blitz was so bad that they couldn't move out. When he got to Winchester he was in a state of semi-shock. He stayed with us for about a week and then he went back. But he died about two days out from Liverpool and they reckoned it was because of the dreadful blitz on the city.

Richard Hancock
Evacuee headmaster, Winchester, Hampshire

Some of the boys lost fathers or had other casualties during the war. I remember being asked to break the news to a boy once or twice. Happily, it wasn't all that familiar, but I think on one or two occasions when it happened the mother had made a point of coming up to see the boy rather than sending a message. If in those circumstances they wanted the boy to go home for a bit with the mother, of course one gave permission with one's blessing.

Many country people who lived beneath the Luftwaffe's flight paths spent disturbed nights in shelters after the siren sounded. There were also instances of indiscriminate bombing and crashed aircraft, which caused death, injury and damage.

Dennis Hayden
Evacuee schoolboy, Highclere, Hampshire

Grotto Lodge was situated on top of Highclere Hill, which gave a commanding view of the countryside. And it seemed to be the turning-round point of the German raiders of London. They would come up through the Thames valley, turn round at Newbury and head back for the coast. We'd wake up and hear a noise and look out of our window and sometimes below us, or even on a level with us, see a plane on fire, flying around. Probably a German raider had been hit coming over London. When one crashed very near to the school, we all cheered and said, 'Hooray, that's the school!' But when we went to school the next day it was still standing.

But in the field, the other side of the manor house, this German plane had crashed there and had burnt out. And I can remember all the schoolchildren – all sixteen of us – climbed over it and looked into it. I don't know what had happened to the crew, but I know we took goodness knows what off this thing: guns, machine-guns, pistols, ammunition, compasses and the stick. We took them all to school. And then about eleven o'clock the police and soldiers turned up and said, 'No doubt you children have seen the plane which has crashed about twenty yards down the road. Can we have anything you've taken?' And everyone was lifting up desk lids and handing back machine-guns and pistols and belts of ammunition! Quite a collection.

Rodney Giesler
Anglo-German schoolboy, Hele, Somerset

The bombers were still coming over at night to Cardiff well into 1941. A bomb flattened a cottage just up the road from us. The morning after this bomb landed, the field over the road was full of little heaps of ash. We were curious, so we dug down about eighteen inches and found the head of the bomb. They were incendiary bombs, which had been scattered by German bombers racing for home. These became war trophies and we used to trade them at school. They also used to drop these anti-personnel bombs. The wardens used to come to school with pictures of butterfly bombs. They had intriguing shapes and lots of kids were killed by them. We also had stirrup pumps to put out fires. They were marvellous and powerful. We used to have stirrup-pump fights. You stuck the pump in a bucket of water, and it had a side arm that you stood on, the 'stirrup'. It was so easy. It had two settings – jet or spray. Every household was issued with one.

Noel Dumbrell
Schoolboy, Ashurst, Sussex

Occasionally there would be the odd one or two bombers coming over, and the night fighter – the FIU [Fighter Interception Unit] – would be up there nice and quiet, flying around, and if he spotted the German, somehow a signal was sent that the FIU wanted all the lights to go out. One of our searchlights from the army camp would then give the sign to all the others in the area by widening its light right out, then closing it back until doused, so that night fighter would then attack his victim unseen in the dark.

On this one occasion, which is very vivid in my memory, I was lying in bed with Mum as I used to do during the air raids – Dad was out on fire duty somewhere – and this FIU fighter came down on a bomber, and I heard short bursts of fire, and then all of a sudden the German bomber was on fire and it circled round and round, round and round. Mum and I got out of bed to watch it, and from where we lived at Ashurst on fairly high ground, I could look down to my grandmother's house in Partridge Green, two miles as the crow flies across the river, and as this plane went down, it blew up over the top of my gran's house and several others just before it hit the ground. So I got on my old bike and just *went*. When I got to Gran's house, there was quite a lot of activity going on. No civilians were killed, but all the German crew unfortunately died. I can remember walking down the path and going in. And as I went into the front door, I remember looking up into the rafters and there was a German body, or what was left of it, hung up in the rafters there. I can picture it till this day. Gran got her hair burnt, and there were lots of bits of aeroplanes and burnt stuff around. The FIU pilot came down from Tangmere, and he shook hands with all the people around and apologized to them for the problem he'd caused, but he was obviously a very good shot, got it with just one burst. So far as I was concerned then, that German was a German and an enemy. It hurt me more to see my grandmother with her burnt head – terrible thing to say, but it was a case of 'We've got one!'

May Moore (George)
Evacuee, Eyam, Derbyshire

There was a time when bombs dropped at Foolow, a little nearby village. I think everybody turned out to walk up to this village to see the crater holes – and that is how distant we were from the blitzing on the towns. You walked up, looked at this bomb crater in the middle of the field, walked back again. We saw the crater, the big holes in the field, and that, I suppose, was as near as the war was to us then. When I look back, Eyam was just *twelve* miles from Sheffield where there were all these steelworks. It seems fantastic: we were *thirty* miles from Manchester and we were *safe*. We were in the hills and in the country, and there was nothing in the country that the Germans would want.

Millicent Morgan (Miller)
Evacuee, Oxborough, Norfolk

They never had any experience of the war in Oxborough at all, really, except the discomfort of having evacuees pushed on them, I suppose.

In 1942 the cathedral cities and other towns of cultural interest were hit by the so-called 'Baedeker Raids', after the series of German guidebooks. Considerable damage was inflicted on historic buildings and hundreds of citizens were killed.

Maureen Smith (England)
Young child, Exeter, Devon

This night, my father was going on duty [National Fire Service] and he said, 'I'm taking you to your aunt's house. I'm on duty and I have a feeling that something is not good tonight.' I remember it was moonlight and we were wrapped up and he took me by the hand, and led my mother and me to my aunt's and then he left for duty. Then, of course, the sirens went. Well, it was *terrible*: the noise of the bombs! I was thinking of my father and my grandparents, who were in the centre of Exeter, and my cousins. I asked my mother if I could go to the toilet, which was upstairs. The house was quite high and you could look down over Exeter.

I asked Mum if I could look out of the window, thinking, Where is Father? And I remember the sight. I will *never* forget it. The sky was filled with searchlights – the noise and the explosions – the whole of the town was lit and you could actually see the fights of aircraft: they would catch them in the searchlight. And you could hear this machine-gun fire, the bombs exploding, and it was horrific, really. I'll never forget it, ever. You could hear crackling from where buildings were flaming, and you could see it all showering up into the air. For three days and nights we didn't see Father again. I remember my mother was very, very worried and, of course, so was I. And then he came home and I can remember so well as he stood in the doorway: his face was black, his clothes were filthy – and his eyes! The whites were absolutely red. And the smell in his clothes! A horrible burnt smell. I remember thinking: Thank goodness Father's back. He had been all around the centre of Exeter and he said it was horrific . . . horrific.

David Gray
Schoolboy, Bootham Quaker School, York

We returned from Bransbury where we'd been evacuated, and settled back into Bootham just in time for the Baedeker Raids, so my memory of air raids on York is very clear. There were high explosives, fire bombs and incendiary bombs and a lot of York went up in flames . . . I remember long, very frightening hours in this brick cellar with my mother reading the Peter Rabbit stories and playing card games, and in term time all the Bootham boys were down there and it got very crowded. My father was up on the roof doing firewatching. Although the main part of the school was never hit, the sanatorium was bombed and burnt out one night, and the houses opposite us, and a huge wooden exhibition building behind them, went up. The whole of the sky was red. It certainly affected my life: I remember being in this brick vault and feeling that there were some people up there trying to kill me, that I was in a dugout and they were aiming to hit *me*. All of us were surrounded by this war propaganda machine with Ministry of Information posters, like 'Walls Have Ears', and Hitler with his little moustache and big ears, listening. I don't remember personal hatred towards Hitler and the pilots up above dropping bombs – it was the bombs I hated, not the Germans.

Jean Greaves (Catchpool)
Schoolgirl, Sidcot Quaker School, Somerset

Bishop Bell had written a letter to *The Times* after Coventry saying there should be an agreement between the belligerents to restrain or abolish night bombing. My father wrote to Bishop Bell, and a small committee was formed, which included Vera Brittain, who wrote a little book recommending an accord to stop the bombing of citizens altogether, but they realized this was unrealistic, and narrowed the field to abolish night bombing. And they put out a lot of pamphlets, giving examples of destruction to try to get people to put pressure on the government. But my father was denounced as a traitor for this work and someone had written, 'Please distribute your pamphlets to all the public lavatories in London.' Herbert Morrison, who was Home Secretary during the war, examined their work quite carefully and decided they were not traitors and their work continued. It was a very courageous thing to do.

Maureen Smith (England)
Young child, Exeter, Devon

I didn't have any hatred towards the Germans, but a fear of them. To me they were monsters. In your mind you had a picture of a horrible monster people who did this to you. But after the blitz on Exeter, in the field behind the houses in St Catherine's Road, one day we looked out of the window and there were a lot of men erecting huts, and suddenly we saw the German and Italian prisoners-of-war arrive and they started to build the road that is now called Prince Charles Road. And I remember my father, although he'd fallen through a burning roof and he had damaged his back and was never the same, he had compassion. Mr Englisch, the German soldier in charge, would talk to my father. Seeing them, it made me think, They're human and look no different from us. And one very cold day Father said to my mother, as they looked out of the window, 'You know, when you look at those young men, if we'd had a son a little older, he could have been one of them.' My father then said, 'Get a quarter of a pound of tea from the cupboard. Those boys are working like mad. I'm seeing they're having another cup of tea to warm them.' So he took the tea to Mr Englisch and told him to make an extra cup of tea to keep them warm . . . I remember the day they left after the road was finished, Mr Englisch came over to see my father. Also, there was another young German called Hans, and sometimes on the way to school I would give him an apple. And when they left, he also came over to my father and gave him a carved heart to give to me. I still have it.

Tony Parker
Teenage pacifist, Manchester, Lancashire

I joined the Civil Defence and remember going into Manchester after a heavy raid and seeing a lot of destruction. I was working with an ambulance, a Civil Defence ambulance. And I was quite appalled. What I didn't have was any feeling of anger specifically towards the Germans. I just thought this bore out what I thought about war: that it was senseless, destructive, wasteful, *awful*.

8. World War: 'The End of the Beginning'

Operation 'Barbarossa', Hitler's 22 June 1941 attack on the USSR, took the heat off Britain and ended the 1940–41 Blitz. On the night of the attack, Winston Churchill, a known anti-Communist, declared his full support for Russia. At first, few felt that the Soviets could withstand, let alone beat, the German onslaught, especially after their dismal perform-ance in the Winter War with Finland, from 30 November 1939 until 12 March 1940. But once it became clear that they were fighting tooth and nail to defend 'Mother Russia', the British became enthusiastically pro-Soviet, mounting fund-raising campaigns to send tanks and armaments. From August 1941, the 'Russian convoys' began their hazardous journeys from northern British ports to Murmansk and Archangel, taking war supplies that Britain could ill afford to her new ally. Many ships were sunk *en route*. After the Red Army had made its stand at Moscow, Leningrad and, later, Stalingrad, admiration for it and the heroic Russian people swelled even further, and Churchill lifted his ban on the BBC playing the 'Internationale' among the national anthems of the other Allies.

But events in the Far East had the greatest impact. The entry of the USA into the war on the Allied side, after the surprise Japanese attack on Pearl Harbor, was a great boost to Churchill and the War Office. Now the British felt confi-dent that, however long the struggle took, with Russia and America on their side, victory would surely come. But in the weeks after Pearl Harbor, the Japanese advance gained pace as success followed success. On 25 December 1941, Hong Kong fell, and in February 1942 the Japanese overran the Malayan peninsula. On 15 February 1942 the surrender of the 85,000 troops in Singapore was, in Churchill's words, 'the largest capitulation in British history'. It was a terrible, humiliating defeat that shook the country and the world. In the following month, the Dutch East Indies fell into Japanese hands. By April Japanese forces controlled a major part of the Philippines, and in May, they penetrated into the northern reaches of Burma, cutting off supplies flowing into China. It was feared that Ceylon, now Sri Lanka, parts of India and even Australia might be next.

As the Japanese advanced, British civilians and other foreign nationals working and living in the Far East were captured and interned. Many wives and children had been evacuated to safety before the invasion but, even so, large numbers of British children spent more than three years in the camps, often in appalling conditions.

Marjorie Bond (Cranshaw)
Schoolgirl, Hull, Yorkshire

I think the [German] invasion of the Soviet Union was the turning point of the war, and certainly in our house we felt very definitely that we would now win.

Count Nikolai Tolstoy
Schoolboy, Bude, Cornwall

We were brought up by my father who, at this time, was married to a Russian woman. So although I had English relatives and an English mother, my upbringing was largely Russian at home because my stepmother and father always spoke Russian together and we even had a Russian gardener, with his wife, who couldn't speak any English at all. They were recent immigrants, and despite twenty-five years of Communism, it was just as it had been in the days before the revolution. They called my father Baron, and the relationships were the same as before the revolution. There are two branches of the Tolstoy family. There was the famous Peter Andreich Tolstoy, who was a minister of Peter the Great, and Leo Tolstoy was descended from him. We're descended from the elder brother, Ivan ...

When I was young, Russian immigration was very strong in London. Whenever we went there, we stayed with my stepmother's parents. They had two floors in Cromwell Place, and we hardly ever saw English people there, just Russians. It was a lovely atmosphere because there were always pictures of the Tsar and icons and Guards officers and so on. To me at that time, the old Russia was very vivid ...

I went to a little prep school in Surrey. And, of course, all children, especially boys, found the war terribly exciting and I still remember it vividly. And when I write about it, people say, 'Well, you were only nine or ten.' But I remember the atmosphere so *vividly*. I was very proud of being Russian, and I knew I was different in that respect – all boys like to have something different about themselves. But I didn't know anything about the circumstances of the Russian civil war and hardly knew about the revolution. I do remember a boy telling me, when I would not have been more than nine or ten, about the revolution and saying, 'Why are you supporting the Red Army when you should be on the other side?' And he told me solemnly about the Whites and the Reds ... But I remember having cut-outs of Russian submarines and so on ...

Ann Barclay (Terry)
British evacuee schoolgirl, Toronto, Canada, extract from her memoir

Letters from the family arrived frequently, though irregularly because of the wartime mails. They [her family] were living a wartime existence and I, particularly when I went to the USA, was living a totally different one, and felt that they did not know any of the people or places or even lifestyle I was writing about. I thought they were keeping pace with the ways in which I was changing (in actual fact they were not) ... I can remember being in a dormitory room at 40 Maple Avenue [Toronto] when a concert was interrupted to report that the Japanese had bombed Pearl Harbor ...

Diana Owen (Houston-Boswald)
Teenage daughter of diplomats, British embassy compound, Tokyo, Japan

I was in bed when the war started. It was a Monday and I was going to start school in the Sacred Heart convent in Yokohama. I woke up with someone banging on the door; I thought it was the *amah*, and I said, 'Come in.' But it was a very frightened little Japanese policeman, who said, 'Excuse, please, there is war, you get dressed bloody quick' . . . Because of the international convention, we all went into the Chancery building to tear up and incinerate secret documents. This was allowed because the Japanese in London did the same. Altogether we were eighty-nine people and then ninety-one because two babies were born – everybody was very angry with the parents: it was considered a *very* inconvenient and thoughtless thing to do! We all had to put up people who came in from outside; we had nine extra in our house.

Jacqueline Towell (Honnor)
British child, Manila, Philippines

After a year in Australia, 1939–40, my father was posted to Manila; he went on ahead of us. We finished the school year and got on a ship and sailed. My mother was concerned as she felt there was a great possibility of war in the Far East. She went to the British consul general and the American consul general and said, 'Look, if you had two children would you go to the Philippines at this time?' And they said, 'We see no reason why not.' And so we left and arrived in Manila about the beginning of December 1941, and settled in almost immediately. Then on 7 December, Pearl Harbor was bombed, and we were in the middle of bombing once again. But this time we didn't have a cave to shelter in, as we had had in Chungking, we were literally just under the dining-room table with mattresses. It was a very frightening time because, clearly, the Americans were leaving quite fast and the Filipinos were panicking, buying food and rushing to the banks to get out money.

My mother was a very practical person. She called the grocery store and had enormous amounts of food sent to the apartment and went to the bank and took out as much cash as she could. Then the American troops withdrew and Manila was declared an open city. Just before that happened, my father was asked to go and destroy all the oil tanks in the Standard Vacuum Depot.

We waited about three days, including Christmas Day – then we heard the Japanese were coming into town and they were going to collect everybody, except Swiss and Italians. We were collected by two Japanese soldiers and taken to the Manila football stadium where we spent a number of days, managing as best we could.

Paget Natten (Eames)
British child, Singapore

All I can remember is being part and parcel of this very hectic, mad crowd, with people lining the whole of the wharf with suitcases and incredible amounts of luggage – we had very little on us – and being caught up in the mad rush of trying to get on to this ship. I can remember my father pushing us on and seeing my grandfather going further away in the distance, waving and calling, 'I'll see you some time.' I was then four years old.

There were quite a number of our relatives on the ship, but not my father. Several hours out into the sea, the ship was bombed. It was just a little old vessel carrying a number of women and children and Red Cross nurses. Despite the fact that it had a red cross on it, it was bombed. The bomb came very suddenly and I can remember screaming and shouting, absolute panic. My mother's skirt was ripped away by the blast and she was a bit embarrassed . . . Then the captain came round and said, 'You've got to jump.' Mum didn't swim and she was absolutely terrified. My cousins were being blasted right and left, and one got half of his body shot off; another was injured badly and soon died. The captain then said, 'Look, I don't want you dead. If you don't jump, I'm going to push you.' So Mum said, 'Put your arms around me, cling tight, we're going to jump.' She had no lifejacket, but a man near us threw a child's lifejacket to me and she put it round me, and we jumped.

In the sea there were a lot of dead bodies floating around us and the water was quite cold – surprising for such a hot country – and that lifejacket kept my mother and myself up in the water. There was an awful lot of screaming and panic, people going crazy and calling out for taxis in the water, and just going down. Mum kept saying, 'Keep quiet, keep calm, we'll be okay . . .'

We were in the water a very long time. The afternoon went by and evening came, and then I fell asleep. I woke up a few hours later and Mum, my cousin Millie, who was with us, and I were still floating. There were funny animals in the water, sharks, I think, and people floating past. All of a sudden I saw this vessel on the horizon and said, 'Look, Jesus has sent a boat.' And this little sampan, with about five people on board, dragged us on and took us to an island where the head of the village gave us comfort for the night . . .

It was then decided that we should travel by night with other survivors and try to get to a place where we could meet up with friends and secure some freedom. The headman was excellent to us. He dressed me in peasant clothes and we travelled from island to island under cover of darkness. They would call out a password in Malay, and if they got the correct response we would land, be taken ashore and cared for secretly until the next sampan picked us up. We did this for a couple of weeks. Then, at one meeting, the signal wasn't the right one and we landed right in the hands of the Japanese. They shot the Malay gentleman who had been looking after us. Then we were taken ashore and found other relatives. This area had been divided into two camps. We were put in one of these . . . The Japanese came with machine-guns and the people in the other part of the camp, including my aunt Sybil and her two children, were mown down. The only logic seemed that they had enough room only for a certain amount of people. Then they put us on lorries and we were taken from camp to camp, meeting up with other prisoners, walking. About a year later we ended up in a place called Bangkinang [Sumatra] right on the equator.

James Maas
British schoolboy, Shanghai, China

I was eight when Pearl Harbor happened. I woke up early one morning when there was a great deal of noise overhead from fighters wheeling about – I suppose bombing the British ships. We lived a long way from the river but, really, nothing much changed for us at that time. Some people tried to get away but there weren't many ships available. We had to wear red armbands as 'enemy nationals', but otherwise life continued very much as normal for us. Some parts were considered dangerous, but I kept going to school. The shops and stores were still open and life was relatively normal so far as I could see it. We'd see the Japanese when we visited friends beyond the railway lines. Then one day we were told we had to pack up what we could, and Father had to end his job. We were bundled into buses and taken about five miles south in the city to a suburb called Lunghuo into Shanghai Middle School, which was now our camp. This had been prepared for us. There were six or seven blocks. We were given a room in D block, but because there were just three of us, two boys from the Kennedy family came at night to sleep in our room.

Doreen Hartley (Saunders)
Teenager, Simla, India

When we returned to India in 1940, no one had any idea that the Japanese were coming – no war at all there. People were still enjoying the good life. True, there was some unrest, and my father would have been involved with the Gandhi riots, but as children we weren't involved. It was only when the Japanese got to Malaya that we became aware of the threat. They came like ants. We were completely unprepared – that was 1942. A great shock, horrible, but they were far away. My father became very ill and we moved down to Bombay near his military hospital . . . Then things changed very quickly. Thousands of troops arrived from Britain and they were going to the Arakan and Burma, where some terrible fighting was going on, and they would come back wounded. There were great movements of people. Then it was suggested by General Cowan's wife, 'Why doesn't Doreen join the Wasbies [Women's Auxiliary Service (Burma)]?' So I took this long train journey right across to Calcutta and from there up to Assam. It was lovely, a beautiful climate. I couldn't believe I was joining the army.

Keith Goldthorpe
Infant, Maymyo, Burma

I don't remember anything about going to Burma at all, just fleeting memories ... I have lots of fleeting memories of the house we used to live in, in Maymyo, and of the dog that used to accompany me at the time. The house was on a slope and there were steps down, and I remember, when the Japanese planes came over, we had to go to a slit trench on the other side of the road below some trees. The cook and cleaner and everybody else would descend the steps at a high rate of knots, run across the ground and dive into the trench. It always intrigued me. I thought it was a lot of fun seeing these planes going over. But I could see the seriousness of the faces, and the fact that a chap came down from the barracks with a machine-gun to set up by the trenches ... I remember asking him what he was doing as obviously one machine-gun was not going to handle several hundred paratroopers if they jumped out, and he said, 'I've got to guard you and the wives and other children.'

My father was with the King's Own Yorkshire Light Infantry. He was fighting the Japanese, later on [Major General Orde] Wingate's side he was a Bren gun instructor and a Bren gun carrier commander. When we walked out of Burma, he was left behind. I didn't see him again for maybe two or three years. We had twenty-four hours' notice to get out. I remember my mother saying that we couldn't take anything, that we had to disappear with a bedding roll each. I found it quite exciting, really. I didn't realize the gravity of the situation. Some people went out on trains. There were twenty-five or thirty people in our party and quite a few children. All I remember about the whole thing are fleeting bright spots that come back to me. One was crossing a river – Chindwin? Irrawaddy? I don't know. But it had an enormous tree felled across it. I was carried over by four bearers in a grass chair and I can remember being held up on their shoulders and sometimes over their shoulders to keep my backside clear of the water – I thought this was *marvellous*. We crossed several rivers and when we got to the side of one, we got into a truck with fold-down sides and my mother was crying. I sat down beside her and said, 'Why are you crying, Mum?' And she said, 'Because I've got a bone in my leg.' I thought that was a funny thing to say, but I did remember my mother was quite upset and stressed . . .

During that time I also remember being carried from one place to another in a large round basket on an elephant, four or five kids on each elephant. I can remember the movement and hanging on as it walked through what were basically jungle tracks. My next recollection is when we lived in Sabathu in a barracks above the village, in India.

June Knowles (Watkins)
Teenager, Nairobi, Kenya

When the war really hit Kenya, I had more or less run away from school and got myself a job in the Meteorological Department, and with Italy in the war, I had to go on to watch systems to be able to supply the RAF and SAAF [South African Air Force] with weather reports. I remember buying some powder and putting my hair up, but was told that I had to be nineteen to take a government post. I said, 'I am aware of that, sir!' But he took me on at sixteen – he knew and I knew, but he wanted people. I found myself in a job I liked. There was a very progressive man in charge. We were all sworn to secrecy once Italy was in the war. I got information on telex, put this on to charts, which were coded, and then I converted it to international measures of centimetres and centigrade and put it on enormous scale charts, one for the whole of Africa and one for East Africa. When the information came in cipher, you had to decode it. I became very quick at this and enjoyed doing it.

When the RAF came down to recruit people later, I passed all their tests but was told I was too young and to go away. But I was eventually taken on although they knew I was underage. So that's how I found myself a WAAF under the age of eighteen, soon to be working on Enigma machines in North Africa.

My father did an extraordinary thing before I left for Egypt. First he taught me how to use a gun. Then he said, 'I hope you won't have to do this, but it's better than being taken prisoner if you've got secret information.' Then he took the gun, unloaded it, jumped on me with it and pushed me to the ground. I said, 'What are you doing?' He said, 'I'm going to teach you how to fight off a rape attack.' And he did. He showed me exactly where to put my knee, and said, 'In order to loosen a man's hands on you, put your arms up as if you're giving in and then put your thumbs in his eyes and press hard. He'll pull back and then you can use your knee between his legs as hard as you can, and put him out of action for quite a while.' I think that was an amazing thing for a man to teach his daughter and it proved most useful later when I was attacked in Ismailia . . .

On the British home front, with the Luftwaffe now heavily engaged elsewhere, the bombing raids continued on London and other cities but with nothing like the scale and intensity of the 1940–41 Blitz. Although many evacuees stayed with their foster-parents, others trickled back, some wishing to be reunited with their families – if, indeed, they had families to return to. Others, having reached the school-leaving age of fourteen, needed to find jobs.

Reg Baker
Schoolboy, Bethnal Green, London

I went home in 1942. I can't recall my dad saying, 'Come home,' or 'Do you want to come home?' But I know I returned 'cause all evacuees still wanted to run away even though you'd been treated nicely. It's still your *home*, whether it's good or bad . . .

And the country was an entirely different environment for us. We was flung in it with no choice. Well, to come home to London! It'd been bombed, which I hadn't seen – the Blitz had hit it badly, you know. But I was back, and with all its bomb damage it was still home. And you go round picking up what was left of incendiary bombs and things like that. You could find the tail fins on bomb-damage places. Although you had two years in the country in a nice quiet atmosphere, you could change completely back to your East End environment. I did miss the animals and things like that – the local park and the zoo was the nearest you got to things like that in London.

Millicent Morgan (Miller)
Evacuee schoolgirl, Oxborough, Norfolk

I think we adjusted to country life pretty well. We were so over-awed by the country and being able to run about and paddle in streams, and it was just a delight to see big fish swimming about in the water and watercress growing and things like that ... But I was coming up to fourteen, I don't know why my mum had us home, probably a lull in the raids and she probably was a little bit more prosperous and could afford to have us back. So she had us home for a week in the spring of 1942. My brother didn't want to go back to Oxborough, and he showed his true feelings that he missed her so much. So she told me, 'Well, you're nearly ready for work so you go down and get the clothes and tell them you're not coming back.'

They were quite cross with my mum because she took us home. I don't think they ever formed a great attachment to us, but they'd probably got used to having us around. It meant the kitchen was going to be empty when Miss Hilary went out to make a pot of tea or coffee, didn't it? Yes, they were quite put out when we came back home.

Gwendoline Stewart (Watts)
Evacuee schoolgirl, Ashby-de-la-Zouch, Leicestershire

I was moved from this old lady to a youngish man and lady, and they had a little daughter about four years of age. Everyone thought they were such kind people, and they weren't. Behind all that kindness they were so cruel, I wanted to get away. I couldn't do my school lessons – they wouldn't let me do my homework because I had to sit with this child. I had to get up before them in the morning to get the child up and give her her breakfast. If we were at school in the morning, I had to rush home from school to start the lunch – peel the potatoes, get the lunch on the go, give the child her lunch. And she was a little *terror*: she would break things and I would be blamed for the breakage because they said, 'Pauline wouldn't do a thing like that.' I was beginning to feel quite demented . . . All right, I was fourteen but I thought, I shouldn't be treated like this. I did *all* the housework, *all* the washing-up. I was the skivvy.

John Wheeler
Teenager, Purton, Wiltshire

My dad wrote to Billy and Kathleen's mother and invited her down any time she wanted to see her children, and Mrs Milcoy didn't reply for weeks. And then eventually, on a Saturday, she turned up at the front door unannounced to say she'd come to see her children. She came with a man that Billy referred to as 'Uncle'. Mrs Milcoy was a lot younger than my mother, and I can remember quite clearly that she arrived on the front door with red high-heeled shoes and a fur coat. They were entertained at home to lunch, stayed the day, left and said they'd be back. I think throughout the years of the war Mrs Milcoy came down to see her children only once after that occasion and their father came down once on his own. So, really, they were to all intents and purposes out of sight, out of mind to their own natural parents.

Vera Bullman (Tipson)
Evacuee schoolgirl, Sherston, Wiltshire

I had a mishap with a soldier and I was terrified. I didn't know about the facts of life, I was only twelve. I just thought he was filthy. I remember I punched him and I was terribly worried. I didn't tell anybody. He was someone who came to the house and came into my bedroom. I was packing up something and he got me on the bed. I was so terrified and I remember calling him 'a filthy dirty terrible man'. Not that I knew what was going to happen. He actually raped me, but because I was shy I didn't tell anybody. When I told my mother eventually, she nearly went *spare*. I was very worried and it took a lot of courage to talk to boys after that. I think children are funny, they keep things to themselves. He went away, I don't know where.

Peter Smith
Schoolboy, Petts Wood, Kent

My mother wished to have us back home as a family – this would be just before Christmas 1942. My father came up to fetch us. This journey from Carlisle to London would probably be typical of many journeys people made in those days. Having arrived on Carlisle station, we decamped with all our luggage. Ten minutes before the train was due in, it was announced it was coming in on another platform. So, up sticks, find a goods lift and dash across to the correct platform. The train was quite full and we were split up along one carriage. The atmosphere was quite horrendous, a lot of smoke, the blinds were down because of the blackout – and that would have been early as it was winter.

We arrived at St Pancras somewhere about ten o'clock at night. People were pouring off the train, trying to find taxis. My father managed to get a taxi for my grandmother, who was going back to her home in Peckham, so that was a weight off his mind. However, we had all our stuff, including two bikes, somehow to get across London to Victoria station. How were we going to do it? No taxis. Fortunately a very kindly porter came to our rescue. He had a word with a naval officer who had a shooting-brake going to Victoria and he kindly agreed to take us. So we got to Victoria and caught a train to Petts Wood. We left most of our stuff at the station and trudged home, arriving somewhere about midnight, very tired. So it was nice to be back. But what immediately struck me was the size of this suburban house compared with the big farmhouse we had been living in ... It took a little while to become adjusted, and we had the Christmas break to do so. In January I started at Bromley Grammar School.

Houses such as ours, which had been badly damaged, were patched up so there were people living in them. The next road where the bomb had dropped was more or less demolished and there were just piles of rubble. A lot of neighbours were still absent.

Margaret Woodhead (Butler)
Evacuee schoolgirl, Winchester, Hampshire

My mother − who had joined me in Winchester to escape the bombing − and I returned to Portsmouth when things were quieter. Mother had let our house furnished while she came away and the people were moving elsewhere. As we opened the front door, this most dreadful smell hit us. We walked in and my mother opened the dining-room door and we stood there, horrified. Before she moved to Winchester, she had bought a beautiful new carpet for the dining room − we surmised that they had cleaned motorbikes and had umpteen babies over it! We just picked the carpet up, went into the garden and burnt it. We went into the kitchen, and where my mother had left her tea services and dinner plates and other china, there was just one cracked cup left on the shelf. It was really dreadful. We had to get rid of the mattresses and blankets, but eventually we put it right.

In 1942 Britain contained a plurality of foreign troops: Poles, Czechs, Norwegians, Free French, Dutch and Belgians. Troops

18. A friendly engine driver greets a group of evacuees at a London station before they travel to safety, April 1941.

19. Lifeboat No. 12 from SS *City of Benares*, which was picked up by HMS *Anthony*.

20. The rescued children on the deck of HMS *Anthony*.

21. The surviving members of the Bech family, with Colin Ryder Richardson, after their return to Glasgow where they were kitted out with new clothes. (*Left to right*) Barbara, Marguerite Bech (mother) clutching Derek, Colin Ryder Richardson, Sonia.

22. Rodney Giesler and brother Neville ready for their four-mile cycle ride to school, 1943.

23. An Oxfordshire village schoolboy displays his National Savings poster to the rest of the class.

24. London evacuees from Streatham enjoying a very different walk to school in the lovely village of Caio, Carmarthenshire.

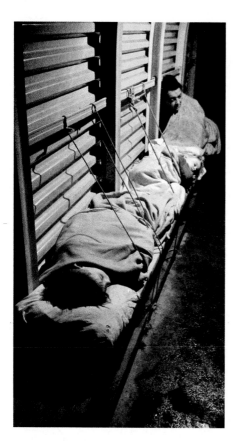

25. A flooded north London air-raid shelter. This mother has tied her two children to the bench to prevent them falling into the water.

26. The Morrison indoor shelter was available to householders from February 1941. It not only provided shelter for families, but could also be used as a table.

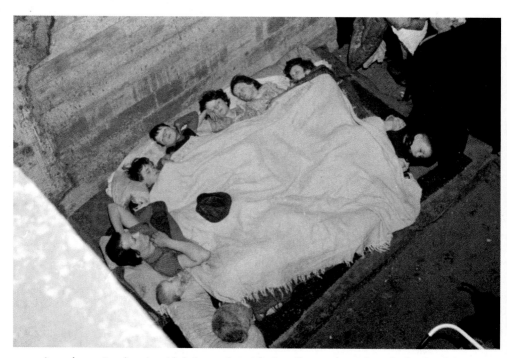

27. A south-east London air-raid shelter underneath the railway arches. Nine of a family of thirteen share a covering while the four older children rest nearby.

28. Undaunted, a young Londoner hangs out the flag over his bombed home.

29. Children enjoy their games among the ruined homes.

30. Evacuee Freddie King of Fulham makes friends with a hen.

31. Three boys in a boat: Rodney Giesler (*left*), with his friend and brother on the river Tone, near Taunton, 1945.

32. Evacuee John Carter helping out on the farm.

33. Pamela Leopard (Brownfield), the proud owner of a new, home-made dolls' pram.

34. London evacuees searching for trout at Farmers, Carmarthenshire.

35. Helping the war effort in Balderton, Nottinghamshire. Boy Scouts do their bit by collecting salvage.

36. Evacuees from Greenwich give the smith a helping hand in Llandissilio, Pembrokeshire.

from the Dominion countries also came to join the battle against Nazism. Canadians had been in Britain since December 1939, and by the end of February 1940 there were more than twenty-three thousand. Generally they were made welcome, regarded as more like 'us' than the American GIs (General Issue), who began to appear in 1942.

By the end of that year, 250,000 American airmen and other service staff had arrived in Britain, their numbers boosted by ground forces in 1943. By May 1944 1.5 million were poised for the opening of the Second Front in France. At first, the British were unenthused by their presence. Surveys conducted at the time revealed resentment that America had entered the war only when she was forced to do so in her own national interest. Attempts were made at mutual understanding and both sides produced advisory pamphlets – *A Short Guide to Britain* for the GIs, and *Meet the US Army* for the British. Nevertheless, opinion was sharply divided, for and against. The GIs were liked and admired by many British women for their healthy looks, glamorous uniforms, relative affluence, generosity and the whiff of Hollywood they brought. They were disliked, especially by their hard-up British service counterparts, for being slovenly soldiers, conceited, boastful, bumptious and materialistic. As if this weren't enough, they bribed British women with Post Exchange (PX) goodies. In fact, as the saying went, they were, 'overpaid, oversexed and over here'!

Their overtly racist attitude to their black comrades-in-arms didn't help. These were often the first black men the British had seen, and the segregation policy then prevalent in America and among Americans in Britain shocked many. For their part, white GIs were disgusted by the fraternization that took place between British women and black GIs. Those who were children in wartime generally speak warmly of the Americans, who were easy-going and generous with sweets, chewing-gum and the odd packet of cigarettes.

Stalin's immediate response to Churchill's offer of aid after the German invasion of June 1941 had been to demand a 'Second Front Now' to take the pressure off the Soviets' dire situation. With American entry into the war, he increased the pressure on Churchill and extended it to President Roosevelt. Eventually, and despite misgivings, on 19 August 1942 Operation 'Jubilee' went ahead. It was an assault by 4,963 Canadian troops, 1,075 British and fifty American Rangers on the French port of Dieppe to test enemy defences. It resulted in the tragic slaughter of Allied troops – 907 Canadians and 275 British. Many more were taken prisoner. This was a blow to a country badly needing a victory, and demonstrated just how difficult and costly the opening of a Second Front in Europe would be.

Peter Smith
Evacuee schoolboy, Bessiestown, Cumberland

It would have been in the autumn of 1942 when I was attending school in Carlisle, that I saw the first American troops and their big lorries – we hadn't seen coloured troops before, this was the first time. The local girls used to get off with them. I can remember them kind of lolling about cuddling in the parks. Of course, this was very much frowned upon, that local girls were cavorting with the GIs.

Peter Bennett
Schoolboy, Godalming, Surrey

We had Canadians in the area and I remember very well my mother being whistled at by soldiers in a lorry. I didn't think she was a whistleable-at person. She was my *mum*. I thought, Stone the crows!

Of course, we used to get gum from Americans in particular. That's when the saying 'Got any gum, chum?' came in.

Audrey Hammon (Cobb)
Schoolgirl, Romney Marshes, Kent

One time, as we were eating Sunday lunch, we realized there was an aeroplane making a different sort of noise from usual. We went outside and saw a Flying Fortress going round and round and round. It had been damaged, and we heard later that it had wounded on board. It wanted to land, but as Newchurch was a fighter, not a bomber, airfield the runway wasn't long enough. However, it landed, outstripping the runway. By the time we got there the crew had come out and were sitting on a grassy bank. I just wish I had a picture of the expression on my face seeing American airmen for the first time in all their flying gear! And one of them saying that he didn't goddamn know where he was, but he supposed he was back in England!

Maggie Lanning (Mundy)
Infant, Earley, Berkshire

One of the amusing things my mother told me was that one day, as she was pushing the pram, some troops stopped by her side and a very large black soldier jumped down from the back of the vehicle and said to her, 'Would you mind if I pushed the baby because I've got a little child at home that I haven't yet seen and I'd love to push the pram?' And she allowed him to push the pram up the hill for her, and he was delighted.

Dennis Hayden
Evacuee schoolboy, Highclere, Hampshire

I think the first involvement with troops was with the Canadians, who came through in preparation for the Dieppe raid. They drove up through this lane between the house and the outhouse in Churchill tanks, then swung off right to go up in the woods. And one of them turned a bit too sharp and went straight through the outhouse – took away the chicken shed and everything else and left the end of our bath-house wide open. They were there on exercise in the woods for about five days. They were very, *very* friendly towards us, and I know we had chocolate bars, tins of fruit, boxes of cheese and things like that given us by these visiting troops . . . The American forces came through asking for eggs and water. There were always tin cans left lying around and petrol cans, which then were a small sort of square brown can, which held about a gallon. They used to punch a hole in each corner and fill up their petrol tanks. But, of course, some was often left in the can. George and Daisy sent us out getting all these cans and I know we siphoned off the petrol that was left. I forget how many gallons we got, but there must have been hundreds of cans. And then we took the tops off, burnt off all the fumes, and fitted wire handles through them and these were used as buckets by everyone.

Margaret Woodhead (Butler)
Evacuee schoolgirl, Portsmouth, Hampshire

The man whose garden faced ours worked in the dockyard. One night he didn't come home but he managed to get a message to his wife saying there had been some trouble. When he did come home at the end of the next day he was very, very quiet and didn't want to eat anything. About three or four days later, she told us he'd said to her, 'The reason I didn't get home and why I've been the way I've been is that I had to pick up the bits of the boys' bodies they brought back and put them in coffins.' I remember going to work myself, and when I went over the railway bridge seeing the trains go through with coffins inside, sometimes blinds drawn, but often not. The coffins were from the Dieppe raid by the Canadians.

John Starling
Evacuee schoolboy, Portsmouth, Hampshire

I remember when I was serving my apprenticeship in the dock-yard at Portsmouth in 1942, at the time of the unsuccessful Dieppe raid, seeing the barges coming back to the dockyard with all the charred bodies on board. It was a *terrible* sight.

Frank Bower

British evacuee schoolboy, Napanee, Canada, extract from his memoir

Gradually the war began to catch up with Napanee. Some of the older boys got their call-up papers and disappeared overseas. Those who were in the air force were already engaged in active flying duties over Germany, and the casualties began. Barbara Kimmerly lost her brother; young George from the bank was killed in the RCAF [Royal Canadian Air Force]; the casualties from the fiasco at Dieppe when the Canadians bore the brunt of the fighting affected many ... Food remained plentiful, but somehow it never occurred to my sister Anne and me to send food parcels home where they would have been so appreciated. Our parents never asked for any and rarely mentioned the war in their letters, although they were having the most intensive bombing in Liverpool. To us the war seemed so remote that, in the careless ways of youth, we hardly thought about it, except when it inconvenienced us in some trifling way.

In March 1942 the new, huge, four-engined Lancaster bomber became available and Bomber Command's new chief, Sir Arthur Harris, backed by Winston Churchill, set out to prove that bombing could win the war against Germany. By the end of the year, spirits rose with British success at the second Battle of Alamein and Rommel's retreat in North Africa, then again on 13 November, when the South Africans reclaimed Tobruk. All over Britain church bells were rung to celebrate what was seen as a great victory and a reversal of fortune. As Winston Churchill told the British people, it was 'the end of the beginning'. Alamein, with the Soviet victory at Stalingrad, and the Battle of Midway, in June, at which Japanese forces found themselves at last on the defensive, is generally regarded as the turning-point of the war.

Joanna Lawrence (Rogers)
Schoolgirl, West Wickham, Kent

One day we heard there would be an important announcement at nine o'clock and we waited and it didn't come. We went to bed upset. Next morning it came: the Battle of El Alamein had started and we were on our way forward again. We were terribly excited. It gave us the sort of excitement that children don't get now. It was *thrilling*. We were then able to go to the cinema and we saw pictures of Italian prisoners surrendering in *droves*. We used to roar with cheering – there was always a lot of cheering and clapping at such news. I never had any doubts about our winning the war. I don't think as children that we knew how bad things were at times ... We heard of the victories, not the defeats. I remember one time when they rescued some prisoners off the *Altmark* in a Norwegian fjord, and the navy went in and we were told they called out, 'It's all right, lads, the navy's here!' Well, that sort of thing was *tremendous* to us, and we couldn't wait to grow up and be in the services.

Rodney Giesler
Anglo-German schoolboy, Hele, Somerset

The Eastern Front was quite well covered in *War Illustrated* and everyone got their tongues wrapped round Russian towns from radio broadcasts. There was one called Veliki-Luki, and there was this racial character in *ITMA* [*It's That Man Again*, a radio programme] who was an Egyptian pedlar: 'I sell you a nice bucket, sir, very leaky, very luki.' Smolensk, and Dnieper-Propetrovsk and Kharkov, remote towns you've never heard of since, were all familiar to us then, like Bihać and Sarajevo now in Bosnia ... I remember German-occupied land was always in black with great black arrows showing advances. Every morning you'd open the paper to see the heavy black line had been rolled back a bit. Our forces were shown in white arrows, puncturing the black. The state of the war was made very graphic. I think I was aware of the war more at an adult level because I took a keen interest in it. I got to know the names of VC winners, the battles, different weapons and tanks. I could spot a Crusader tank from a Matilda or a Churchill. I got to know most German tanks from photographs, particularly during the Normandy landings – those horrendous tank battles in the Bocage.

Peter Smith
Schoolboy, Petts Wood, Kent

On many days at school we'd see our own bomber raids going out. I can remember one sunny afternoon there were just streams and *streams* of Fortresses and Liberators – American aircraft – going over, and later in the evening, of course, our own bombers, the Lancasters, Stirlings, Wellingtons and Halifaxes. We were quite good at aircraft recognition and these were, of course, the forerunners of the thousand-bomber raids . . . On the morale-boosting theme, a great event was the Dam Busters' raid led by Guy Gibson. I also remember our convoys to Russia – the Arctic convoys, as they became known – and the terrible conditions under which they were undertaken, supplying war materials to the Russians. Even when we were in Carlisle, I remember collections made for aid to Russia. I can recall a big shop window with a huge star outlined in red, white and blue to show the link between Britain and Russia. So we were conscious of the suffering of the Russian people, and what they were undergoing, but also of what we were trying to do in some small way to bring aid to them.

As for the Germans, I think I lapped up a lot of the propaganda – they were all evil and had to be beaten. The heavy raids were reported, including Dresden later, but the import of it and the scale of the destruction of the city didn't come over at the time. Speaking personally, at the time I knew the Germans had done terrible things and they deserved what they got.

Dennis Hayden

Evacuee schoolboy, Highclere, Hampshire

We weren't directly involved with bombing. I think there was only one bomb fell on Newbury ... I don't think we appreciated the war as such. It was never mentioned at school. And if I listened to the wireless they said, 'Well, what's the news then, boy?' I'd say there was another raid on a south-coast town, or aeroplanes struck deep into the heart of Germany and five of our aircraft failed to return. And Daisy would say, 'Oh, them poor dears. Oh, them poor dears!' But other than that, it didn't mean anything to me – what the state of the war was, who was winning, who was losing. We were tucked up in an environment where we were quite safe. It didn't bother us.

Peter Bennett

Schoolboy, Godalming, Surrey

At nine o'clock on Sundays, they used to play on the radio all the national anthems of the countries that had been overrun. And it really meant something to me. One thought about those people in other countries listening on their illicit radios to their national anthem. And it was done quite nicely, I think: 'To all our comrades in France and all our comrades in Poland ...' and it went right through the lot.

It was only when we started winning, which, of course, we did in North Africa, that I started taking an interest in the war. We were always impressed with Winston Churchill's speeches. I remember also there used to be national days of prayer ... I don't remember that we took a great deal of notice of the people out in the Far East. That was a war that was entirely different. I don't remember anything about that, or very little. I think that's what they complained about too – the Forgotten Army. Well, they *were* forgotten ...

Doreen Hartley (Saunders)
Women's Auxiliary Service (Burma), Shillong, Assam

The Wasbies, having got out of Burma, were now helping the troops' welfare. They started with one canteen and were serving the troops convalescing there. We were trained and got our uniforms, then were posted. I was sent down south, to the Arakan area, near Chittagong, which was a vast transit area, with huge numbers of troops coming and going. We lived in straw huts. The troops were pouring out from battle, and as they passed our centre we gave out tea, cakes, coffee – whatever they wanted. Suddenly they'd see two young girls there and they wouldn't *believe* it. They had just been in hell, and I'll always remember their faces when they saw us: the relief! 'What are you doing here?' You see two young girls – it must be a peaceful place! The canteen was a big thatched hut so that hundreds of troops could come, sit and rest there and drink our lemonade or char. They'd had a terrible time in the Arakan. They always wanted char, mugs of very strong tea with enough sugar for the spoon to stand up in it. We had vast tin baths and we'd put a bath of water on the fire, and when it was boiling I would pour a whole packet of tea and all the milk and sugar in and we'd stir it with a piece of wood. Then we'd call out, 'Come and get it!' They loved it: strong, sweet soldiers' tea.

At one point the Japanese surrounded us. You never knew where they were – they came very fast. But I was never frightened because we had the commandos and the marine commandos with us. I went to Kohima just after the battle. There was still some fighting going on and I had to stay the night. I hated it – it was very eerie. I had to get to the Wasbies at fifty milestone; Kohima was at forty-seven.

All this was hard work, yes. When we got to a camp, you'd hear the sergeants say, 'Watch your tongues!' The troops always behaved well and really wanted to talk about their girlfriends and wives, but not to me – I was still a very young girl – to the older Wasbies; they would cry on their shoulders when they were homesick or if the wife had gone off with somebody. That was part of the job, to talk to them. The 14th were called the Forgotten Army. I once wrote a letter to a parson in England whom I knew, asking him to remember the men of the Forgotten Army.

Diana Owen (Houston-Boswald)
Teenage daughter of diplomat, interned in the British embassy, Tokyo, Japan

On one occasion the Japanese ordered us all to stand round the gates and watch a shot-down aeroplane – either British or American – towed through the streets. It was reputed to have the dead pilot in it, but my mother didn't encourage me to look. I was guarded from nasty sights. But I do remember that aircraft going past and how we were furious. All the grown-ups were saying what a terrible thing to do, and what yellow devils they were, and there was a great deal of cruelty towards the Japanese servants at that time ...

Then one day an air-raid siren went off, and the air attaché got terribly excited and told us to go into the basement, but nobody would believe it. I was in the Chancery, typing lists, and we rushed and climbed up on the flat roof. It was a Saturday afternoon, in April 1942, and the Japanese were watching baseball in their equivalent to Hyde Park ... I do remember seeing the fires in the most Japanese quarter of Tokyo. These would be paper houses, caused by incendiary fires, and I think quite a few people were killed. Considering the distance they had come, I think they were quite successful raids, by the aircraft-carrier USS *Hornet*, known as the 'Doolittle Raid'. We thought it terribly exciting, a break with routine and very good for morale. After the raid, we had a bad earthquake and that petrified me. It was far more frightening than the air raid.

Lady Thurle Folliott Vaughan (Laver Eriksen)
British child, Copenhagen, Denmark

The Germans had captured a lot of the top patriot people and the Danes were extremely worried because, under torture, they might give away all sorts of secrets, so they sent an SOS to England, explaining that they'd been put on the top floor of the Shell House, which was a building in the middle of Copenhagen, please could they do something. Well, the British sent in Mosquito bombers on one of the most famous bombing raids of the war.

They came in very low, hedge-hopping over the houses, and they threw their bombs in on the bottom floor of the building, a brilliant bit of bombing. On the top floor, one of the cells was burst open by the blast and the Dane inside got out. He found the jailer, who was quaking with fear, got the keys off him, unlocked all the cells and the patriots got away. The Danes were over the moon about this. One of the Mosquitos got its wings caught in some wires and went straight into a school and some children were killed. What I found so remarkable about this was that the Danes all said roughly the same thing: 'Wasn't it marvellous that all the patriots got out? Terribly sad about the school but these things happen in war ...' I thought they'd be terribly cross at the RAF, but they weren't at all. As the bombing was happening, all of us in the convent school went on to the roof. It was marvellous because we saw the Mosquitos come in, and we could literally look in and wave to the pilots.

After the war I met one of the pilots and he said he'd never done anything more terrifying in his life because these damn Danes were running up and down the street, waving anything they could that was red, white and blue. He said, 'Quite frankly, it was very sweet of them, but I had a difficult job to do and didn't want to be put off.' This bombing boosted the morale of the Danes enormously – they liked nothing better than being bombed by the British!

9. Wartime: Daily Life

At the outbreak of war the Ministry of Food had been given power to direct and control food distribution and soon realized that a system had to be devised to ensure fair shares for all. Booklets were issued in September 1939, but rationing did not begin until 8 January 1940. Each family member was given a ration book, which contained a number of coupons, and was required to register with a food retailer. Butter, sugar, bacon and ham were the first items to be rationed, then meat, cheese, preserves and syrups, tea, margarine, cooking fat, sweets and chocolate. The supply of egg and milk fluctuated, so rather than being rationed they were 'allocated'.

Towards the end of 1941 the 'points' system was introduced: each person was issued with a number of points to use when buying non-rationed goods, which were ranked according to their scarcity or value. Invalids and certain groups were entitled to extra food and concentrated orange juice – pregnant women and nursing mothers, for example. Children of school age received almost the same rations as adults and were entitled to extra milk and eggs, and cod-liver oil. A degree of bartering occurred and there were many under-the-counter deals, as well as a black market in most areas. Many children recall the excitement of receiving food parcels from Canada, the United States and other countries, which contained unusual items such as peanut butter.

The 'Dig for Victory' campaign encouraged people to supplement their rations with fresh fruit and vegetables. All available land was commandeered for allotments, including public parks, recreation grounds, football pitches and even the moat at the Tower of London. After the Blitz, children dug and planted bombsites with vegetables. Sections of school playing-fields were cultivated, and gardening became a part of every child's life across the country. By the end of the war 1.5 million allotment holders were responsible for 10 per cent of Britain's food production – and not only fruit and vegetables: they kept hens, rabbits, goats, pigs and bees, for honey, too.

Generally, rationing was regarded as a fair system and has been credited with providing a healthy diet. Controlled prices meant that even the poorest could afford their rations, and the better-off were unable to hoard. Paul Addison has noted that the ration book, with its 'fair shares' ethos, had far-reaching political effects: it was a forerunner of the welfare state set up by the Labour government between 1945 and 1951.

Marjorie Bond (Cranshaw)
Schoolgirl, Hull, Yorkshire

I never felt that we were any worse off with rationing. In a sense my parents had prepared for the war. When it began we had quite a hoard of sugar – and working-class women had always had the ability to make food go a long way. We were never short of bread and potatoes – the basic things in the English diet, really. At one time during the war, my mother and I cycled out to Skidby, a village outside Hull, and gathered fruit from the fruit farms there. We picked raspberries, gooseberries, blackcurrants and redcurrants, and then we used the sugar we had and bottled them, so we were never short of fruit. Of course, you didn't get many bananas or oranges, except on the famous occasion when a ship went down in the Humber – all the crates of oranges fell in the river and these were rescued and Hull got all the oranges.

Thomas Houlton
Schoolboy, Hull, Yorkshire

As a lad I had hollow legs and a very healthy appetite, but I wasn't particularly conscious of being half starved. One tended to fill oneself up on whatever was available at the time. I certainly remember at school dinners we were well aware of horsemeat being served, it being very stringy in texture and bright yellow in colour. On one occasion we had both horsemeat and whalemeat on the plate at the same time, which wasn't very pleasant. The whalemeat was oily and smooth and brown and the horsemeat was stringy and yellow. Needless to say the staff would never admit what it was, but we all knew. Often mothers would sacrifice their rations in order to supplement the rations of their children. Two ounces of butter wasn't a lot for a week, but I don't think my health suffered from the food.

Peter Bennett
Schoolboy, Godalming, Surrey

We used to sit round as a family and peel onions for pickled onions. And we used to salt beans, which tasted horrible when you had them later. Rhubarb, which we used to grow, was bottled, and then later it was turned into jam when we ran short. And my dad used to have a 'relationship', shall we say?, with a lady who kept ducks, so we used to get the odd duck egg, which was all right for making cakes. I think everybody must have had their own 'friends' . . . Another thing, our little greengrocer's shop used to sell cleaned carrots. And I often bought a quarter of cleaned carrots instead of sweets and chewed those . . . I think it's probably true that people were a lot healthier. I know that there were people who couldn't afford to buy their butter ration. So we used to have butter all the time rather than part-margarine and part-butter because there was an arrangement one made with the shop. Not that we were affluent, but others were worse off than we were.

Even the shops were different from today . . . Our little village shop used to bake their bread and make their own sausages. And we worked the sausage machine for them many times. They had some damsons in their back garden, which we used to pick for them. It was a very nice life, I think, in many sorts of ways . . . My mother liked entertaining and we used to always have people for tea on Sundays right through the war. And then if anybody came to stay they used to bring a little bit of butter and a little bit of sugar, a sort of mini food parcel.

Rodney Giesler
Anglo–German schoolboy, Hele, Somerset

We had a sweet ration, but it wasn't enough. We also got tins of condensed milk on points – points were more flexible than coupons and could be used for different things, depending on what the grocer had in, tins of jam and so on. Rationing made it fair for everyone, rich and poor. You would have been deemed very anti-social if you'd tried to get more than your entitlement. I'd get condensed milk, cocoa powder and vanilla essence from the kitchen, mix them up in a bowl into a sticky mess and we'd go and sit in our fort on the island at the bottom of the garden, and my brother Neville and I would spoon it down and feel thoroughly sick. That's how we satisfied our craving for sweets. And then, of course, there were the Americans. They introduced us to Hershey bars and Juicy Fruit chewing-gum. Whenever you saw an American truck you'd shout, 'Any gum? Any candy?' They were very generous. They'd shower it on us.

The British Restaurant – that was a great institution! We used to cycle into Taunton and have lunch at one of these. You bought little coloured tags – green for soup, blue for the main course, and yellow, to match the custard, for the puds. You could eat ration-free very wholesomely for a small amount of money. We'd have this lunch, go to a film, and that was our outing. There were lots of brilliant films made during the war: *Western Approaches*, *Desert Victory* and *The Way Ahead*. We'd catch up with these during our holidays.

Kathleen Schaller
Schoolgirl, Belfast, Northern Ireland

My mother came from south of Dublin. We went down there once or twice, mainly to shop, because [Eire being neutral] you could get things there. We bought clothes and put on several layers and took boxes of chocolates and stuff that we couldn't get in the north. There was Customs, but because we were wearing all the clothes, we got through that way. People would be handing round these huge boxes of chocolates just so they were broken into to get through Customs ...

Sylvia Townson (Limburg)
Jewish schoolgirl, Paddington, London

I remember when I was back in school in London, the sailor son of the headmaster came home with a case of bananas. The headmaster cut them up so that every child should have a taste of a banana ... In Wales, where I was evacuated later, I remember going to the chemist in Mountain Ash and buying liquorice root – it looked like a tree root, and you sucked this stale piece and it was *lovely*. You could get great quantities of it.

Joanna Lawrence (Rogers)
Schoolgirl, West Wickham, Kent

We used to do a lot of shopping for Mother. We were registered with Sainsbury's and we dealt with the coupons. Fish was never rationed. My father had an allotment and we used to grow all our vegetables, and he had beehives too. We had to give part of our sugar ration up to get special sugar for the bees when he took the honey out, but he could sell the honey. Spam was usually put in sandwiches, but Mother served it up as meat too. By and large we did well for food. Dried egg was a saver – you could do a lot with that.

Marguerite Patten (Brown)
Adviser to the Ministry of Food

'Potato Pete' was a clever thing. Potatoes were home grown, they were filling and versatile, so 'Potato Pete' became a symbol – he was a character. If you can imagine a big oval potato with a funny little hat on his head and a cheery grin, that was 'Potato Pete'.

Children loved him and if you said to them, 'Now "Potato Pete" would like you to do this or that ...' I don't think it worked every time, but it was an encouragement. I think the Ministry of Food did an excellent job during the war. They didn't mind making a joke of it, jollying people along ... If a child was hungry between meals in wartime, the mum would say, 'Well, go and have a carrot, darling.' You can't imagine mothers saying that to their children today! ... Oranges came into the country very, *very* rarely, but when they did come in, they were reserved for children, and each child would have a pound. The peel wasn't wasted and most mothers would save that and make orange-peel marmalade, and you made it up with good old cooking apples.

Country dwellers had obvious advantages, with more abundant supplies of eggs, milk, rabbits and other game. It was also much easier to find the land to Dig for Victory. At harvest time, the hedgerows provided rich crops of hips and berries for jam, syrup and home-made wine; there were mushrooms, too, and acorns were fed to pigs. Children shared and enjoyed the picking, evacuees joining them and learning country lore in the process.

Noel Dumbrell
Schoolboy, Ashurst, Sussex

I know we were better off for food than people in towns, because when the evacuees saw what we had to eat compared with what they had, they said it was absolutely different. No one went shopping. The only time my mum and dad went shopping was Christmas to get us a few presents. Everything was grown or reared: we had our own pigs – half had to be given up to the ministry, everything had to be shared, and quite right too – and chickens too. Potatoes and everything else was grown in the fields or in the garden. Our main meat was rabbit, pheasant and partridge. I could catch rabbits from an early age. I used to go out with our ferrets and always had the dog with me. Didn't shoot because of the noise, and cartridges, of course, were expensive. So we used to snare or wire them. I used to breed tame rabbits – Old English and Flemish John, because they were big and meaty. But we would never eat our own rabbits, *couldn't*. So, for a little bit of pocket money, I would sell them to the butcher. People probably wouldn't believe this, but there was rook pie, made from baby rooks, and something which you never hear talked about, what we called 'spar catching'. Sparrows, hundreds and hundreds of them, we'd catch, and, believe it or not, we used to have sparrow pie. Very tasty. Rook and sparrow meat were white and very sweet, done mostly in stews in the copper. Vegetables: fields of mangels and turnips and swedes. You could go on any farm and pull yourself a swede or turnips. You only took what was wanted ... All told, in the village, there was nothing you couldn't eat, and the evacuees loved our food.

Dennis Hayden
Evacuee schoolboy, Highclere, Hampshire

We were self-sufficient. The fact that our foster-father, George, was a gamekeeper meant there was no shortage of food ... They always used to keep a pig and every pig was always 'Chuggie'. During the interim months, before they were slaughtered, one got to love the pig quite well. One particular pig always seemed to know when we were going to school and would jump out of the sty and come with us – most unusual, I suppose, to take a pig to school! But he would trot the mile to school and, having followed us there, he would get down in the pine tree, which was in the middle of the playing area, burrow into the roots and rest there. Then, when we were ready to come home, he'd get himself back up on to his haunches and on all fours. Because he realized it must be feeding time, he'd to start to run. But being a pig he was not built for running and he'd sit down and would give what sounded like a hearty laugh as he was trying to catch his breath. When I first met my wife and I heard her laugh, it reminded me of this pig getting its breath back. Since then she has always had the name of 'Chuggie'.

Reg Baker
Evacuee schoolboy, Weston-on-the-Green, Oxfordshire

Country people are right genned up, you know, 'cause they're self-sufficient, really, ain't they? But I missed my pie and mash – that's an East End dish, very tasty. But Grandma Dorling used to do spotted dicks – suet puddings in a cloth. I put on weight there. I come home with red chubby cheeks, you know, which people took the mickey out of, 'cause they remembered me as a skinny little so-and-so. There was plenty to eat there and fruit was in abundance. At first we used to jump up and pick the apples. Then they said, 'Don't do that, there's the windfalls.' You only had to cut off the bruised part, which was logic to me.

Clothes and cloth were rationed from June 1941; only hats and working clothing were exempt. Although large children and adolescents were allotted extra points, clothing caused problems for parents, who found it particularly difficult to provide shoes for fast-growing feet. The WVS came into its own, opening clothing exchanges for children, and offering advice, in connection with the 'Make Do and Mend' scheme, for renovating and altering clothes. The Utility trademark ensured strict economy in the design and production of clothing, furniture and household goods.

Acute shortages inconvenienced everyone. Baby necessities, from prams to rubber teats, were hard to find, and from February 1942, you could buy just one three-ounce tablet of toilet soap or four ounces of household soap every four weeks. Crockery, cutlery, glasses, combs, lighters, razor blades, cosmetics, tobacco and toys were almost unavailable. Paper was in short supply, which meant that every tiny scrap was used for writing or drawing, paper bags were saved and reused, and newspaper cut up for use in the lavatory.

With pre-war memories of treats at Christmas and on birthdays, children missed new toys, but improvised. Those that were in the shops were often related to the war effort:

lead soldiers in khaki uniforms, guns, camouflage helmets, and aeroplanes. Playing cards were printed with wartime themes and characters, and board games involved war operations. Dolls were often dressed in uniform. Comics were still printed, and the wartime *Just William* and Biggles books referred to wartime events and conditions in the stories and situations. The collection of wartime souvenirs became a popular pursuit, and shrapnel, bombs and shell parts were highly prized. It was considered sinful to waste anything and salvage drives, arranged by teams of volunteers, were commonplace. Children collected rags, waste paper, metal, bottles, jam-jars – anything that could possibly be used for the war effort. The wartime recycling of food and other materials would hearten today's conservationists.

Joanna Lawrence (Rogers)
Schoolgirl, West Wickham, Kent

Clothes became a problem – things were mended a lot. We had thick lisle stockings which used to last well. The biggest problem was shoes: my feet were growing fast. We were fairly hard up for fabrics and nothing was renewed in the home. Windows were broken several times: someone would come and inspect and you'd get new glass and it was repaired. We did keep rabbits and it was heartbreaking when one was killed, but we did have rabbit-skin hats and gloves. Rabbit was quite a part of our diet then.

Patricia Fitzgerald (Stringer)
Schoolgirl, Sidcup, Kent

I made a whole coat by unpicking and turning it. We had nothing new. We were encouraged to make things. You couldn't buy much material unless you had the coupons. I can remember someone had brought home a bag of rags, and Mum got a horrible puce evening dress from it, but I made something out of it.

Maggie Lanning (Mundy)
Infant, Earley, Berkshire

I can remember being dressed up in a beautiful dress, which was made from parachute silk. That was so luxurious and has stuck in my memory – the *smoothness* of the material was absolutely wonderful. I must have been four-ish then.

Peter Bennett
Schoolboy, Godalming, Surrey

Pencils were plain wood, no paint on and not easy to get either. And tins of fruit didn't have pictures of the fruit on them, just plain white labels – usually plums because that's all we seemed able to buy. And silly things like elastic were difficult to get ... There were shops in Godalming where we knew the person – I suppose you'd term it a sort of under-the-counter black-market operation. Some people would say, 'We've got the coupons, we haven't got the money.' And others would say, 'We've got the money, we haven't got the coupons.' And it used to work out quite well, mainly between friends. Petrol was bartered, just through friends. But everybody used to do it. Even when I was eight, I used to cycle seventeen miles each way to visit one grandparent and twelve miles to visit the other. Tyres were difficult and you couldn't get paint to brighten up your bike. I suppose life was very drab. People didn't go in so much for bright colours in those days. Clothes weren't so bright – materials were rather brown and uninteresting.

Pamela Leopard (Brownfield)
Schoolgirl, Gravesend, Kent

I had a wonderful surprise one Christmas when my parents wheeled a dolls' pram in. This was made by my father who was a carpenter. It was made of wood, all lacquered black – it was *wonderful*. It would have been very difficult to buy toys. I know my mother had difficulty in getting a doll for me and she met a lady in a bus queue who said, 'I've got one at home.' That's how I got my doll. I loved it and treasured it.

Peter Smith
Evacuee schoolboy, Bessiestown, Cumberland

We had very few toys; they were hard to come by. But this shop in Carlisle had a superb set of Dinky toys – all military things, tanks, lorries, Bofors guns, field guns, etc. They were in a long cardboard box, which cost thirty shillings – £1.50 today. I used to get sixpence [3p] a week pocket money from my grandmother and half a crown [13p] on a birthday or special event. I saved and saved and used to go and look at this set every week, hoping it hadn't been sold. Eventually I was able to go in with a pocketful of small change and buy it. I beamed with absolute joy that I had it. When I got back to Bessiestown and they saw it and asked how much it was, they were absolutely aghast at spending so much money on toys. But I kept it for years and had a great deal of fun and entertainment from it.

Rodney Giesler
Anglo-German schoolboy, Hele, Somerset

Once my father had to go back to our house in Kent to see that everything was all right. We had filled our garage with everything we couldn't take with us: our toys, glass, plates, bits of furniture. When he got back there, the place was empty. The Military Police, of all people, had been occupying it and my father was *incensed*. He roared: 'The SS couldn't have made a better job of it!' It was totally looted ... We lost the lot and never got a penny for it. Anyhow, it was unpatriotic to complain. The authorities had better things to do than process insurance claims ...

Evelyn Fee (Moss)
Evacuee mother of five, Byworth, Sussex

My husband met some of the Canadian troops during his leaves and there were two or three nice fellows we made friends with and they were very kind to the children. Their wives used to send things from Canada for them. That was when they first started to get toys, and they sent me food and a baby layette. I had my baby, Roy, while we were in Byworth; he was born in November 1940. There wasn't all the care and attention they get nowadays. I just went and booked the nurse and I never saw no more of her, not till they went and got her the night I had the baby. She was a wonderful woman, Nurse Alan, absolutely lovely, and so kind.

Janet Shipton (Attlee)
Schoolgirl, Stanmore, Greater London

We had no privileges [as Deputy Prime Minister Clement Attlee's family]. On the contrary, Mother was mad when Father knew they were going to introduce clothes' rationing, and he didn't tell her. We had few sheets, just a few old linen ones from my grand-mother. They lasted because Mother sides-to-middled them. She always did that, we were a very economical family. We hadn't bought anything after the depression so it was a struggle. No, we didn't have any privileges at all. The only thing we had was a green telephone in Father's study, a secret telephone to be used when he was home, that was all. He lived just like an ordinary person in the basement of number 11 [Downing Street].

With disrupted schooling, fathers away in the services and mothers busy with war work, firewatching and endless queueing, children were left to their own devices far more than they ever had been before. Many got into mischief, especially during the Blitz, as the rise in recorded rates of juvenile crime illustrates. In the first year of the war, for instance, there was a 41 per cent increase in children under fourteen found guilty of criminal offences, and a 22 per cent rise for those between fourteen and seventeen. But generally, in city streets and on bombsites, in the woodlands and fields of the countryside, in homes and in shelters, wartime

children continued to play and squabble much as they always had, but with the war providing an added dimension for their games.

Peter Bennett
Schoolboy, Godalming, Surrey

I went in for a fancy-dress competition when I was about seven. I dressed up as a gardener and put some vegetables in my little wheelbarrow and wore an apron and an old straw hat and I had 'Dig for Victory' on the side of the wheelbarrow. I got first prize and I got one of these old Brownie box cameras and it had a film in – films were virtually unobtainable then ... There was a painting competition for the children in the school and I drew and painted some warships and wrote: 'Our ships that sail the seven seas, Will bring the Nazis to their knees.' It was highly commended. I didn't get a prize for it, but we always used to join in with whatever was going on.

We used to go to what's called a Crusader Class. It was like Sunday school but for boys only. And we used to have a party at Christmas, which was a BYOG affair. BYOG stood for 'Bring Your Own Grub'. Everybody brought something and it was all put out on a table and you shared what you'd brought. There was no icing for cakes but something they called American frosting, made out of granulated sugar – a bit runny.

Peter Smith
Evacuee schoolboy, Bessiestown, Cumberland

One of the things I did get to like and still love, much to the consternation of the family and friends, was the bagpipes. There was a chap called Jockie Wylie who used to play the pipes. It used to be so plaintive, especially in the evenings, and I really took to this. One of the customs they had up there over the New Year was 'first footing', where they would go off visiting farms or homes and knocking on the door as soon after midnight as possible and be the first foot over the threshold and, of course, be invited in for a dram or two – then the whisky used to flow.

Rodney Giesler
Anglo-German schoolboy, Hele, Somerset

My brother and I used to swim in the river Tone. There was a bit of wasteground at the bottom of the garden that was a peninsula lying between two streams. We built a fort there and had fights with the village boys, not vicious. 'You be Germins.' 'No, you be. We was Germins last week.' We had our bicycles and we'd load mudballs in the saddle-bags and be dive-bombers ... Later in the war my mother bought an old boat with a canvas bottom advertised for ten shillings. We'd take that out on the river and row up and down, and that was our fighting fleet against the local boys.

May Moore (George)
Evacuee schoolgirl, Eyam, Derbyshire

In the village we had the Girls' Training Corps, the GTC, and we used to have these little forage caps and a navy blue tie, white blouse and navy skirt. The boys would go to the ATC, the Air Training Corps, and after our meetings, we'd wait for the boys to come out and we'd all wander home together. We also had this picture-house in the Mechanics Institute – it was the picture-house to end all picture-houses because it was a travelling cinema, and on Friday nights everyone would converge on this hall ... The children would sit in front and watch the old silent films. Hilarious looking back, because you'd pay your money and sit on the floor in front. And if there was still a queue outside and they had paid for their tickets, they'd come round, 'You, you and you, you're making a noise – outside you go!' and three would go out and three would come in. And Daisy Barlow, a village lady, used to get these concerts up in the village hall, and she'd have the children singing and dancing. And the village coalman would get up and do his songs and recitations. One girl, Frances, was fantastic at saying these monologues – in this lovely Derbyshire accent. They were such happy times.

John Gibson
Teenager, Belfast, Northern Ireland

We had the *Belfast Telegraph* delivered every evening, and my mother would sit in front of the fire and she'd go through the paper and read the notices of death. Even now I can hear her saying, 'Oh, my *God*, look who's gone!' And I would say, 'Who is it, Mummy?' And she'd say, 'Ach, my God, it's *terrible*! It's Willy So-and-so. We'll have to go to the wake – it's no good, we'll have to go. Put on your coat and we'll go over.' And we'd go by tram or bus or walk, wherever it was in Belfast ... My mother's aunt died during the war. Her husband was a market dealer and he brought half a side of bacon home to hang on the back door of the kitchen for the wake. This was ready cooked and everybody was going to where it was hanging and getting slabs of bacon off with bread and butter and drink galore – Guinness, beer and whisky – and very often they'd have a sing-song with the corpse lying in the corner ... I went to one where the corpse was standing up in the corner in the coffin. All of a sudden there would be 'Bang!' and one of the buttons on the shroud would fly off and nearly hit someone in the eye. 'Oh, my God, we'll have to sew that a bit tighter!' It was hilarious, really ...

Noel Dumbrell
Schoolboy, Ashurst, Sussex

We used to go off on day outings, not organized, but Mum and Dad would pack us up some sandwiches. Chanctonbury Ring was about eight miles away, and we'd say, 'Right, today we're going to walk dead straight there. Bye-bye, Mum,' and off we'd go as straight as we could, with the streams, the ditches and the lake. And we'd light a fire – we were trying to be soldiers, remember – and we had our mess tins, and we'd all have some tea. We knew which fruit and hips we could eat on the way from the hedges. If you stung yourself, you'd rub your leg with a dock leaf. And that's what we called a day's outing. Mum would say, 'They'll come home when they're hungry.'

Rodney Giesler
Anglo-German schoolboy, Hele, Somerset

There was also a huge German PoW camp at Norton Fitzwarren and we'd come home from school that way sometimes for Jerry-baiting. We'd get there just as these prisoners were being marched back into the camp with black American guards – I think that was deliberate to antagonize the Nazis among them. We'd shout, '*Sieg Heil*,' and do the Nazi salute at them, and sing, 'Whistle while you work, Hitler is a twerp ...' Some grinned; most of them ignored us. It was rather nice, because in those days you weren't rude to grown-ups, but German PoWs were grown-ups you *could* be rude to. We could say, 'Get stuffed, you horrible men.'

Margaret Woodhead (Butler)
Evacuee schoolgirl, Zeals, Wiltshire

Near the Rabbitz cottage was a field in which there were two trees that at one time had been struck by lightning and the tops were hollowed out. After we'd finished our daily chores, the daughter of the family and I would get some apples from the tree and she'd go up in one tree and I would go in another with our apples and books. That was our world. I can remember looking up and seeing the sky and the clouds, so clear and so peaceful – nobody to shout at you, nobody to worry you, just beautiful. A great contrast with my home in Portsmouth where you always had the town, the pictures, the shops. There weren't any shops in the country, but it didn't worry me. I had this lovely peaceful field, and the trees ...

227

Noel Dumbrell
Schoolboy, Ashurst, Sussex

One day old Arthur, the gamekeeper, came up to the school and said, 'Any of you kids like to play some music, learn the drums or banjo?' So I did, and I started playing the drums when I was ten. Arthur taught me, and he played the banjo and there was a woman – we were a three-piece. We used to play every two weeks at the dances in the village hall on Saturday nights – everybody out by ten thirty! Couple of bob [10p] to go in. And I remember I used to get half a crown [13p] for this.

On alternate Saturdays in the village hall when we weren't playing, we used to dance to Victor Sylvester's strict tempo and that was very popular. I can remember us all doing the quickstep and then the jitterbug. And then, of course, in came the big bands, and Glenn Miller was my favourite. So, good memories, especially of Vera Lynn. I know she used to buck up the troops, but she also did us youngsters. I often had tears in my eyes with some of the songs she sang. She was doing it for the boys who were fighting – she was the Forces Sweetheart. She probably doesn't know it, but she was the younger ones' sweetheart too!

Millicent Morgan (Miller)
Evacuee schoolgirl, Oxborough, Norfolk

We got on quite well with the local children unless any of the village boys hit my brother and then I'd have to go after him. Actually, I think we did look on them as village bumpkins a bit because they wasn't as bright as the Cockneys were ... If my mum sent me a modern jumper or a skirt or something that was a bit unusual, they would all remark on it because they just dressed for the sake of dressing. I was always proud of being a Londoner. Whether it was the community I came from, this little cul-de-sac street where we were all such great friends, I don't know, but I've never gone anywhere where I've not been proud of being a Londoner.

Reg Baker
Evacuee schoolboy, Weston on–the–Green, Oxfordshire

We had fights, a couple of little set-tos. I had one with a boy by the village hall. He was bigger, but East-Enders can manipulate themselves. Fights were usually familiar to us, being Londoners. And this morning he said something and I took umbrage and we had this little set-to. But all of a sudden the school bell went and we knew we'd be late so it finished then and there. He was the gypsy type, a very poor villager by their standards ...

I used to help the village blacksmith, mostly working the bellows and other little things, pulling the horse's leg up, that sort of thing ... It was fascinating to watch him. We also used to help the farmers during the school holidays, which again was fascinating. They'd cut a cornfield gradually, in squares. And people would stand around waiting for the rabbits to run. How quick they were with their guns, shooting rabbits running at speeds like that! I suppose the thing we noticed mostly was that there was so much *space* – like being at the seaside where you've got a bloody great ocean in front of you. Another thing I remember is that Grandma Dorling bought wellingtons for us. I'd never had them before, and they were nice and you had to leave them outside after you'd scraped the mud off with one of those scraper things.

Mary Whiteman (Walker)
Wife of chief billeting officer, Saffron Walden, Essex

The country was completely strange to many of the evacuees, and to be able to explore fields and get your feet in brooks was wonderful ... And there was a kind of safety in those days, and although you couldn't go into the woods [where ammunition was stored] to go into fields and the open spaces was a lovely outlet for small children who were not used to it. It impressed them so much. I heard of a child who wrote a letter home to his mother saying, 'They've got something lovely out in the country, it's called "spring"' – he thought it only belonged to this part of the world.

Dennis Hayden
Evacuee schoolboy, Highclere, Hampshire

Within a couple of days, I had become nameless. From then on I was always known as 'Boy'. 'Come on, Boy, we're going out in the woods to get a pigeon!' Or 'Come on, Boy, clean out the pigsty!' I became a nameless person ... When George took us out, he would try to teach us the gamekeeper's way of life and he was an excellent gamekeeper and very, very patient. He would tell us where to tread, when to stand still, when or when not to breathe, what to look for, rather than go blundering through the woods and making a noise and frightening everything away. He was an excellent shot. He never wasted anything and never killed unnecessarily – just purely to keep things down, or vermin.

In this outbuilding where the fire and the copper was, there was this toilet. This was a very large bucket and it was always the responsibility of George. He always dug a very large hole in the woods and emptied the bucket into that and filled it all in. I suppose being kids and completely uninhibited, if one wanted to go, there being such a large wooden seat atop the bucket with the hole in the middle, we all used to sit there together and read comics. And whosever turn it was to sit in the middle was the one that went. It would be brother one side, Pamela the other, and we shared the comic between the three of us. It became a very cosy family affair!

We had one Christmas at Grotto Lodge, otherwise we went back to Portsmouth. I remember there was a small tree with tinsel on it, no lights. It was a very romantic Christmas, just oil lamps and candles. I know there was deep snow outside – what one would generally imagine a Christmas *should* be.

Peter Smith
Evacuee schoolboy, Bessiestown, Cumberland

It was whilst living with the Armstrongs in Bessiestown that I became interested in the farm work. It was expected of us, and my parents said that we would help. So I learned to milk cows and Jean and I had to feed the hens. We also helped at weekends or in the school holidays in planting potatoes. One field grew oats, which were used to feed the horse and the chickens. It was a big sheep-rearing area. After lambing, the lambs had their tails docked. Then during the summer there would be the dipping, then the shearing – this was done by hand with metal shears. Then, of course, there was the rounding up in the autumn for the sheep out on the hills. It was while I was on holiday with some other relatives in Newcastleton that I learnt to work with a team of lovely Clydesdale horses and I did some harrowing of the fields. It was an interesting time and I enjoyed the life.

As well as organizing the collection and sorting of salvage, Boy Scouts and Girl Guides took on Civil Defence duties: firewatching, learning to put out incendiary bombs, detecting poison gas and giving warnings; they acted as messengers for the Home Guard too. Other teenagers joined cadet forces or worked for the Red Cross, St John's Ambulance Brigade, the Boys' Brigade and other such associations.

Peter Smith
Schoolboy, Petts Wood, Kent

Back home I joined the local Scout troop. This was a good education in itself. One of the things we became involved with was the erection of Morrison shelters. These were the indoor shelters, steel frame with a steel top and mesh sides, the idea being that people slept in them or got into them in an air raid; the shelters would be strong enough to withstand a ceiling and roof collapsing upon them. They arrived in kit form and were quite heavy, and we were asked to assist householders erecting these. In many families there were no menfolk available. Usually two or three of us worked together because they took some manhandling. I know our troop put up just over a hundred altogether. Ours was in a small bedroom on the ground floor and when the sirens went at night we would troop in there.

Reg Baker
Evacuee schoolboy, Weston Green, Oxfordshire

We learnt to knit for the soldiers. Believe it or not, I can *knit*! Plain and purl only, but I *can* knit. We learnt in the village school. You know, just straight scarves, khaki wool. But I'd hate to think of any soldier getting *my* scarf. It was the war effort, you know.

Leslie Alexander
Evacuee schoolboy, Girlington, Yorkshire, extract from his memoir

One of my fondest memories was collecting books that were sent to our prisoners-of-war. The amount of books collected entitled one to a rank in the army, i.e. 25 = Corporal, 50 = Sergeant, etc. I was made 'Field Marshal Alexander' and had to attend Bradford Town Hall to receive an embossed certificate from the mayor of Bradford.

Thomas Houlton
Schoolboy, Hull, Yorkshire

As a boy I was an avid collector of shrapnel and bits of aluminium wreckage, which I used to take to the ARP stations to help the war effort. It was my undying ambition to find a complete incendiary bomb, which I did after the second night of the blitz. It was underneath a tree about half a mile out into the country, in thick mud, and after about half an hour's effort I managed to pull it out. I put it over my shoulder and marched a mile and a half up Preston Road to the ARP post. I presented it to the warden, who nearly died a thousand deaths. Apparently it was the explosive type of incendiary. I was ordered to place it very gently on some sandbags, then told off with some choice words which are not repeatable. I used to pull out literally hundreds of tail fins of incendiary bombs and take them to the ARP. I thought it was useful for the war effort.

Noel Dumbrell
Schoolboy, Ashurst, Sussex

To help the war effort, we used to take sacks out with us, and we used to pick up what would have been loads of acorns from the trees for the farmers to feed their pigs. And we used to go out picking hips and berries for making jam – things the evacuees knew nothing about. I can remember this charabanc coming along and stopping outside the Fountain Inn and we were actually milking the cows in the cow stall there when the evacuees got off. One of them went by the buckets – no machines then, it was all done by hand – saying, 'We don't get *our* milk from these dirty old cows, we get ours from a nice clean dairy.' But then they got used to the cows and the animals. We used to take them round and show them how to collect moorhens' eggs from the ponds, and plovers' eggs – they were beautiful to cook. But there was nothing like vandalism, you never ragged [tore to pieces] a birds' nest. We'd watch for these birds and if, say, the moorhen had laid today – they would lay anything from fifteen to thirty eggs – you'd keep taking them one by one. You never took them all. They were really our chickens. But with plovers, and there were plenty about in those days, we'd only take one. There were many different species of birds and we used to make collections: we'd take one egg from each nest, take it back home, mark them and blow them to get the contents out, lay them in this cotton wool and they were all there, with the names of the different birds – you'd probably get shot for it today!

The radio, or 'wireless', as it was then called, came into its own during the Second World War. With people confined to their homes by the blackout, the BBC gained a vast new audience, and the nine o'clock news was the high point of the listening day. The BBC adapted quickly to popular taste and scheduled regular variety and comedy programmes, with comedians like Tommy Handley and Jack Warner. Singers, including Vera Lynn and Anne Shelton, became very

popular, as did the Americans Bing Crosby and Frank Sinatra. Glenn Miller's band was enjoyed as much by children as it was by adults, and the older ones would practise the jitterbug to 'In The Mood' and other catchy tunes with their older sisters. Radio assumed tremendous importance in the war. It was a godsend for lonely housebound women and a source of entertainment for children, who listened to *Children's Hour* but today remember the comedy shows – and, of course, Lord Haw Haw.

William Joyce, 'Lord Haw Haw', was an American citizen of Irish parentage who had resided in Britain during the 1930s, then fled to Germany in 1939 on a fraudulently obtained British passport. He took German nationality a year later. His snide, hostile bulletins on Britain's weakness before Dunkirk, as well as rumours he mentioned relating to specific landmarks and events, meant that at first many Britons took him seriously. Gradually, though, his 'Jairmany calling, Jairmany calling . . .' which announced the start of his broadcasts, was greeted with great hilarity.

Along with radio, the British cinema became a significant feature of wartime life, even during the Blitz. Flash-up signs warned of raids and it was left to members of the audience whether they fled into shelters or took their chances. 'Going to the flicks' became a regular twice-weekly event, and a chance to escape the war, although newsreels and Ministry of Information shorts brought audiences back to reality. Theatres had closed for a brief period at the start of the war, but were soon back in business and, like the cinemas, remained open throughout the Blitz.

Donald Swann
Evacuee schoolboy, Exeter, Devon

Michael Flanders said to me, 'Let's do a revue called *Go To It* – this was one of the great slogans of the war, 'Go To It.' His mother actually wrote a song called 'Go To It, That's the Order of the

Day', and set it to music. I was known to be one of the school pianists who could extemporize – usually on hymns! This was our first collaboration and Michael played most of the parts and was very funny and, of course, he was not disabled then; and dear old Anthony Wedgwood Benn was the stage manager. We travelled up from Exeter and did two nights at the Everyman Theatre, Hampstead. That was the first full week of the Blitz. There was an air raid at the end of the show, and I spent the rest of that night in a Hampstead shelter ... It never occurred to me as a pacifist that there was anything funny about being in a show whose title was a war slogan. You know, even as a youngster I was taken over by the war mood. You just got on with it. Maybe I was 'going to it' in my own funny sort of way ... In many ways children stop thinking they're children at all, and just get on with what is immediately around them.

Evelyn Fee (Moss)
Evacuee mother of five, Byworth, Sussex

The highlights of the week for us were Monday and Thursday nights, which were picture nights. We all enjoyed the pictures. It was only a little cinema in Petworth, but it was nice and had good pictures. Sometimes they'd lay things on for the village children in the vicarage that we used to go to ... I used to get a bit fed up in the winter and with the blackouts, when we just used to sit indoors and read, knit, listen to the wireless, go to bed early, get up early. It wasn't much but, well, you never thought anything about it then. It was what we were used to.

Peter Smith
Schoolboy, Petts Wood, Kent

There were some wonderful shows on the wireless. I suppose the main one was *ITMA* with Tommy Handley and these wonderful characters, and the great verbal dexterity and word-play. You'd get the sound effect of a door rattled and being opened and, 'Can I do you now, sir?' 'Oh, it's Mrs Mopp ...'

and he would rattle off all these funny little anecdotes. Then there would be 'You know, I think that chap's got a double chin.' 'Double gin, sir? I don't mind if I do!' That was Colonel Chinstrap. Then the telephone would ring: 'This is Funf speaking.' Funf, the German spy. We used to look forward to this very much, as people later did to *The Two Ronnies*. There was also Jack Warner – he had a show and his favourite thing was a bicycle bell ringing and him saying, 'Mind my bike, mind my bike.' And, of course, there were the songs: Vera Lynn, of course, and another who used to belt her songs out with much more oomph – Anne Shelton. And we had Bing Crosby's records and Frank Sinatra was coming in . . . Glenn Miller. His music would have been on the American Forces Network, or something like that – 'In The Mood', 'Moonlight Serenade'. There was also this chap, William Joyce, Lord Haw Haw. He was in Germany and used to broadcast this propaganda from there. It used to be 'Jairmany calling, Jairmany calling.' We took no notice of this, really, it was just a big joke.

Noel Dumbrell
Schoolboy, Ashurst, Sussex

I can remember Lord Haw Haw making a terrible mistake over the radio. You see, in 1936, they struck oil in our village of Ashurst, and then it turned out to be seawater. The well was closed down in '36, '37. And he broadcast that they'd bombed Ashurst oil wells. We all laughed and it was the talk of the village . . .

May Moore (George)
Evacuee schoolgirl, Eyam, Derbyshire

During the war Uncle Jim's mother used to come to visit from Wigan. She had a little pub, the Crossed Keys, on Wigan pier. Wigan pier was always a joke – all the comedians used to joke about it. One day Uncle Jim took us to Wigan and we walked down to the little river, full of sludge, and we stood at the end

From *The War Weekly* by Guy Barnett and Derek Tongs

of these little planks and he told us that Lord Haw Haw had put it over [on the radio] that the Germans had bombed Wigan pier! That was hilarious.

Rodney Giesler
Anglo-German schoolboy, Hele, Somerset

Radio drama was terrific as well as documentaries: Richard Dimbleby doing a live broadcast from a bomber over Germany. War correspondents – they brought the war alive. Radio was fabulous, no television then. Radio was better in a way – you could imagine things for yourself. *ITMA* spoke for its time. Tommy Handley was a *god* for me. I loved radio comedy ... All these sayings got into everyday language. You'd go into a pub: 'Another half, Charlie?' 'Oh, ta, I don't mind if I do.' You still hear it today.

Brian Ryland
Schoolboy, Sidcup, Kent, extract from his memoir

One man I loved to listen to on the wireless was Ed Murrow, an American journalist and reporter who kept the American public informed of what was happening here. He had a distinctive voice and a dramatic turn of phrase. He would always start his broadcast with 'This is London, and this is Ed Murrow reporting.' The way he said it always thrilled me, and he would describe exactly what was happening, with the sound of bombs coming down in the background. It was exciting stuff, and he did a great deal in getting American public opinion on our side.

For children lucky enough to live near American camps, Christmas, Thanksgiving and other celebrations meant parties for them, with sweets and presents handed out by the GIs. Their teenage sisters delighted in the cosmetics and nylons from the PX stores and many young girls, despite their parents' disapproval, started to date Americans.

Margaret Woodhead (Butler)
Teenager, Portsmouth, Hampshire

We had lots of troops stationed around the Portsmouth area and we had the Americans stationed in the barracks there. 'You don't talk to Americans,' my parents told me. Well, my friends talked to them and went to their dances and I thought, what they can do, *I* can do. My friends came to me one day and said, 'There's a big concert at the American camp tonight. We don't know whether we can get in but do you want to come?' I said, 'Yes, but don't tell my mum . . .' Well, we were told at the camp, 'Only American troops.' But we pestered until we were told, 'Well, sneak round the back, but if anybody finds you . . .' And that was the night Glenn Miller came to Portsmouth and played, so I actually saw Glenn Miller and heard his band.

Eileen Woods (Cox)
Schoolgirl, Spelding, Kent, extract from her memoir

My sister was very glamorous and these gentlemen from the States were like bees around a honey-pot with Joan. She must have found life hard as a fashion-conscious teenager and was very good with the needle and thread, making do and mending. She even used to recycle lipstick by melting down the last stubs of lipsticks in a tin over the hot plate and as the mixture began to set she would roll the lipstick in Cellophane, making little sticks that she would pop back into their containers to set hard.

Joanna Lawrence (Rogers)
Schoolgirl, West Wickham, Kent

We *dreamed* of nylons and occasionally someone had a pair. It was easier if you knew an American. My mother and the nuns at school thought we'd be *contaminated* by them. Mother thought they were terrible people, and they had a reputation with the ladies. I was quite frightened of them, really. I was so green. They told us the Americans were dangerous and we had no idea why. We were very carefully watched.

Mary Whiteman (Walker)
Wife of chief billeting officer, Saffron Walden, Essex

But the American invasion had a great effect upon the town – a lot of drama, colour and romance. Social life certainly bucked up for girls, teenagers, young women and wives whose husbands were away – all sorts of things happened in Saffron Walden. I know two middle-aged women today who work in the baker's shop; they giggle when the Americans are spoken of. As teenagers, they used to try to get out in the evenings against their fathers' wishes to see them. 'Oh, we *did* have times,' they said, and they did. Some frowned upon it – there was a bit of anxiety about them. They were generous: they always had sweets to give to the children, and if a fair came to the town – this did happen during the war – they'd treat all the children, but at the same time I imagine teenage daughters' mothers did worry and, of course, many did marry and go out to America. The GIs couldn't understand the life over here. They certainly couldn't cope with the cold, and when they were billeted anywhere the coloured Americans went *khaki*, they were so cold. The great meeting place was the Rose and Crown – burnt down in 1969 – and in the minds of the Americans the inn *was* Saffron Walden.

Rodney Giesler
Anglo-German schoolboy, Hele, Somerset

Just prior to D Day, the US Army Signals Corps had to lay a lot of telephone wires. This was a black unit – I never saw any mixed units. They were nice – we used to ride up and down on their trucks. They were so friendly and lonely. They missed their families and they enjoyed our company. My father frowned on it. Not only was he anti-Semite, he was also anti-black. I think a lot of people were, in those days. They referred to them as 'blackies'. It wasn't racial hatred or anything. It was a culture of ignorance.

Countess Mountbatten of Burma, Lady Brabourne
(Patricia Mountbatten)
WRNS, Southampton, Hampshire

There's one lovely story about the Americans during the build-up to their invasion of Europe. They were posted right round the coast; therefore they were in remote little villages. And one old lady was asked what she thought of the Americans. 'Oh,' she said, 'they're very nice, really charming, very considerate, and they have such lovely manners. I like them *very* much. But,' she said, 'I don't care much for some of the white officers who come with them!'

John Leopard
Schoolboy, Deptford, Greater London

I remember whilst in Norfolk chasing after American airmen: 'Any gum, chum?' One was friendly with a local young lady. I was inquisitive and went around where they were. He said, '*You* again! Got something for you.' He gave me a small parachute and said, 'Find yourself a big tree and jump off.' And, being a silly boy, I tried to, but I didn't get far as I got caught up.

Joyce Reeves (Peach Vaitkus)
Teenager, Teddington, Greater London

At the time I was doing clerical work at what is now called British Aerospace. Teddington was Eisenhower's headquarters so we were absolutely surrounded by Americans there. Most people that I've met didn't have a hard word to say about them. They were welcomed into most homes because of their generosity . . . They had their first Thanksgiving dinner just after I met my GI and they opened it up to friends, and I think it was the most exciting day of my life when I saw this huge room with a table down the centre and a turkey about every five or six feet with all the trimmings . . . I think they did have an impact on the area because suddenly the pubs would be full, so the piano would be going and we'd be in there for a sing-song.

We were both sixteen when we met − he had changed his age to get into the service so I was always under the impression that he was older. When I look back I think, Well, probably we were just young kids . . . But there was a lot of glamour. After all, the Americans had all the money they wanted to spend on a girl, and I think this was what caused a lot of jealousy in the English men when they were home on leave. They obviously couldn't afford to spend as much on girls, and the American uniforms were so neat compared with the British ones at that time . . . I didn't feel that I was 'picked up', as they say. I was *introduced* to him. I brought him home to meet my family in the proper way . . . Times were very different then. You wouldn't even think of living with a man, like they do today, or sleeping with him. That would be *unheard* of. Women were expected to be virgins when they married and you'd better make sure you were married for nine months before you had a child! . . . I think my parents were getting a little upset when we started to become serious. It was the thought of the future, I suppose, because I was so young. I remember my dad saying at one time, 'Are you sure you know what you're getting into?' Of course at that age you just say, 'Yes.'

Pamela Winfield (Witcher, née Phillips)
Schoolgirl, Wimbledon, Greater London

My first encounter with the Americans was at the dances in the Wimbledon town hall. I was still at school then. We collected buttons off fellows' uniforms and I went to school one day with an American air-force button on my gymslip. My friends were horrified because nice girls didn't go out with Yanks. I found that very funny – that sort of thing never bothered me, but this was when I resolved I would like to meet some more Americans. How was I going to do it?

That was when I heard that if you joined the American Red Cross, it was a nice way to meet them. So my friend and I signed on in a place in Grosvenor Square [London]. We were assigned work in Portman Square, down in the basement, where we became waitresses. After a while we got a bit bored with this. Then we saw girls passing us all dressed up, and they were going to dances as dance hostesses. The American services had decided by then to try to get a better class of girl into the clubs to stop their men picking up girls in the streets. Marie and I decided that was what we were going to be. Our parents had to sign forms. 'Dance hostesses' sounded rather bawdy, but I managed to convince them that it wasn't going to be like that. We were then sent to the Mayflower Club in the Edgware Road. We had to make something special to wear and clothes were rationed. I don't know how, but we both got hold of enough material to make ourselves pleated skirts. Being pleated, they would twirl and just show a tiny hint of the knickers, which was as daring as we would be at that time. We didn't know how to jitterbug, but we saw it in the movies and had a bit of practice.

So we went to the club. Marie was a much better dancer than I and she was having a whale of a time, and across the floor I noticed this sailor ['Red' Witcher] who was jitterbugging like mad – a fantastic dancer. And he came and asked me to dance. I nearly passed out. I never thought I could keep up with him, but I managed somehow. And to cut a long story short, this was the man I married. Only it wasn't that simple because I had to take on both my parents *and* the United States government.

10. Wartime: Education

When evacuation started in September 1939, schools in reception areas had to cope with vast numbers of extra pupils. Evacuees joined pupils at the local school, regardless of space, staff or resources and often with scant notice. The result was massive overcrowding. One solution was to educate children on a shift system, alternating weeks of morning or afternoon schooling, with hard-pressed teachers, both local and evacuee, having to arrange activities to keep their charges occupied while they weren't being taught. When evacuated schools remained intact, the *ad hoc* premises allocated – church halls, vacant shops, saloon bars of public houses – were often unsuitable. Usually the disruption meant a more limited curriculum for all. Secondary-school city teachers worried about the lack of science facilities in rural schools, as well as the shortage of books, especially for pupils preparing for exams.

Public schools made their own arrangements, as did many smaller private schools, and tended to relocate intact, although many had to share accommodation – Westminster, for instance, shared the premises of Lancing College in Sussex, which caused overcrowding and pressure on resources.

The pastoral role of teachers was pivotal, particularly with younger children trying to cope in a strange new environment. Teachers worked far beyond normal school hours, writing letters to anxious parents and sorting out difficult billeting cases. Often male teachers were accompanied by their wives, who took on the role of social workers, mediating between foster-homes and evacuees.

Those children who had stayed at home when their schools

were evacuated were often left with no education as premises were requisitioned by Civil Defence, the Red Cross, the Auxiliary Fire Service or the armed forces. Some schools reopened when evacuees returned during the Phoney War, but many could not because their premises were being used for other purposes. Emergency schools were set up, but many children were uneducated.

During the Blitz of 1940–41, and the second wave of evacuation, schools that had reopened were once more depleted. During the worst raids they were closed, and for those that remained open, children spent most of the day in the basement shelters. Inevitably lessons were interrupted with a dash to the shelters, which undermined everyone's ability to concentrate. Exams were often taken in difficult circumstances, sometimes in classrooms during air raids or in shelters. When children drifted back after the Blitz had ended, they found their schools had again been requisitioned, so once more emergency schools were opened. Often only part-time attendance was possible, and children of varying ages and ability were taught together. It is estimated that 290,000 children in England and Wales were not receiving full-time education by April 1941.

When married women had been recruited in increasing numbers for war work, the need for infant care became acute. Often groups of mothers made informal arrangements, but the demand was recognized by the government, and by July 1943 1,245 officially sponsored day nurseries were operational, a vast increase from the fourteen that had existed in late 1940. Also, in evacuee reception areas, premises were sometimes found to relieve evacuated mothers of their young children for a few hours every day. The great majority of these wartime day nurseries were closed when the war ended.

By June 1944, when there were still 237,000 schoolchildren in the capital, things had improved, but then the V1s began to arrive and another wave of evacuation left 136,500. Those who remained in London once more found lessons disrupted. Many schools had inadequate shelters, so the indiscriminate bombing meant that children were permitted to stay at home. More than a thousand London schools were damaged during the war, and many had to be demolished. The disruption meant that many children were never able to catch up in subjects such as maths. Education was regarded as a major casualty of the Second World War.

Peter Bennett
Schoolboy, Godalming, Surrey

War was declared in September and we didn't go back to school because the army had taken it over. And it was about three months after that we found out that the school was running in the church hall. Nobody had bothered to contact us or tell us. After that we used the Congregational church – there was a hall at the back – and sat on hard benches. One half of the school came in the morning and the other half in the afternoon. After a period of six months or so, we went back to school. It was a junior school, all lady teachers, a very nice school. We had lessons in gas masks for some time, to get used to wearing them. They used to smell pretty horrible and the eyepieces would cloud up. And, of course, you could hardly hear what other people were saying.

Richard Hancock
Evacuee headmaster, Winchester, Hampshire

First of all there was to be half-time schooling for everybody – equal shares of misery for Peter Symons School and us. The assumption was that we should use the textbooks and facilities of the host school. Well, obviously this wasn't *on* for a long service ... In due course, after a lot of badgering for our own books, Portsmouth rang to say, 'If there's not an air raid on Sunday you can have the mortuary van on Monday to bring up your books.' So we were able to get our textbooks and get some real work done, to keep in fact to the essential timetable we had always had, but spread out in all sorts of ways, boys being taught in odd corners and so on. But we ran that way for the whole of the five years we were there.

John Starling
Evacuee schoolboy, Winchester, Hampshire

Education did suffer in the early days. We shared with Peter Symons School: they went in the morning and we had the afternoon. School was for six days a week in order to get the curriculum in, so both schools had problems keeping their pupils occupied in the free time, and set an awful lot of prep. Sometimes supplementary classes were held in church halls. I got the feeling that the masters of Peter Symons School rather resented having to share their premises, and the groundsman wasn't very happy as we played soccer, not rugby, and he had to dash around putting up soccer posts. There was a degree of isolation so far as the public school was concerned because they had a lovely swimming-pool in the grounds, which was strictly *verboten* so far as we were concerned. You can imagine in the hot summer that we were rather envious of these lads. There was no interaction between us and the public-school boys, we hardly ever saw them, and no interaction between the masters. They tolerated each other and that was it.

That situation lasted well into July 1940. Then the authorities in Winchester decided that we could have class accommodation at Winton House to supplement Peter Symons, so there was a complicated timetable from one place to another. It was more satisfactory in that a five-day week was set up, better for staff and pupils. But Winton House had corrugated-iron classrooms, very sparse, no science rooms as such. The swimming-pool was boarded up to make one big classroom, which was sub-divided. Initially I think standards declined: some of the masters were called up and had to be replaced. A lady teacher joined us, the first ever in the grammar school, but the older masters provided the continuity and did very well. We all adapted to the problems of accommodation and did remarkably well, when I consider the success in the Oxford School Cert [O Level equivalent] in 1942, when I had nine passes, with one or two credits, really all to the credit of the staff.

Richard Hancock
Evacuee headmaster, Winchester, Hampshire

It was never formalized and certainly there was not the same sort of pastoral organization that you now have in schools, but I think it was generally accepted that teachers stood *in loco parentis* particularly when, like us, you were running a kind of very odd boarding establishment. There was a twenty-four-hour series of contacts, and certainly it was an intensification and extension of the process that we'd all met at a school excursion or camp when you do get a different relationship. But it makes confidences greater and the willingness to ask for help – directly or indirectly – greater. This certainly happened ...

Boys are extraordinarily resilient creatures ... Obviously one had the odd disciplinary case, though I would say, on the whole, less than one had in normal circumstances. There was a case I had quite early of a small boy who was discovered shoplifting in Woolworths. I had him in my room and requested a list of what he'd pilfered. I wrote it down – it went on and on and on. Eventually I said, 'Bless my soul, boy, what did you have? A pantechnicon?' And he said, 'No, sir, I asked the lady for a box.' That boy would go far, I thought! Consciously or unconsciously – consciously, I think – we maintained the concept throughout that we were a *Portsmouth* school. We were *not* a Winchester segment. We were very grateful for what Winchester had given us, but when the troubles were over we were going back to our own home. We were Portsmouth and we wished to remain so. I think it would have been unfortunate to try to make them into a sort of hybrid Wykehamist.

Charles Kemp
Evacuee teacher, East Dereham, Norfolk

We started teaching immediately. It was a much older school than ours and without the modern facilities, but we didn't really need them. We had very few materials; mostly it was chalk and talk. Because it was a question of teaching two or three hours instead of five, we had to concentrate on maths and English. I was mainly teaching maths. We were given two rooms. The big trouble was that with fifteen staff and only about two or three classes going, the staff had no staff room, so one taught a class with about six teachers being quiet behind us, which was rather disconcerting at first. But it did enable me to pick up some tips from one of the best teachers I've ever met, a chap called Callum. There was this boy who was the biggest nuisance we had at Gravesend and he carried on in that way during evacuation. But Callum treated him individually, kept him in at night and gave him individual attention, and it was *amazing* the difference in that boy in a couple of months. He was almost a reformed character. Unfortunately he returned to Gravesend because he was coming on fourteen and got work on one of the ships in Gravesend. On his first journey out, his ship was mined in the Thames Estuary and he was killed. But it shows what *can* be done. I think some did gain from evacuation: they lost in education, but I think they gained in knowledge of life.

Because of the part-time teaching system we worked out, it was a big problem having to spend a morning or afternoon out of school. So unless the weather was really bad, we took a group of boys for football or country walks, the wives did the same with the girls, and we talked generally about educational matters with a group of twelve boys or so. If the weather got really inclement, there was a railway bridge under which we'd shelter for a while without getting wet, and we'd carry on talking there. We stood in groups and talked. We became used to it. Children were returning home every week. We returned on 21 January 1940, but left several staff and children there.

Ena Kemp (Drinkwater)
Evacuee helper, East Dereham, Norfolk

A great fellow-feeling developed between teachers and children – we came from Gravesend and so did they, so there was this bond, we were all in it together. This great danger thing that had come upon us, we shared it because we came from the old home town . . . I took them out for long walks in the countryside. Some of the wives were trained teachers and they would take the children for certain subjects. I took them for games, needlework and knitting. I mainly took the girls. It was good for them to have feminine company. They used to come and talk – we were an important link with home.

John Hammon
Schoolboy, Stowting, Kent

I had just begun at grammar school when the war started and the evacuees arrived, and I started school on just one half-day a week. On Monday mornings we went from nine until noon and we were given homework for the rest of the week. This slowly increased because they found other buildings we could go to, so we would be doing three half-days, another set of boys would have the second half of those days, then we progressed to a full week of half-days, and eventually we attended full-time. Very often a full day would mean that we got to school and went straight into the shelter and often wouldn't come out again until four o'clock. We stayed in the shelter all day.

Dorothy Lester
Evacuee primary teacher, Cricklade, Wiltshire

Cricklade was just a small village then, hunting country at the source of the river Thames. I landed up with children aged from five to eleven. I was given a hall connected with the church. I had nothing. I hadn't got a book, a pencil, *anything*. The children sat with *nothing*. One morning, in comes this man all dressed in hunting pink. He looked around and said, 'I suppose you've got everything you need?' I was flabbergasted! The children were sitting on the floor, we didn't even have chairs! I went into Swindon and bought some little sixpenny [3p] reading books, pencils and paper. Then it was decided that this place was unsatisfactory and I was given the Methodist church hall with a stove, which had to be lit every morning. Often we'd go in and the place would be filled with smoke. I'd dash to the pulpit – which was my desk – grab my register, and dash out again. The children sat in the pews. I had little tots, oh dear! I didn't know anything about infants, so I just did my best. Eventually the headmaster from the village school came to see me and I begged some books, some with arithmetic, which I badly needed.

All the children – about thirty by then – had to be examined by the nurse. I had to trail the whole school along the main road of the village to where that nurse inspected them. She turned out to be the daughter of the man in hunting pink who had come to see me. Her name was Lady Mary ... The worst thing was that some of these children had got nits. She dressed their hair with some awful stuff and their little heads were bound up with some white cotton material and I had to walk them back through the village streets like that. Some of them were crying, it was *awful*. People had this image of London evacuees – they thought we were dirty.

There was a huge culture shock: the London children missed the shops and the streets, and so did the mothers who were evacuated with babies. They were horrified at the conditions in the country – no shops, no cinema, no nothing. The local people didn't really want the evacuees and who could blame them? In the country they were right out of the war. Eventually, after a lot of the children had drifted back, a London inspector came and I begged to go home. I went home. When I returned, Cologne School was used by the fire brigade so no education going on there. I was sent to a Jewish school where I taught for quite a while. By then we were having a lot of bombing ...

Margaret Woodhead (Butler)
Evacuee schoolgirl, Zeals, Wiltshire

The village school in Zeals was really nice; there were just two classes. Miss Farthing was a typical village-school teacher. She had never married, was very tweedy with flat shoes, and she used to ride an old sit-up-and-beg bicycle. She took all the little ones and you didn't hear children crying ever because she would sit and talk to one and cuddle another. This was her school and her *life*. Mrs Hollis took all the classes in one room: one set of desks for the first year, another for the second and so on up to the fourth, and each one was taught at their level. When you think about it, she must have been great. Our own teacher was there, but they had an arrangement where one would take one group and one would take another, and the evacuee and local children were all integrated together. I would think there were about twelve evacuees and thirty village children in the big class. Each child had little jobs to do – one did the inkwells, another got the chalks, another made the coffee for the teachers in the morning and tea in the afternoon. Most of the time we had slates with the old grey pencils. Paper was a luxury so you didn't waste it.

I had always had the impression that country children didn't have the same education as we'd had, and our reading standards were a bit higher with more advanced books, but they could teach us an awful lot. Walking to school, they would notice if a plant was appearing and what it would be. We didn't know any of this because we'd never seen it. To sit in the churchyard and observe the birds, or learn the different trees, was part of their education. That was something I appreciated. It wasn't considered a waste of time. It was very different to the school in Portsmouth where we were all girls and where we had separate classes for each subject. Here, the teachers had to know every subject, even first aid. When you think of how people would say, 'Oh, country school teachers!' But in many ways they were more advanced than those in the cities. Then for playtime, whereas we'd go out to the playground to play, in Zeals we weren't just seeing a play-ground and a brick wall: they'd take you on walks in the mornings around the lanes and you'd discover all sorts of things. So I think I received a much wider education there than I would have done in the town.

One of the most fascinating things was the Dorset accent. Miss Hoare, our teacher, couldn't bear to hear the way the local children spoke. The local children would come in and say, 'Where be to Mam, where be to?' instead of, 'Where are you, Mum?' I can hear her now saying, 'You Hampshire children speak very badly as it is; you should say, "How now brown cow?" not "Howe nowe broen coew".' When my parents heard me, they would say, 'Would you mind saying it again? Don't speak like that.' So we must unconsciously have picked up their accent.

Sylvia Townson (Limburg)
Evacuee Jewish schoolgirl, Great Tew, Oxfordshire

It must have been difficult for the local teachers. First they had a group of children all of the same background and roughly the same standard and then, suddenly, this influx of foreigners with obviously different outlooks who would query certain things and create problems for them, but they coped very well and I enjoyed that school. The school itself was on the village green so it was very easy to get into the lanes. And, of course, we all went to Sunday school. We also occasionally went to church on Sundays with the Panting family. Religion didn't enter our home in London at all. The Jewish part of my life wasn't obvious until later on. I don't think there was ever any overt anti-Semitism towards me. Maybe there was to my father when he came to the village with a name like ours. I suppose it could have had some bearing on the frigid way I was treated by the Pantings, but I wasn't aware it had anything to do with my Jewishness . . .

Later, when the rockets started, I went to Wales. The school was very nice and I progressed very quickly. I was definitely advanced when I returned to my school in London. The Welsh are proud that their academic education is second to none. I had a lot to make up when I went there, but at the end of my time I was up with the leaders. I certainly gained a lot. We were able to stay in school from the moment we went in until we left in the afternoon. I wasn't able to do this in London, with the air-raid warnings, so I was able to concentrate for much longer in Wales ... There was never a problem with the local children, more trouble with the evacuees among ourselves. We were perhaps jealous of each other, what sort of houses we were in, whose parents visited more often and what kind of parcels we received from home. I think the local children were surprised by our conflicts and that the different parts of London didn't mix with each other.

Dennis Hayden
Evacuee schoolboy, Highclere, Hampshire

School was the Crux Easton village school. This was about a mile from Grotto Lodge and we had to walk both ways, no school buses, across fields. The school was a large hall – or so it appeared to us – in which there were sixteen children whose ages ranged from five to fourteen. There were two teachers. One, Miss Scott, who taught the infants, used to come to school on a very ancient bike, which had a skirt-guard on the rear mud-guard. And she always reminded me of the wicked witch out of *The Wizard of Oz* – very upright on an upright bike. And she seemed very ancient. The other lady was a Mrs Cudby and she was rather overpowering and overbearing. And everybody did the same thing at the same time. If we were learning tables, depending on your age, you only learnt them, say, as far as the three times table. If you were seven or eight, you learnt the five times table. Come dinner time, no school dinners being available, we had a large aluminium kettle, which was put on the pot-bellied stove and we always had a cup of Horlicks, but this was only in the winter. There were always house-martins flying around inside the school and swallows or swifts coming in as well ... The playground was mainly shingle with a large pine tree in the centre. And beyond the pine tree was part of a field which the local farmer had stuck a fence across; on the other side he kept his cows. One day some aircraft were practising aerial gunnery at a target towed by another

South Road

~~N~~ S Devon

18 6.40

Dear Mummy and Daddy

I am happy in my billet ~~the people are nice but at school~~ it is horrible everything is different we have french names sing french songs. Three ~~othed~~ boys are billeted with me the name of the landlady is Mrs Milbourne I have a lot off homework to do so I will write a longer letter later on

Yours

Graham

PS
there is ~~not~~ the dinner are horrible ~~a lot of cutlery~~ so I had to eat my first course without a knife and my second without

Graham Willmot writes home, having been evacuated from vulnerable Suffolk to the safety of Devon aircraft and they were flying rather low and suddenly one of the cows in the field, much to our delight, leapt up in the air, did about three paces, then fell down dead with all four legs sticking up. We thought this most amusing at the time.

I think possibly in the beginning we might have been a little bit higher in standard, and I suppose our level did drop down quite a bit till we came to their level. Desks were primitive, the sort of two-seater upright type of thing with a lid. There wasn't any electricity, just oil lamps suspended from the ceiling. I think we may well have finished earlier during the winter but, of course, sometimes during the daytime we did have to turn the oil lamps on. My parents, when they came to visit, noticed a vast change in the way we spoke. I remember one day I said to my father, 'I aster about it.' And he said, 'Asters are flowers. You *asked* her about it.'

Peter Smith
Evacuee schoolboy, Penton, Cumberland

We were enrolled in the local school, which catered for all ages from five to fourteen. It was mixed education, just two main groups, something like five to eight and then eight on to fourteen – those that continued to fourteen. This was a farming community and often the children were away from school, particularly boys, at harvesting time. Mr Reah was the headmaster and there were one or two teachers. I was looking forward to sitting the scholarship and I think Mr Reah did his best to try and keep me ahead, but, with respect, most of the children were well behind us. We also had a number of children who had been evacuated from the Newcastle area and they were just as rough as the farm children. However, it was a very happy time there although the education was a bit sparse. The boys used to dig the headmaster's garden in the mornings and we grew the vegetables for the school dinner. And the girls used to prepare the school lunch, which basically used to consist of minced meat, potatoes and root vegetables. As I've said, the children were rather rough and I came into contact rather abruptly with a lot of swearing, and I suppose this was when I first heard the F word. A lot of those youngsters were semi-illiterate and so the effing, effing, effing went on.

The winter time was quite interesting in the deep snow because the corkers on the clogs were great for sliding on ice, and there were a number of ponds we'd go sliding and skating about on. The school also possessed two superb sledges. One of these would seat about four children and it had a small bogey sledge in the front between the two front runners and you could steer this with two ropes. We had good fun there. Otherwise, we used to kick a football around ... Eventually I sat the scholarship in Carlisle and went to Carlisle grammar school, a long and arduous journey. In the first term or two we only had schooling in the mornings because boys from Newcastle schools attended the classrooms in the afternoons. By that time we were living with a different family in Bessiestown, the Armstrongs.

Noel Dumbrell
Schoolboy, Ashurst, Sussex

Education? Well, I didn't even get up to fractions and decimals, didn't get that far. Looking back, they [the teachers] wore many hats: they were air-raid wardens, they used to feed us, bring the milk, ushered us right the way down to the church when sirens went to hide us underneath the pews ... I would say that our education was affected. It was quite a shambles when the evacuees came. How the teachers managed, I don't know. So much time was spent, when the air raids came, running down to the shelter – a big one was dug for us near the school by the soldiers. When I think of it, the teachers didn't have much time for lessons ... Later in life I found my education not so good from the formal point of view, but we had a marvellous education of going on nature walks. The local boys and girls knew all about the coun- tryside, but the evacuees – God bless them – didn't. And we used to go right across the fields, by the old Dutch barn and the ponds, deep in the country, down the rivers, and we could show them all the different animals and creatures – otters, badgers and foxes were all there ... The river, a tributary of the river Adur, was so clean that we could drink out of it and did. It was a beautiful sight to see a grass snake swimming across the water with his head up. You'd walk through the woods and see a nightjar or a woodpecker – they'd never seen anything like that in their lives. A lot of the evacuees were so distressed and would cry for their parents, and I think this probably helped.

The rich people in the country realized their children weren't being educated, and because they could pay their children went to the grammar school in Steyning. I wasn't worried at all. My mum and dad couldn't afford it and most of us didn't go. But half a dozen or so went there, the first school uniforms we saw and the caps – it was a bit of 'them and us', I suppose – 'the edumacated ones', we used to call them. But I was 'edumacated' at Ashurst University, which was our tiny little school. But a funny thing, later on in life I turned out to be better off than them.

David Gray
Evacuee schoolboy, Bransbury, Yorkshire

I'd gone to a kindergarten in York and then a private fee-paying school, a pretty sheltered schooling. And the rough and tumble of the village school! Well, I didn't understand the language to begin with – it was very broad Yorkshire. I wasn't very happy there. A big lad used to take it out on me and beat me up on the mile back from school we had to walk. But the other children were very nice to us. There were *huge* teenage farm girls, thirteen and fourteen, totally foreign creatures to me, and the ribaldry that used to go on in the back desks with the big farm boys, who were also jammed into those tiny desks! I became aware of things I wasn't in any way knowledgeable about. The teacher was a genius because she taught eight-year-olds until fourteen and she had a great leather strap hanging from the blackboard and it got used sometimes on the big'uns when the boys staged a raid on the girls' lavatory at playtime. It was real life. It reminds me of Laurie Lee's *Cider with Rosie*, this growing up in a village school.

Kathleen Schaller
Evacuee schoolgirl, Lack, Northern Ireland

We started to attend the village school, which had only three rooms. Every morning the Protestants of all ages would gather in one room with the headmaster, and all the Catholics in another room with the Catholic woman teacher. And when we'd had our little religious service, we would then be mixed. My younger brothers and I were all in one class, so it was very backward for us. I had passed my eleven plus at that time, and the headmaster used to give me private lessons in his house at night. This went on for about a year, but it was very unsatisfactory ... My father was living in a house in Essex, which we had moved into in 1939. It was his stroke that forced us to go home ... When we got back, I immediately went to the good grammar school I should have gone to and the headmistress tried to make sure that I made up what I had missed.

Joan Reed (Chantrelle)
Evacuee schoolgirl, school camp, Itchingfield, Sussex

Our age range at the camp was eleven to sixteen, all from the Thomas Hood School, with one small dormitory of children just below age, not our children. Teachers came from our own school, and there were some local people working there, including the cooking staff. We had house-mothers who were the masters' wives. We had darning nights and hair-washing nights and we all had to look after our own dormitories. It was very civilized, really. We did the boys' darning and mending and they mended our shoes. Discipline was firm, very strict timing for everything. As it was co-ed, it must have been a responsibility, but we were so naïve in those days that there wasn't any harm done, although we did have one fourteen-year-old girl who was made pregnant by a boy from the village. She left the camp and went home. We had a choir – I was the school soloist – and dances, and sports in summertime, all the games.

Towards the end we started a farm with pigs and chickens and one of the teachers brought bees and we had allotments. There was plenty going on and lots to do. I had my own little garden. I loved the outdoors, and in the springtime the woods and spinneys and the bluebells and primroses to me were out of this world, the place was carpeted with them, and there was plenty of wildlife in the woods.

We had the curriculum right across the board, all the lessons we would have had in London. We had musical appreciation and domestic science, too. I was made head girl during my last year at school. I was over sixteen when I left in the summer of 1942. I didn't take the School Certificate, it was the boys who were mostly encouraged to take this, but I was more interested in outdoor life and extra-curricular activities. I stayed as long as I possibly could, I would have stayed *for ever*. I felt very important. I was very popular with the others and the staff, and I had glowing reports. I would never have had the same excitement or freedom at home, coming from such a puritanical background. I had such fun there. It didn't start out that way, but if there hadn't been a war I wouldn't have had such fun.

Gwendoline Stewart (Watts)
Evacuee schoolgirl, Ashby-de-la-Zouch, Leicestershire

The school didn't mean much in those days because it was hit and miss, hit and miss. Your teachers weren't always the same teachers. You go from your own school to sitting on your bottom on the floor of an hotel's ballroom and trying to work on your lap, then going into a strange school and strange surroundings. It means that you lose the continuity ... I had liked school until evacuation, but after that school just became something you had to go to and you were glad when you got back out ... When I took myself home to Birmingham, the school had closed down. So by this time I was fourteen and a half ... A few weeks went by and I got myself a job working as a trainee telephonist-receptionist at a little factory in Birmingham.

Joseph Stagno
Gibraltarian evacuee, Kensington, London

Until we got to school we just played about. We were taken by
the WVS on little sightseeing tours of London. Eventually we
started school. It was in the Victoria and Albert Museum in
Brompton Road. One small part, half facing Exhibition Road,
was open as a museum, the rest of it, with the main entrance in
Brompton Road, became our school. Some of the rooms in the
museum were fitted out like classrooms. It didn't compare at all
with what we'd had in Gibraltar: they tried to put us in groups
of the same academic level and taught the basics, tried to keep
us occupied. I definitely think my education suffered, very much
so. It probably stopped in the early part of 1940, started again a
year later, early '41, and finished in the middle of '41 when I
went into the navy, although we did have schooling there. Had
I carried on where I was in Gib, my education would have been
better.

Rodney Giesler
Anglo-German schoolboy, Hele, Somerset

King's College was mainly a boarding-school. We day-boys were
in a minority and we were heavily resented by boarders because
we went home every night. There was a lot of antagonism there.
The other thing concerned my German background. At the time
they were sending foreign nationals to the Isle of Man and Canada
[for internment], and plain-clothes police turned up at our house
one morning. My father still had a sister living in Germany. I can
remember them taking our house apart. No warning. This deeply
upset my father. At the same time my half-brother was thrown
out of the RAF. And that was compounded by the bullying we
had at school. Two or three mornings a week in school assembly
there'd be an announcement: someone's father missing in action,
someone's brother, an Old Boy killed. And with German names,
my brother and I took the brunt. It was usually after games in
the afternoon, back in the showers – the wet-towel treatment.

The usual devilment: throwing our clothes in the showers so we couldn't get dressed. This is why I've always boiled at any discrimination, whether it's anti-Jewish, anti-coloured or anything. That went on for quite a long time. They couldn't understand that we were equally patriotic, and never condoned anything. The staff turned a blind eye to it ... I never told my parents and, anyway, my father would've been heartbroken: he was so sensitive about his German roots. There was also the public schools' ethos. It wasn't manly to complain: 'Bullying made a man of me.' We took the rough with the smooth.

Donald Swann
Schoolboy, Westminster School, London

Westminster School was evacuated to Lancing College. We shared the school and we were very edgy about it, and the idea of being on top of another school must have upset the Lancing boys no end ... And then, of course, it was right opposite France, and there was endless trouble over there by then ... What eventually happened was that London was considered the safest place. That was the Phoney War. So we were all going back to delightful Westminster and the strange, archetypal, medieval environment that we lived in. And, of course, just as we got back there was the Blitz, so off we went again. This time it was Exeter University. And then finally we went to Bromyard and finished up outside Worcester, trying to keep our identity going.

That last year at school was the happiest one, war or no war. To rise through the ranks, as it were, and find that you can more or less choose your own work! I was now studying languages, which I loved, and messing about ever so much with music ... On my last day at school, I remember going and telling the headmaster, John Christie, that I had become a conscientious objector, and I knew he strongly disapproved. I then went on to do a 'wartime year' at Oxford. That was an extraordinary time, a depleted Oxford. I remember walking into a room and a boy said, 'We're finished.' And I said, 'What do you mean, "We're finished"?' He said, 'The aristocracy.' Of course they weren't finished. But they weren't to know that. I do recall feeling uncomfortable at times. I remember being called utterly idealistic and certainly recall being called a coward. I think it did affect me. I think it made me feel as though I was pinned back in some way, made into a sort of minority thing, which I am sure has survived to this day ... But I felt that by non-violence, there was something I *could* do. I had a sure glimpse of it. But it wasn't pleasant, no, certainly not, because some of my friends were about to go into very dangerous places ... I wanted to find a position where I could say, 'I'm going to do something at least as brave as you lot.' I was ready to join an ambulance unit or participate in a non-violent humanitarian war effort.

Tony Parker
Schoolboy, Manchester, Lancashire

Friends of my own age thought I was completely mad to be a pacifist. I remember I used to argue with them at school about war. I certainly didn't know anybody else at school or of my own age group who held these views. Then, as we got older, they started going into the forces, and they used to come to see me when home on leave, and not one of them held it against me. We used to argue the rights and wrongs of it, but they never changed their friendliness towards me, which I thought was remarkable.

Peter Bennett
Schoolboy, Godalming, Surrey

School was never boring because we were always doing different things. And, of course, there were air-raid warnings and we used to go into the air-raid shelter that was under another building. And we used to do what was called 'French knitting', which was a cotton reel with four nails in the top, and you wound the wool round and the wool goes through the hole in the cotton reel ... I never got much further than that. You were supposed to be making something out of this long tube of knitting. Must have been dreadful being a school teacher in those days, trying to keep the kids happy.

I can't remember at any time during the war having new books. They were always old books, and dead boring, no coloured pictures whatsoever. Everything was boring from that point of view. And we had to supply our own pens and pencils and look after them, because they were virtually unobtainable. And, of course, after the war – because the effects of war go on a long time afterwards – when people came back, a lot of them did a one-year teacher training, and some of them were all right and some of them were dreadful and had a very difficult time.

Peter Izard
Schoolboy, Civil Defence messenger, Beckenham, Kent

It was being indoors and listening to the bombs and hearing the shrapnel rattling on the roof that was so awful. In the midst of all this we did our School Cert. And every time the warning went we ran to the shelters. We were under the trust of the headmaster that we wouldn't talk about the answers, and we didn't. And during that time, if you weren't taking exams, you were on the school roof spotting the flying bombs and pressing a bell if you saw one coming.

Mary Whiteman (Walker)
Wife of chief billeting officer, Saffron Walden, Essex

Miss Garry, the principal of the training college, felt that a nursery school would help the town, the evacuees and her students. The Friends' Meeting House had a big room upstairs and a smaller one, which was used as a kitchen, and so a nursery school was founded there for twenty children. These were very rare before the war. They did the cooking there, which meant the mothers could find jobs, and it was run throughout the war. The health of the children improved so much. It was visited by R. A. Butler himself, who was busy with his Education Act, to whom it had been recommended as a simple, good nursery school. The children all slept in their little beds after lunch and, as my friend Molly who worked there told me, you'd get a golden-haired baby sitting up and swearing like a Billingsgate porter. The language was simply wonderful! Local children went in, too, before the end of the war. We also had three residential nurseries in three big houses. They were a great help.

Joanna Lawrence (Rogers)
Schoolgirl, West Wickham, Kent

Looking back, our education was pretty basic. We had a very narrow range of subjects during the war years, unless you were at a big public school that was evacuated with all its staff and kept them. If we had stayed at one school I think we'd have had a better education. It was getting used to new schools all the time and teachers who didn't know you. We kept getting these upheavals ... Then the big difficulty was that after the war the universities were full. People were coming out of the war and the chances of getting in then were practically nil. You had to be at a very good public school to get in. I got in later.

Dennis Hayden
Evacuee schoolboy, Highclere, Hampshire

I felt that at the end of my school life, my standard of education was so low that I had to do a rethink and a reteach on myself. Literally by buying a book and starting to re-form letters and join them up together to teach myself handwriting because mine looked a complete shambles. I certainly don't hold this against anyone. At least we did get *some* education, which possibly people in a town that was being bombed didn't have.

Brian Ryland
Schoolboy, Sidcup, Kent, extract from his memoir

I had my 14th birthday in December and during the last week at school I was summoned to the headmaster's study. I still have the reference he gave me to give to any prospective employer:

just a small piece of paper upon which he wrote, 'Brian Ryland has attended here for the last three years. He is a quiet lad who tries hard.' This would make a good epitaph, with one word altered: 'a quiet lad who tried hard'. That was all I had to show for my years at school: I had nothing to offer anyone, and was worn out by the experience of the last few years, thin, undersized and shy beyond belief. I did feel a great relief that one nightmare had now come to an end, but what lay ahead seemed another long, dark tunnel . . .

Sylvia Townson (Limburg)
Jewish schoolgirl, Paddington, London

I did well at school after the war and passed the scholarship with a very high pass and got entry to the local grammar school. I was the first year when they had non-paying students, the time of the reorganization of the educational system.

Reg Baker
Schoolboy, Bethnal Green, London

Oh, I think my education would have been the same without the war. See, in the East End you're not looking to any future, you're just doing it as it's coming to you. You wait 'cause you want to go to work; going to work seems a lot better, but you realize afterwards it's not. But they used to write you out, you know. You'd go and see the headmaster before you leave and he'd say, 'Been a good boy?' 'Yes, sir.' 'Played truant a lot?' 'No, sir.' And yet, being wartime, I could have stayed away – I've done it – *weeks*; if I wanted a week off, I could do it and they really couldn't challenge you.

Millicent Morgan (Miller)
Schoolgirl, Hackney, London

I don't think as far as my parents were concerned that education played a major part in our lives at all. But when I went back to school in London I found it all so exciting. Everything was exciting, you know, because I'd missed that two and a half years of growing up in London. Yes, I was thrilled to be back and go back to school and see some of the girls I'd been evacuated with now grown-up, and some of the old teachers that I'd started off with.

Evelyn Fee (Moss)
Evacuee mother of five, Byworth, Sussex

When we moved to Byworth the children used to go to school in Petworth for the full day. Jean was in the infants' and Eileen and June were in the big girls'. June, the eldest, was unhappy at Petworth School. She used to get very upset when the children used to say things about 'vaccies'. The others didn't notice it so much, perhaps because they weren't so old. I forget how old Juney was when I took her away. I got her into the convent school at Midhurst, which she liked very much. The children all passed scholarships, and my youngest son, Roy, passed for university. The boys went to Midhurst grammar school and Jeannie and Eileen to Horsham high school. No, I don't think their education suffered because of the war. In fact, I think they've got a lot to be thankful for. I've often wondered to this very day what would have happened to all of us if we'd gone back to London ...

Sylvia Taylor (Bell)
Schoolgirl, Hook, Surrey

We were ostracized to a certain extent [as children of a conscientious objector] and it was quite obvious that the teachers at school knew of our background and were therefore a little awkward with us. Afterwards my mother claimed that I never won a scholarship in the eleven-plus exam because of what my father had been. Obviously one would doubt that, but I think it *could* have been possible ... The war certainly disrupted my education because I don't really remember learning anything in the war years at all, and I've been backward ever since. I've done all my learning through reading books since then.

Peter Smith
Schoolboy, Petts Wood, Kent

My contemporaries at Bromley grammar school seemed to have streaked ahead of what I had done at Carlisle, although we were using very similar textbooks. Otherwise I was able to hold my own fairly well and usually came within the upper ten in the class at term's end.

Margaret Woodhead (Butler)
Evacuee schoolgirl, Zeals, Wiltshire

The papers for the exam you took when you were eleven were sent by the Hampshire authority to Zeals. We just sat down in the village school and took it with all the village children looking at us. I passed and so did my friend Mickey, and this was why we went on to Winchester . . . I don't think my education suffered. I think we still had the same chances of education that they have now. I know when I went back to my old school in Portsmouth, those who wanted to take the examination for the municipal college were given special privileges at the school to study for this examination, so we were given every chance to do what we wanted. The main drawback was that as colleges were evacuated, even if you passed there were only so many you could get into – the colleges couldn't take so many. I actually left school at fourteen and went into floristry, which I enjoyed.

Charles Kemp
Evacuee teacher, East Dereham, Norfolk

Evacuation improved my teaching. Six teachers standing at the back [there was no staffroom] while one was teaching, and hearing what these very good teachers said and did, enabled me to improve my teaching. The children lost educationally, but gained socially. They remembered it for many years afterwards.

Richard Hancock
Evacuee headmaster, Winchester, Hampshire

We brought back at the end of the war almost exactly the number that had been evacuated in the beginning, which was quite remarkable. We could have done this, of course, only with the generosity of the people of Winchester. We did our best by running what was in effect a boarding-school when we had these premises at Winton House in which we had a hundred boys, along with some other biggish houses, which staff members ran. This made it less of a burden for Winchester people.

Gwendoline Stewart (Watts)
Evacuee schoolgirl, Ashby-de-la-Zouch, Leicestershire

My father was a great one for saying, 'Study, study, study.' But I don't think I've missed a lot by not continuing school. I've always gone to night school. I speak French and German, which I've picked up by travelling. I've always travelled, I've liked to move around ... And I find travel is a better education than sitting at a desk reading about it – get out there and *see* it!

John Leopard
Schoolboy, Sidcup, Kent

Tuberculosis, TB, was prevalent at the time. I was given just three months to live, my aunt later told me. I was first put into an isolation ward but I responded well to treatment and they transferred me to the main ward. They were amazed at my recovery. I was left with a large hole in one lung and the other was like a sponge ... So, I had no schooling after the age of twelve when I was diagnosed with TB. My father's regiment and the Ford Motor Company, where he had worked before the war, paid for me to go to a commercial college for eighteen months to further my education. The then Labour government did nothing at all. My local Labour MP tried, but there were two departments arguing between themselves as to responsibility ...

David Pritchard
Infant, Trevince nursery hostel, Cornwall, extract from his memoir

Had I been a normal child, no doubt I would have handled my
stay at the nursery better. As it was, my early upbringing, under
such stressful circumstances [blitz in Plymouth] had not fitted me
for a lengthy stay away from my family. All the disturbed nights
and stress of my father's absence at sea and subsequent loss had
taken their toll on my nervous system, so to find myself apparently abandoned in an isolated country house along with a crowd
of other children must have been quite disturbing to me. Consequently, no amount of care would have made up for the loss that
I must have felt. One of the results was the bed-wetting, which
was a more obvious and embarrassing scar I brought back with
me from the nursery ... In my case this went on for many years.
Another problem that I can only attribute to my stay at Trevince
was my acute shyness and my low threshold of embarrassment.
Not that I would in any way want to blame or condemn the
staff of Trevince, they did the best that they could in very trying
circumstances. Thousands of children of all ages found themselves
sent away and separated from their families during the war for
safety reasons. Some enjoyed this time and even benefited from
it, but there were many like me who found it difficult and even
worse. We were just as much casualties of war as the sailor lost
at sea or the soldier killed on the battlefield. In fact, we were part
of a whole generation who experienced things that children of
our age should never have had to go through.

11. Wartime: Life Overseas

Wartime life for overseas evacuees was very different from that of their counterparts in Britain, the uprooting far more dramatic and severe. While the majority of children evacuated within the British Isles could exchange regular letters with their parents and even enjoy parental and home visits, overseas evacuees were often thousands of miles from home. Mail contact was usually erratic, with letters taking weeks or months to arrive, if they reached their destination at all. Many children heard news of the war and were anxious about their families, wondering if they'd ever see them again. Before 1939, few British people had travelled abroad and, apart from what they saw in films, knew little about the United States or even the Dominions. The culture shock evacuees experienced was huge. And, of course, they met the reverse on returning home in 1945. After such a long separation, many were reunited with strangers, and some found it impossible to restore old family relationships.

The billeting experience seems to have mirrored that in the UK: some children were hosted by kind families, while others found themselves at the mercy of cold foster-parents, and were even abused sexually. With their parents so far away, these children felt helpless and abandoned, which left in some a long-term legacy of insecurity and lack of self-confidence. However, the majority seem to have settled happily and adapted well to their new environment. Although food and other materials were rationed in most countries during the war, this was nothing like the austerity experienced in Britain, and most overseas evacuees had access to fruit, sweets and other goodies, and far better clothing and shoes than they would have worn at home.

Derek Diamond
British evacuee schoolboy, Hamilton, New Zealand

Hamilton was a nice, friendly place. The house we lived in backed on to a small lake and a park, which was used by all the people in the town, a nice place to play ... One episode that perhaps epitomizes this time is that I became ill. I contracted jaundice as a schoolboy, and I spent something like five weeks in hospital recovering from an infection of the liver. When it was time to leave the hospital, it was arranged through my cousins that I would go and recuperate on a sheep farm two or three hours' drive from Hamilton. I remember spending a wonderful four or five weeks being completely wild. No one asked you to have a bath at night, no one told you to change your clothes, no one worried, and I simply travelled with the sheep farmer on his rounds and played with the children in the farmyard. All this had to come to an end, and I was made to have a bath and my clothes were washed very thoroughly for the first time in ages. New Zealand farm life was a very simple affair then.

I don't remember any hardship or rationing in New Zealand – we could get milk, butter, eggs, meat. I think these were in excess supply during the war since their markets had been cut off from them. There were only a couple of things that made me realize the war was on: one was that my father was far away in Britain. Correspondence was very difficult: my mother used to write to him once a week and it was a great day when the mail arrived from England and we had news of what was happening to our family there. The other way I learnt about the war was occasionally seeing troops in the town. It was obviously a training area because troops came on exercises in these extensive, unoc-cupied bush areas ... I don't recall any conflict occurring in New Zealand, but the Japanese involvement in the war, the invasion of New Guinea and the bombing of the Australian city of Darwin must have made a difference for adults. It certainly didn't make any impression on a primary-school boy in Hamilton during those years.

Literally just up the road from the house we rented was the

primary school I attended. I don't have any other than happy memories of going to primary school, playing football and rugby. At school our class was about thirty children, and we sat at small wooden desks. I shared mine with a pupil who was always late to school and often arrived at ten or eleven o'clock after school started at nine, then promptly went to sleep. I remember the teacher telling me, 'Be careful not to wake him up. He has walked a very long way to come to school.' He was one of the Maori children, who had obviously walked for one or two hours to get there.

Marjory Mingo (Ursell)
British evacuee schoolgirl, Victoria, Australia, extract from her memoir

Then Fremantle, Western Australia, greetings, and we had arrived at our home for the next five years. I lived on a dairy farm in the Gippsland area of Victoria staying with the brother of one of my father's colleagues. It was a new world to me – I cycled four miles to school each day along country roads. The two daughters of the family did the same and we all went to the technical school there. I was someone special and everyone had just that bit of sympathy and really looked after me. So healthy to spend my early teens in such fresh air, such exercise, such fun trying to ride that horse – the Saturday ride along the road a couple of miles to collect the daily mail and deliver it to the neighbours on the return. More often than not I was chucked off Mahonga's back. He just hated this chore ...

Elizabeth 'Bussie' Grice (Hearn)
British evacuee schoolgirl, Nova Scotia, extract from letter, 5 July 1940, to her mother

I will tell you what struck me most when I first landed: the town is neither town nor country. You keep coming to a very towny sort of place and then to a very countrified place. The roads are marvellous but are hilly. Halifax has some marvellous old houses with drives leading up to them like country houses do in England.

The flashy way people dress and talk put me off at first but I suppose I will get used to it. This is a marvellous hotel and this is certainly a wonderful experience but I don't think I could face another trip, it is too much like hard work saying goodbye.

Countess Mountbatten of Burma, Lady Brabourne (Patricia Mountbatten)
British evacuee schoolgirl, New York, USA

I was very homesick in the beginning. It took about six months to get over the feeling, rather, of resentment: your food piled high on your plate, every light was turned on, and no account was taken of the reports of what was going on in the war. And at home they were sitting there, waiting to be invaded ... I think the Battle of Britain did hit people's consciousness. You saw it on the newsreels, and in those days the newsreels were great. There were 'isolationists', who certainly didn't want America to have anything to do with the war, but there were many people who were very pro-British. There was a wonderful organization called 'Bundles for Britain', which was sending over all the things that were short in the country.

The Blitz was horrible. My mother's life then was going off to the shelters at night to see what she could do to help as soon as the air-raid warnings went. Being so far away, it was awful, because you didn't really know, and one just prayed that nothing would happen, and luckily nothing did happen – but a really anxious time. Then, on 23 May 1941, I was coming home from school and I saw a news placard. I forget the exact words, but something like, 'The [HMS] *Kelly* has been sunk.' Of course that was terrible. I assumed that if the *Kelly* had been sunk, then very likely my father [the captain] would have been lost with the ship. The next day the message got through that he was one of the crew who survived. That was a very sad time. I adored my father, we were very close ...

Sheila Cooley (Westcott)
British evacuee schoolgirl, Montréal, Canada, extract from her memoir

I think I settled fairly well as I was not the only evacuee in my class. There was another English girl, a Jew from Holland and another from France, and a Yugoslav. Educationally there were some stumbling-blocks. Canadian history and geography were unknown to me but I found that very interesting to learn. French was quite unknown to me and in Québec that was something that had to be learnt fairly fast ...

I was homesick after the first novelty of being there wore off. I felt a complete outsider and my clothes, accent and manners were all wrong ... Some things in the house were new to me, the ice-cream maker, the toaster, washing-machine and, strange though it may seem now, I don't think I had seen a shower ... At the end of October I experienced Hallowe'en for the first time and went up the hill with Joan and the twins, all dressed up, to get goodies from the various houses. Years of experience had taught them where you got the best offerings from the houses at the top of Westmount ... My first winter was learning to adapt to the life and the snow and its attendant sports. I made friends at school with both Canadians and evacuees, and I was often asked back to their homes but was always diffident about asking them back. Some time in the autumn the present Queen, then Princess Elizabeth, broadcast to evacuees everywhere. At school all the British evacuees were gathered in the library to listen and afterwards someone had to write a letter to the Princess thanking her for her words and we all signed it ...

The war went on and I heard from my parents irregularly – letters came in batches. Things had changed at home. The bombing was bad, over 300 bombs within a quarter of a mile of my home. One landed in the nursery garden next door and my home was badly damaged ... In 1942 Father joined the RAF ... My parents rented their home to some Belgians and Mother went to Rochdale to live with Granny and started as a full-time aide in the local hospital there. All this was a bit hard for me to comprehend as I could no longer visualize my parents in their home as I remembered them.

Frank Bower
British evacuee schoolboy, Napanee, Ontario, Canada, extract from his memoir

We got on with Mrs Russell like a house on fire and became firm friends. She supported us when people in the town tried to talk about 'how unruly those English evacuees had become'. She had no children of her own and, quite simply, we became 'her children'. She said to my mother, 'Thank you for lending me the children I could never have.' She holds a special place in my life for all her kindness. I loved that tall, gaunt-looking lady with the severe appearance that put off some people, but beneath whose apron there beat a heart of pure gold. She was my friend.

Geoffrey Shaw
British evacuee schoolboy, Waterloo, Ontario, Canada, letter to his parents, 21 June 1942

Farmer G. Shaw!!!!!!!!!!!! Believe it or not, I am working on the farm for the summer ... We (the farmer, Mr Weber, and I) go up to the second farm, Point Clark, about five miles from Kintail, about once a week for two or three days ... Here is an outline of a typical day on the main Villanova Farm at Waterloo: 6.10 a.m. – arise and shine, feed calves, start milking machine, finish milking – breakfast, clean out horse and cow stables, work in field (hoe thistles, corn, fix fence, etc.), come in for dinner, work in fields (or mow lawn – which is considerable), finish work in field – fetch cows on bicycle, supper, milk, finish milking – clean out stables. 8.45 p.m. finish work. By that time I am ready for bed, I assure you! On Point Clark we have to work like the deuce to get everything done in a hurry – usually work from 5 to 10.30 at night – sometimes 12.30 in the season. What a life! Well, anyway, it's a healthy life, and I'm paid a minimum of $15 (more than £3) a month ...

Keith Goldthorpe
British schoolboy, Sabathu, India

We moved to Sabathu. It is south of Simla, about 6,000 feet high, a beautiful area to live in. We lived in a two-storey barrack upstairs and a few people who came out [of Burma] with us lived there too. There were little cookhouses at the back, the rooms were very big with big verandas all around. I remember the monsoons: for a long time it wouldn't rain, then suddenly the clouds would come up and we used to cheer because it would start to rain. We would stand out in the rain, in the hailstones. As they say in France, 'It rained like strings.'

There were steep hillsides from the veranda and zigzag paths going up this hill, and with my father's binoculars I used to watch these people walking up these paths. I remember going into the village and the people were very friendly ... I was aware, particularly as I was getting older, that my father was fighting the Japanese. I realized that we were safe but my father wasn't. He would arrive usually late at night; I would be asleep in my mosquito-netted bed. I remember him in uniform, looking very gaunt and drawn, and then he'd recover and start looking normal and then would be off again. My mother was always very worried. She knew what would happen to Japanese prisoners and she knew he was always very close to death. I detected it in the strain and stress, and think that had an effect on me, particularly as I became a teenager.

School was mainly for Europeans – a long, low, single-storey building. Most of the children I was at school with were British officers' children although there were a few Indians ... A vivid memory was the snake-charmer who used to travel around the school fields; in his wheelbarrow he had sacks and pots and things and he'd get all this out in the middle of the school field, and I remember this massive python in a sack, and we used to stand and let the python go through our legs – it was very tame ... I was at a disadvantage when I returned to Britain because I didn't really have constant schooling, it was intermittent. Going to the local school at Ludgershall when we returned in '45 was a bit of an eye-opener for me. I integrated quite well and had a lot of friends, but it was different and gaining qualifications was slower. But eventually I found my little niche, got on and went to University College in London. But what I experienced in Burma and India was *really* education.

British children trapped in Germany and countries under German occupation had to keep their heads down. The Channel Islanders spent four years under German occupation – an experience they shared with France and the rest of occupied Europe. In Guernsey, approximately twenty-five square miles, there were 20,000 troops and the same number of local people. As the war progressed, conditions became increasingly severe, and the population was strictly controlled.

Hunger became so acute on the Channel Islands that by the middle of the war no cat, dog or horse was safe, and potato peelings were sold in the market for twopence [1p] a pound. Food and commodities were sold at controlled prices, and generally people lived by scrounging. School continued, cinemas were open, but the curfew meant that social life was curtailed. Although radios were banned, an underground organization of five men, the Guernsey Underground News Service (GUNS) circulated BBC news around the island from May 1942 until they were caught by the Gestapo in February 1944.

The Channel Islanders were close to the reality of atrocities: Jewish friends were deported, and there were hungry, bedraggled lines of slave labourers for all to see. But they were not subjected to the Blitz or V1 and V2 raids. In common with the peoples of occupied Europe, the islanders were confronted by the moral complexities of war. British propaganda presented the Germans as a race of disciplined robots, cold, pedantic, brutal. This was vastly oversimplified, as the islanders found at first hand. Living side by side with Germans, they discovered that although some lived up to

278

the stereotype, others did not. The islanders were inclined to see the Germans, especially those billeted in their homes or with whom they worked, as ordinary human beings.

Ron Hurford
Baker's boy, Guernsey

The Germans confiscated my father's car and the rule was that you had to be in by nine o'clock at night – that was rigidly upheld. Once my dad was standing outside on the footpath near where we lived and it was just turned nine o'clock, and the German soldiers picked him up and threw him in the Martello tower and left him there for three days. Having the curfew was difficult for me as a youngster.

We had identity cards issued by the States of Guernsey when the Germans arrived. We all had to have our photographs taken and different disfigurements marked – that was your passport for the Germans. The bailiff and other islanders who organized things had a very awkward job to do; people say that there was collaboration. I suppose there was a little, but not a lot, and I think they did things the Germans didn't know about – you had to make out that you were helping them but in the end do what *you* wanted. We gave up one of our wirelesses and kept the other in the cupboard under the stairs, well concealed with crockery in front of it. If we wanted to listen, we only had to move a little bit of wood and we were into it. Quite a few got caught with them, and then they made these crystal sets.

Really, it paid to keep a low profile: least said, soonest mended ... Everybody on the island worked for the Germans. No matter what you did, you were involved in some way or other. The state told you what you had to put in your greenhouses, might be potatoes, some had to grow peas, tobacco, beans ... My father was growing tobacco plants and potatoes, and you had to give so much to the state.

Marion Tostevin (Letissier)
Schoolgirl, Guernsey

The Germans were quite lenient, really, and they liked children. Sometimes they would give us sweets or a lump of their horrible bread – so sour, oh dear! We didn't talk to them, as my mother always told me not to get friendly with the Germans, not to get involved with them, and I never knew a German personally. Some of the other children did. They used to go to where they were billeted and beg for food, but I never did, no. Generally, their behaviour was correct. Having heard about all the things that happened on the continent, I think we were treated very respect-fully. And, of course, we didn't have resistance going on here. If we just carried on and minded our business, they didn't bother with us. But the island was *saturated* with Germans. Oh dear! German signs everywhere, even on the road. And, of course, with their fortifications being built, we had massive machines going along the road and horse-wagons and the Germans singing and marching along – that was lovely, I can hear them to this day. There's one song that sticks in my memory, 'Ayee, aye-oh, oh, ooooho.' And then all the slave workers they brought over, they were pitiful, so wretched. I was so sorry for them. They had lost their dignity. They were taken from their homes with only what they stood up in and, of course, they were in rags. It was pathetic. We lived opposite a soup kitchen and every evening they were queuing for their little bit of watery soup with their cans, after their hard day's work building the fortifications. Many of them just had sacking on their feet because they had worn their shoes away.

We did know some people who were very friendly with the Germans – they had them into their homes. But to me, being so young, I didn't really know what that meant. Definitely young girls went out with the Germans. I still remember them to this day. Every time I see one, it comes into my mind. It would have been frowned upon by the population, definitely. They were known as 'Jerrybags'. Quite a lot had babies . . .

Molly Bihet (Finigan)
Schoolgirl, Guernsey

Some [Germans] were billeted on local ladies, mostly widows or those who used to take boarders ... We didn't really talk to the soldiers except those who lived along our road. Two of them stopped my mother once; they were being sent to the Russian Front, which they hated. And they had been living in my evacuated aunt's house and mentioned some photographs of our family, which they had found in the house, and offered them to my mother. They said if other soldiers came they might destroy them. We thought they were two good Germans, not at all like the German who once gave me a kick. This was when I stole some potatoes. These had to be brought over from France. They would take them off the wagons and lorries into the stores near our home, so we children went down with our prams and came back with maybe half a basket, according to which German was on. We had to be very careful. On this particular day this Otto was there. He was a *horrible* German, a real Nazi. Nobody liked him. I thought I'd be clever and stand on the board of the lorry as it was easier to fill my basket, but Otto came round, shouting in German, and I thought, Oh dear, this is *it*! and I started running down the road with my basket. He chased me and gave me a whopping big kick. I was running home and crying. Well, my father, he just wanted to get out and get hold of Otto! But I wasn't any of the worse for it. My pride was hurt, but I still had the potatoes and I went down the next day. That's what we did all the time, scrounging for anything: we'd get wood shavings, and one day we ended up with a bag of cement that had fallen on the road. Another time when the coal boats used to come into the old harbour and the tide was out, we'd go down to the slips, very quietly, and pick up bits of coal.

Ron Hurford
Baker's boy, Guernsey

I worked for a baker whose business was then taken over for

bread for the soldiers and officers. They had their own flour, brown bread for the men and white for the officers. Nobody pinched more than I did. I had two brothers at home and Mum and Dad, and I used to take a brown loaf when I could. I was courting at the time and would take some down to my young lady and her mum and dad, and if I saw anybody on the road on my way to the different German billets, I'd pass them a loaf occasionally. It was asking for trouble, but I was at the age when it didn't worry me. The Germans were in charge of the bakery – and to work for them! Well, lummy, it was '*Raus! Raus! Raus!*' [Out!] always chasing you. We were three shifts a day. I had a permit for the night shift. I always took a mac with me and had it over my arm, and I would put a loaf down the sleeve – the daft things you do! And we always had a box on the back of our bikes for when there were no Germans around.

Some areas were restricted: there was barbed-wire and tank traps, and you weren't allowed to go on some of the beaches. The fishermen had to have special permits to go fishing, and when they went, they had a German with them nine times out of ten. Fortifications were built all around the coast. I was allowed to keep my bike, that was the only way around. I used to smoke what they called 'coltsfoot', which used to grow wild around the island, and we'd have bramble tea and ersatz coffee.

Molly Bihet (Finigan)
Schoolgirl, Guernsey

We had a rationing system. It was a gradual rationing, lessening of food, but it started off fairly well. I remember Mum stocked up a bit in the beginning, but gradually it got less and less, and soap was non-existent. Luxuries like sweets and biscuits we didn't see for years ... As schoolchildren, we were lucky in having an allowance of half a pint of milk a day, and I remember once we were given a biscuit each with our milk ... We were very hungry towards the end. We had no bread for three weeks, that was the worst time. Come the end, a lot of the older people must have died of malnutrition because they couldn't get around like the young people to get some nourishment. Yes, I know what it's like to go hungry.

The only time I went to see a film was one that was all German propaganda: Germany winning the war, 'Victory in the West', and I was sitting there with my father. All the Guernsey people were on one side, the Germans on the other, and a long pole in the middle . . . On the film there was a direct hit – the Germans had sunk *another* boat, and my father just laughed. Four Germans swooped on him and he was fined and told to get out and we never went to the pictures again. He was fined for laughing: he just saw the funny side of this propaganda.

Ron Hurford
Baker's boy, Guernsey

We went roller-skating in St George's Hall. The Germans would come as well. Being young and devil-may-care, we'd say to them, 'Come down this way, there's a big learning room down there' – we all spoke a bit of German – and we'd give them a push towards the end, and trip them up when they were skating, saying, '*Entschuldigen mir, mein Herr*.' Sorry!

Eventually I was deported to Germany. One day there were two loaves missing from a case and these were supposed to go to the German officers. They wanted to know where they were. I said I didn't know. He said, 'You will tell me.' I said, 'I don't know.' And with that he hit me and, being a Guernsey man, I retaliated: I hit him back. He was down on the floor and shouted out for Rudi, and here comes Rudi, and they pinned my arms behind my back and gave me a hiding with their belts – see? I have the scars over my left eye to show for it. After that there was more or less a free for all . . . I was put in prison and eventually deported, having been classed as an 'undesirable'. About two to three hundred of us went on a clapped-out old banger of a boat. We landed at St Malo, then it took us three days on a train to get to a camp in Laufen, Germany. It was a big *Schloss* containing Americans, Poles, Guernsey and Jersey men, all civilians. I was with Jerseymen, Guernseymen and Englishmen . . . I was better off in Germany, far better off, because I had a Red Cross parcel every week, half a parcel when things got difficult to make sure they lasted out. But the worst thing for me was the lack of freedom.

Marion Tostevin (Letissier)
Schoolgirl, Guernsey

When the occupation started I had to change schools. Because most of the teachers had left, we were left with a tomato grower who had no qualifications to teach us. Anyway, we got on with education and I had a whole new group of friends, a completely different bunch ... We had normal school hours. There was a head teacher who was qualified and she'd visit the classrooms, which were scattered in different places. Lessons were mainly the three Rs, and we learnt French – I came top of the class for that. When we were about eleven or twelve, the Germans made it compulsory for us to learn their language. We had another local man to teach us and I got top of the class for that as well. One day the German *Kommandant* came to award a prize. He had two armed guards with him. They stood in front of the class and they addressed me, as the top in the class. They asked a simple question like, '*Wie alt sind Sie?*' I didn't have a clue and I was absolutely petrified. I thought they were going to shoot me. Then one of the girls behind me whispered, 'How old are you?' and I answered, '*Ich bin dreizehn*' – thirteen. Then they gave me a book, which was all in German so I've never been able to read it.

I remember the sinking of the HMS *Charybdis* in 1943. I was then thirteen or fourteen. All the crew were drowned. Most of the island turned out at the funeral, which was held in St Peter Port. Oh, it was really a big thing, there were crowds – I can see us standing by the cemetery wall, crowds of people, it was really something. I think the people wanted to show the Germans that they were thinking about the British. They wanted to show their loyalty. They've all got memorial stones and a lot of their families have been over since the war to see the graves. Every year in October we've honoured them.

Madge Howell
Mother of five, with her Service husband, Valetta, Malta, extract from her memoir

Every Christmas since has brought back to my mind that Christmas Eve 1941. During the day we had to register for bread – a sign of things to come. In the evening I was packing the children's stockings, but there were several bad air raids, and so the children had to be carried down to the shelter and then back to their beds when the all-clear sounded. In between I was listening to Rediffusion. Someone in England was saying in what a very desperate plight Malta was now that Crete had fallen and there did not seem to be any hope for us. My spirits dropped but, strangely enough, my thoughts were all to get through Christmas Day happily, no matter what happened afterwards ...

At 6 p.m. came the third and worst attack. The Hun was very precise in his timing. We were again in the shelter, feeling like rats in a trap. This time the back of the hotel was hit and practically all the windows and doors were blown in. The girls' room was cracked right across and our room was a shambles. It was impossible to take the children back, as no one knew if the floors were safe. We had to sandwich ourselves in the shelter for the night. When I had settled the little ones I returned to our room to pack our belongings as best I could. Everything was full of plaster and glass. There was no blackout as it was blown to bits, and I dared not light a candle. Thank heavens Jerry left us alone that night. For days afterwards I found bits of debris in my shoes and belongings ... Food became scarcer and scarcer. The electricity and gas were bombed. There was no gas for a year and no electricity for about six months. Our only means of cooking was our Primus stove and even this was restricted as paraffin was very scarce. The rationing was so strict that one could not go out for a meal, or even for a cup of tea or coffee. We knew things were very desperate, but we did not know that at one time there was only one more ration to issue and then Malta would have had to capitulate. It was then that a convoy struggled through. With dismay we heard Mr Churchill's voice announce on Rediffusion:

'A vital convoy has reached Malta.' We knew only too well what would happen. That night, the German bombers came over in full force and the supplies so bravely brought to us were lost in port.

Lady Thurle Folliott Vaughan (Laver Eriksen)
British child, Copenhagen, Denmark

After a time, the Germans got fed up with the Danes because they were not being co-operative, so we had a curfew and had to be indoors at nine o'clock. If you were found outside after that time, you were shot, as simple as that. And at five to nine most nights there was an explosion. It was patriots blowing up something of the Germans' and it was called 'Hitler's goodnight kiss'. You could literally put your watch to it. The Germans realized that Denmark was an agricultural country and they used it as their larder. The great thing was to keep back as much food as possible so that they couldn't get hold of it, so an enormous barter system went on with the farmers coming in and selling their produce round the back door.

Yes, I was frightened of the Germans. You always had to get off the pavement if a German was coming or they'd push you off, and you always had to get out of the way if they were getting on a bus. They were arrogant more than aggressive, and they had a sick sense of humour too. One day we were playing in the park and a couple of German soldiers arrived and pretended to shoot us with their guns. We were absolutely *terrified*, but they thought it enormously funny. As an English child, I didn't have a Danish identity card. One of the interesting things is that when the Germans walked in the Danish police burnt all the archives of foreigners in Denmark so there were no records. My mother went to the mayor, whom we knew as a good patriot, and explained the situation to him. He said, 'Why didn't you come before, my dear? Of course she can have an identity card.' Out came a clean one and he wrote on it 'Thurle Eriksen, born in Copenhagen' ... This gave me confidence and I felt safer. All the girls knew I was English but nobody ever said a word about it.

Ann Thornton (Helps)
British schoolgirl, Copenhagen, Denmark

We knew all about Nazi anti-Semitism because we got a huge package of propaganda about Jews in England delivered to our villa. It said how everyone important in England was Jewish, Churchill and so on, and this amused us very much. That was before there was any trouble with the Jews. Jewish people went on living quite happily in Denmark, people like Nils Bohr; his children were of our generation but a bit older and we had, and still have, some connection with them. The Danish Jewish bourgeoisie have been there for many generations and are completely Danish yet keep hold of Jewish traditions. They have a very fine position in Danish cultural life. Denmark is highly civilized in that way.

Michael Hart
Anglo-German schoolboy, Berlin, Germany

We had no divided loyalties. My father spent a lot of time in England and the family position was very clearly and unambiguously anti-Nazi, which wasn't difficult for us because that was the school atmosphere, and virtually all the German families, too, were of the same opinion. We certainly lived in a sort of generally agreed oppositional way. It was a cocoon to the extent that you didn't talk about it in public. My father would remind me, time and time again, 'For God's sake, keep your mouth shut in public!' I had to take a train to get to school in the centre of Berlin and he would say, 'Be careful on the train how you talk.' It was very risky to offer any defeatist opinions, even more risky to mention that you listened to the BBC or something like that. But the moment you were in private houses with friends, you talked quite openly. We listened to the BBC regularly. My father certainly considered it risky. He was not himself persecuted, but he was known to be a person of great anglophile leanings and with no commitment to the regime, so it was quite likely if there were certain suspicions that they would bug us, so we had to be careful.

It was in 1943 that some very good friends of ours – the woman was half-Jewish and well informed – told us in great confidence horrific stories about concentration camps. These were not the local well-known German concentration camps – Oranien-berg, near Berlin, and Dachau, near Munich, most people knew about these as they had been there for a very long time and were used mainly for political opponents and homosexuals. They told us about the infamous concentration camps associated with the Holocaust – Auschwitz and the others in [Nazi-occupied] Poland, designed for the extermination of the Jews. Even in our circles, and we reckoned we were relatively well informed, very little was known, and the first really concrete information you got was mid or late '43, not earlier ...

Ann Thornton (Helps)
British schoolgirl, Copenhagen, Denmark

There was still plenty of food, but nothing like rice – my family having lived in the East liked that. It was difficult to get, but we had some friends at school who were in the Italian embassy and they got us rice. Coffee was very bad. There was no chocolate, but plenty of cream and meat. In fact, we were very well fed. Clothing wasn't so good, but we were given lots by kind Danes and would swap clothes too ...

When we changed schools at the start of the European war we went to an international convent school – the Convent of the Assumption – outside Copenhagen with wonderful French nuns. You didn't learn much there, but it was absolutely enjoyable and the nuns were so sweet. It was really a very posh place, and the Queen would visit informally. There was a German cripple girl there, who was the daughter of the German commander of Copenhagen. And the SS officers, with their leather coats to the ground, used to come and bow to the nuns. At the same time the Reverend Mother was helping Jews, taking them in and hiding them ...

We went on listening to the English wireless all the time. It was supposed to be forbidden, but the Danes wouldn't have dreamt of stopping. The BBC news was awful: there was a moment when Singapore fell and everything seemed to be going wrong. My sister wrote in her diary, 'This was really a black moment.' You suddenly thought, My God, we might lose the war ... We listened to Churchill's speeches and were very impressed with all that. It was very important to have that radio link. I remember *ITMA* and all sorts of stuff. German newsreels of Dunkirk and other events were shown and my mother would get very upset by them ... There were demonstrations in the cinema. Once they showed *The Scarlet Pimpernel*, and there came that moment when the actor said, 'This England!' and the entire cinema cheered, very moving, actually. Another time there would be a picture of Hitler and someone would say, 'Who *is* that man?' Roars of laughter! Nothing happened, no retaliation for that cheek. One of our diplomatic friends had a connection with a Danish aristocrat who regularly went to Sweden and, without his knowledge, we smuggled stuff into his luggage, which he posted when he was in Sweden and we got letters back [from England] that way, in toothpaste tubes and things.

Michael Hart
Anglo-German schoolboy, Berlin, Germany

The French *lycée* was really an island of peace and quiet and international understanding, and during those early war years, virtually no Nazi propaganda or anything of the sort. And I remember not only among the pupils but at home with our families, as long as you were certain that you weren't overheard, discussion ranged very freely and very, very critically over everything that was happening in Germany in general, and the war in particular ... In late 1942, not surprisingly, the schools were asked to help with the harvest, which meant that in the autumn they were closed for a fortnight and the pupils were sent to all different parts of the country to help the farmers bring in the harvest. But not our Jewish friends. They were kept in Berlin and made to sweep the streets, and this was the first time that one realized things were getting very unpleasant and there was a great wave of indignation in the school. And when we came back we collected for a present for the Jewish child in our class. So it was relatively secure until 1943 – it was only then we noticed suddenly that some of our half-Jewish children were obviously distressed. In the morning I remember someone would come in and say 'they' had collected his grandparents at two in the morning. You then knew that things were going from bad to worse. At this time you could physically sense the change in war fortunes and this was obvious in the German war propaganda, which had been very optimistic and blatant right through '40, '41 and early '42. It was only with the Russian campaign that disillusionment set in. There had been a certain degree of tolerance *vis-à-vis* foreigners, and even towards those who were half- or quarter-Jewish at the time, but all this ended in 1943.

I was then hidden in a private boarding-school in Bavaria, which was run at that time by an anti-Nazi, Dr Reisinger, who had written a quite well-known pamphlet against Hitler in 1932. He was a marvellous old boy, an arch-liberal and highly intelligent. There were about two hundred pupils. Reisinger was not going to trumpet the fact that I had British nationality, and there were other pupils whose ethnic backgrounds were not to the liking of the regime. Certainly there were one or two teachers who were quite openly anti-Nazi, and one of them was thrown out during my time there. A relatively high percentage of German aristocracy sent their children there; we had one or two extremely nice young people from quite well-known German families. Again it's intriguing that Dr Reisinger was allowed to run this school until 1944 when, not surprisingly, he was thrown out and replaced by a very intelligent, but very radical, Nazi headmaster. When the new Nazi headmaster took over, it became more military and focused on preparing us to do our duty in the German Army, so a great emphasis was placed on military style – short hair, physical exercise and so on. But that was only one aspect. The whole tone changed: there were constant appeals at school assembly to patriotism and a great emphasis on Nazi ideology.

Ann Thornton (Helps)
British schoolgirl, Copenhagen, Denmark

Martial law and the rising tension in 1943 meant that, eventually, we escaped by boat. It was a large open boat with no bung in the bottom. My poor mother had to sit on that hole with her knapsack full of butter, which we had masses of. She thought in Sweden she could barter it ...

We thought the Swedes awful. The saying went: 'Norway had taken ten days, Denmark had taken ten minutes, Sweden had taken a telephone call' ... The Swedish soldiers gave us coffee and buns, then put us in prison. My mother rang up the English consul in Helsingborg, whom she knew; she'd had the sense to bring all sorts of papers and the receipts for the passports so that the Swedes didn't think we were spies. So, this man turned up in a car and drove off with us. And there it was *heaven*, out of the war, but there was rationing there too. And ordinary Swedes were so kind to us and equipped us with clothes. We stayed in Helsingborg for a couple of days, and then we were lent money by this consul friend and my mother said, 'Let's go to Stockholm, start making a nuisance of ourselves and try to get back to England.'

Eventually, in 1944, my mother did get over, and we followed a few days later, landing at a military airport in Scotland. Then we had a terrible train journey. We got to Baker Street and there had just been a flying bomb so it was all pitch-blackness. Then a train to Amersham, where my grandmother lived, and that was it: we were back in England. I had missed out on all formal schooling since the age of eleven so I had a bit of a difficult time fitting in. I just seemed to be very bored, going back to being a schoolgirl.

By June 1942, six months after the first Japanese attack, with Hong Kong, Malaya, Burma and the Dutch East Indies occupied, the last American resistance quashed on Corrigidor, Japan was in possession of the whole of South East Asia.

Along with captured service personnel, civilians were rounded up and placed in internment camps: missionaries, business officials, engineers, surveyors, journalists, nurses and teachers. Though mainly in Malaya, Burma, Hong Kong, Shanghai and other parts of China, the camps were scattered across almost all of South East Asia, with Britons in most of them, including many children.

Those children interned by the Japanese were the most deprived of all young Britons in wartime. Denied liberty, they were in camps guarded by Japanese or Koreans, and were often subject to threatening behaviour. Overcrowding was the norm and there were few facilities for eating, cooking and washing. But in some camps recreational activities were organized and educational classes were held. Food consisted of a little poor-quality rice, supplemented with whatever vegetables could be found and occasionally a small amount of meat. The lack of protein, fats and vitamins caused malnutrition. By the time of liberation, the majority were well below normal bodyweight and many people had deficiency diseases.

Diana Owen (Houston-Boswald)
British schoolgirl internee, British embassy compound, Tokyo

The first day we had a detective, shared between my father, mother and myself. He was so keen that he even came to the loo with you. He would sit on the edge of the bath with his back to you, but he got embarrassed with having to do this and that stopped. Our servants were sworn into the *Kempei*, the Japanese Military Police, so they had to listen to everything we said. Also they had put microphones into the wall switches, a pretty advanced technology then. If anybody was going to say something slightly dubious, we would take a cushion, walk over to the light switch and cover it with the cushion before we spoke ...

We almost got into a routine with our lives: our meals would be served in our dining room, waited on by the butler, great style with all the silver out – still gracious living, the servants went on as before – and you had people to lunch. It was really business as usual, but on a reduced scale. Fresh supplies of food didn't decrease because the Japanese were terrified that if they took out anything on us, it would be taken out against their own in London and Washington ... There was a tremendous amount of sharing. People were absolutely incredible, and there were no major rows, small dramas, yes, but nothing major. Lady Craigie, the ambassador's wife, was very American. She didn't take an interest in what was going on, she only appeared rarely as a sort of royal figure. She was a pain in the neck for my mother, a considerable problem ...

We were allowed out of the compound after war had started. For some extraordinary reason, the Japanese thought very highly of going to the dentist and I had lots of my lower teeth filled with the most advanced fillings, which fascinated British dentists when I got back. During these outings, you could evade your detectives. For instance, I once popped into a bookshop and I remember buying the *Noh Plays of Japan* there. We were taken to a Buddhist cemetery when the cherry blossom was at its height because they wanted to strike the analogy between the Samurai warrior who fell in his prime like the cherry blossom – in other words to show us what a rough enemy we were up against. Fear was unknown and Bushido was the thing.

Jacqueline Towell (Honnor)
British internee child, Santo Tomas University camp, Manila, Philippines

It was a large stone building with little towers and gargoyles and various outbuildings, surrounded by a cement wall, so it was an ideal place for us to be. We were divided up: women with children under ten, I think, were put into the annexe, women with children over ten in the main building; boys from the age of twelve and men went into another building. We slept on the floor for quite a while. Our cook was able in due time to push some mattresses over the wall for us, we already had our pillows, and we all slept on floors and tables. Almost immediately we had an earthquake – all we needed! I remember the room sort of dancing around as I tried to hang on to the top of the table. We had no mosquito nets or anything like that, and very, very poor washing facilities. So, rather an unpleasant time . . .

Then we were suddenly allowed to live as a family. So we started off under a mango tree. My parents made the mangoes into jam and sold it, and we slowly got money together and my father built us a shack – literally a shack. It had to be on stilts because of the flooding, and the roof was a special kind of palm leaf. We were not allowed walls, as the Japanese had to see into the place, so we had an overhanging roof. Father made four bunks and he built a table with a bench either side of it. Then we had a *punka* – a sort of fan, which you pulled with bits of string and it brought air in. This sounds extraordinary, but seen from the angle of a child: here we were in this shack and life was very primitive – I mean, we'd lived in very comfortable, even luxurious places before – but it did not bother us one little bit. My brother and I were not a bit put out that one day we had a lot, and the next we had nothing. We were perfectly comfortable with it.

We had a loudspeaker system for our instructions, and an American circus troupe had managed to keep a radio receiver hidden and would give us the news from this in a way that sounded perfectly innocent. When the island of Leyte fell, for instance, we were told that we had to do something that day and it was 'Better Leyte than never.' This roar went up through the camp. But when the Japanese looked at the transcript, it said, 'Better late than never.' We knew that Hitler was dead when the music they played in the morning was 'Hail, Hail, The Witch Is Dead!' from *The Wizard of Oz*. In the evenings, we would have singalongs and little amateur theatre groups. Whatever role people had in civilian life they took it there: we had doctors, nurses, but very little medicine, and as the war progressed, the doctors were being required to sign death certificates for people who had clearly died of malnutrition, but were not allowed to put that on.

So, thinking of the daily life, it was a question of *surviving* and of the children trying to learn. Eventually I started to faint all the time, and it was discovered I had a heart murmur caused by malnutrition. A lot of people got beri-beri, and my parents got desperately, desperately thin, but they didn't have anything physically wrong with them, and you can be sure they gave us more food than *they* had. There was a lot of dengue fever. We all got it, you just ache *screamingly* all over and get a very high fever. The desperate worry was any sort of infection. People also got TB, and there was a lot of dysentery because the conditions were really so primitive. There were a lot of single people in the camp, most of them under thirty-five or forty. They died because they had nothing to live for. Not a single parent died in the camp because they *couldn't*. Their big worry was 'What if we die? How do the children get back to their homeland and families?'

Paget Natten (Eames)
British internee child, Bangkinang camp, Sumatra

The part that I remember most vividly in Bangkinang is how I lost the command of English, my native tongue, because we were with so many Dutch. The British contingent was very small. There were also some Eurasians, some Indians, a lot of Tamils, Chinese and Malays. We were kept within this final place, which had wire around it and a wall. The Japanese even made the children work – we had to go and tend their gardens and collect buckets of water for them. We had to bow every time we saw a Japanese soldier and my friend and I would bow but we swore in Dutch under our breath as we did so, and we always had to say, '*Nippon bonsai! Nippon bonsai!* [Japan ten thousand years!]' If anyone committed an offence, they were made to stand out in the sun for a very long period. But every day my mother said to me, 'Look, we're going to make it.' She also told me to keep the idea of my father with me, because we didn't know what had happened to him.

The work they put upon the women was utterly unbearable. Then one day the Japanese came into our camp to choose comfort girls to take away with them. We had some very pretty girls ... A small group of women in the camp intervened and they hid the young ones. The Japanese only wanted virgins so Mother was quite safe, and when they saw there weren't any young women there, they got very angry and demanded volunteers ... There was a group of Indonesian and Malay prostitutes, who finally got up and said, 'Look, this is just another job to us, let us go.' But the Japanese weren't satisfied as there weren't enough of them, so some strapping Dutch ladies volunteered. Hours later this same truck came back, and we heard that these big Dutch ladies had stopped the truck, beaten up the drivers and had driven the truck back to the camp. We all waited, wondering what was going to happen to us ... but the Japanese were embarrassed about being beaten up by the women and we didn't hear any more about it. The girls who wanted to go went. No one made any judgement about that. The important factor was staying alive ...

Sometimes the Japanese were very kind, they could give you the odd sweetmeat and sometimes show you pictures of their families. They were especially understanding to children. Sometimes we got the impression that they were, in the main, not happy with what they were doing but had to do what they did ... There was a great deal of kindness among the prisoners there, very little ratting on people. You needed each other and therefore you stayed with each other. We just kept very busy. I can remember – this is very vivid – running across the camp yard just before sunset and looking at this whole camp, so much space, and very few people around. It was at that moment, in complete isolation, that I wondered, What am I doing here? What's happening? You grew up very quickly. You learnt to fight your battles very quickly. You learnt to steal and lie. You had to. You *had* to.

James Maas
British internee child, Lunghuo camp, Shanghai, China

We were allowed to take our clothes and took as much as we could. I took some toys and books. We used a heavy trunk to sit on and had a folding table and three folding canvas chairs, which had our numbers on the back. Mine was 15/207. I was then ten years old. It was a change, true, but we were with the same people, our friends, all together. So a boy of my age adapts pretty quickly and I took it in my stride.

We had inspection twice a day – roll-call. We all had to stand to attention outside the door and a very small Japanese with a very big sword would come clattering along and check off the list. If you weren't standing up, it was *very* serious. One lady, the wife of the Belgian consul, was feeling a bit rotten one day and sat down. Another guard spotted her and came up and gave her a *tremendous* slap. Her son had to be restrained ... All the while, that violence was under the surface. If people escaped – on the whole this would be the few younger, single men, who would escape into mainland China and join the war – we'd be confined to our room and down to one meal a day. But as it was a family camp, there were not too many young men. We got the crew of an American ship, which had been seized at the beginning of the war. They were transferred to the camp to do some work. The Americans weren't too co-operative, but they produced a little bit of colour and excitement when they played softball and would get angry and noisy, which amazed us kids. To us, this was un-British behaviour!

When the Japanese had defeats, we noticed that things got a bit difficult in terms of food and worse behaviour by the guards. They would be changed and a more brutal lot brought in. But on the whole they didn't treat children badly. I honestly didn't take it all in as a child, we just lived in our own little world and got on with each other.

Paget Natten (Eames)
British internee child, Bangkinang camp, Sumatra

Hunger was the main thing. We didn't get any Red Cross parcels. During the day we had a can of cooked rice for the adults, half for the children and virtually anything that you could grab hold of. Towards the end you were picking grass. When I went to work for the Japanese, tending their gardens, Mum would say, 'Okay, you can steal.' So I used to take back in my knickers anything that was green. By this time Mum was quite resourceful: she would take eggshells from the Japanese dustbins and put them on

the coal fires and powder them down to make calcium for me
and make me swallow it, whether I liked it or not.

Jacqueline Towell (Honnor)
British internee child, Santo Tomas University camp, Manila,
Philippines

The really vital part of our day was getting food any way we
could. You could grow a bit. My brother had a spinach garden,
and we grew ginger, which seemed to do well. The Japanese kept
pigs and they would put out their pig swill and I'm afraid the
kids would go and get it if they possibly could. My brother told
me that he remembers me sitting with this bowl of ghastly porridge
stuff, which was just packed with weevils, and I was delicately
picking out each weevil and putting it on the side of my plate,
whereas he was eating it all and saying, 'It's more protein.'

A typical day would be getting up in the morning, having
ginger tea and anything we might have to eat – part of a banana,
if we were lucky. Then we had to go on roll-call, and that would
consist of us all standing in a line in the sun where we would be
counted. The officer would go up and down with his long sword,
and we would bow. They were never cruel or nasty to us, to my
knowledge. But I know that people who tried to escape had a
bad time. We used to play skipping-rope games: two children
turning the rope and somebody jumping in. Sometimes one of
the guards would jump in and we would deliberately tighten the
rope to trip him up and he would go down with a splendid
clatter, but he would laugh. Then after roll-call we went to school,
where we had our main meal. A lot of the time this was very,
very tiny dried salt fish, some sort of protein, and rice. We had
about four food parcels from the Red Cross in total, and that
saved our lives. They contained powdered milk, corned beef and
stuff like that, all good protein. The rice became more and more
watery as time went by until it was a teacupful of rice a day, and
that was it. We all became obsessed with food, rather like anorexics.
There were a few recipe books in the library and, even at the
age of ten, I could copy out recipes – you know, you were sort

of mentally eating. The last six months I was bedridden as I was not able to walk from malnutrition.

James Maas
British internee child, Lunghuo camp, Shanghai, China

We were two thousand in all. We children just played our games together – we were always outside shooting or exchanging marbles. We had a strict code or rank of marbles and that took up a lot of our time. And then there was football and softball – the American influence. We were always kicking a ball around because there was a big playing-field right outside the block. The camp would have covered forty-three acres, so plenty of space to wander but not too close to the boundary. Certain parts would have been out of bounds ... We didn't mind being restricted to camp. We kept busy all the time and we just accepted it, up to my age anyway. I adjusted. Also, in the earlier days, we put on plays and revues. Father rather liked doing this: he was in *The Pirates of Penzance* and *Twelfth Night*. Those rather died out in the later months when things were getting very difficult. Mother used to play bridge in the evening – she had a bridge four. I watched this and learnt how to play ...

My mother once told me that I said, 'Oh, Mummy, I'm *so* hungry!' I don't remember saying that, but I remember being hungry. But on the whole it wasn't too bad because parents were very sacrificing, and we did get the Red Cross parcels, which were a godsend, and I got most of the contents of those, and there were a few treats in them. I have a photograph, which was taken in August or September '45, of Mother looking very cheerful, although very thin, and I look entirely normal.

Jacqueline Towell (Honnor)
British internee child, Santo Tomas University camp, Manila, Philippines

They started up a school in the camp, with American-style education. We had no books, no writing materials, but we had a lot of people who had been teachers before the camp; we had blackboards from the university, and we had some books, a library of English books. We had school every day from about nine until twelve and we had different grades, according to our ages. My mother, being English, was given the class of twelve- to thirteen-year-old boys, who were running very wild. We had a tremendous mix of nationalities, some well behaved, some not . . . They really did their best at school, but of course everything had to be learnt by rote. Then there came a time when we didn't have school any more. I imagine we were all too weak to get there, so school just stopped.

Paget Natten (Eames)
British internee child, Bangkinang camp, Sumatra

We were not allowed education. The Japanese would not allow it. We had some nuns who said, 'Right, we think the children ought to be educated.' But the Japanese came and took down the boards . . .

James Maas
British internee child, Lunghuo camp, Shanghai, China

There were a lot of ex-missionary teachers and the headmaster was Mr Osborne. My mother was also a teacher, and we kept up quite a good standard. They kept to the normal curriculum and everything was quite well taught – maths, English, French, history, geography, all the usual subjects, science and biology . . . It was fairly relaxed, but I began to work quite hard for the exams when I was about twelve, I began to realize I worked for *myself*, not for my parents or the teacher. They did give exams. Whether they counted I don't know. There was a building set aside for the school, and we had desks; we didn't have much paper to write on. We had to open cigarette packets and bind them together for paper . . .

Diana Owen (Houston-Boswald)
British schoolgirl internee, British embassy compound, Tokyo, Japan

The Swiss became the intermediary power who got everything

arranged for our return from Japan. Quite suddenly the removal man became enormously important in our lives. Everything was packed up, possessions and clothes, and taken off to the ship. Then into taxis for Yokohama where we got into the most luxurious liner, but nobody was allowed on deck. We were all battened down below because of naval activity. All the portholes were blacked out. The ship had the most enormous white cross on the deck, which was lit up. We travelled under lights because of the international convention, and this made you feel an absolute target. At every meal we had these beautifully painted menus and there would be a little gift, a paper parasol or fan, laid at your place. The most fantastic food was served and the waiters were bending over backwards to be nice. It was the most *extraordinary* time. We had a lot of people on board that we didn't know because they'd been let out of the Meiji prison in Tokyo. Then we stopped at Saigon and Shanghai and took on people in need of repatriation because of their medical state. One old priest, Father Ward, came on board and died two days later. He was buried at sea. We had quite a few burials at sea because some of the people who came from the prison were in a terrible state. They told of the appalling things that had happened – they were well into the 'Tenko scene' and made you feel quite guilty for being so comfortable all the time.

We eventually arrived at Lourenço Marques, our trans-shipping point where we would leave the Japanese ship and get on to an English ship, and the Japanese who had come from England and America would get on the Japanese ship and return [the exchange of diplomatic staff and their families]. It was quite funny because the Japanese and English knew each other, and we caused quite a scandal among the Portuguese by rushing around and greeting each other in Japanese when we should have been cutting them dead and walking past with growls and snarls. It was then on to Liverpool where there was an air raid, then up to London by train where we met up with relatives and life was suddenly as if all this had never happened. Our belongings arrived, faultlessly packed, down to the smallest ornament.

12. Wartime: Work and Service

As the conflict dragged on, many who had begun the war as children now faced the prospect of finding jobs. In 1939 the government had intended to raise the school-leaving age to fifteen, but war had put paid to that, and many whom we would now consider children were in full-time work. Their jobs were sometimes dangerous – for girls as well as boys – in industrial plants, dockyards and steelworks. Others, coming up to eighteen, entered Cadet forces or volunteered for the services, many before their call-up was due.

John Starling
Dockyard apprentice, Portsmouth, Hampshire

The initial period after I went home was very traumatic. I had no break from the time I finished my School Certificate and started work in the dockyard. It was a bit of a shock having to start at seven in the morning, and as I was working on torpedoes and other essential war goods, there was a degree of productivity required to churn out the goods for the navy, so although we were on apprenticeships, there was no time for things other than work. It seemed to be all work and no play, as I was also in the Royal Dockyard School for continuing education, equivalent to a degree, two whole days a week.

Joan Reed (Chantrelle)
Clerk, Woodford, Essex

When I left school and the camp in Sussex, I went straight away to an office opposite Euston station and I *hated* it. I was basically an outdoor person and longed to be back at school. It didn't take me long to adjust to life at home with my mother, although I missed the freedom I'd had in the evacuee camp at Itchingfield. I was home for just one year. In the summer of that year I went off on a Dig for Victory potato-picking trip, out in the open again, under canvas ... I was only at home for a short time and then I joined the services.

Irene Mead (Weller)
Trainee, printing firm, Birmingham, Warwickshire

Eventually we went home and made arrangements with this relative on the outskirts of Birmingham, which was then countryside. By this time the war was getting into its stride and I went straight to work the week I was fourteen. Previously you had to wait until the end of the term, but because of the wartime conditions, if you got a job you could leave straight away. I had a job in the printing trade.

Gwendoline Stewart (Watts)
Trainee telephonist-receptionist, factory, Birmingham, Warwickshire

The next morning you'd come out of your shelter and there'd been incendiaries everywhere. The trams weren't running but you had to get to work. No matter what happened, you *had* to get to work. My job was right across town and I had to walk through the city centre of Birmingham as best I could, going round craters, stepping over hosepipes. Chaos everywhere, the smell of burning, just picking your way through. And even if you arrived at the office at eleven o'clock they were still pleased to see you because everybody else was making the same effort. And everyone was so cheerful. People spoke to each other then. You'd start trudging with somebody you'd never seen before and before you got into town you'd be the best of friends. And this went on for many, many months. And the same thing trying to get home at night. Everyone was worried if you didn't show up for work. They would think, What's happened? And if someone else didn't show up *you* would think, What's happened?

John Wheeler
2nd Lieutenant in the Wiltshire Regiment, Sandhurst, Berkshire

Bill's cup was full, really, when I was commissioned in the Wiltshire Regiment. I went to Sandhurst and I know he used to brag about me being in the army and going to be an officer – it gave him some ascendancy over his friends. And I recall when I first came home on leave after being commissioned, in a brand new uniform with a shiny pip and a Sam Browne [belt], Billy's cup was over-flowing. And if he could have got a band to lead me from the station up home he would have done so. That was the sort of relationship that Billy and I had. He was a likeable lad and really became like a brother to my brother and me. But I was particularly his idol because I was in the army and we were fighting a war. Eventually, in 1944, I went to north-west Europe.

Janet Shipton (Attlee)
Women's Auxiliary Air Force, Cardington, Bedfordshire

From 1941, when I was eighteen, I was in the air force. I volunteered and went to the Air Ministry, took a test, and joined the plotters. I went to a camp in Gloucester and met the most interesting people, a very diverse group. We did boot camp – as the Americans would call it – and I liked it. Then I was selected for work involved with mental testing of air crew, so instead of going off to be a plotter, when I'd probably have had pilot lovers who were killed, I missed all that. My peril – peril that my children can't even *conceive* – was the married man who didn't wear a ring and got many girls pregnant, only for them to discover afterwards that he had a wife. It didn't happen to me, but I was so naïve that it was a real, grave risk. I knew nothing about the world, had never dated a boy in my life, and all of a sudden I was *free*. I could go out until ten o'clock every night and until midnight at weekends!

After joining up in 1941, I was really out of the home and political circuit, but when I was at Cardington, Bedfordshire, the wing commander called me one day. I wondered what I had done wrong. It turned out that Father was coming to one of the British Restaurants in a small village in Bedfordshire and wanted to take me with him. So he came with his driver and picked me up. They had taken down all the signs so you didn't know the way, and Bedfordshire is full of crossroads and T-junctions and we got lost and were over an hour late, which didn't please Father or those who were waiting. But that was just the one time. I didn't go everywhere, like Mary Churchill did with her father, nothing like that. I just stayed and did my job in the WAAF. I wasn't special at all, just me. I hardly ever had to play his daughter in the war; that was the one occasion when I did.

Myra Collyer (Murden)
Women's Auxiliary Air Force, Whitehall, London

I was going to be called up at nineteen, so on my eighteenth birthday I went with a friend and joined the WAAF. When my father, who by now was back in the army, heard, he wrote, 'My dear girl, I'm so pleased you're patriotic enough to join up. I wish you well, but don't ask me to bale you out. You've made your bed, you lie on it and toughen yourself up . . .' After being tested for our future roles, we were all shuttled off to Morecambe Bay. We were a very mixed group – some of the girls said they were 'ladies of the streets', and therefore 'reserved occupation', and they were out. The first night one or two of the girls cried, but I quite enjoyed it, and loved meeting people. Remember, even to go from Reigate to London was a big journey then! After the basic training I was stationed at the RAF War Room, in King Charles Street, London. This was underground, almost under the Cenotaph. I did shorthand and typing there. We had to have sunray treatment once a week because we worked twelve-hour shifts, nights and days, with two days off every eight days. The building was very eerie. I remember an RAF officer saying that if the Thames was bombed, we'd drown, and if there was gas, just put the gas mask on because there was nothing else you could do . . .

Jill Monk (Holman)
Mounted messenger with Auxiliary Units Special Duties Section, Aylsham, Norfolk

I was riding in the woods, doing my spying, and Mark, Colonel Collings's [organizer of the Auxunit in the Aylsham area] Alsatian dog, was with me. There was a whole collection of military vehicles camouflaged in the woods. A couple of soldiers came along and were chatting me up. I decided that I had to get away, and one of them took hold of the horse. 'Oh, you don't need to go yet!' I said, 'I do, and Mark will make you let go of my horse.' 'Mark? Who's Mark?' I called, 'Mark, attack!' And Mark went roaring for him and he let go in a hurry. Yes, there were risks, but a horse was useful for getting out of the way. I mainly rode my chestnut stallion for daytime spying work, but my black horse, Merry Monarch, for when we had exercises in message-carrying at night.

One night I was nearly rumbled when carrying a message about two a.m. I had tied the horse up and was hiding behind some rhododendrons when a man suddenly came and leant against a nearby tree and lit his pipe. You can imagine! You want to sneeze, you want to cough. I didn't know who he was, only that there were lots of people out to catch us. Was he one of those, or was he a gamekeeper or a poacher? I couldn't actually see him, just smell the tobacco. Eventually he knocked out his pipe and went off. I didn't spend any more time trying to find where to drop the message. They were placed in split tennis balls, then you put them down the pipe to the operations room underground. I had no idea where these were, just the drop place. People say, 'Weren't you frightened?' I say, 'No, in some ways it was all a game.' But it was my *war* work. I suppose that, really, I was too young to think of what it might be like if the Germans *did* come. I remember saying laughingly to John Collings, 'What happens if I'm caught and they decide I'm a spy?' He said, 'Well, you'll be put up against a wall and shot.' I knew that, but I suppose one felt it was such a remote possibility. The government informed us that we were fully prepared to repel an invasion. I, in my innocence, believed them.

Pay? Good Lord, no! *No!* Good heavens, no! We would have been insulted had it been offered. We did it not as a duty but as something we *wanted* to do. We were volunteers. We felt it was something we *could* do. We weren't able to fight so it was the next best thing. My work with the Auxiliary SDS was good training for my work with radar in the WAAF, which I joined later in the war.

Elisabeth Small (Fabri, née Hadfield)
Secretary, French section, Special Operations Executive, Baker Street, London

I arrived in London and found an employment agency somewhere at the top of Regent Street. It was rather a depressing place with a depressing lady there. I walked in and said, 'I want to be a WRN. I've got my secretarial diploma and I speak French.' She said, 'Well, you can't go into the WRNS, no room! You can be a cook in the ATS, or perhaps there are vacancies in the WAAF.' That was a dreadful shock: my wonderful plan was going quite wrong! Then she peered through some papers and said, 'You say you've got a secretarial qualification. There's something here asking for a French-speaking secretary at the Interservices Research Bureau, in Baker Street.' She rang the number and said, 'If you go round someone will give you an interview.'

I took a taxi to 64 Baker Street. I walked round the back to the entrance and went in. As I waited I saw people in different uniforms, walking in and out, so I thought it must have *something* to do with the war. Then I was told to go up to see this civilian woman of about forty. She was in a very bare office, which didn't give any indication of the type of work expected. She took my CV and said, 'Oh, we have something here which I can't tell you anything about except that you would find it very interesting. French is essential. You would work long hours, six days a week, sometimes seven. I can't give any indication about leave and the salary would be five pounds a week.' That sounded *enormous* ... I started the Tuesday after Easter, 1943, in what I later learnt was the Special Operations Executive – SOE ...

When I arrived on the first day, this woman said, 'I would like you to sign the Official Secrets Act,' which I did. She told me, 'You'll be working for the French section, for Captain Noble, in Norgeby House across the road.' That was that. She hadn't told me anything about the work and said she couldn't. I went across and was introduced to George Noble – a captain in the British Army [Major Georges Bégué, 'George One']. Two RAF officers were there as well as the secretary to Colonel [Maurice] Buckmaster, who was head of section. I was welcomed by the RAF officers, but nothing was said about what was going on. Then George Noble said, 'I would like you to type this for me, please.' It was a page of numbers and alphabetical figures, which made no sense at all. He said, 'I want one copy and then you must go and get it reprinted and you have to ask them to put it on edible paper. You won't make a mistake, will you? Somebody's life may depend upon it.' I then typed it and afterwards went over to Buckmaster's secretary and asked her if she would check it, which she did.

Captain Noble realized I knew very little and said, 'Look, we have a filing room in here, and when I don't need you to type, I give you permission to go in. They're all files belonging to agents who have been sent to France. You can pick a file, read it, and that way you'll learn more about this section than anyone can tell you. This is a section in which we keep to ourselves. The less you know about other people's work in the building, the best.' That was the ethos that went through the whole of SOE: the less you know the less you can divulge. Each agent was an operator in the field. The files contained their life histories, how they got there and much more, they were very, *very* fascinating. I did my typing and listened to the other, mainly older, people there. This helped me a great deal to understand the work.

Countess Mountbatten of Burma, Lady Brabourne (Patricia Mountbatten)
War work, London

The minute my school graduation was over, I expected to come home and did so. My ambition was to join the WRNS, the

Women's Royal Naval Service, but it took me a whole year to get in. They always had a waiting list and I was not privileged in any way, despite my father's high position in the Royal Navy [then chief of Combined Operations]. I was determined not to be, and my father didn't want that either. I knew I'd have to wait my turn and that it would take some little while. In the interim I did war work in a depot, packing wool that was knitted into garments mostly for sailors – jerseys, mittens, scarves. Then I started working in the bar at Combined Operations Headquarters, but somebody complained that the daughter of the chief was working in the bar so I was demoted to the canteen. I wasn't very good at that, but it was fun. When I eventually joined the WRNS, I chose Signals. It was an interesting department at the heart of what was happening.

Iris Hobby (Cutbush)
Land girl, near Croydon, Surrey

My father dropped me at Halliloo Farm. The farmer and his wife greeted me and he took me over to Mrs Grummet, my billet. Her address was 1 Bughill Cottages – enough to put a seventeen-year-old off! He said, 'You can come over once a week for a bath,' and told me I would receive twenty-three shillings [£1.15] and sixpence a week and out of that I would have to pay twenty-one shillings and sixpence [£1.08] for my billet. So I had one and sixpence [8p] for working seven days a week from five in the morning until six in the evening, with three-quarters of an hour for a lunchbreak. And in the summer you were expected to help with the harvest and everything else. This was for seven days a week and they didn't have to give you a day off. They were supposed to give you over-time pay for over sixty hours a week, but I never got any.

Mrs Grummet greeted me on the doorstep with 'My husband did the milk round on the farm but he was called up. If I want to keep this tied cottage, I have to take two land girls, so you'd better behave yourself or you'll be out.' I went in the cottage, and there was a growling dog called Jack, who tried to get me. She gave me a candlestick to go upstairs with. I was so cold as there was no heat upstairs and I used to wrap my feet in my green sweater. The water was from a well and, of course, the toilet was outside. After a week the other girl turned up and she was greeted in exactly the same way. She'd been brought up on farms, a tall girl, nearly six foot, but she just burst into tears on the step.

I was told to report to the farm at four forty-five a.m. and I would be met by the head cowman. And, it being wartime, no lights and pouring with rain, with boots that leaked, I couldn't find him. I wandered into a shed and saw a cow who looked as though she might be calving. I rushed out, tripped over a lump of corrugated iron and fell into a puddle of filthy water and that was how the head cowman found me. I said, 'I think there's a cow having a calf in there.' 'What do you mean "think", don't you *know*?' And he told me I must go with him and watch ...

We used to feed the cows with brewers' grain. This was delivered in a big lorry and put in a pit, and you used to get a big wooden shovel and shovel it all in. This was the first job I was given after I came back from my breakfast. I really had a struggle with it and I heard the farmer say to the lorry driver, 'Well, they said they'd send me a land girl, but they've sent me a b— schoolkid.' I thought, *Right*. I'll show you. I worked twice as hard as I need have done just to show them all ...

If the cows were in service they were turned out into the yard with the bull. I used to find this most embarrassing. I would be washing up the milking-machines and I could see out of the dairy, and the men working there would hold my head up so that I'd got to look. But I soon got used to it ... We had to be very careful with the bulls – there were two on that farm. Occasionally the smaller one would get in with the cows when the bigger one was there and we used to have to separate them. It was quite frightening. We had forks but we had to get him out otherwise the bigger bull would have got him. But I must tell you this: when I went into the [Women's] Land Army, I took my ukulele and my mouth-organ and I'd sing the cows a song, playing my ukulele because I was sure they'd let their milk down better in the milking-machines.

Joanna Lawrence (Rogers)
Schoolgirl, West Wickham, Kent

When we stayed with my uncle on his farm in Buckinghamshire, we felt sorry for the Land Army girls there. They used to mutter about my uncle to us – they were treated as second-class citizens: they lived in the mews in the yard and weren't allowed in the house, although there were plenty of rooms. We thought they were very nice, but my uncle thought they ought to know their place. He was a very wealthy farmer with a big farm.

Audrey Hammon (Cobb)
Schoolgirl, Stowting, Kent

My uncle had four land girls on his farm and they helped enormously. They would come to our farm for the threshing. This was done in the winter and it was very, very cold. Mother had a lot of compassion for the land girls, and she would invite them into the kitchen where maybe she had a milk pudding of some kind. She also let them use our toilet facilities. Farm workers were away in the forces so the land girls did a good job, as far as I could see.

May Moore (George)
Evacuee, Eyam, Derbyshire

Fourteen was the official age to leave school, if you hadn't passed the scholarship. It was at the back of my mind that I would have to go home. But Uncle Jim said, 'I think I'll try to get you a job at the View.' This was a large house that Edgar Allen's [the Sheffield steelworks] head office had taken over. They didn't want people from the village rushing up there wanting jobs: they brought their own specialists out from Sheffield. To get a job at the View was really something. My sisters Enid and Myra joined me later. We worked together in an office there until we went home.

37. Children at Moorside Road School, Bromley, in south-east London, survey bomb damage to the school premises.

38. An open-air sewing class in Pembrokeshire for evacuees from Battersea, London.

39. Women's Land Army girls clean a cattle-fodder mangel, on a farm at Cannington, Somerset.

40. Jill Monk (Holman), ready for her auxiliary messenger job, on Merry Monarch.

41. Donald Swann sunning himself in Greece while on humanitarian service in 1945 with the Friends' Ambulance Unit.

42. Ready to tackle that bull! Land girl Iris Hobby (Cutbush), Farnham, Surrey.

43. Conscientious objector Tony Parker, experiencing the life of a coal miner, Lancashire, 1942.

44. 'Farmer' Geoffrey Shaw, Ontario, Canada.

45. Some anxious moments for overseas evacuees.

46. British evacuees in the United States speak with their parents on a radio link jointly organized by the BBC and the National Broadcasting Company of America.

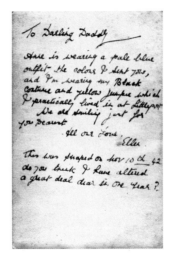

47. Maggie Lanning (Mundy), photographed with her mother in November 1942. On the reverse of the photograph there is a message to Maggie's father, who has yet to see his daughter.

48. Fran Whittle (Casselden) clutches her father George's finger as sister Nadine holds the pram. George was killed during the D Day landings while serving with the Royal Navy.

49. After being buried for three hours following a V1 'incident', a young girl is rescued from the debris of her family home.

50. PC Frederick Godwin of Gipsy Hill Police Station comforts a shocked elderly man whose wife has just been killed and home destroyed in a V1 attack, Upper Norwood, London, July 1944.

51. The ship's company of HMS *Belfast* entertain a group of young British ex-internees, including James Maas, at Shanghai, October 1945.

52. One of the many bonfires lit to celebrate VE Day.

53. It's all over! At Piccadilly Circus, a cheerful London girl and two happy GIs are among those celebrating VJ Day and the war's end.

Carmin Sidonio
Cinema rewind boy, Blackheath, London

Back in London, as I was approaching fifteen, I was told that I'd better start looking for a job ... I loved the cinema and thought I'd like to work in one. The Prince of Wales in Lewisham had been converted from a theatre to a cinema and I went in there and got a job as a rewind boy. I shot out of the cinema, ran all the way home, burst in to the shop and said to my mother, 'I've got a job, starting tomorrow. I'm going to be a rewind boy in the pictures and, Mum, I'm getting *fifteen shillings* [75p] a week!'

We were showing a film three times a day, so at least fifteen times a week. Although most were in black-and-white, Technicolor was being introduced at that time. The film I remember most vividly is *Gone With the Wind*. It was so *wonderful*. We operators used to pick the films to pieces, but that was such an *impressive* film. I show off to people now and say, 'Oh, yes, I saw that about twenty times,' and then have to explain to them. There were also a lot of wartime morale-boosting films – the one Noël Coward did about the navy [*In Which We Serve*]. The newsreels were a *must* and we always started off with one.

The cinema itself was a little world of pleasure for people, especially at night in the blackout. It was dark at four o'clock and people would flock in. Something that always stuck in my mind was that, within an hour of the showing, there was a haze of smoke in the cinema. I would say about ninety per cent of people were smoking, every seat had an ashtray. I would look out of my operating box and there was a sea of glowing cigarette ends. The smoke was *incredible*: the beams from the projectors were like searchlights trying to pierce it. There was some audience participation too. When air raids on Germany were shown, there would be clapping and cheering – people were very involved as well they might be. War was a way of life. It took over everybody's life.

If there were raids, we used to flash 'Air Raid' on the screen, but it was left to people whether they wanted to stay or go. I was always surprised at how many stayed. We used to keep watch from the balcony. We could see the sky and flashes of gunfire, and if we knew a heavy raid was starting, we would have to close the cinema and go down to a public shelter.

Colin Ward
Teenager, Ilford, Essex

Curiously enough, for a headmaster's son, I left school at fifteen. I don't really know what ambitions my parents had for me but I was a dreamy child and wasted my time at school. Then the war broke out and I got a job. You will laugh at this [later he was anti-war and an anarchist]. My first job was working for a small firm of builders who were putting up Anderson shelters. The local council was employing small contractors to erect these things at the time of the outbreak of war in backyards and back gardens. My employer was a rogue. These things were supplied free but he implied to householders that they needed to pay him for the labour of putting them in. Then I had another job with a builder, and then I went to work for an architect, working on the drawing board. Of course, in wartime, he only did plans for repairs to war-damaged buildings . . .

I went into the army in 1942 and began to question things in 1943, by which time I was in Glasgow where there was an active anarchist movement at that time, but I think I became interested in propaganda through reading the publications of Freedom Press, the anarchist publishers. Probably the first I read was a pamphlet called *The Philosophy of Anarchism*, by Herbert Read.

Paul Eddington
Window-dresser, Birmingham, Warwickshire

So I left school not knowing what to do. Employment wasn't all that difficult for a young man at that time because most men were away at the war. We happened to know somebody in the personnel department of John Lewis, in Birmingham, and she got me a job in the display department. I didn't enjoy my time there. It was an extremely autocratic regime. I was told that, shortly before the war, the assistant general manager used to go round the departments every Saturday morning and sack a few people '*pour encourager les autres*' [to encourage the others]. And poor men with families and mortgages were seen queuing up to go to the lavatory to be sick before he made his rounds – this fired my own radicalism.

I can remember being asked to contribute to the Spitfire Fund, and I refused to do so. This caused a considerable frisson in the department. Eventually I was called by the assistant manager who said, 'Eddington, you don't appear to be enjoying your job.' I suppose any normal employee would have said, 'Good heavens, yes, I *love* it, sir.' But I wasn't able to do this, so I said, 'No, I don't very much.' Poor man, all he could do was say, 'Well, do try to pull your socks up, old chap.' However, I remember hearing one day that a girl with whom I'd been at school, and with whom I'd acted occasionally, had decided to become an actress. And suddenly it was like the road to Damascus, a tremendous *revelation*. I realized one could earn one's living at this enjoyable activity, and from then on nothing would stop me but that I must be an actor ... And so I joined ENSA – Entertainments National Service Association. Eric Portman had been in this company and so had James Mason, but before my time.

Joseph Stagno
Gibraltarian boy seaman, Royal Navy

I was fifteen when I entered the navy. This was September 1942. Then I went to the boys' naval training place in Douglas, the Isle of Man, until July 1943. We knew political prisoners, mostly Italian, were billeted in hotels there, interned for the duration. We met them and used to chat to them.

I joined HMS *Belfast* and my first trip was escorting Winston [Churchill] to the Quebec Conference in Canada. He travelled across in the *Queen Mary*. We escorted her so far and then the American and Canadian warships took over. I was also on the Russian convoys to Murmansk. This was quite a regular thing – you went from Scapa [Flow] to Iceland, then Iceland to

Murmansk and back. I was on HMS *Belfast*, which was defending the convoy, and we escorted them back. Our role was ahead of the convoy, more to shelter or protect it from surface craft, which did materialize in the shape of the *Scharnhorst*, in December 1943. They started off the day before Boxing Day, chasing off across the North Sea. Eventually she was engaged and the last we saw of her was when she was completely on fire. Then the destroyers picked up survivors. This was a huge boost to morale. There had always been the possible threat to the Russian convoys, not only from the *Scharnhorst* but the *Tirpitz* too. We always expected them to come out and the senior officers *hoped* they'd come out.

The conditions on these convoys were very cold and there were constant alarms for aircraft and surface vessels, which didn't always materialize, so you were kept on the hop all the time. We were issued with special warm clothing, but the guns would get iced up and you had to chip it off all the time and this made life more difficult. Really, it was just the monotony of it: being on your mounting, going down getting something to eat, then back again on your mounting. There was very little chance of survival if you fell into the water around the north cape – just four minutes. That was proved by the *Scharnhorst* – thirty-six survived out of the whole complement.

Later, on D Day, we went over with the main assault on 6 June. We laid off Arromanches and supported a Canadian division ashore. At first it was very quiet; we just kept on bombarding the shore. We were there until early August because we were the flagship of the cruiser squadron. Later on we had some clashes with the shore batteries, but by and large it was just a question of being there and bombarding. The whole invasion was very well organized: if you looked across the Isle of Wight into the Channel, you could walk across the ships and landing craft – a real armada going across to the beaches for the following morning. We arrived about two o'clock in the morning. We were lucky with our landing: it wasn't as bad as other sectors.

Jesus 'Cai' Martinez
Spanish teenager, Dudley, West Midlands

Franco wanted us back because he wanted to say in the papers,
'Oh, look, the children are coming back to a glorious new Spain.'
But we were growing up and had to find our own way. And as
I had received some art education and was drawing and painting,
the obvious thing was, 'Oh, we'll send him to a painter and
decorator in Dudley.' The decorator there had eight or ten men
and they had all been taken into the army and he was only left
with an old boy, who used to push the cart with all the gear on.
I had no training with this physical work and during my time
there I used to do everything – painting Midland Red bus signs,
without any signwriting experience, spraying helmets for the
Military Police, doing black-out in the factory at Dudley, huge
windows and we had to black them all out, signs in pubs ...

Luis Sanz
Spanish teenager, London

I came to England in 1937 with a group of Spanish child refugees
from the civil war and I refused to go back after the fall of Bilbao,
when children started to return ... I got a job when the Second
World War was declared. The homes we had been living in were,
of course, closed down and we had to go and earn our living.
My first job was to the Argentinian embassy, sharpening pencils
and filling inkpots and acting as messenger. Fortunately the ambassador was a member of the World Refugee Committee, and he
took special care of me ... I didn't have British nationality for a
long time as I thought that Franco would die sooner or later and
we'd go back to Spain, but of course he didn't die for a long
time. Very few, if any, decided to take up British nationality until
each of us was called to Scotland Yard to be interviewed by the
Home Office. Among the many questions they put to us – perti-
nent and impertinent – was why we hadn't become naturalized.
The seed was planted and from that date I became naturalized

and many of my friends too. Several of us joined the British forces during the war and some were killed, but I didn't.

John Gibson
Teenager, boarding-house worker, Belfast, Northern Ireland

When you were fourteen in those days you had to find work. I got my first job in a boarding-house in Belfast near my home. The south was neutral during the war. It was a strange situation in some ways because we had a Customs set-up then, which we'd never had before. The gentleman I worked for used to take me down to Dublin to buy things we couldn't get in Northern Ireland, and we'd smuggle them through. You know, clothing was very, very scarce in the north during the first part of the war, and we used to buy three or four pairs of pyjamas and put them on with our clothes on top. The train would stop at the border, the Customs men came on and searched you everywhere, and we'd have all the pots of stuff hanging outside the carriage door – a wartime dodge!

Iris Hobby (Cutbush)
Land girl, Farnham, Surrey

When I moved on to the big farm at Farnham, the head cowman became very ill and I worked completely on my own for three months, no time off at all. And I had to clean out the bull's pen, nobody else about but me. I used to clean him out on my own every day, which was against the law. But I did it because I was trying to prove I could do these things ...

Sometimes I used to hear shed doors creaking and it used to be the Italian prisoners-of-war creeping up behind me. They gave me a lot of sexual harassment and I used to carry a pitchfork around with me permanently and swear that I would stab them, and would have done so too. One of them made me a ring – 'Thees, Mees, for you.' I thanked him, then he said, 'One kees, Mees.' I said, 'Get out!' One day I heard this girl, whose husband was a prisoner-of-war in Italy, screaming, and I rushed in to see one of these Italians attacking her. I went at him with the fork. They were apparently a bad lot of Italian prisoners. They had a civilian with a rifle looking after them, but he was never about.

Peter Izard
Teenager, Civil Defence messenger and BOAC trainee traffic clerk, Beckenham, Kent

I had left school by the time the flying bombs came. I was in the ATC [Air Training Corps]; I wanted a job but didn't know what I wanted to do. Eventually I went to BOAC [British Overseas Airways Corporation] at Croydon and started with them. I was in uniform as a trainee traffic clerk with what the navy would call a 'tiddly' uniform, double-breasted with one wing on my sleeve – at sixteen, very good for the girls and dances! So then I had three strings to my bow: a messenger in the Civil Defence, in the airlines, and in the Air Training Corps ... One of my jobs with BOAC was to look after the diplomatic mail. Every afternoon after lunch I had a small crew-bus and a driver, and I used to go to the Foreign Office, the Home Office, the Colonial Office, the Air Ministry, the Admiralty and the War Office, and collect the diplomatic mail – and here am I just sixteen and a half! All this would be taken back to the centre at the air terminal where it was sorted out and taken to various places overnight on sleeper trains by retired army officers. Every so often one of us would have to go. So at sixteen and a half, seventeen, I was on a train, maybe from Paddington to Bristol, going to the old airfield with diplomatic mail and suchlike, every now and then managing to get a flight back to Croydon.

Kenneth Sparks
*Survivor of **City of Benares**, boy seaman, Royal Navy*

I joined the navy in 1944. You could look at it two ways: either the last thing you'd want to do, or, oh, well, I've been through this before, so it won't happen again, will it? I went as a boy bugler to the Isle of Man for training, and from the day I left the island I never touched a bugle again! But I still got my sixpence [3p] a day for the job. I was then nearly sixteen. In a battleship, we were a long way from what we were firing at as we chased up and down the Mediterranean, and we did see a little action with the Americans in the Pacific, where we assisted the 7th Fleet. At one time we were based at Sydney and I received a call to report to the captain. I wondered what I'd done wrong, like all sailors do. But 'Someone to see you.' This was Rory O'Sullivan from one of the lifeboats [from the *City of Benares*] who had kept track of us. All the boys on our lifeboat, apart from Paul [Shearing], went into the navy. We'd already had a taste of what the sea was like and I thought, It can't do any worse than it's done already.

Would-be conscientious objectors (COs) had to face a tribunal that would determine whether they should be given unconditional exemption from military service, non-combatant duties in the armed forces, or undertake some form of 'alternative' civilian service. Sometimes an application was turned down altogether. A refusal to obey any directive was punishable with a fine or prison sentence. In all 1,891 COs went to prison, including many women. The total number by the end of the war was 59,192.

Rodney Giesler
Anglo-German schoolboy, Hele, Somerset

I don't think many people had much time for 'conchies' because they wanted to opt out of everything – they wanted others to do the fighting on their behalf. But you don't have to take lives to support your country. I got involved with Quakers when I was studying at home after the war, when I had time to think about it. I used to go to meetings. Many of them had joined the Friends' Ambulance Unit, and the FAU had a lot of casualties during the war. They went just where the fighting troops went. They carried no weapons and they were in the line of fire just as everyone else was, except they couldn't defend themselves. If

I had been a pacifist at that time, I think I would have been in the Friends' Ambulance Service.

Dennis Hayden
Evacuee schoolboy, Highclere, Hampshire

We had conscientious objectors – they were working on the farms. We didn't know they were conscientious objectors, we just knew that they didn't want to fight. There didn't seem to be any ill feeling towards them, and they seemed very good farm workers. The second youngest daughter, Jean, was a land girl; sometimes they escorted her home and had a meal ... We even met Italian prisoners-of-war, who were put out to farmwork. Again, they came home and were welcomed quite happily, simply because they were doing farmwork. I think it was this love of the land – whatever one's beliefs, or one's enemies, didn't bother the Bakers one little bit.

The only interesting person who lived in the village was Sir Oswald Mosley, the Fascist leader. I think he was in exile in the manor house, next door to the school. Not that we ever saw him. If we had, he would have been in a closed car, in and out of the village ...

Audrey Hammon (Cobb)
Schoolgirl, Stowting, Kent

We did have conscientious objectors working on the land in this area – the local term for them was 'conchies'. I think most people treated them with scorn. They weren't popular at all. I think they were shunned by most people, held in contempt.

Carmin Sidonio
Conscientious objector, Beare Green, Surrey

In late 1943, when I was coming on for seventeen, conscription was looming. I had no intention or desire to go into the forces. My brother George was a pacifist and he used to come home and tell me what he was doing. I was pretty sure I didn't want to fight. One of the reasons why I didn't want to fight was that I didn't want to fight Italy and Italians, although we didn't identify with Italy at all. We were concerned for our many relatives in Italy and we just thought of the war as a horrible thing that was breaking things up ... I remember when I was seventeen saying to George, 'I don't want to go into the army.' He said, 'Well, why don't you object?' I said, 'What do I do?' He said, 'Join the Peace Pledge Union.' I contacted the London office and in February of 1944 they notified me that there was a hostel opening in Surrey, which was taking on land workers and conscientious objectors and there were vacancies.

I gave in my notice to the cinema, and on a cold morning in February 1944 I travelled down to the hostel in Beare Green, Surrey. I was only five foot four, weighing about seven stone, although wiry and energetic. I was the youngest to report. I was given a job helping in the kitchen, preparing food and cleaning the rooms ... I fitted in well, but I wanted to become more involved with the men and said I'd work on the land with them. They tried to put me off but I said I wanted to try, so I was fixed up in a gang. The job then was threshing corn – dirty work but I loved the physical side of it and the camaraderie too ... When I was called up, they let me continue as I was already doing work of national importance. I never experienced hostility as a CO, but I know a couple of others were turned down by farmers because they were 'conchies'.

Jean Greaves (Catchpool)
University student, Somerville College, Oxford

I was a very innocent child, a bit of a swot, and doing German in the sixth form. I got into Oxford with an exhibition, which pleased everybody, I was given a place to do PPE [politics, philosophy, economics], but the exhibition was for German. It didn't work for me. I remember a very painful evening when I was trying to write an essay about Schiller's guilt complex and feeling very guilty about being at university at all. We had to do war work once a week, and mine was at the Radcliffe Hospital, helping on the head-injuries ward and I remember thinking, This is where I *ought* to be. But for some strange reason, when I left Somerville at the end of that term, never to return, I didn't think of becoming a nurse. I missed that opportunity. Instead I joined the Friends' Relief Service. For me, deciding *not* to be a conscientious objector would have been difficult. It would have given my [pacifist] parents a great deal of grief, had I joined the ATS or gone into munitions, so I did a great deal of heart-searching about whether to register or not.

Tony Parker
Pacifist, mine worker, Manchester, Lancashire

When your call-up time came, you either went for your medical to go into the army, or you asked to be put on the register of conscientious objectors and this was what I did when my call-up date came ... I did feel very alone. I think most conchies did because it was never a clear-cut issue. All the time one was saying, 'Am I doing right or wrong? Ought I to rethink this?', especially if a friend had been killed or injured in the war. That was the time when you felt rather bad, rather guilty about it ...

It was extraordinary that I thought of going into the coal mines, because I didn't know anything about them with my middle-class background. But I thought it would be such an unusual experience. That's why I went. And what a turning-point it turned out to be because I was working in a pit and living in a mining community and, of course, to someone with my background, it was a whole new world. I never knew what work was like, and when I say 'work', I mean manual work, *physical* work, and how people could spend their lives doing this.

I worked on what was called the screens – long mechanical belts in very low sheds. The coal came down the chutes at the end of the shed on to the screen and then went along on these fantastically noisy mechanical metal belts. And there were people standing at each side picking out the lumps of rock ... and you would pick out these pieces of rock and put them on a conveyor belt behind you and they would be carried off. Most of the men doing this had been injured down the pits and were no longer fit for work of a very strenuous nature, and some were very young lads like myself. From time to time the belts used to break down and stop suddenly, whereupon everybody would fall over because they'd been standing there, eyes down, looking for these rocks, which were covered with coal dust. And we'd all fall on top of everybody else. This was very disconcerting.

There was a young lad opposite to me and I noticed that his lips were moving while he was working. At the end of the day I said to him, 'What is it you're saying to yourself all the time?' He said, 'Oh, I recite poems.' 'What sort of poems?' I asked him. 'Oh, you know, Wordsworth, Keats, Shelley.' So I said, 'Go on, tell me some.' So he said, 'Still glides the stream, and shall forever more ...' I said, 'How the hell did you learn that?' He said, 'Oh, I got it from a book in the library.' I used to pass the time by whistling, and this same lad said to me one day, 'What's it you're doing?' He couldn't hear but could see my lips. I said, 'Oh, I whistle.' He said, 'What do you whistle?' 'Music.' 'What music?' So I said, 'Well, chiefly Beethoven.' He said, 'How does it go?' So I whistled a bit of the Emperor Concerto and hummed a bit. He said, 'Where can I get it? Where can I hear it properly?' I said, 'Well, look, do you have a gramophone?' and he had. I said, 'Well, I'll bring it to you.' The following week he said to me, 'Have you got any more stuff by that bloke?' I never knew the result of that because eventually I went underground. But it's always seemed to me that this set-up of two young lads, one from a rather prissy middle-class background, myself, and the other from a working-class background, swapping bits of poetry and bits of music and so on – it's something I've never forgotten – it stopped me getting any ideas that there was something special about having a middle-class education.

The only incident of hostility I experienced there was when one of the young boys came up to me and said, 'You're a fucking conchie, aren't you?' I said, 'Yes, that's right.' And he hit me. Otherwise, no hostility and quite a few of the older men were very sympathetic, particularly those I worked with underground

... But what impressed me most was the feeling of solidarity amongst the workers. There was this big poster at the pit head as you got into the cage and it said, 'You are the commandos of industry.' I remember the sour remarks of the colliers. They'd say, 'Oh, yes, that's not what they said before the war. We were "the scum of the earth", and if we didn't do a decent day's work, we'd lose our jobs and many of us did.' So they were very cynical about it and that's one of the reasons they accepted a conchie because they didn't swallow this 'you are the commandos of industry' at all.

Paul Eddington
Actor with ENSA, Birmingham, Warwickshire

About half-way through a tour in the Orkneys with ENSA I was called up for national service. I was seventeen. I always knew I would register as a conscientious objector and I did so. I went along to register with some trepidation. I expected some show of hostility from the clerk or the people who were around me, but I didn't meet any of that.

After one of our shows on this tour some of us went to the officers' mess for the usual little party, a little drink. As luck would have it, I found myself having a drink with the commanding officer, of all people, under a little blue blackout light. And the CO said to me, 'Well, young man, and what branch of the services will you be going into?' And I said, 'None, sir.' 'Ah,' he said. 'On medical grounds?' I thought, Oh dear, this is going to put the tin lid on the whole evening. I said, 'No, I've registered as a conscientious objector.' 'Oh,' he said, and turned various shades of purple under this little blue light. 'Don't agree with you, admire your stand, don't agree with you.' And I think that was an education for me in a way. I understood for the first time, I think, why people were prepared to die to enable the sort of conversation that we were having to take place. I didn't think there was any other country in the world − at war, of all things − where that conversation could have happened between a commanding officer of a military unit and a conscientious objector. Most *extraordinary*.

It didn't alter my views, but I think it broadened them considerably. I hope. Anyway, because I had registered as a conscientious objector, I was told that there was no longer a job for me in ENSA.

I was prepared to go to prison and thought I might have to, and I was prepared at my tribunal in Birmingham to be asked all sorts of trick questions on obscure parts of the Bible and things like, what would I do if a German were to rape my sister? Attempt to fight them off, I suppose. As far as I could see, there was a fundamental difference between that sort of reaction and dropping a bomb from a mile high on somebody. Judge Finnemore was chairman of my tribunal, flanked by various city worthies. He was a most impressive man, very, very old – he must have been about forty-five then, but you must remember I was seventeen. He read my disposition. I was at a considerable advantage because I had been preceded by a dozen Christadelphians, all of whom said exactly the same thing. They had the same person to speak for them all. They were obviously well schooled in their Bible studies, and they answered all the questions as if by rote. And they were sent pell-mell, one by one, down the mines or into the ambulance service or something like that. I was asked my details, and I spoke in an educated voice and sufficiently loudly to be heard. I could almost sense a slight feeling of relaxation on the bench. However, when we had done with all that, the judge looked me squarely in the eye and said, 'What are your objections to military service?' And, put like that, I hadn't the faintest idea. I was expecting all sorts of tricks. I remember I gave a gulp, which ricocheted off the wall behind the judge's head, and he actually came to my rescue. 'Are they religious?' and I said, 'Yes,' with relief, and we took it from there. I thought myself to be a Christian, and being a Christian to try to live one's life as Christ lived His, and I couldn't imagine Christ donning a uniform and shooting someone. It was basically as simple as that.

Donald Swann
Pacifist, hospital porter, Orpington, Kent

Although I was in no form a medical worker, I wanted to do something to help, though not to join the army. And, of course, that was the beauty of the Second World War position *vis-à-vis* the conscientious objector – on the whole they approved of you if you were willing to do *something* ... My most important time was in Orpington, a branch of Guy's Hospital, where the Friends' Ambulance Unit, which I had joined, did all the orderly work. There was a lot of conviviality between us, mostly men, a section of about eighteen. We called ourselves 'conchies' – that was our jokey name for ourselves. We learnt ever so quickly. I was a mortuary-trolley operator and then, most interesting of all, I worked in an operating theatre for about four months and saw most of the operations. I was the one who pushed the patient in, then helped, watched the whole thing and cleaned it all out, then pushed them back to the ward. Perhaps the only other thing I remember vividly is bathing chronics – very sick old men. We each had to bath nine a week in our own time, and that was, I suppose, my introduction to sick old people – what a hard finishing to life that is, lying in beds very close to each other. If they asked, we told them we were pacifists, but they didn't worry. You see, this is the thing: a medical passport is one of the most wonderful things. Everybody relaxes very much. I think this was the beginning of this *entente*. I knew then I could talk to soldiers, and to ill soldiers. I was not a Quaker at the time ... I went abroad in 1943 to the Middle East and then Greece, doing humanitarian work with the FAU.

Deryck Moore
Pacifist, porter, Hammersmith Hospital, London

There was one particular ward where one of the patients called me a 'dirty conchie', and asked why wasn't I at the front. And this does jolt you momentarily. Some of the other patients told him to be quiet, and if I wasn't doing it someone else would, and it was only part of a training that would probably take me abroad. But this chap had a thing about 'conchies' and you had to respect his views.

Ronnie Huzzard
Pacifist hospital stretcher-bearer, Hull, Yorkshire, extract of letter to evacuee sister Dorothy

I am glad to hear from Mother and Dad that you are keeping very well but am sorry to hear you want to come home. Things are no safer now than when you went away, and as I write this letter at 1 o'clock in the morning the planes are overhead and the anti-aircraft guns are booming and Mother and Father are in the shelter. I am afraid the quiet weeks we have had since the last two 'blitzes' will not come again until the new moon has finished ... Mother tells me that conscientious objectors are boycotted in Pickering and ignored by a large number of the people. It is a good job I don't live there. I think if Pickering had been as much hit by the war as Hull, those who refused to support the war would have been respected. After all everyone has a right to his own views ...

13. 1944: 'The Beginning of the End'

Nineteen forty-four was a momentous year in the Second World War. By the spring, everybody was expecting the opening of the long-awaited Second Front – an Allied invasion of Europe, which would take the pressure off the Eastern Front and drive the Germans out of occupied Europe. With the Russian advance from the east, it would lead to the final Allied victory over Germany. The time and location of the invasion were kept secret, but it was impossible to disguise the magnitude of its scale. In the ports of southern England, 4,126 ships and landing-craft were berthed ready to sail for France, and roads were clogged with convoys of military vehicles, making their way to coastal areas. Every bit of spare land was occupied by camouflaged vehicles and troops poised for embarkation.

Operation 'Overlord' – the code name for the landings on the Normandy beaches on 6 June 1944, or D Day – started at 12.16 a.m. with planes and gliders dropping 23,400 men at both ends of the fifty-mile assault front. These airborne troops held their ground until seaborne forces landed. The news was announced on the BBC at 9.30 a.m. to great rejoicing. But the cost of the landings was soon brought home to British civilians: by the end of the day fourteen thousand had been killed, wounded or were missing out of the 152,715 Allied troops who had landed. Despite the losses, the success of the Normandy landings was a huge boost to civilian morale – but there was a long, hard slog ahead.

The Channel Islanders saw the planes flying over to liberate France and expected that soon they, too, would be free. But to their bitter disappointment, the invasion forces swept past, leaving them to starve alongside their German occupiers, now under siege from the Allies and cut off completely from supplies.

Elisabeth Small (Fabri, née Hadfield)
Secretary, air operations section, Special Operations Executive, Baker Street, London

After I had worked under George Noble for a time – a very happy association – Colonel Buckmaster asked would I like to transfer to air operations? This was under [Major Gerard] Gerry Morel, who was a very experienced officer who had been an agent ... The operations were only in force during the moon period. You got prepared for them in the non-moon time when the agents would send in details of the ground where we could drop either personnel or arms, the idea being to try to equip the various resistance groups ready for D Day ...

We had quite a lot of success. Of course, D Day was the great time. We were very busy before that, a three-day shift system, including nights. One of the reasons for being there all night was to listen to the BBC messages that were put out ... Each operation had a particular message, something quite innocuous like 'The cockerel has two wings', which the agents themselves had given when they gave the co-ordinates for the drop. We listened every night for when the BBC were putting out these messages, and the agents were listening too. When they heard it, they would think, Oh, tonight there'll be an air drop because we've heard our message, and that was the way we communicated.

Before D Day two messages had been arranged: one was message B, which was to tell all resistance workers to be prepared, that D Day was coming soon; the A message told them that the invasion was on the way. The weather turned dreadful, and some of the boats were at sea and had to be recalled, so that was an awful blow. But they got away twenty-four hours afterwards and we had to be prepared to send out the A message to say that the invasion was taking place. That night I was on duty and rigged myself up something to sleep on, and Major Morel came in and

said, 'Come on, get off your bed. I want you to type the A message.'
I said, 'Oh, great – *great!*' He said, 'Yes, Airborne are *en route* and
the boats have started.' Then he said, 'That's something nice for
your grandchildren!'

John Starling
Dockyard apprentice, Portsmouth, Hampshire

There was a tremendous build-up of American personnel, tanks,
lorries and guns of all description around the Portsmouth area
because this was one of the main embarkation places for the
invasion of Europe. There was no mistaking what was in the wind
because Eisenhower's headquarters were at Purbrook nearby, so
by the end of May 1944 we knew things were happening. I don't
know how they kept that secret from the Germans because any
casual observer would have noticed this tremendous build-up
around the Portsmouth and Southampton areas, and all roads
going back as far as Winchester were chock-a-block with troops

From *The War Weekly* by Guy Barnett and Derek Tongs

camped alongside lorries and tanks. And, of course, all the invasion barges were in the dockyard ready to take on troops from the beaches of Portsmouth at Southsea.

I remember on 6 June news coming out that the invasion forces had taken off at dawn and we heard all the transport rumbling through the streets of Portsmouth on the way to Southsea and the aircraft buzzing around, accompanying the ships over to the other side. Of course, when they landed there was a great deal of elation amongst the civil population that at last we had entered Europe after all that time. The ships were anchored off Spithead. Southsea was a restricted area so you could only see a small amount, but I remember going down as far as I could and seeing this great armada of ships in the Solent ready to go off. The build-up continued afterwards. They also built a Pluto pipeline to carry the fuel. It started at the oil terminal at Netley, went across to the Isle of Wight, and then to the invasion beaches of Arromanches. I remember seeing the Mulberry harbours being towed out – great big concrete blocks to act as artificial harbours so that ships could land well offshore and troops could come in on smaller ships once the bridgeheads had been secured.

Margaret Woodhead (Butler)
Florist, Portsmouth, Hampshire

We lived near Langstone harbour and I used to walk the dog up by the playing-fields and along by the harbour at night. I remember seeing boats suddenly appearing in the water and you realized that if you stepped into one you could walk right across to Hayling Island, and suddenly troops appeared in the playing-fields.

On the day before D Day, I was walking the dog past soldiers sitting outside tents, and one fellow came over and said, 'Can you post a letter for me? We're not allowed out of here and I would like my wife to get this.' I wasn't in the habit of talking to strangers and I wondered if I should take it. Supposing he's a spy telling the Germans where he's stationed? If so we'll have bombs here. But I did take that letter and I posted it. The next morning when I took the dog for a walk, there was not a soldier to be seen, not a tent, not a boat. That was D Day. And coming over Portsdown Hill we saw all the gliders and the troops going out. That was really a *fantastic* thing. I've often wondered whether that fellow came back, what happened to him ... oh, yes ...

Peter Smith
Schoolboy, Petts Wood, Kent

Of course, the big event in the early summer of 1944 was D Day – the Normandy landings by Allied troops on the north coast of France. I recall very vividly being in class and the headmaster coming in and announcing, 'Our troops have landed in northern France.' And we all got up and shouted, *'Hooray!'* – a great event that was, *so* much excitement.

Joanna Lawrence (Rogers)
Schoolgirl, West Wickham, Kent

By May 1944 we were seeing much more military activity. The Canadians had come and were billeted in empty houses all around us then, and my parents were beginning to get more strict about where we were, and we had to draw our horns in. There was a half-built road behind us – work on it was stopped at the beginning of the war – and camouflaged tanks and guns were put there. We used to see planes practising and war traffic was everywhere, mostly tanks on low-level loaders, and there were soldiers in camouflaged tents. During May, every lane had *something* down it or moving down it, and we used to see a few gliders. Obviously something was going on – everyone around us knew. The weather was bad and we waited, glued to the radio, and we knew they'd gone even before there was an announcement. On the day of the invasion we were *thrilled to the core.*

Noel Dumbrell
Schoolboy, Ashurst, Sussex

D Day! I'd never seen anything like it! More and more troops were coming into the area. Every field, every wood was packed with things I'd never seen before, these huge tanks and other vehicles. Whole roads were blocked with camouflage netting from one side to the other. Nothing could get through – just a mass of men and machinery. And troops of every nationality you could think of. I remember Free French and some Poles. A special tank road was made through the fields with a Bailey bridge over the [river] Adur, from Ashurst to Henfield. They had all this equipment I used to ride on. And, of course, this bridge gave us a short-cut and we could use our cycles. But it was later blown up by the Canadians. Then I woke up one morning, very disappointed. The lot was gone! In the night, *gone*. Just a few petrol cans, a few cigarette cartons left. All gone, gone to war. I know it was said, 'The boys have all gone, we'd better say some prayers for them.' Then, of course, we heard on the radio about the invasion, but I can't remember it being called D Day then.

After D Day it all ground to a halt, very quiet indeed. Jerry left us alone. The bombing suddenly stopped and we didn't have to be so careful at night. Then, of course, the troops down the army camp eventually went. I didn't want them to go, but my schoolteacher let me have the day off to watch them, and they towed everything away. I cried my eyes out when they went. They gave me the Royal Artillery badge. But I was very upset, I missed them ...

Rodney Giesler
Anglo-German schoolboy, Hele, Somerset

People say that D Day came as a surprise. Maybe to the Germans, but not to us! For about three weeks before D Day I can remember playing cricket at school and about two o'clock every afternoon the skies would darken with Dakotas towing gliders, heavy formations practising. It wasn't a surprise when the news broke. But there was a *tremendous* sense of excitement. The build-up was so strong. You couldn't hide it: the convoys, the trucks – endless Studebaker trucks loaded with men and supplies, tank transporters. Military Police were everywhere – they were called 'Snowdrops' because of their white helmets. The trains were packed. The weight of troops was such that you couldn't hide them. And when D Day happened, everyone got a lift, although there was this terrible fighting in Normandy ... Then everyone got depressed about the Battle of the Bulge ...

Countess Mountbatten of Burma, Lady Brabourne (Patricia Mountbatten)
WRNS, Southampton, Hampshire

I was in the Combined Operations base on the river Hamble, Southampton Water, for D Day. There was this extraordinary build-up of ships in Southampton Water across to Cowes, on the Isle of Wight, and I think you really felt you could walk across from ship to ship to Cowes. It was absolutely *extraordinary* that they never got bombed – they were there for quite a few days ... Then one morning we woke up and they had all gone. That was extraordinary too. We heard distant gunfire, and we waited to see who was going to come back. A lot came back and a lot didn't come back. They were people we knew very well because they lived on our base and worked with us. That was very sad ...

Marion Tostevin (Letissier)
Schoolgirl, Guernsey

One day the skies were absolutely *black* with planes. I shall never forget it – this was D Day! And the *drone*, day and night, was continuous. We knew there was something going on and we could see the fires in France and we thought, Oh, this is *great*, we'll have our turn soon. But it was so disappointing that they bypassed us. I can see their point now: they didn't want to make it bad for us as they would be destroying the island, really. But it was bad for morale. We were *so* disappointed at the time and then we had *nothing* in the way of food. I really don't know how we existed that last year.

Fran Whittle (Casselden)
Infant, Lewes, Sussex

My father was reported missing on 25 June 1944, nineteen days into the D Day landings, three days before my second birthday. He was in the navy and had served on the Atlantic convoys as communications officer. I have no memory of him at all. My mother still talks about the way she was notified: a telegram, 'Missing presumed dead.' Nothing else, that's *it*. I had an elder sister, Nadine, and my mother was pregnant with my third sister, Georgina, named after my father. So she was left with two small children and a baby. We were classed as 'war orphans', even though we had only lost a father. That continued throughout our lives in so far as it meant getting a bit of extra money.

Michael Hart
Anglo-German teenage schoolboy, Berlin, Germany

News of German successes at the start of the war would be announced with a note of *tremendous* triumphalism. All the military news was introduced with a famous fanfare from Liszt's Preludes, and you knew immediately that another victory would be announced. This went on right into 1943, but as the war changed from being very successful to being increasingly disastrous, Liszt disappeared from the radio. But it would be wrong to suppose that the German public was given any accurate information about the military reverses. They admitted the loss of Stalingrad and the general retreat from the Russian front, et cetera, but morale was kept alive by constant references to secret weapons. This was a *very* powerful propaganda instrument telling people, 'Yes, the war isn't going as well as we'd hoped, but ultimately victory depends entirely on the secret weapons ...'

I remember around Christmas 1944 and early 1945, it was clear to any intelligent person that the war would be lost, but a very large number of the general public would still talk about the secret bomb that would annihilate London and force Great Britain to come to terms overnight and produce a dramatic reversal of war fortunes. In the same vein, the parallel was constantly drawn with Frederick the Great, who had been on the verge of total defeat in his wars against Austria and Russia, and then came the sudden death of the Russian empress and the change in Russian policy, which saved Frederick the Great. That was quoted as an historical parallel of how a war that seems to be lost can still, at the last minute, be turned to success.

But what one has to remember – and this is extraordinarily difficult for someone who has not lived under those circumstances – is the total absence of any alternative view to government propaganda. Only the Nazi Party line was broadcast, and except for the very small number who listened to the foreign news, particularly the BBC, there was no way in which you could immediately find a corrective for what you knew to be misleading reports. And listening to the BBC became increasingly dangerous. If caught, people would be put in a concentration camp . . . The news of the famous July Plot, for instance, which we now know was a very complex and widespread comprehensive attempt to bring down the Nazi government, figured for just one day, maintaining that some criminals had attempted an assassination of Hitler and only a few names were mentioned. The fact that half the senior army generals and people from other services, including Intelligence, were behind it was never revealed. Another example of the German public being kept completely in the dark about events.

The heavy bombing of German cities such as Nuremberg, Munich, Bremen, Essen and Berlin had started in the spring of 1942. The German government promised reprisals, which came in early 1944 in the form of the 'Little Blitz' on London. Although it was not of the scale and intensity of the raids of 1940–41 it was a setback, especially when London schools were beginning to recover, and Londoners had thought that the big raids were over.

The German government maintained people's morale with the promise that 'miracle weapons' were to be launched

against Britain and would bring victory. In September 1939, Hitler had spoken of 'a weapon with which we ourselves could not be attacked'. The British public had been warned that the Germans might use chemical or biological weapons, which had failed to materialize, but now the reprisal weapons were ready to launch on London.

The first V1s – Vergeltungswaffe 1 – arrived on 13 June 1944. They were pilotless flying bombs and were soon known as 'buzz bombs', 'doodlebugs' or just V1s. They were launched from the French coast and the unique terror of the weapon lay in the last seconds of its flight when its motor cut out. Then it glided silently and fell, causing a huge flash and a vast crater. Once more for Londoners life became one long alert, as well as for those living under the robots' flight paths in the south. They flew at low altitudes, and at first the anti-aircraft guns had difficulty in dealing with them. Later, with the repositioning of the batteries along the south coast, many were successfully exploded in the air over the sea. RAF fighters attacked them too, either tipping them over with their wings, or trying to shoot them down over the area known as 'Bomb Alley' – the English Channel, Kent and Sussex. V1s carried 1,870 pounds of explosives and travelled at 400 m.p.h. From June until September 1944, 10,492 were launched; 7,488 reached Britain, but only 3,531 fell on target, the rest being destroyed by anti-aircraft guns and the RAF. They caused 24,165 casualties, of which 6,184 were killed and 17,981 injured – a crushing blow to the morale of Londoners. Later, 1,600 were launched from planes and scattered over a wider area of the country, some landing as far north as Manchester and Yorkshire.

After five years of danger and austerity, war weariness had set in and the new sinister weapons began to corrode British resilience. But life, work and entertainment carried on much as before. Another wave of evacuation took place: this time about a million women and children left the London area. Ironically, many children who had been evacuated abroad

338

for safety were now returning home, in time for the new wave of attacks. For those who remained in threatened cities, Underground shelters were opened again. Deep shelters and the indoor Morrison shelters, which had been too late for the 1940–41 Blitz, now came into their own.

Then, on 8 September, Londoners experienced another shock with the arrival of the V2s. The first fell on Chiswick, and the explosion was so great that people heard it all over West London. It was passed off as a gas-main fracture, but on 10 November, Churchill revealed that a new weapon, a rocket, had been launched from Holland. The V2 was a huge steel canister, forty-five feet long. It carried a ton-weight warhead, and was far more powerful than the V1. Supersonic, it gave no warning of its arrival, so evasive action was impossible; 1,403 were launched and over six months 517 fell on London, killing 2,754 people and badly injuring 6,523. The damage to housing was tremendous: when the V1 and V2 attacks ended, London had lost 130,000 homes. The last V2 fell on 27 March 1945, the last V1 on the twenty-ninth. By then, Allied troops were across the Rhine and the end of the war was in sight. In all, 60,595 civilians were killed during the war, 86,182 were seriously injured and nearly 4.5 million homes were destroyed or damaged.

Michael Hart
Anglo-German schoolboy, Bavaria, Germany

Schöndorf, where the school was situated, is near a lake north-west of Munich – very rural, no likelihood of the area being bombed. Munich was very heavily bombed and on one or two occasions we were called up very early in the morning, put on a lorry and driven to Munich – a matter of an hour and a half's drive – to clear up after raids, save what could be saved from the burnt-out houses and so on. So we did see the effects of the '44 raids. But I had seen a great deal of this in Berlin in '41, '42 and

'43 so it was nothing new. There were shelters at school, though, and if there was a raid you had to go into them.

Rodney Giesler
Anglo-German schoolboy, Hele, Somerset

We weren't aware of the tremendous casualties in the bombing raids in Germany and weren't in touch with our relatives there. All the news bulletins said the targets were military or economic. The marshalling yards at Hamm were always mentioned. It was a great gag of Tommy Handley, 'A lovely piece of Hamm' – brought the house down. Our bombers always hit the target while the cowardly Germans bombed civilians. So, we didn't really care what happened to them. I don't think anyone in Britain did, or anyone fighting the Germans did: 'Flatten Dresden? That's Hitler's fault. He shouldn't have started it.'

Robert Needham
Schoolboy, Trent College, Long Eaton, Derbyshire

This sounds unbelievable now. In 1944 the rate of usage of cannon shells in aircraft based all round Leicestershire and Nottinghamshire was so fast that the RAF ammunition dumps on the airfields couldn't cope, and they were in piles at the roadsides. And we used to go and collect twenty-millimetre cannon shells, and in the engineering lab we would take the cordite out of the back and put it in empty Heinz baked-beans and spaghetti tins. Then we would make rockets and put cordite in the rockets and launch them from the grids outside the library ... One famous day we hadn't taken account of the difference between British and American cordite, which was in long white sticks. We filled one rocket with the American granules and left one of the British strands sticking out and set fire to it so that it would burn its way up. And as it was American granules, we hadn't worked out the maths right and the entire thing blew up spontaneously with an *enormous* explosion during a cricket match against Worksop ... The headmaster, sensible chap, didn't do his nut. He stayed calm and said he'd give an amnesty to all of us if we handed in the ammunition we'd got; he'd go down to his house for two hours so he wouldn't see who'd done it. All he wanted was the ammunition: he thought we were decent chaps. He was playing the game and wanted us to play the game. We took the ammunition into his study and we laid it out in an enormous swastika. He came back and was absolutely deadpan.

John Carter
Schoolboy, Walthamstow, London

In February 1944 the Luftwaffe conducted a mini-blitz on London. One night a bomb fell on my aunt Carrie's house in Clapton, killing her and my two-year-old cousin, Margaret. I can remember a policeman came to our house the following morning and told my father what had happened, and he and his sister, Aunt Nell, went to Clapton. The following day I went over to Clapton because all the family were there. And to this day I remember the scene in Glenarm Road: the houses with the roofs torn off, the great mess, and my father and his two brothers dressed in black overcoats, black ties, talking sombrely between themselves. And Aunt Nell, my mother and a couple of other aunts standing in another group with handkerchiefs in their hands, crying. I didn't know what to do ... I think it was the first time the war had really come home to me: people got *killed*, you know, even small children ...

Joanna Lawrence (Rogers)
Schoolgirl, West Wickham, Kent

The morning of 13 June, we heard this funny noise. It sounded like a motorbike, but it was a little plane flying low, but we knew our planes well and this looked like a meteor and it had flames coming out of its tail. We were standing by the front door and my sister Elizabeth said, 'Look, it's on fire!' and then its engine cut out. And, being children, we didn't rush in, we rushed *out*. It landed about a mile up the road and we thought it had exploded.

We thought it was a plane but it had funny chopped-off wings and was making a funny noise. That was the only one we saw that day, but we heard others and we realized it was something different.

Daddy came home late from work that night. Nobody had said anything on the radio, but everyone local knew something different was happening. We went to see the one that had fallen up the road within about half an hour of it falling. It was the house of somebody we knew. They hadn't been killed, but they were hurt and this was really when war began to hit us: we saw hurt people, people cut and bleeding, and the firemen getting them out. That was the first time we really *saw* things and we began to get a little bit frightened. Daddy told us it was something secret and new, and soon these doodlebugs came over day and night, falling short of London and coming down around us all the time. And, really, at that stage we were a little bit windy. It was all right when you could see them, but it was when you couldn't see them but could hear them that you got frightened. We had big barrage balloons around us and occasionally you'd see one catch a wing on it, and down they'd come. We'd also see planes trying to tip them with their wings, but not successfully. My parents realized they had to get us away again. For us this was the most dangerous time – they were over regularly, day and night, and there weren't alerts. They were just coming. So, once more, the school was evacuated, this time to Dunblane, Perthshire.

John Starling
Dockyard apprentice, Portsmouth, Hampshire

It was an *eerie* experience. It would go pop-pop-pop-pop-pop and then the engine would stop and it would go into a steep dive. You would count for twenty seconds and the thing would explode on impact with the ground. That time between the engine stopping and the moment of impact was frightening, not like bombs coming down. There was an eerie silence just after the engine stopped and before the explosion. We had a lot of damage in Portsmouth from these during the latter part of the war until we managed to overrun the rocket sites in northern France and Belgium.

Leslie Alexander
Schoolboy, Islington, London, extract from his memoir

Everybody in the shelter was very quiet when we heard the rasp of the engine as it approached, because we knew that if the engine continued running and stopped overhead, or after it had passed over, we were safe as it dived away from us. However, if the engine stopped as it approached, then everybody seemed to look up in complete silence with their hands over their ears, counting the seconds and awaiting the explosion, praying that it would not land on us. After the explosion there was a general discussion about where it might have landed, and we waited anxiously until my father or one of his colleagues, who were air-raid wardens patrolling the streets, called in to give us the sad news about the street or buildings destroyed.

Evelyn Fee (Moss)
Evacuee mother of five, Byworth, Sussex

We had an anti-aircraft battery near our house and they didn't start using it until the doodlebugs started. One night one was shot down. Fortunately it fell in a field a short way from us, on the other side of the bank leading to the waterworks. If it had fallen on our side . . . The police came round because it blew my door off, blew my windows out, blew all of us down the stairs. I landed at the bottom with all five children on top of me – I was black and blue for weeks afterwards. And we had a big bit of metal come right through the window. If it had hit one of us . . . That was an *awful* night. I'll always remember it. Good job I wasn't watching out of the back door, as I usually did, because I would have had it – it blew the door right off. The whole top part of the house was full of gravel from the drive. We were treading on it for ages. Oh, it was awful!

Meg Oliver (Adams)
Schoolgirl, Mottingham, Greater London

Then the rockets were starting and one of my friends was killed. I had heard it when I came down the hill. We weren't counselled in those days, but our form mistress let us cry and sob, and we had assembly and we went back still crying and sobbing. And then the geography mistress came in. 'All right, girls, come along, life must go on!' She had a First World War background. That was how you coped: you couldn't be crying because there was a war on. My mother said that my brother used to jump in her womb when those rockets landed. We had two doodlebugs at the end of the road. But you never thought, Oh dear, I shall get caught like that ... or, I'm never going into Woolworths again – somehow the news didn't impinge on you too much, and they didn't show the horror of it on the Pathé News.

Peter Smith
Schoolboy, Petts Wood, Kent

There were just a few doodlebugs to start with, but within days they had built up quite intensely. The sirens would give a warning that they were coming over. The lady next door to us in our semi-detached house, Auntie Vi, was very deaf. She had her elderly mother staying with her. During the day, when her husband was at work, she couldn't hear the sirens and we would bang on the wall to give her warning. We had an interconnecting door in the fence so that when the all-clear sounded we'd go through and tell her. Well, one day the sirens had gone, and later the all-clear, and we had forgotten to tell her. It was about an hour or so after that when we thought, Oh, gosh, we haven't told them! So we went through and there was poor old Vi's mother sitting under the stairs with a cushion on her head all huddled up, and poor Auntie Vi with her, and they had been sitting there all that time. Poor souls. We felt dreadful although we couldn't help but laugh about it afterwards ... One dropped on a tennis court less than a mile away. It was a very close shave. So having stuck this out, going to school in the normal way, it was decided that Bromley schools would be evacuated to Loughborough. I was taken to a family, also called Smith, who lived in nearby Birstall.

Peter Izard
Teenager, Civil Defence messenger and BOAC trainee traffic clerk, Beckenham, Kent

The doodlebugs were quite something. We were patrolling all the time and I got very involved. I pulled an old lady with her throat cut out of a house. I recall vividly coming away from an incident at the other end of Beckenham and noticing some big old double-fronted houses, with everything missing down to the tops of the windows. As I looked up, I saw this flying bomb coming. As I watched, it stopped and the nose went down and it was coming *straight at me*. I just stood there. I couldn't move. I heard this pounding of feet and this huge fireman, in his old-fashioned kit, took me in a beautiful rugby tackle round the waist and we both went under this little wall. The bomb exploded on the other side of the road.

Sylvia Townson (Limburg)
Jewish schoolgirl, Paddington, London

One day my father came home from work covered in dirt and blood, with little pieces of glass in his clothing. A buzz bomb had dropped in Tottenham Court Road, very close to the building where he worked, and the front workroom had taken a direct blast. A couple of female dressmakers had been killed and several were injured. My father and others in the back workroom had to take part in the rescue. It was at this time it was suggested that my mother and I should go on yet another evacuation, this time to Wales to a family we'd known for many years. This was in the summer of 1944.

Rodney Giesler
Anglo–German schoolboy, Hele, Somerset

When the doodlebugs, the Vis, started in 1944, there were re-evacuations. There was a large farmhouse next door and a bunch of Cockney families arrived. My parents were *outraged* – 'They'll come and dig up our cabbages!' The Military Police were always calling because the blokes in the families were always on the run. And when the Americans arrived, the wives went out with them. More trouble.

May Moore (George)
Evacuee, Eyam, Derbyshire

I think we used to hear about the bombing and we did go home to Manchester for a weekend. I remember being in bed at night and lying there with my elder sister. And Joan said, 'Oh, we'll probably have an air raid tonight.' I didn't know what an air raid was, although we'd heard about them. This particular night it was when the buzz bombs were coming into Manchester, we were settled into bed and suddenly we heard this 'wrrr–wrrr–wrrr' and it stopped. And Joan said, 'Oh, it's only a buzz bomb, it probably won't land on us.' She knew from the time the engine stopped, you see. And I lay there in bed and thought, This is what Joan's going through and we don't know all this.

John Hammon
Schoolboy, Stowting, Kent

As soon as we saw a doodlebug come down or heard a bang-crash, we were there. One fell between two local houses and knocked them about very badly. We arrived there and a young lady was sitting with her head sticking out of all this rubble. We started digging to get her out and realized a carpet was completely over her. I got my knife out and said, 'I'm going to cut this carpet because we can't get you out without cutting it.' And she said, 'Oh, John, this is Auntie's best carpet. You really mustn't cut it!' But the house was completely destroyed and it was amazing that she was alive, amongst all this rubble. I think the carpet had blown up over her and saved her – she had a broken leg and was cut quite a bit, but nothing serious. So we got her out. Then she said, 'Auntie's in the kitchen,' but we looked at where the kitchen had been and there was nothing above six feet left of that house. We found Auntie and got down to look at her. Just then a doctor came and he put a stethoscope on her and said, 'It's no good, she's dead.' We then went up to the other house to see if we could help there, but people had already arrived. The main part of the bomb had gone, but the propulsion engine was propped up by some poles with a Union Jack flying from the top of it.

Kathleen Schaller
Schoolgirl, Aveley, Essex

It was the first week of the summer holidays. My brother's birthday was coming up and I was knitting him a sweater. He was fifteen then and working in the City. I had finished it that very morning and was free to go out, which was a miracle, otherwise I would have been killed. I remember putting this big rice pudding into the oven and taking a bus to my friend's house where I played tennis. We saw this doodlebug come over, we heard it stop and fall nearby. But I stayed there until early evening because it was light. Then, as I was waiting for my bus home, they dragged in the remains of the bus which had been near where the doodlebug had gone off. It was on my route, and that was when I *knew*. I didn't panic. I got on the bus and said to the conductor, 'I've just seen a 371 being dragged in. Where did the bomb fall?' He told me. Ah, that journey was terrible . . . It seemed *so* long . . .

The V1 had fallen in a field directly opposite our house. They had cleared the road. I got off the bus and there was no house, of course . . . There were Civil Defence people around and somebody grabbed me and said, 'Oh, she comes from that house.' And they gave me a cup of tea – oh, that NAAFI tea was wonderful! I didn't cry. I was just speechless. I didn't dare ask what had happened, but somebody did say, 'Your family are all in different hospitals and tomorrow you'll be able to see them.' No one told me how much they had been injured or that there had been a death. I was taken into an Anderson shelter in somebody's garden. I couldn't sleep. I lay there waiting for morning. In the morning, this person gave me breakfast and said, 'Go and see your father. He's in the primary school [which had been turned into a rest centre].' I set off up the hill and went past the house of a friend of my father's. His wife came out of the front door, came to the gate and said, 'Where are you going?' I told her. She said, 'I'm sorry about Frances.' Well, Frances was my mother's name. It certainly sounded ominous. I said, 'I don't know what you mean.' And she said, 'Don't you know your little sister was killed?' That . . . that was really a shock.

Then I went to this centre and my father came out. His earlier stroke had affected his speech, but now it had *completely* gone. Then we were told that we had to go and identify my sister's body . . . I think an American jeep took us. As far as I could see, there was no mark on her. I think the blast had killed her . . . I didn't cry . . . I was so shocked . . . When we went to see my mother, she was in a terrible state, full of glass, which kept coming out of her body in small pieces until she died at an early age. She had sent Babs [Frances] in the bus into the village to buy something. My brother who worked in London was on the bus, and got off at the stop. He had a piece of the bus in his head. Fortunately they removed it and it didn't touch his brain. My younger brother was in the kitchen, and when the doodlebug stopped, he and my father went to the door so the top of the door fell on him and broke his leg. I think my dad had plaster fall on him . . . We weren't allowed in the house because it was a shell, but I persuaded them to let me go up the stairs to get some clothes. I can't remember when I discovered that our coal had been stolen, but later I found out who'd taken it – some old bag along the street.

Maggie Hantken (Edwards)
Schoolgirl, Hounslow, North London, extract from her memoir

It must have been soon after 11 p.m. when a doodlebug cut out practically overhead and dived into the back garden of the Hollies, just a few yards from us down the London road. The noise of the explosion was deafening! I was awake in seconds, sitting bolt upright, heart pounding. The bedroom looked like a building site. There was the familiar taste of plaster dust and soot in the air, a carpet of broken glass and plaster on the floor, and a rush of cold air through the bay window. For a few terrifying seconds I knew the true meaning of the words 'quiet as the grave'. The house was deathly silent. No cries, screams or even groans. We all seemed suspended between life and death and I feared death would win.

Then I heard Mum call out: 'Where are the children? The children!' and I swung out of bed and went down the passage on my bare feet, dancing over the debris as though it were a bed of pine needles.

The kitchen – which was really our living room – looked like something out of a horror film. As usual there was no light, the bulb and flex having collapsed with the ceiling. The sash window had blown in and was lying across the back of Mum's armchair where it had fallen over her head, smashed into hundreds of tiny lethal pieces and framed her like a hunting trophy. She said Dad had managed to lift it off and that she was all right, but I could see her face was badly scratched and streaked with soot. The kitchen door had been wrenched off its hinges and had fallen on Dad, where he'd been sitting at the kitchen table. Hitler had certainly been gunning for both of them that night. Dad said it would take more than that to beat us and what about a nice cup of tea? 'Don't be daft,' said Mum. 'All the cups will be smashed.' But after about ten minutes, Dad stumbled back from the scullery, carrying a tray with a half-filled milk bottle, slightly chipped round the rim, three cups, a full teapot with a saucer for a lid and a pint of Guinness. The Guinness was for Dad and we reckoned he deserved it.

Homeless but together, we set out for Gran's ... From the alleyway beside our house, we could see the trail of devastation, about 630 other houses had been damaged. A few had had their exterior walls sliced off, exposing lopsided pictures on papered walls, broken staircases and rumpled beds – backdrops to a crazy drama in which the players were long gone.

Elisabeth Small (Fabri, née Hadfield)
Secretary, air operations section, Special Operations Executive, Baker Street, London

Word went round that we had to come with night attire and washing equipment and we were told we were going to be put in a tunnel under St Paul's. Well, this really scared me. I was scared of being underground, I had slept five floors up in my digs throughout the raids and doodlebugs. But we knew something else was coming – these were the V2s. They really were *awful*, you couldn't do *anything* about them, they were faster than sound ... If they had come in greater numbers, I think there would have been a very great difference [to the war's outcome] and I person-ally was scared in a way I hadn't been with any of the other bombing. People said, 'Why are you scared because when you hear them you know you are safe?' But I said, 'Yes, but that sudden great crash somewhere unannounced is *so* frightening – a devilish thing.'

Peter Smith
Schoolboy, Petts Wood, Kent

Things had quietened down by the end of the year and it was decided that all the children would return to their homes in Kent. But no sooner had we got back than the V2 rockets started. These were a different kettle of fish as there was no warning, just one almighty *crash*. I remember being in class one day when I just happened to glance out of the window to see this streak of light go through the sky, like a shooting star. After that I could see this great pall of smoke and dust rising, followed by an explosion. This was the one that fell on Catford. We had several in our area. Houses were demolished and there were one or two fatalities. I think we were quite phlegmatic. There was nothing you could do about it and you just put your trust in fate or God; if your number was on it, you were a goner and that was all there was to it.

John Starling
Dockyard apprentice, Portsmouth, Hampshire

The V2s entered the upper region of the stratosphere and went at such a speed that you never heard them coming. Therefore they were much more devastating than the V1s. There was no defence at all as they went ten times the speed of sound. Had we not overrun the launching sites when we did, it could well have brought a German success at that time in the war. Had the D Day operations been deferred for another year we would have had it, quite frankly. We had nothing to counter that sort of weapon at the time.

Reg Baker
Schoolboy, Bethnal Green, London

It was a lovely clear night – I'll always remember it – and being the age I was then I could stay out late. And I was looking up, and all of a sudden I thought there was a shooting star. East End people always say that a shooting star means another baby born. And it didn't stop: it just carried on over Silvertown. It was a V2, one of those big rockets. Fascinated me.

Sylvia Townson (Limburg)
Evacuee Jewish schoolgirl, Mountain Ash, Wales

There wasn't much war activity in Wales, but they had one dreadful experience when a German aeroplane is thought to have seen the coal fire of a train and followed it, thinking it was going into an industrial area, and dropped bombs as it travelled between Mountain Ash and Aberdare. But it was a goods not a passenger train, and nobody was killed. That was as close as they got. But, of course, the young working women and men too old to be conscripted or work in the mines were taken to the munitions factories, which were deep underground in the Merthyr Tydfil area. Everybody knew what kind of weapons were being made and that there was a war raging somewhere, but as far as everyday living was concerned, apart from the fact that evacuees were living with them, their lives went on much as they had during the twenties and thirties.

Thomas Houlton
Schoolboy, Hull, Yorkshire

What isn't very often recognized is that Hull was a key port in the Russian convoys. While bombing seemed to end for the rest of the country in mid-'41, Hull's troubles continued for a good year after that, a lot more people being killed. Even after a year, intermittent raids went on. In fact, Hull experienced the very last manned raid in the country when a plane dropped splinter bombs in the vicinity of what was then the Savoy Cinema, just as the people were walking home. A lot of women and children and some men were killed, twelve on that occasion, 17 March 1945. A week after that the last V2 landed on London. Hull had quite a lot of strafing – machine-gun bullets hit the ground in front of me as I walked to school one day. We had oil bombs too. They were designed so that when they exploded lots of oil would run and make the whole place more inflammable.

We must have had longer under air attack than possibly anywhere else. That feeling that we were a 'forgotten city' is still very common today. People feel the city has never been properly recognized for what it went through. They get very frustrated with places such as London and Coventry getting a lot of publicity when Hull's death rate was higher than any other city's. I think it was mentioned twice, possibly three times, in the whole of the war. We weren't the only city that complained, I know Liverpool felt the same. They had a large number of raids, almost as many as Hull. There was a tremendous feeling of pulling together and that's the only way people got through it, really.

Kathleen Stephenson (McManus)
Teenager, Hull, Yorkshire

My grandfather was killed in the last air raid on Hull, March 1945. They printed a paragraph about him in the *Hull Daily Mail* and they wrote that he'd thrown himself over a young boy to save him. The bomb dropped just when everyone was leaving the Savoy Cinema and my grandparents lived nearby and my grandfather had come out of the shelter and apparently had tried to save this young boy.

Patricia Fitzgerald (Stringer)
Schoolgirl, Sidcup, Kent

I was sixteen when my brother was killed. I had picked up the letter at home when I got back from school and left it for my mother and went to the local cinema with a friend. We were sitting there and a notice came up on the screen: 'Would Pat Stringer please come out to the foyer where her parents are.' I went out, my mum and dad were there, and they told me that they had got a letter saying Wilf had been killed. I went to my friend and said, 'I'm going home. My mum and dad are here. My brother has been killed.' I remember her coming up and holding on to my arm. She knew what it meant, but it hadn't sunk into me. Then I saw Mum and thought, Been killed . . . ? and we all walked home. It then hit me, I kind of grew up then. It was 1944, nearly the end, and he had been through so much. He was only twenty-five. That was wrong. War had come.

Frank Bower
Overseas evacuee, returning to Liverpool, extract from his memoir

My feelings were of complete apprehension as to how it would be to meet Mother and Father again. Four years was a long time to be away and I had grown from a schoolboy into a man whilst they had gone through a very tough war. Granny would be missing as she had died in 1942. Would we have anything to say after the first flush of excitement? Should I kiss my father? Where could

I possibly begin to say what had happened to me in Canada? What would Waterloo be like after the bombing? ... Mr Connolly, my father's colleague who was accompanying me, was talking to me. I just wanted to be quiet for the sights I was looking at through the train window: miles of ruined buildings; streets with no houses, just piles of rubble at each side of the cleared cobbles; small gardens almost filled with the half-buried air-raid shelters; ruined warehouses that had been gutted by fire, without roofs and with the charred shutters swinging on broken hinges at the different loading levels. Everything looked so drab and depressing. The trains were filthy; the stations had not been painted for years and rust was showing through what remained of the paint on their cast-iron columns. What on earth am I coming back to this for? I wondered.

We arrived at Waterloo station ... only a few hundred yards to go, and my stomach was turning over with apprehension and excitement. We turned into Victoria Road and walked over those familiar flag pavings that I knew so well. As we reached the gate Mother and Father and Anne came running out and it was all hugs and kisses. No need for words, and indeed I was too choked to speak anyway. It had been a hard war for my parents. The house had been occupied to the full with neighbours who had been bombed out. Father had been in charge of the air-raid wardens in the district as well as running his shipping and forwarding business. Rationing, bombing, anxiety over the last four years had taken their toll and they looked tired and drawn, much more aged than I remembered them. Had I eaten? was the first coherent thing Mother said. My God! I'd been away four years and that was the first thing that came into her mind, as if her last meal served to me in 1940 had been the last time I had eaten! But it was a start, and we had to begin somewhere.

14. Victory and Aftermath

On 15 April, the British entered the Bergen-Belsen concentration camp. Shocking newsreel images of emaciated corpses being bulldozed into mass graves appalled the public: although the Nazis' persecution of the Jews was well known by now, no one was prepared for the scale and nature of the barbarity. On 7 May 1945, Germany surrendered, and the next day, VE Day, Winston Churchill addressed the crowds from a balcony in Whitehall, receiving rapturous applause. Bonfires were lit all over the country, bells pealed and bands played. It was a day of joy, mixed with sadness for the many who would not return. Others had continuing anxiety for men still fighting in the Far East and for those in Japanese captivity, for whom the war did not end until the Japanese surrendered on 14 August 1945.

Count Nikolai Tolstoy
Young child, Bude, Cornwall

I remember that when I heard the Soviets had seized Berlin I was so excited, I ran upstairs to tell my father, who was dressing in the bedroom. And I remember that he looked strangely disconcerted. I think, with hindsight, he probably saw what I didn't see and what lots of people were nervous of [Soviet expansion westward]. But I thought it *wonderful*.

Lady Thurle Folliott Vaughan (Laver Eriksen)
British schoolgirl, Copenhagen, Denmark

When she heard the British were actually coming over the border, my mother was absolutely delighted, and she went into the centre

355

of Copenhagen to wait for her countrymen to arrive. She wouldn't let me go in because she thought it might be dangerous ... It was marvellous when they arrived. The Danes went completely and utterly mad and we had party after party. The Angleterre, the main hotel in the middle of Copenhagen, became the British headquarters, and every morning my mother would walk into the officers' mess there and say, 'You, you, you, you, come home to dinner tonight.' For three solid months we had dinner parties every single night. We had all this meat and stuff, and the officers loved having a proper meal ... I was very lucky because on my fifteenth birthday the Royal Navy threw a party for me on board a destroyer and I was allowed to ask all my friends. Now, can you think of anything nicer than a fifteen-year-old being able to do that?

Pamela Leopard (Brownfield)
Schoolgirl, Gravesend, Kent

I remember a very nasty experience. I went down into the cellar with a friend and saw some magazines there. We opened them and there were all these pictures of concentration camps with the Jews. I've never forgotten what I saw. It has been with me all my life – these pictures of starvation in the camps and of these poor souls, skeletons, really. I shouldn't have seen them as I was only six or seven then.

David Gray
Schoolboy, Bootham Quaker School, Yorkshire

The first time the Belsen photographs were published in the *Illustrated London News*, I felt physically sick and I remember talking about this with other Bootham boys in my bedroom, and looking at the heaps of corpses, gas chambers and the rest – incomprehension that this had happened in *Europe*.

Rodney Giesler
Anglo-German schoolboy, Hele, Somerset

I was fourteen when I saw pictures of Belsen. We saw the news-reels of the skeletons. There was a wave of revulsion. I think by that time we knew Hitler was capable of anything. And I remember the Nuremberg trials well. They went on for over a year. They were covered on the newsreels. I remember seeing in *Picture Post* all the death photographs: Himmler, who'd taken poison . . . Keitel, Goering, Ribbentrop, Streicher . . .

Michael Hart
Anglo-German teenager, Munich, Germany

At the end of the war I joined the American forces in the south and worked for them as an interpreter because I was pretty much bilingual . . . When I was with the Americans in Munich at the end of the war in '45, I returned to my school in Bavaria. I had left about two months earlier. I found two things that were both shocking and revealing. One was that the school was being used for survivors from a concentration camp. And there they were, figures reduced to skin and bones, still in their old concentration-camp dress. For the first time they were being properly fed, but unable to keep food down and being sick all over the place. You suddenly saw – I mean, you'd seen ghastly things during the war, but you saw this *total* misery and inhumanity, and *humiliation* of human beings who were only just beginning to recover. They had survived, but were in a very poor state. The second point was that our Nazi headmaster was still there and working quite humbly in the school gardens. His world had collapsed. He'd been basi-cally a decent man. He had accepted the consequences, had resigned and said, 'This is where I live. Will you allow me to work in the garden?' I don't know what happened to him. He wouldn't have been a war criminal, but he certainly had a very heavy Nazi past.

Richard Hancock
Evacuee headmaster, Winchester, Hampshire

Of course the householders got tired – five years is a long time and their own circumstances changed. But we received an enormous amount of warm-hearted hospitality, and lots of boys kept very affectionate memories of places they'd been in and kept contact for a long time ... Thank God – and I don't say that lightly – no boy at the Northern Secondary School was killed. When evacuation ended, we asked the vicar to conduct a service so we could all say thank you and he did that very nicely for us ... We also had an occasion in the city's Guildhall at the end when we invited all the householders to come to tea so that we could say thank you together. It was simply a tea, not an enormous affair, but it was an acknowledgement.

Dorothy Lester
Evacuee schoolteacher, Corbis Bay, Cornwall

I was still in Cornwall with the handicapped children when the war ended. My fiancé had been killed, and there was all this jubilation. I didn't feel like celebrating. My head was very good – she said, 'Would you like the day off?' I said, 'Yes, please.' So I went off walking by myself from Corbis Bay to St Ives along the moors ... We hadn't had much time together. He had arranged for me to go to Rugby, and we were going to spend the weekend there with an uncle. And I had this telegram, which said, 'Don't come.' That was all, and for some time I didn't know what had happened. Anyway, that was the end of that, and what with being bombed out ... It was awful for my parents at their age. I remember my father kept a diary and after he died I found it. He must have had it in his pocket when we were bombed and he'd written that day in September when the bomb fell, 'We've got no home ...'

I WISH TO MARK, BY THIS PERSONAL MESSAGE, my appreciation of the service you have rendered to your Country in 1939.

In the early days of the War you opened your door to strangers who were in need of shelter, & offered to share your home with them.

I know that to this unselfish task you have sacrificed much of your own comfort, & that it could not have been achieved without the loyal co-operation of all in your household. By your sympathy you have earned the gratitude of those to whom you have shown hospitality, & by your readiness to serve you have helped the State in a work of great value.

Elizabeth R

Mrs. Stafford Smith.

Queen Elizabeth's personal message of thanks to the hosts of evacuees, 1939

Pat Arrowsmith
Schoolgirl, Cheltenham Ladies' College, Gloucestershire

I had been at school just over a year when VE Day occurred ...
On VE Day we were told that we wouldn't do very much, not
to go out in the town, and we weren't to wear red, white and
blue rosettes at prayers – really a list of what *not* to do! ... I said
to myself, 'I hope we're never going to celebrate another victory
day in my lifetime – it would be awful to have another war, so
I intend to make the most of this one.' I decided that I would
go out on the town. At a suitable time after lights out, I put on
my 'mufti' clothes, my civvies, and I went down into the playroom,
out through the window and into the town – *unheard-of*!

First of all I found myself riding around on an American army
jeep. It seemed to go quite a long way and I became more and
more aware that the other women in the jeep were, if not on
the game, very nearly on the game – not a phrase we would have
used then. I was sophisticated enough to be conscious of things
like prostitution, and I felt uneasy so I got off and wandered back
into the town. I wanted to see the fireworks and the lights and
so on. A young fellow of about my own age latched on to me
so I had an escort for the time I was out. He told me he worked
at a factory. I don't think we did very much, just wandered about
... At any rate, about one or two in the morning he escorted me
back to the school. Then I had my first sort of, in a sense, excitement: he kissed me goodnight – an experience I didn't get a great
deal of pleasure out of, but it seemed the proper thing to do, a
long, lingering kiss. This was quite a way-out kind of thing for a
young Cheltenham lady. I was just fifteen.

Reg Baker
Schoolboy, Bethnal Green, London

I thought, I'm going to stay up all night, live it up, like. We had
a party in the buildings, which was okay 'cause you got all the
usual gubbins, as we say. You got cakes and fancy hats and blow-
outs and streamers – I think the mums were more pleased. And

then you got signs up all over the East End, 'Welcome home Harry' or 'Welcome back son.'

Peter Izard
BOAC trainee traffic clerk, Beckenham, Kent

On VE Day I went from Buckingham Palace to Trafalgar Square in my BOAC uniform, wearing an American air-force officer's hat and he had mine on. I went the full length of the Mall and back, met him again and swapped hats again – quite incredible. That *was* a day! So was VJ Day.

Peter Bennett
Schoolboy, Godalming, Surrey

I hadn't remembered much of what life was before the war as I was quite young then. I do remember at the end having oranges for the first time. That was when we were having VE Day parties, street parties. I ate the peel and was sick because I didn't realize that was a thing you didn't do. I remember having my first peach after the war and bananas and, of course, ice-cream. The first ice-creams that came back were water ices and they were pretty diluted and didn't taste particularly good, but they were new and they were different ... And then [later, for Victory Day] we all got a letter from King George VI, sort of thanking the boys and girls of the country for coping during the war and reminding us of what had been done by our older brothers and sisters. It was a nice thought.

Evelyn Fee (Moss)
Evacuee mother of five, Byworth, Sussex

VE Day – no, we didn't have anything, no people up our end of the village to celebrate with. Just damn glad that it was all over. I know I was ...

Noel Dumbrell
Schoolboy, Ashurst, Sussex

On VE Day, we went out in the garden with all our neighbours; we lit a huge bonfire, the first time ever, very unusual then. Everybody made wine: dandelion, rhubarb, mangel wine. They got all that out and we had a wonderful celebration in the garden.

Patricia Fitzgerald (Stringer)
Schoolgirl, Sidcup, Kent

It was a marvellous feeling, when the war ended, of everybody enjoying themselves and letting go. Suddenly you thought that everything was going to be beautiful tomorrow. Actually, it took a long time, but there was definitely a feeling of lifting, the feeling that you could start to live again.

Sylvia Taylor (Bell)
Schoolgirl, Hook, Surrey

We didn't know what was coming because we couldn't remember what there was *before* the war, we just knew that something great was coming; things were going to be different, eventually we would have sweets and there would be things like heating and coal – no more power cuts. I think every street had a party. We were not included [as the family of a conscientious objector] in ours, we had to stand on the outskirts, we weren't really wanted. There was a great big bonfire – we were allowed to stand and watch that ... And, of course, we were always remembered as 'that family'. My father didn't go back to his job in the City. Perhaps things might have gone back to normal if he had done that. Yes, I suppose up until then *war* was 'normal'. But now there was this great adventure ahead of me: no war. And we didn't really know what was coming. We just knew that everyone was happy, very happy ...

Count Nikolai Tolstoy
Schoolboy, Bude, Cornwall

I remember the atmosphere of VE Day vividly. We were taken by the headmaster to see a huge bonfire, and there were Canadian soldiers being carried away drunk, and people were singing in chorus, 'Adolf Hitler lies a-mouldering in the grave ...' And I thought, Now the end of all troubles has come, and it's a wonderful world coming – we all thought that – but for everybody it was an anti-climax, of course.

Carmin Sidonio
Conscientious-objector teenager, Beare Green, Surrey

I was still on the farm when the war in Europe ended. And when we had VE Day, we were all given a holiday, everybody – even us. We travelled to London and I went home. London was *seething* with excitement and I wanted to see it myself. I went to Trafalgar Square and it was a tremendous experience. There were crowds as far as the eye could see, and girls in dresses, girls in uniform, mothers and babies – everyone who could be there was there. I don't know where we were all going, just milling around, really, aircraft flying overhead and everybody cheering. For VJ Day we just carried on with our work. But it was a marvellous experience to go home and say, 'Thank God that's all over.'

Thomas Houlton
Schoolboy, Hull, Yorkshire

Almost the whole of Hull was badly damaged, but it didn't prevent the festivities going ahead. I well remember people dancing in the Queen's Gardens around the fountain – in fact, I was one of them. Also street parties, dancing elsewhere in the parks, mostly just homemade fun.

Maureen Smith (England)
Schoolgirl, Exeter, Devon

When the war ended, yes, of course relief and joy. The joy of your parents and grandparents was so great, and there was an air of excitement, of wondering what was going to happen, and not of always being afraid when you went to bed.

David Morrish
Schoolboy, Plymouth, Devon

There was this great sense of relief when war came to an end. Although there was austerity and the centre of Plymouth was flat, there wouldn't be any more bodies, or any more up at night and air attacks. During the war, we had this very effective lord mayor, Lord Astor, and Plymouth distinguished itself by being one of the first cities to have its post-war reconstruction plan ready. You see, the morale of Plymouth was badly shattered by the Blitz . . . The city was employing planners and architects to rebuild the new city, which kept morale up. After the war Plymouth was able to make a claim on any steel or whatever was available for rebuilding purposes. Jill Craigie, Michael Foot's wife – he was then the Labour MP for Devonport – made the documentary film *The Way We Live*. And we all took part in the mass film scenes in the Guildhall, and King George VI and the Queen came down to Plymouth and inaugurated the Royal Parade with the symbol of Drake's Drum at the centre, and we all felt that something was happening and life was all right again.

Vera Schaufeld (Löwyová)
Refugee Jewish Czech schoolgirl, Bury St Edmunds, Suffolk

I remember the day the war ended. We were sitting in the classroom, the teacher was reading and someone came into the room and spoke to her and she said, 'I have something to tell you: the war has ended.' I said, 'Hooray!' She sent me out for causing a disturbance. I remember standing outside the classroom with all these mixed thoughts. My parents are going to be cross because

I can't speak to them [in Czech or German]. Will I be able to take my School Certificate? Does it matter? I just want to see my parents again. I just want to go *home*. Then, later on, realizing there was nothing to go back to ... My parents and grandmother had been taken to Theresienstadt. My grandmother stayed there because German citizens over eighty were kept there. But my parents were sent 'on a transport going east', that is, to Auschwitz. And that was the last that was heard of them.

Little had been known about the conditions on the Channel Islands until after D Day when a number of escapees made it across the narrow stretch of sea to liberated France. Throughout the war the islanders had felt badly let down by what they perceived as London's unconcern for their welfare and lack of resources. As VE Day was celebrated on the mainland and in liberated Europe, the Channel Islands were still awaiting liberation. The Germans did not surrender them until 9 May, when the arrival of the first British troops in Jersey and Guernsey was greeted with immense joy and relief. Sark was liberated on 10 May, Alderney on 16 May.

Molly Bihet (Finigan)
Schoolgirl, Guernsey

There were rumours that we were going to be freed. A radio came out from somewhere in Les Canishers on a window-sill, and we were listening. And the Germans were just passing by, ignoring us – that was 8 May, and Winston Churchill told us we'd be free tomorrow. The next morning my sister and I woke up *very* early in the morning. We looked out of the window and could see all these boats along the shoreline. We got Mum and Dad up and said we were going down to the harbour. When we got there, the police and constables were there to keep us back. We were right at the front of the people there and we had to wait very patiently – an hour, two hours. Then you could see this little party walking up from the bottom of the harbour. I shall *never* forget it. We had been trying to edge our way through these police and constables, and all of a sudden we knocked them flying, we thought we just *had* to get down to them. I think I was one of the first with my long legs. That was wonderful because these soldiers – there must have been about twenty – headed by a Guernsey man, well, we just flung our arms around them, we kissed and cuddled them, we were crying and they were crying. Their hats were off, they were overwhelmed when they saw us all running down ... I can't talk about this without getting very emotional ... I don't think anyone who was there will *ever* forget seeing those boys coming up. We hadn't seen a soul in British uniform for five years, and *knowing* that the Germans were going to be off the island ... I was just fourteen and I never knew I could feel so happy.

Marion Tostevin (Letissier)
Schoolgirl, Guernsey

Liberation! Oh, that was the happiest day of my life! Oh, it was *wonderful*! Oh, the *atmosphere*! I went down to the harbour with my father and saw the British soldiers arriving – oh, it was wonderful! My mother had always promised, 'When we have plenty of bread and butter, you can eat as much as you want.' And I had a whole one-pound loaf to myself and a tin of Spam. That was *great*. The crowds just *flocked* to the harbour, kissing the English soldiers and cheering them on. They brought those big landing-craft as near as they could get and were throwing out bars of soap, sweets and chocolate ... The slave workers all looked very happy. They were repatriated as soon as possible and could wander around on their own. The funny thing is that we didn't see any Germans. They remained hidden the whole time. It was a great surprise when we saw all the fortifications and realized how many there were on the island. We couldn't wander off because of the mines. It took time for the British Royal Engineers to clear them.

Ron Hurford
Inmate of prisoner-of-war camp, Laufen, Germany

We were liberated by the Americans. The first we knew of it was when their tanks smashed through the great big iron gates. I got back to Guernsey and my brother was waiting for me at the harbour. He had a bike for me and I rode with him back home. Oh, yes, that was quite something coming into harbour, all singing 'Sarnia Cherie', our local song: 'Sarnia Cherie, gem of the sea, isle of my heart [*sic*] . . .' I always get upset when I think of it.

The Japanese surrender came on 14 August 1945. On 6 and 9 August the Americans had dropped atomic bombs on Hiroshima and Nagasaki, killing more than 150,000 Japanese civilians and maiming thousands. Later, many suffered from radiation sickness. The exact nature of the atomic bombs was not apparent for some time, but in effect it marked the opening of the nuclear age – an 'exclamation mark for the world', as Melvyn Bragg put it in his book *Speak for England*. For wartime children about to enter National (military) Service, it presaged a new, terrible dimension to warfare, and reinforced the anti-war commitment of conscientious objectors. They now faced tribunals for permission to undertake non-military service, unless they took an absolutist stance, which could mean prison.

The emaciated state of returning Far Eastern PoWs and civilian internees, with stories of the brutality they had endured, hardened public attitudes against Japan, just as the liberation of the concentration camps had against the Germans. However, it is interesting that those who suffered internment – children as well as adults and PoWs – are often those who today feel less bitterness. VJ Day was celebrated with a two-day public holiday, street parties, fireworks and bonfires, but in comparison with VE Day it was muted. It didn't make as much of an impression on children –

demonstrating, perhaps, that the Far Eastern theatre was indeed the 'forgotten war'.

Jacqueline Towell (Honnor)
British child, Santo Tomas University camp, Manila, Philippines

The end in the camp was so awful that it has cancelled out a lot of the other part. During the last six months, I was in bed in our shack with weakness from malnutrition. If I got up and tried to walk around, I fainted. Then we started getting American dive-bombers coming in to attack the harbour of Manila, and they were very, *very* accurate because not one bomb hit the camp. The whole of the town was very badly bombed . . . The Japanese were becoming more and more scared and they replaced a lot of our guards with Koreans, and our parents warned us that they were much tougher and crueller, we must not tease or play games with them and take as little notice of them as we could. Then one evening we heard this great rumble outside the walls. It was five hundred tanks from the 1st Cavalry Regiment and they literally burst through the front gates of the camp and took it over. This was an advanced column as they had heard that the Japanese intended to shoot all the occupants because they couldn't feed them and were losing the war . . .

Life became very dangerous then. The shelling started and we had mortars in our camp, and after a few days of this my mother developed some sort of nervous thing whereby she couldn't walk and we were having to try to carry her and drag ourselves into this main building to get shelter. It really was a very fierce battle and I should think we were in the front line for three or four weeks and some of my friends were killed . . . We tried to live any way we could. The American wounded were brought into the main building on stretchers to what became their field hospital. Everyone was in this building and we had soldiers at the windows firing out. And that was the first time that this eleven-and-a-half-year-old said, 'Are we going to live through this? Are we going to survive?' Which we did, thank God. I've seen people shot, I was right there. I've seen all that, which is why I'm so anti-war. Slowly but surely, the Americans took the outside, by which time the town was completely destroyed, and then they started to organize to get us away.

Paget Natten (Eames)
British child, Bangkinang internment camp, Sumatra

At times the Japanese seemed so kind and at others so volatile. It must have been the war situation. Once, towards the end of the war, they made us go and dig holes. My mother said, 'Why are you making us dig trenches?' And they said, 'Because we're going to shoot you all.' That scared the living hell out of us children and we started crying and running away ... I can remember being told one day that we were free. And this marvellous feeling, but also people crying and I wondered, Why are they *crying* when we're *free*?' But it was quite an emotional time for the women, who didn't know what they were going back to – so, a lot of crying and a lot of apprehension. But the liberation was wonderful, you had this feeling of euphoria, but we children, our main concern was that food would come in.

James Maas
British child, Lunghuo camp, Shanghai, China

Our liberation seemed to be a rather indefinite affair. Nobody was quite sure that the war was really over. I think the Japanese were pulling out very quickly and there were rumours that the war was going very badly for them. When they left, we felt the war was really over. But we were still uncertain whether to go outside the gates. I remember it was at least a week before I went off with a friend to Shanghai. The city seemed pretty normal. The Chinese ignored us – they lived their lives, we lived ours. The Americans came in very soon after that.

Later on, all the children were taken to the USS *Nashville*, which was anchored in the river, and we were filled up with ice-cream and all sorts of goodies that we hardly remembered, and they took us round the ship and brought us back to camp. Later, not to be outdone, HMS *Belfast* arrived and we had the same event, and today there are one or two photos of this trip on the *Belfast* ... Other people were living in our house and we had nowhere to go, so, like most people, we stayed in the camp until the ships were ready to take us back to the UK. I remember the B29 bombers dropping parachute supplies on the camp and we got to know things like K rations and Spam, *wonderful* Spam! We really started tucking in then. Journalists came in telling us of certain things and using words we'd never heard of, one would say, 'Oh, we rolled up in our jeeps ...' and we would say, 'Excuse me, what is a jeep?' I think we sailed home on 5 November 1945 and got back just before Christmas of that year.

Donald Swann
Pacifist relief worker, Friends' Ambulance Unit, Greece

I believe it was in a camp called 'Efialtis', which is the Greek for 'nightmare', where I heard about the atom bomb. I was just about as far away from Hiroshima and Nagasaki mentally as I've ever been in the whole of my life, largely talking Greek and trying to help these peasants and work out what was happening to them. Our war had, of course, ended. So I think the fundamental thing I experienced was the feeling of it being over and that somewhere, a long way away, they were trying to work it all out ... That's how the war ended for me.

Diana Owen (Houston-Boswald)
Schoolgirl internee, British embassy, Tokyo, Japan

As for the atomic bomb, I felt uneasy about it, rather sad and horrified. Delighted because it meant the end of the war, but horrified when we thought of people like our *amah* of whom we were terribly fond, and also of the kind and friendly Japanese who had been so nice to us and now were meeting this terrible death.

Peter Smith
Schoolboy, Petts Wood, Kent

We had always been told in our chemistry and physics lessons that the atom was the smallest thing in the universe and the fact that it had been split threw the theory we had been taught into disarray. We knew about the huge explosion that had flattened Hiroshima and caused thousands of deaths. The morality of this comes into question, but I've always taken the view that it did shorten the war and saved lives, not only of the Allied troops but of the Japanese as well.

Marjorie Bond (Cranshaw)
Schoolgirl, Hull, Yorkshire

The atom bomb was the thing that demonstrated the change in morals throughout the war. At the beginning of the war it was considered to be very immoral to bomb innocent citizens: bombing should be on military targets only. When the Germans were bombing Britain, the news was always put about that they were bombing indiscriminately and that they weren't attempting to hit military targets and this showed what a wicked enemy we'd got. Eventually all this changed and it became quite all right to drop these bombs on innocent civilians in Japan – the end was justified by the means, which was the ending of the war and getting the prisoners out of Japanese camps. Certainly it was a big shift in attitude. I thought it was a terrible thing to do. I was only eighteen when it happened and I wasn't sure of its impact, but I can remember my father saying, as he heard the news, 'This changes *everything*.'

Pat Arrowsmith
Schoolgirl, Cheltenham Ladies' College, Gloucestershire

I think it was when I was seventeen, getting near to preparing for university, that the atomic issue began to make an impact on me. We had an essay set for us: 'The pen is mightier than the sword.' And the teacher concerned, a very learned lady, picked my essay out for commendation because the theme of my essay was that, certainly, in the past, the pen might arguably have been said to be mightier than the sword, but in the atomic age, it plainly wasn't. I began to realize that one had to water down one's pleasure at the war ending with anxiety of what the bomb portended for the future.

Sylvia Townson (Limburg)
Evacuee Jewish schoolgirl, Mountain Ash, Wales

I was home in London for VE Day, but I was in Wales for the VJ Day party and my parents came down for that. This was certainly an event in the history of Mountain Ash. They had an *enormous* street party in our terrace. I don't know where all the tables came from but they had an enormously long one all the length of the terrace and masses of food and bunting and drink, and *everybody* participated. And the children wore fancy dress. Because I had just come back from London, I didn't have a fancy dress, and this dear old lady dug into her attic and managed to produce a beautiful Japanese kimono and wound that around me, and she had a fan and a parasol and those Japanese shoes with ribbons attached and some artificial chrysanthemums, and I went along in it. How extraordinary when you think about it – celebrating the end of the war with Japan dressed as a Japanese lady!

Andrew Salmon
Schoolboy, Marlborough College, Wiltshire, extract from his memoir

VJ Day remains firmly etched in the memory. It was holidays and coincidentally we were having a barbecue on the Mendips, called then a 'sausage sizzle'. I was told, in true Victorian style, that as the youngest male my task was to propose the toast to the King: 'The King, God bless him.' It was something of an ordeal for a stuttering youth, which made a lasting impression. But there is a better reason for VJ Day being memorable for it touched the family directly. Brother Bernard would be coming home from Burma. It may be all the more surprising, therefore, that the preceding VE Day, signalling the end of the nearer war in Europe, hardly seems to have registered with me, at least in the long term. It was during term at Marlborough College and the cricket term at that. It is perhaps another illustration of how little the horrors of war had touched us. It is indeed true that school, as well as home, had protected us, so that life was a world away from reality.

Peter Smith
Schoolboy, Petts Wood, Kent

I think, with VJ Day, it was more a feeling of relief. Subsequently, of course, the news of the terrible conditions of our prisoners-of-war was very worrying. There was a family living opposite us who had escaped from Singapore, but the father was a prisoner whom they hadn't heard from for years. It was some time before they heard he was safe. Obviously they were relieved to have him home, but he was emaciated and had had a very rough time. I think also that it affected him mentally and he was somewhat withdrawn.

Reg Baker
Schoolboy, Bethnal Green, London

But then, later, the victory parade! The King and Queen, old Queen Mary, they came along and they waved. And all the soldiers and tanks came. The King and Queen visited the East End after-wards and I sat on top of a pub that had been bombed. And I remember the Queen – the Queen Mum – waving to me and there's a *thrill* . . . The East-Enders were *very* loyal to their queen and country.

With the end of war, life wasn't suddenly transformed into the 'sunlit uplands' Churchill had evoked at the end of the Phoney War. Austerity continued for some years: clothes were rationed until 1949 and food until 1954. Worse, some items, such as bread, had been unrationed during the war

but now were included in the scheme. The end of the war with Japan, in August 1945, and the abrupt termination of the Lend-Lease arrangement by which the Americans sent supplies to Britain resulted in even greater shortages.

Many men did not come home, others were severely wounded, and those who returned in their demob suits faced huge challenges of adjustment, given the general uprooting that had occurred since 1939. Thousands of women had brought up their children as single parents, and had relished the freedom to have jobs, their own money and a social life with their workmates. Many resented having to return to the kitchen sink and look after a man once more. Plenty of returning men were not used to the austerity civilians had experienced throughout the war, and yearned for the freedom and camaraderie the war had provided. Children who had been evacuated when they were eight or nine returned home old enough to leave school. They, too, often found the old family life erased. They had learnt different ways and values, and readjustment was tough – particularly when fathers had been absent throughout the war, which applied to all war children, not just evacuees. Much depended on pre-war relationships, and the communications maintained through a father's occasional leave and letters. There was also, of course, a terrible housing shortage, which often meant that families had to share their homes with others. It is no wonder that the divorce rate in England and Wales shot up with 24,857 petitions filed in 1945, compared with 9,970 in 1938.

Evelyn Fee (Moss)
Evacuee mother of five, Byworth, Sussex

At the end of the war my husband said, 'Well, now what are we going to do? Are we going to try to get a home in London or what?' And I said, 'Oh, God, *no*, I don't want to go back to London.' And the children were old enough to understand and, oh, my, no, they were proper up in the air. No, they didn't want to go back. I said to my hubby, 'Well, what about *you*? Do you want us to go back?' 'No fear,' he said. 'The sooner I get back down here the better.' No one was more surprised than me when he agreed to take this cottage in Fittleworth, because he was a Londoner, born and bred. I mean, he was a Cockney to his fingertips. I thought he'd be off like a rocket. In fact his transfer [from the Post Office] came through very quick, which was a blessing because we were keeping two homes going for a time after the war.

Dennis Hayden
Schoolboy, Portsmouth, Hampshire

I think we were glad to get home. It was something new, something of a challenge, and it made us appreciate what we had missed by being away – our own kind, our own people, our own type of life. It's only in later life that I've realized how much I miss the country life and would like to go back to it.

May Moore (George)
Evacuee, Eyam, Derbyshire

I can remember the day we went home and it was very sad. They looked upon us as their daughters, I'm sure. We were always known as 'Mrs Sharples's girls'. On my part, there was some conflict in my affections. Mother sometimes came to visit us and I'd seen her get on the bus and go home. Then I had a twinge. I used to think, There's Mother going home. She's on her own there ... I used to feel ... yes, torn, you are *torn* ... I got so much from Auntie Mollie as a giving, loving person, very much, from both of them, very much, yes, *yes*. And I should say they drew quite a lot from us. We drew them into the village life. Yes, I think it was give and take on both sides. But with me being the oldest one I always had that feeling that you shouldn't love them *too* much. Like Uncle Jim was always saying, 'Remember that Fifth Commandment: honour your father and mother.'

I did miss my life in Eyam at first, although a city like Birmingham had different things to offer: I loved the Hallé Orchestra, which was beginning to come back. But village life was so different. You never walked out without saying hello to somebody. And suddenly you were in a city where you didn't know people. And there was another difference: you hadn't grown up with your parents over those war years ... I'm sure in their wildest dreams they never thought we'd be grown-up when we came back but we were.

Maggie Lanning (Mundy)
Infant, Earley, Berkshire

I remember this shadowy figure appeared in our lives one cold, foggy January evening. We knew he was coming and my mother was obviously very excited, but it didn't really spill over to me. I can remember sitting up with my mother at the upstairs window, me ready for bed, and seeing this figure in uniform with a kitbag over his shoulder walking up the slope of the street to the house. And a little later on there was this person saying hello to me, and then Mum tucking me up and sending me off to sleep. The significance didn't really make an impact on me ...

A little later that year, I can remember sitting at the table and asking to taste the Marmite that my father had wanted and my mother had managed to get. She put it on some toast. I wanted some. I remember sitting there. 'I don't like it!' 'You wanted it, you *eat* it!' he said, in a stern voice. And I had to sit there and sit there, and *sit* there, and I kept on trying to eat it and it was *horrid*. Eventually when my father's head was turned the other way, it was whipped away by Mother – she was on my side over *that* one! ... I can remember a little later in the year when he was home on leave, my father and grandfather sitting down to tea one day and there was cheese on the table. My father dug into it. 'Any more of this, Ellen?' I can remember him saying, 'No, dear, you've just eaten the family's cheese ration for the *week*!' Of course, India didn't have the same deprivation and I don't think the returning troops understood the lack of food that we'd endured. It came as quite a shock to him. Certainly he was very quiet ...

I think our relationship was very strained for a long time ... My sister arrived in 1947. He figured much more in her early years. She was diabetic from the age of five, and being involved with medical matters in his work, his focus was much more on her – the things he did and the way he acted. I became very much the older sister, having to take more responsibility than I should ... My mother was a lone mother for four years, it probably made her stronger in some ways and self-sufficient. We were always very close and this continued until she died.

Fran Whittle (Casselden)
War orphan, Lewes, Sussex

At school there was always the feeling that we were somehow different. This was particularly so when my mother remarried: her younger children had a different name from us as we had retained my father's. We'd constantly have to explain it, 'My father's dead.' 'How?' 'He died in the war.' I have this memory of my mother working terribly hard, but when you think that you lived with someone who was in a terrible state of grief, with all these little children, you don't quite understand what's going on ... Of course I wondered about my father, but I didn't talk about him until I was much older. My mother would be going on about something and I would say, 'My father would *never* have treated me like that.' And she'd say, 'Oh, you have a graven image of him.' I would think, No, I don't have *any* image, really. Yet to me he was always some wonderfully embellished person, not a parent who might say, 'No, you're not going out tonight.' Also, I clung to the idea that had he been there we wouldn't have been so poor, we would have had things, especially in the early fifties when people started getting a bit more money.

Peter Bennett
Schoolboy, Godalming, Surrey

We thought with the end of the war it would be back to normal – we didn't know, couldn't remember, what 'normal' was, but we thought it was going to be entirely different. In fact, I think it got worse for a time. And I think that was when we got a bit fed up. I suppose it must have been about 1948 when we had a holiday in Paignton, Devon, the first proper holiday when you could go into the sea.

Patricia Fitzgerald (Stringer)
Schoolgirl, Sidcup, Kent

It was going to be marvellous tomorrow. You could have all the bananas and ice-creams you wanted, and you could go and buy clothes and sweets too. But of course you *couldn't*. We had to wait a long time for these things. I started work in September 1945 and there was still clothes and food rationing and I still made my clothes to wear to work, which I would shudder at now – but so did everybody else. Even then we bought silk parachutes at Gamages in London, and we spread them out on the office floor and made underclothes and nightdresses from them. And because of the power cuts when we were so cold, we'd go out and buy the fire-service trousers, which we wore to work and changed into skirts when we went in to the boss.

Brian Ryland
Schoolboy, Sidcup, Kent, extract from his memoir

Foods that had never been rationed throughout the war, like bread, became so scarce that they could only be obtained with a ration book. Everything was in short supply, and the situation remained like that for several years. Like 1944, Christmas 1945 had to be the most austere Christmas we experienced. Clothing remained strictly rationed, and even to a young person like myself I remember how drab everyone looked – and it got worse during the coming year.

If adjustment to home life was difficult for children evacuated within Britain, it was even more so for those returning from overseas and particularly acute for those who had been interned.

Ann Barclay (Terry)
Evacuee to Canada and the United States, extract from her memoir

My family were strangers. In spite of all the letters, I was not the daughter who had left them 4 and a half years before. I was an independent young woman. I think it was hardest for my mother: her only child had grown up and she had missed a lot of it ... after the war I could not adjust to civilian life in Great Britain. I'd got used to the hustle and informality of US life. Just as I had been impressed by the openness in Canada – open spaces, open communication with all sorts of people, not waiting to be introduced or making friends only within 'one's own class'.

Sheila Cooley (Westcott)
Evacuee to Canada, extract from her memoir

I had a Canadian accent and a lot of strange ideas. This was brought home one day when a great-aunt asked us for tea and her granddaughter of my age was to be there. We were supposed to make friends but she was in her school gray and I was in one of my Canadian dresses and high heels and I joined in the conversation and she just sat. We had nothing in common ... Life at home was not easy either. Although my parents wanted me to keep in touch with the Turcots, out of gratitude, they really seemed to want me to forget all about my life in Canada and not be too friendly with others who had been overseas. Perhaps this was in the hope that I would settle down and become an English schoolgirl again.

Derek Diamond
Schoolboy, Milford, Surrey

On returning to Britain it seemed a grey and colder place – this would be autumn and the winter. The rationing made an impression because of the absence of rationing in New Zealand during the war. I remember sugar and meat being particularly scarce. The other story I remember well relates to the fact that in New Zealand no primary-school children wore shoes. It was thought healthy for children to go around in bare feet: you played football with bare feet, went to school, shopping, rode your bicycle in bare feet. And I remember after our return to England, going to the local shop in bare feet and the shop mistress saying, 'Oh, you poor boy, don't you have any shoes?' In fact, my parents had a job persuading me to go to grammar school in shoes ... This and the rationing were the two main contrasts I recall.

Jacqueline Towell (Honnor)
British schoolgirl, Southend, Essex

We got back from the Philippines to a different way of life. Our grandparents were living in Southend and I think they were a bit horrified by us. We didn't know how to use a knife and fork and we seemed pretty uncivilized to them. My brother was in very good shape, but I had by that time developed corneal ulcers and couldn't see for a long time – it took me two years to recover. Because I was so young, I didn't lose my sight as so many of the young men in the prison camps did. It was an extraordinary experience when I think back on it now, but at the time we didn't talk about what had happened to us to anybody. When I finally went to school in Britain, I was fifteen.

Paget Natten (Eames)
British child internee, Singapore

We were flown back to Singapore and from the airport we were put on trucks and we congregated outside Raffles Hotel. My uncle Philip, who had been in Changi and also on the Burma–Siam railway, was there to meet us. My mother was looking all around the trucks for my father. The sad thing was that he had passed us and hadn't recognized us because we were so thin and indescribably dirty. I said to my mother, 'It's Daddy, *Daddy!*' She said, 'No.' But it was, and we went into Raffles and he booked us in. Uncles and cousins were there to meet us. They said, 'What do you want to eat?' I said, 'Coconut, banana and rice,' and I had this lovely feast. I remember in Raffles having a bathtub all to myself and being cleansed. And my father standing away from the door, looking at me and wondering, Is *this* my daughter? Is this my beautiful child? Then we were put on a troop ship to Liverpool, then to Southampton, where my mother was taken to Broadlands. Lord Mountbatten had opened up a special wing for the internees, and she was operated on for cancer and was fattened up. By this time she was virtually a shell. I can remember the humiliation of being taken to the baths in Southampton and being deloused and cleansed, and the fact that I couldn't speak my own language . . . The fact that you are suddenly eating good food had peculiar repercussions – your body started breaking out in sores and rashes. So it was most embarrassing going to school not knowing the English language and having all these bandages around you. It was explained to the teachers what had happened, but the children, being children, made fun of you so you retreated into yourself rather.

James Maas
Schoolboy, Britain

It was quite a culture shock being back in Britain. I went to school in '46. They had been told that this Maas was coming a term late and was just released from a Japanese prison camp. There were only three of us [new boys] that term. And one of the boys was extremely thin, and I wasn't thin at all. This boy who'd been in Britain all the time looked far more as if he'd come out of a prison camp whereas I looked quite fit. They thought, Gosh, we've got the wrong boy! My [academic] level was pretty much the same. I was put in the bottom form but managed to get out of

381

that after one term. There was a lot of interest in me for the first two or three terms, but we all got used to each other after that.

Luis Sanz
British civilian of Spanish origin, London

My parents stayed in Spain. I never saw my mother again. I saw my father once, across the French frontier. I couldn't go to Spain because I would be taken for not having done military service and other things, so my father and my [Spanish] wife's father came to the French frontier.

Ann Thornton (Helps)
Schoolgirl, Amersham, Buckinghamshire

I remember telling my father when he turned up, 'I *hate* it here, it's *horrible*.' We did suddenly get everyone's chocolate ration to eat, but what concerned us was the *grimness* and the *tiredness* of the people. Ooh! Coming back to England, even after the war, was *terrible*. These were the people who had really suffered, but of course they couldn't understand what it is to have no law and order and suddenly be taken off as a hostage, but it was an awful life they had had of privation and terrible food. The excitement of living in occupied Denmark was something you never forgot and life never came to that pitch again. And the English never understood, even our brothers. A European had such a different experience from the English.

Separations continued into the post-war period. During the war British women had married Allied servicemen, and with the end of hostilities it was time for them to go overseas and join their husbands. Eighty thousand British women left for America and their GIs.

Pamela Winfield (Witcher, née Phillips)
GI bride, Wimbledon, London

We were married in August 1945. My parents were not at all keen and I had an additional problem: I was Jewish and he wasn't, and certainly my father was against me marrying out of my religion. He kept saying, 'He's so nice. Isn't it a shame he's not Jewish?' In the end he realized that I had made up my mind, but they would not come to my wedding, which was in a register office, and then we had it blessed by a chaplain because we both wanted a word of God involved. And we had a reception in the English-speaking Union ... I trotted into that wedding very happily. I was saddened that I had this hostility from my parents, but when you're a teenager, you're very interested in yourself. You really don't care about anybody else at all ...

I knew a lot about America from the books I had read, and I adored Hollywood, but I was aware that it wasn't all like that. My husband was always very honest with me and I never really had any of the GIs' spin-line. My sailor told me that he came from a small town and that they had no running water in his home and no toilet, and I didn't think that was important. I loved him and that was all there was to it. So, he didn't tell me any fairy stories ... I don't think his mother was very thrilled. The only way I can explain it now is if a girl came home and said to her parents, 'I've met this smashing guy from Siberia and I'm going to marry him and go and live there.' I think that all the parents in this country and the parents in the United States must have felt like that about it. We were foreigners to Americans and certainly the USA was the end of the world to British people.

At dinner parties in England, I can sometimes feel a man bristle once he knows I was one of those girls who went out with Yanks and married one. So the resentment between British and American men was there and still is.

Joyce Reeves (Peach Vaitkus)
GI bride, Teddington, Greater London

Recently I heard another GI bride say that she didn't realize what a big step she was taking until she saw her family on the dock, waving goodbye. And that was my first reaction when I left Waterloo. The whole family came to see me off and it wasn't until I saw my dad cry – which I had never seen in my life before – that it hit home. I remember I waved until they were out of sight, and then I immediately sat down in tears . . . I can remember my first sight of America: it was evening and we had to wait for morning for the tide, so we sat in New York harbour all night. I can remember seeing Coney Island, all the ferris wheels and the lights on them going round, and on the other side possibly Long Island, because there was a long stretch of lights. After being in the blackout for six years, it was a wonderful sight, all those coloured lights. When we came in the next morning, it was very misty, so we could hardly see the Statue of Liberty, just an outline, that's all . . .

I had a picture of him in civilian clothes so I did know what he would look like, but I didn't expect him to turn up in *jeans* – that was another adjustment I had to make because we didn't wear jeans in Britain in those days, and here I was being approached by a husband in jeans. I said, 'At least you could have put a suit on!' He said, 'I've been travelling all night [from Berwyn, Illinois], I had to be comfortable.' So that was another impression: they dressed more casually.

When Britons looked back at life during the 1920s and 1930s, images that came to mind were depression, unemployment, hunger marches, dole queues, the humiliation of means testing and 'the panel' if they were ill – all of which could be blamed on Conservative politicians. Now they wanted something better and were offered a real chance of getting it. Debate had been ongoing throughout the war about the

post-war order. J. B. Priestley's popular radio programme, *Postscript*, urged Britons to fight not only the Nazis but for a more just and equitable society. The Army Bureau of Current Affairs (ABCA) organized lectures and printed pamphlets to prompt discussion, all of which led to a vigorous questioning of the status quo.

The Beveridge Report of 1942, drafted by Sir William Beveridge, was, in the main, received enthusiastically by all politicians. It advocated a comprehensive policy for social welfare and to abolish the 'five giants' of want, disease, ignorance, squalor and idleness. A comprehensive new health service, free for all, was a very popular element, while R. A. Butler's Education Act of 1944 had opened educational opportunity for thousands of British children.

On 5 July 1945 the British public went to the polls. Given the popularity of Winston Churchill as a wartime leader, the result seemed a foregone conclusion, but 12 million people voted Labour (47.8 per cent of the vote) and 10 million (39.8 per cent) Conservative, which gave the latter 213 seats against Labour's 393. Only twelve Liberal MPs were returned to the House of Commons. Ironically, one of those defeated was Beveridge. Despite continuing austerity and the problems of post-war adjustment, there were great hopes for a new start and Britain's wartime children were poised to be the beneficiaries of Beveridge's 'Utopia'.

Marjorie Bond (Cranshaw)
Schoolgirl, Hull, Yorkshire

I think when the war ended people felt they mustn't go back to the old days of unemployment and inadequate care of the sick, and especially that we must have decent housing – that the bomb damage must be repaired and new houses should be built very quickly. I remember being very pleased with the results of the '45 election. It wasn't expected: we all thought Churchill would scrape home. When there was this big Labour majority, it was a very pleasant surprise. I couldn't vote as I was only eighteen. You had to be twenty-one to vote.

Kathleen Schaller
Schoolgirl, Aveley, Essex

I remember when the election came, one of my brothers, although he was only thirteen, was terribly interested in it and I remember he and I talked politics a lot. He was very excited about the complete change of government, even more so than I was. Churchill was very important during the war, an emblematic figure. Politics was at a kind of standstill then, wasn't it? And we didn't know much about it, being young, so after the war politics was very exciting.

John Carter
Schoolboy, Walthamstow, London, extract from his memoir

One summer evening during the [election] campaign I went down to Hoe Street to see Winston Churchill riding in a big open car, complete with his stiff bowler hat, cigar and V sign. Even a man beside me wearing a hammer and sickle badge in his lapel joined in the cheering from the crowds, which lined the route. I also remember the Labour posters and leaflets promising a new future with splendid new houses and towns, schools and hospitals, with full employment and a cradle-to-grave welfare system, plus, of course, world peace through the United Nations – no wonder Labour won with a landslide victory!

Joanna Lawrence (Rogers)
Schoolgirl, West Wickham, Kent

To us Mr Churchill was such a hero. We were shattered at the end of the war when he lost the election – we couldn't believe that we would have a Labour government and not Mr Churchill. He meant so much to us.

Countess Mountbatten of Burma, Lady Brabourne (Patricia Mountbatten)
WRNS, Chatham dockyard, Kent

The election result was not a surprise to anybody with a finger on the pulse of what was happening. Mary Churchill, who was in the ATS, lived an army life, and she warned her father, 'You know, you're not going to get in next time.' The war happened very soon after the Depression, and people's memories of a Conservative government were very, very poor indeed, and quite rightly. It was a terrible time, unemployment and all that, and they said to themselves, 'We've fought this bloody war, we've survived, we're not going back to the same conditions that the Conservatives supported.' It was sad, poor man, for him [Churchill], and to a lot of people it seemed tremendously ungrateful. But nobody was ungrateful to him. Everybody thought he'd saved the country. But I think it shows the good sense of the British people – they were grateful to him on the one hand, but they were going to have something better than they'd endured before.

Jean Greaves (Catchpool)
University student, Somerville College, Oxford

My mother, like my father, had this remarkable gift for friendship and it was really due to her that I kept in touch with my German schoolfriends during the war, because she would send Red Cross letters to their families. They had to go via Holland, and it took six months to get an answer ... I do have personal difficulties about the war – I became very mixed up in my attitude to Germany. I loved the people I knew and remembered as my friends, but the war was a problem for me especially as I was good at German – I was seven when we went to Berlin and twelve when we came back, so I was there just at the right time to make it stick.

We were making food parcels for Germany after the war and my parents had been asking among their neighbours for rationing points to buy foodstuffs as some of the goods were so much needed and they had been a sort of collecting depot for food parcels for Europe. This was called 'Famine Gollancz', famine relief. Oxfam had started by that time too.

Michael Nicholson
Schoolboy, Emden, Germany

After the war, my father was put in charge of the inland waterways of a certain part of north-western Germany, and we were the first British family to arrive in Emden, in 1946. I remember it very well. The devastation was *absolute*. I remember being on my father's shoulders and him saying, 'If you look carefully, you'll be able to see from one side of Emden to the other.' I remember the Germans living in cellars and my father organizing a hare shoot, and they brought in hundreds of hares and rabbits, and my mother and other wives made huge stews to feed the Germans. I was then nine . . . I went around a lot with my father. I remember one horrific experience when he was asked to supervise the exhumation of the British dead for transfer. One hundred or more bodies were in one grave and I remember the smell today. Then we travelled the roads and there would be the debris of war and everything else smashed to pieces, and every so often a rifle stuck in the ground, barrel down, with a German helmet on top, so we were as close to the war as we could be. The Germans, of course, were very hostile, but not the children. I remember the children playing outside and hearing them laughing, and thinking, Good heavens, German children laugh the same as we laugh!

15. Child of That Time

Between 1939 and 1945, 7,736 British children were killed and 7,662 seriously injured within the country. When these statistics are compared with child losses globally – 1.2 million in the Holocaust, four hundred thousand in the siege of Leningrad, or the thousands killed in the last phases of war in Germany and Japan – they may seem light. Yet it was an unprecedented number for Britons at war, and given that 60,595 British civilians perished on the home front, thousands more children's lives were blighted by the loss of parents, siblings and other loved ones. True, British children at home were spared the humiliation and fear of enemy occupation, the thud of jackboots on their streets, but they endured six years of increasing deprivation, uprooting and long separations; and many were exposed to physical and psychological suffering. They witnessed and endured intense air raids, both through conventional bombing and the new terror weapons, the V1s and V2s. Many saw injury, death and destruction, and were forced at a very young age to cope with sorrow at a time when counselling was unheard-of. Those stranded abroad or coming under enemy occupation had their own special uncertainties, sufferings and fears, adding another, often neglected, dimension to the story of British wartime childhood.

Uprooting

Margaret Woodhead (Butler)

When you think back, you realize that war took a big chunk out of your life. In some ways I think we missed an awful lot because things were so upside-down. But it was an experience, and I suppose it's one that you're glad to have had the chance to take part in. When you see youngsters today who are bored, well, we didn't have *time* to be bored. And I think people were a lot kinder to each other than they are now. You did get to know people during the war – there was that spirit, everybody looking after everybody else. Families were split up, of course, but in some ways that brought them closer, because when they did come together again, they appreciated *being* together . . . To be a successful evacuee, you had to be a child who would adapt to anything. I was an only child, possibly a bit solitary, and for me it was hard to accept other people's ways. I don't think I was happy to be an evacuee, but looking back now, it's something I wouldn't have missed.

I wouldn't have sent my children away because I do think it has an effect on a child when they are sent away from everything they're used to. I agree that some separations are good for children, but you could never see an *end* of it. People didn't explain what was going on. You were shipped away and told, 'You'll come back when the war is over.' But you didn't even know what a war was! I mean the day that someone came out of their cottage and said to me, 'It's just been on the radio that war has broken out,' it didn't mean a thing. I just expected that any moment there would be gunfire and bombs. When you heard people talking about it lasting five or six years, you couldn't *imagine* what it was like to be away all that time. I think it must have been a very hard decision to make because parents were torn – wanting to keep their children but realizing what could happen. A very big decision, not one I would have liked to make.

Patricia Fitzgerald (Stringer)

I would have hated to be sent away without my parents, but to go with my parents was just like going on holiday, really. Without Mum and Dad I would have known there was a war on and I would have been unhappy. As it was I enjoyed my little war and I did a lot of things I wouldn't have done otherwise. But the reality of war didn't touch me until much later. Even when my brother was killed and we had been told what happened – that he had parked his jeep near a haystack that had been mined – even then I imagined a pleasant farm field with a haystack, but obviously it wouldn't have been like that because it was at the Battle of Monte Cassino. But even then I saw the world through rose-coloured spectacles – it makes the war seem glamorous, doesn't it? It was for me at my age, but it wasn't for others ... Looking at my daughter now, she had a less exciting childhood than I did. I found the war exciting and my experience definitely made me more grown-up. You learnt how to cope, how to get on, how to mind your Ps and Qs. If there was a raid on, you had to use your brain, but we enjoyed it, *yes*.

Sylvia Townson (Limburg)

Evacuation was a very important time for me. I don't think I would have remembered those years with such clarity if they'd all been carried out in one place with a set routine, as so many children lived their lives. I was taken out of my environment on three different occasions and met very different types of people and because I was a child I had to enter into them very, very quickly and go to their level ... If I felt there was definite danger from attack then, yes, I would send my children away. But I would make sure that I had a close connection with the people they were staying with, and that I liked and understood them. I couldn't let them go, as I did to Great Tew, to an absolutely unknown family. I think in those days the quality an evacuee needed was quiescence. Everybody would love you so long as you didn't cause problems and you fitted in with their routines and way of life. They wouldn't, I think, have expected to come some way to meet you ... At four and a half you're not able to say that above all you need love.

391

May Moore (George)

I think I would send my own children away if I ever thought they'd go to a place like Eyam, a village that opened its heart and its lives, its schools, *everything* to us, integrated us – Eyam, thank you very, *very* much. It was an epic that I think the village should be thanked for, the *whole* village. It was a wartime experience for them I'm sure, and I think a lot of them will remember it. But for evacuees it was *fantastic*.

Peter Bennett

I think parents need to bring up their children. I wouldn't like anybody else to have the responsibility of bringing up my son, *no*. Regardless of what the risks were I would certainly want to keep him with me. Yes, *definitely*. But the next war? Evacuation must be to Iceland or somewhere like that, wouldn't it?

Gwendoline Stewart (Watts)

I think evacuation was wicked because to tear the children away meant the parents were upset, the children were upset, you couldn't lead a *normal* life. And most of these children came back before the bombing started so in a way it was a wasted exercise and it was an *unnatural* experience. Mothers would tear their hearts out at the thought of their children living in another person's house ... Well, my mother had three of us to think about in different towns. You multiply that by thousands of mothers and you have a very unhappy situation.

Bess Cummings (Walder)

A great number of people thought that the parents who sent their children away [overseas] were being scaredy-cats. One lady I know, not only had she lost her children but the neighbours said she couldn't possibly have loved them because she sent them away. I felt my parents were *brave* to let us go, that they had hidden their own true feelings to allow us to go sailing off with such joy. That's a sacrifice. It was a symptom of their love.

Geoffrey Shaw

There is an enormous difference between being evacuated abroad and in your own country. Although Stamford seemed a long way at the time of my first evacuation in 1939, basically we knew we were in touch and, if necessary, could go home tomorrow or my parents could come tomorrow. And although the people I was with in Stamford were of a rather higher social class, basically life was the same – the buses drove on the same side of the road, and so on. Canada was absolutely different: the standard of living was generally much higher there, the architecture was different, the society was different . . . In Canada I was completely cut off from four vital years of adolescence . . .

Joan Reed (Chantrelle)

What an evacuee needs to be happy is kindness, understanding and sympathy, particularly a mother figure, someone you could go to as your own mother. But I think it's the words 'kindness' and 'understanding' most of all. It doesn't matter about the trappings of a home, it's the people who matter, what comes from within, not material things. If you've got that, it makes up for everything, doesn't it?

John Wheeler

Imagine looking at evacuation from their point of view – kids, six and eight. They get their little gas masks thrust around their shoulders. Somebody ties a label on them. They get pushed into a bus and then on to a train and transported to a place they've no idea where they are. And at the end of a long and tiring day there they are, sitting hand in hand. And some big lad, as I was, that they don't know, says, 'Right, you're coming with me.' And they go off to a strange house ... So, looking at it from their point of view, it must have been the most *awful* experience.

Charles Kemp

Adapting depended on the evacuee and the type of home they came from. If they could accommodate themselves, they got on well. If not, then it was difficult. But was evacuation a good thing? At the time, yes. If I had been prime minister I would have done the same.

George Whiteman, billeting officer, Saffron Walden, 1940–43, extract from his report

It is easy to be wise after any event. Looking back at the great experiment one can see some of the factors which were left out by the authorities. They did not recognize the factor of goodwill and the need for fostering it. They do not seem to have antici-pated the astonishing outpouring of hospitality to be expended generously if given the right channels. They made little allowance for the essential difference between billeting schoolchildren and billeting mothers and children together. There was apparently no allowance for the different character of different reception areas, so that people from the dirtiest evacuation areas were quite possibly directed into the cleanest reception areas; or cities with a known preponderance of, say, Irish Catholics in their danger areas allocated to country areas of rigid Protestantism. I even suspect that Whitehall, in planning the reception of evacuees, never contemplated that they would need to be transferred from one billet to another. In at least one district I know that any request for a transfer was refused: 'You've got your billet; if you don't like it, go back.' Transfers were, of course, inevitable. The record in my district was held by one boy whom we tried out in seven different billets ...

I used my evacuation, and that of thousands of other children who were sent into the countryside to save them from being blasted by the Luftwaffe, as one of the reasons I decided to take Natasha [Mihaljcic] out of Sarajevo. When I went there in 1992 for the first time [as ITN's special correspondent], it was very much a *political* story. We were full of Miloševic this and Karadžic that. I went back a second time and suddenly realized we were pursuing the wrong story in Sarajevo, that it wasn't a political story but a story of people living under siege. I remember it was a Monday morning, there had been a mortar attack and some children had been killed and others badly injured. We rushed to the hospital and there was a lot of pandemonium and chaos, and I remember this young doctor said, 'Here, here, here! Look, look, *look!*' and we saw these kids, badly mutilated, bleeding and crying. And he said, 'Show the world. I want you to show the world. These are *innocents*, these are the children who are suffering here. We are to blame, but ask the world to protect our innocent children.' And I started to campaign for the whole week: let's get the children out of Sarajevo. The UN planes were coming in with food and supplies and they were leaving empty. I said, 'Let's fill these empty planes with children. There will be plenty of helping hands at the other end to look after them until this war is over, just as I was looked after by the people in Somerset during the Second World War. Save the children and they can come back after the war.' But it fell on deaf ears. Nobody wanted to know . . .

I had actually done a few stories about the children in the orphanages along the front line. The Serbs knew very well what they were hitting, deliberately targeting the Ljubic Ivezic orphanage of two or three hundred kids. One of the children I met doing that story was a little girl with a pretty face and a very cocky attitude, and I suppose I fell in love with her, and when I had to leave, I thought, Well, if nobody will take any of these kids out, I'll take at least one . . . But, of course, I couldn't do it legally, so I smuggled her out. I'm sure this was my subconscious telling me, 'Look, it happened to you, mate, and you're alive as a consequence of it. At least help *one* person survive this war.' Over the last thirty-odd years, many of my stories have been about children in war . . .

The Legacy

John Starling

I think I did gain from evacuation, I think it made me more self-reliant. Not having brothers and sisters, I feel my mother might have cosseted me a bit too much. But at the age of eleven I was made to stand on my own feet, so I think by and large the experience of evacuation was beneficial. The first night was the worst. I was in a strange house sharing a bed with a stranger, and I must admit that I shed a few tears wondering what I had come to. But after that I tended to accept it, and made the best of it.

Joan Reed (Chantrelle)

I think my wartime childhood moulded my life: I had two totally different experiences, the Ongar time being mostly sad, miserable, unhappy, bewildering, and the school camp being totally different, very happy. I think that formed my character. People were interested in me, the teachers brought out my interest in music and my acting ability. I belonged to a debating society, I was standing up and making speeches – the experience really helped to mould me. Had it not been for evacuation, I would have been a totally different person because my own family background, which was very puritanical, wouldn't have led me into these things. So the war had a *tremendous* effect on me.

Patricia Fitzgerald (Stringer)

It's getting a bit far away now and you tend to forget the horrors and the nasty things, but I think everybody must have gained something. My mother certainly did by going out to work again at the age of forty-four, and in her factory she came *alive* again, making things and having a completely different life. From the days of 1938–9, when we lived here in Sidcup in comfort, with the flower shows and all the rest of it, suddenly to be thrust into a war, and having to think and make do, and go out to work, mix with different people, different ideas, she was useful again. This sounds horrible, but the war must have done a lot of good for a lot of people. It changed the world, didn't it? But I wouldn't like my children to go through it. I wouldn't like another war. It did a lot of good and a lot of harm.

Joanna Lawrence (Rogers)

We gained a tremendous amount of freedom during the war, and gained a lot by being away from Mum as well because she was so repressive, but we lost out educationally – although we did catch up and I think you learn a lot out of school anyway ... We went about the countryside on our bikes, got out to Biggin Hill – we used to go up to the big gun and soldiers would talk to us and we never had trouble of any sort. My children would have given a lot to have my childhood mainly because of the freedom ... I'd rather have had my childhood than theirs, definitely ... For me the war was *fun*. The three years after were rather dull and grim, and all the good things we were promised didn't happen. We'd gone through all this excitement and it seemed very flat afterwards.

Evelyn Fee (Moss)

The beginning of evacuation was *awful*. Leaving London and then not leaving, going back and forth, that part was shocking. And when we got on the coach with the rest of the evacuees, I just wasn't with it. But I can always remember the women and their bottles of drink, singing – more like a Sunday-school outing. And when we ended up where we did, I thought, Oh, well, nothing after this can be worse. But, thank God, I was very lucky, so very lucky. I've got a lot to be grateful for, not all the time ... a lot of worry. I'm sure it was the making of us all, especially the children. I mean we lived in a lovely part of London, not far from Dulwich Park. We had a lovely house, but where we lived was bombed so we would have gone in these awful flats that they put up. God knows what the end would have been. No, I think I was one of the luckiest people out. I do, really. Even the looting of my home in London and the loss of all our stuff, it never worried me. The only thing – and it's funny to say this because the war was so awful for some – it was the happiest time in my life, even though my husband was away. No, I've got nothing bad to say about the war, nothing whatever, and that's the truth.

Dennis Hayden

I think my evacuation experience certainly helped my army career. And when I got married we decided that we would stay together and that my children wouldn't be deprived of their parents' love in any way whatsoever. So even when we went abroad and they said it would be best if we put our children into a home or boarding-school, I'm afraid we said no. We took them with us. And I think that's why we're so close-knit.

My brother, on the other hand, holds our evacuation very much against my mother, that it was the undoing of his career, his schoolwork and his upbringing, that he didn't have the benefits of a normal child's upbringing with his parents. He failed to appreciate that our parents also suffered: they lost two infants who came back almost as teenagers.

Bess Cummings (Walder)

The result of this experience [the sinking of the *City of Benares*], I must truthfully tell you, is one of great advantage to me. I felt that, having survived this, I could survive all sorts of things – it gave me confidence, the feeling that if you tried hard enough you could overcome almost anything. That every human being has a depth of ability which is seldom used – a bit like an iceberg, which has so much underneath.

Reg Baker

I don't think those two years being evacuated were lost. I'd say I was treated well and was with decent people. I'd say it opened your eyes a bit more to seeing things, 'cause you was in your own little East End environment before that . . . I look back now and the only thing that gets to most of us who were evacuated was that we were picked out like prize cattle. And, also, you still had the tendency to run away no matter how good you was treated. Because it wasn't home.

Derek Diamond

I think I was very fortunate to have a very safe and happy five years in New Zealand. But as an adult I feel intensely interested in the events of the Second World War, particularly as they affected people in Britain. I personally cannot recall having heard a bomb explode or a V2 go overhead, or anti-aircraft guns, and many of the people whom I work with recall these noises, events, air-raid shelters and so on, very vividly. So I feel, in some ways, I had a distinctive and different childhood experience during that five-year period.

Sheila Cooley (Westcott), extract from her memoir

I cannot say enough about the generosity of the Turcots for all they gave me, material and otherwise, taking me into their home as a daughter for four years and continuing their friendship for the rest of their lives. It cannot have been easy for them. I don't regret going to Canada, though it was hard there at the beginning and harder coming back, but I learnt a lot and had a lot of experiences that have made me what I am today.

Geoffrey Shaw

I arrived at Nottingham station and hired a taxi – an ancient Daimler – which delivered me back to the family home. It was difficult. Not terribly difficult, but cold, and awkward, I suppose, is the word, because I didn't know them, and they didn't know me. My sister told me recently, 'We were afraid of you, I don't know why.' Afraid because I was unknown . . . I know the only thing that was familiar to me was the dog – Bob. I hadn't seen him for four years and when I said, 'Fetch slippers!', he went over to where my slippers used to live. That was good because Bob had been my real companion and comfort when I was a child, and there he was. That was the continuity, really.

Sonia Williams (Bech)

That experience I had of almost drowning makes me think that when dying comes it won't be so awful. The whole thing has given me a bit of philosophy. We were so honoured by the Almighty that we survived and had happy lives and are so healthy. I think it has made me a bit more tolerant. Also, it gives one the feeling that one mustn't take things too seriously. This disastrous thing turned out all right for us, and I have enjoyed my life. But, then, I'm an optimist – what about that red sail?

Diana Owen (Houston-Boswald)

I think our internment experience in Tokyo was an extraordinary segment of forgotten time. We had a life that was completely detached from any outside circumstance. We were sort of insulated from the outside world and I think one felt, when they started to repatriate us, almost apprehensive of what the outside world would bring because we were all so used to our own little day-to-day relationships. It was a sort of encapsulated time. We were in our own little world . . .

Joseph Stagno

My evacuation to Britain made a great difference to me. Joining the Royal Navy altered my whole outlook on life, which wouldn't have happened if there had been no war and I'd stayed on the Rock. I joined the navy for twelve years, fifteen if I include those years as a boy. So, in 1944, when the evacuees went back, I was in the Far East, so no question of my going back then. It's hard to assess the evacuation from the British government's point of view at the time. Because of the danger of Spain coming into the war, and then of having to feed a civilian population ... with hindsight, I don't think there was any sense to it. They could have taken us somewhere a bit more safe. But that was the way things turned out.

James Maas

I don't think my internment had any lasting effect on me – I was probably too young for it to have affected me a great deal. Many children, or more sensitive children, might have been affected. I think Ballard [J. G., author of *Empire of the Sun*] could have been affected like that, but the average kid, he adjusts to most things up until the age of twelve or so and I don't think it's affected me too much.

Fred Steels

For quite a number of years the experience affected me. Always on the anniversary of the sinking [*City of Benares*] I'd have bad dreams, but over the years it's all passed, all water under the bridge. I think the most traumatic part was as we were drifting away from the ship and hearing all the other children screaming and knowing you couldn't do a thing about it. Eighty-one children went down with her. In fact, two of the boys on our boat lost their five-year-old brothers on her ... You look back on it and think, Wouldn't it have been as safe to stay in this country as to attempt crossing the Atlantic? With hindsight, it would have been.

Keith Goldthorpe

I think my whole education suffered from my being moved about so much – Burma and then India and then back to Britain – and seeing my mother's stress early on. I've never been a very confident person. I think this early stage of my life had a pretty profound effect on me. I was a bit of a loner in a way and only became gregarious when I went to university.

Peter Smith

I had just had my ninth birthday when war was declared and I was just approaching fifteen when it ended, so I was old enough to know what was going on and compare with pre-war life, unlike a lot of younger children who probably had no memory of pre-war days. In those days, although money was always in short supply, we'd had a comfortable life. We always had plenty to eat, and as children we enjoyed sweets and ice-cream – we had sweet rationing in the war and we *never* saw ice-cream. But it didn't seem to *matter*, and I didn't crave these things. Being evacuated to Cumberland, we had a very peaceful life there. It seemed that they didn't really know there was a war on. They didn't experience any bombing and they were rather dismissive at times of what we'd been through. But, of course, it was a *totally* different culture for me. I met people with different ways of life. When I think of it, the war shook me out of a secure but *insular* suburban life. Cumberland was a great culture shock but, being adaptive as children usually are, it proved to be a greatly enriching experience – my love of the countryside and interest in agriculture has lasted to this day and has certainly affected my working life. Also, the austerity of wartime has made me far more appreciative of what I've gained materially. I *hate* waste, especially food, and I have to admit that it's made me very critical of the throwaway society we have become.

Dorothy Lester

The children who went to Wales came back speaking Welsh. A long time before they could speak Cockney again. Evacuees had missed out on scholarships, missed their chance in many places where there were no exams. But the people they went to, having thought of them as dirty little things, discovered they were quite nice.

Mary Whiteman (Walker)

We were very conscious of questioning: what was a country like this doing to allow people to live in such squalor? ... We knew for the first time what slums meant, what they'd done to people and what they'd been obliged to live in, the only life they knew. They were almost used to living with impetigo, scabies and bugs – these were part of life. There is poverty in the country, there are plenty of homes that aren't clean, but there was never that *depth of life* where children thought they had to sleep *under* the bed ... The point is: why did they have to live in that way? That was a thing that was exposed to the whole country through evacuation ... And to have seen the improvement in the health of children living in better conditions with better feeding was a good thing. There was heartbreak, homesickness and so forth, but this was a lesson we all learnt. In a way it *shamed* us, it shamed the country, that people could live like that.

The Enemy

John Tatum

I hated the Germans and the Japanese. My grandmother was of German origin from Danzig; we also suspected that she was partly Jewish. She certainly didn't like the Germans. I remember her running out one night when they were overhead, and shaking her fists at them, crying out, 'Those bloody Germans!' My own feelings continued for a while, and then they changed. I've had

German friends and even Japanese. But I still feel uneasy when Germans walk into a room – my hackles go up ... But I feel that you can't blame people. It's the politicians and arms manufacturers who create wars. I mean, Hitler wouldn't have got anywhere without the support of Krupps and other industrialists. Germans today weren't even alive at the time, and they seem to be one of the most peaceful peoples in Europe now.

Kathleen Schaller

After the war, in 1950, I cycled around Europe with a friend. There were still many signs of war, a tremendous lot. We had Union Jacks on our bikes as we went through France, Belgium and Luxembourg, but when we came to the German border, we took them off. When we got to German youth hostels there were lots of very friendly boys. They made sure our bikes were oiled and everything tightened up as we headed for Rome. We cycled with this group which we called the Glee Club, for a couple of days, and I remember being with them in the ruins of Cologne and Munich. A terrible sight, awful ...

Ron Hurford

We have lots of German tourists on Guernsey today. It doesn't worry me. Occasionally when we talk to them, I tell them I was in the war. At the time I would have killed every one of them, bar the women, although some of the women were just as bad. They've tried to beat us twice and they haven't succeeded, and never will because of that strip of water God sent for the English people, and the navy too.

Sylvia Taylor (Bell)

I didn't know about the Nazis, I only knew about Germans and that Germans were the enemy and that they were loathed, and they'd sent horrible things like V2 rockets and bombs over ...

When I was older I did have books and read a lot and was fed statistics about how millions of Jews had died and many millions of Russians. Seeing it in figures, I then realized just how *appalling* war is. And I began to understand as I grew older the reasons for my father's pacifist opinions, and why he took the action he did. But I think really one can never forgive completely. You can shut things away and you can forget, but it's difficult to forgive.

Rodney Giesler

I used to go over to Germany after the war to stay at my father's place. I learnt German very rapidly because one of the caretakers was a refugee from the East and she was so graphic that even with my basic German I could understand what they'd suffered when the Russian Army arrived. How they just helped themselves to sex, including this lady. The only words they knew were, '*Fünf Minuten, Frau*' [Five minutes, missus]. These were the spoils of war. You couldn't blame them after what Russia went through. I didn't feel sorry for this woman. I thought she'd been lucky to get away from it. The Germans had looked on the Russians as sub-human. It was kill, kill, kill, all the way through ... No, I didn't give a sod about it. I wasn't sensitive to the German half of me because I wasn't aware of it.

Peter Cox

After the war I lost none of the hatred I felt towards this enemy who could intrude upon the lives of so many people and who, therefore, had to be eliminated. Given a gun and an opportunity, even as a child, I would have shot Hitler ... It was not until the seventies that this began to fade and I could permit myself to buy anything German. I bought Japanese products, which is totally irrational except that I excused myself because they had not harmed ME directly ... Then came an amazing breakthrough. My wife Joy and I were running a guesthouse in York, and one of our guests was a German in his mid-seventies. We were talking generally and he asked me what part of England I came from. When I told him it was Coventry he asked if I was there during the war and, of course, I said yes. I saw tears in his eyes as he admitted to being a bomber pilot in the winter raids of '40 and '41 and how distressed he had felt as a young man having to perform a terror raid as distinct from aiming at military targets. We spent some time in each other's arms ... For me the words of Edith Cavell, just before her execution, are all-embracing: 'Standing, as I do, in the view of God and eternity, I realize that Patriotism is not enough. I must have no hatred or bitterness towards anyone.'

Jacqueline Towell (Honnor)

I don't feel any dislike of the Japanese whatsoever. I feel they had a terrible time too. I'm very pleased that I had the opportunity to go to Japan and see the devastation caused by the atomic bomb. We personally never had a problem with the guards and they couldn't have been nicer to us. A lot of people do have a problem, but they probably have a reason, and I don't.

Paget Natten (Eames)

I dislike Hirohito [the Japanese emperor] because he was aware of the situation and could have helped, but I do not hate the Japanese, no, and neither does my mother ... You can't blame the present young generation for what went on in the past. There were things done on both sides, it was the war situation. I just feel sorry that it had to happen to us ...

David Morrish

When we were living in emergency housing, it was suggested by a farmer's wife we knew that I go and spend a weekend on her farm, and I took this up and greatly enjoyed it. It had a significance beyond that because I found myself working on the farm with German prisoners-of-war ... This was quite a shock to the system, because I had come through the Blitz, hating and loathing the Germans who were trying to kill me and had succeeded in killing quite a few of my friends, and here I was actually meeting them and expected to sit down and eat with them and work with them. And I realized that they were very nice people, concerned about their families and their kids. I suppose I didn't become a pacifist at that point but, looking back, I began to ask myself some rather awkward questions that I wasn't finding easy answers to ... I took the decision to become a conscientious objector in 1956 when, after university, national service was looming. I had a tribunal and went into the Friends' Ambulance Service. Their motto, following that of the FAU China convoy during the war, was 'Go anywhere, do anything' essentially to help humanity in times of strain and conflict, and that's what I did.

Carmin Sidonio

I had realized, sharing arguments with my conscientious-objector friends in the hostel, that I was very much in agreement with some of the points they made. I knew then that whatever happened, whatever war, I would not take part in one. No war is *ever* justified and this feeling stemmed from that war when I saw that people who had lived in neighbouring countries could go and kill each other. I don't know if there's an alternative, but I feel that there is never enough *talking*, and always too much aggressiveness.

John Tatum

I thought at the end of the war, *Surely* there can't be any more wars after this! And I'm very disappointed that there have been, even in the twenty-first century. I'm very anti-war today, very cynical about it. I think wars are fomented by power-hungry politicians and arms manufacturers, and resources like oil come into it – it's all about the territorial imperative, and the working people are conned into it. But I *do* think we had to go to war to defend ourselves against Hitler.

I was fifteen when the war began, and I think I had a fatalistic view of it and what was going to happen. There is a phrase used in the First World War by a writer called Randolph Bourne who talks about how in wartime the state and nation become what, unfortunately, they can't become in peacetime, and he talks of the nation 'lumbering into the great peacefulness of being at war'. It's a phrase that has always stayed in my mind because there is truth in it. Not only people like me, but I'm sure plenty of people thought their destinies were being solved for them: they didn't have to think for themselves and act for themselves. And, of course, people do cherish the sense they perceive of national and common initiatives in wartime. And the war was, in that sense, a peaceful period.

War Child

Kathleen Korybut (Daly)

Trying to see myself as the stranger who might one day read this, I find it hard to credit the extraordinary sense of happiness which fills me when I look back on that night (of our first big raid in Dunkirk) and the days which followed. Surely I should be filled with sorrow and hate as I think of all the things we lost and shall never see again, the lives that were lost, the homes that were destroyed. But because I am the child whose heart thrilled with excitement those five years ago (is that all?), I know that I was happy because my life was filled with danger and adventure, as it has never been before or will be again.

Pamela Leopard (Brownfield)

I was a war child, yes, but I was happy and there was excitement. War for me was *normal*. There was austerity still after the war but they were special years. People were looking up, and things were going to improve and of course they have. Things could only go up for us war children.

Rodney Giesler

I was so locked into the war. My involvement was really as a schoolboy, and it was *exciting*. The fear I felt at the outbreak vanished very quickly – it's the Dennis Potter *Blue Remembered Hills* thing. When I aimed my bicycle down a hill and took my feet off the pedals and put my nose on the handlebars, I was a dive-bomber, and there was a U-boat about to crash-dive at the bottom. All kids were the same. Yes, it was a small boy's involvement. We never saw any suffering ...

John Leopard

Most of the time the war was exciting for us. My childhood *was* war. I don't know if children would put up with it, these days. It was a case of keeping your pecker up and getting on with it. I think it was normal life to us: seeing soldiers in uniform everywhere, air raids going off, ambulance and fire engines all over the place – this was *normal*. It was a brutal war for me in that I lost my father and mother, and with my bombing experience, I saw a lot of death. But this would be quite normal for those living in London – people in the docks and Bermondsey and other areas experienced traumatic times, some far worse than I experienced. My experience was not unusual at the time. No, a hell of a lot of people, children especially, experienced *far* worse. You remember the good parts, or try to, but funnily enough, from the age of twelve or thirteen, people always considered me a lot older than I was, so whether the experience made me grow up that much sooner, I don't know.

Fran Whittle (Casselden)

I hadn't really accepted that my father was gone. I remember looking at pictures of the soldiers coming home from the Korean War and thinking, He might be here. I was searching newspaper photos ten years afterwards for a man I never knew, and from a war that wasn't actually connected to his loss. I have this almost unnatural love for men who represent my father: they are the same age, they were in the same war, and when I see elderly men now, I want to go up to them and *hug* them, and thank them for what they did ... And then the kind of memorial things that go on: I remember coming across one when I was in college, suddenly seeing all these poppies falling down. It just *hits* you like a thunderbolt. I suppose that's what they're all about – triggering people's emotions and not letting them forget. But they're *searing* for those who *are* trying to forget and these wounds keep coming back ... I'm a member of the Peace Movement and I always feel that in a way I do it for my dad – he and all the others who gave their lives so that we could live in peace. So, despite my lack of direct memory of the war, it's had a *huge* impact on my life. It's a point of reference which stems from the loss of my father and the effect it had upon my mother, as well as the pathways that were set for us all by his death.

Thomas Houlton

I think for a little boy of eight, nine and ten, the war was really exciting. It wasn't until you realized at school that your friend had lost a mother or father or some child had been killed, that you knew it was more serious. But I would actually crack jokes about it. When bombs were dropping I would say, 'Number seven is ours!'. The neighbour who came into our shelter got very hysterical about me and my little jokes, which of course made me all the worse.

Peter Izard

I suppose the strangest thing for me about the war was going from the warden's house one night in the Blitz to take a message. I stopped outside my house on my bike. Everything had gone quiet, people were talking, and there was this strange person outside the house wearing a fire-watcher's steel helmet – this was big and quite different from anything else – and this person, a woman, was wearing slacks and smoking a cigarette in *public*. It was my *mum*! She said, 'I've taken a leaf out of your book, I'm much calmer being out here ...'

John Tatum

I do feel a certain nostalgia for aspects of the war – people pulled together a lot and shared hardships. For me war was my *normal* experience. That's what we grew up into – war.

Noel Dumbrell

I don't talk a lot about the war. I didn't really do anything apart from being a boy and growing up, but I *think* a lot about it. It did mean a lot to me to be a war child: if I had my life over again, I'd like to go through the same type of thing again. I think it did me the power of good, made me a good, honest citizen. It helped me. I had to use my brain a lot, the survival stuff. And meeting other people like the evacuees, they were lovely people and really appreciated what we did for them. But I dream occasionally, especially if I'm not very well, the same dream of aeroplanes crashing. I think it's because of that one that went round and round in the field and crashed on my grandmother's house. Always aeroplanes crashing, because I must have seen dozens and dozens falling out of the sky on fire.

Geoffrey Shaw

War child? I don't know what that is. I consider myself a child who did a lot of interesting things. Canada changed me, changed my life. What would have happened to me if I hadn't gone? I was a pragmatic sort of person, took things as they came. It came from our home situation and surviving in a very difficult time pre-war, and accepting that we had to get on with things. Life is what happens, really.

Paget Natten (Eames)

I was under four years old when Singapore fell, so about seven at the time of liberation. You grew up so very, *very* quickly. You didn't have a childhood and later you found it very hard to assimilate because you were so independent and so wild and shrewd and cunning because you missed a very valuable part of your childhood ... My mother said that one of the most peculiar things for her was watching this tiny person go round the camp looking for ways to get over the wall. All the time I used to pace the place, wondering, How can I get out of here to the other side? And Mum used to take me and say, 'Just for now, you can't go over.' Evidently I turned round one day and said, rather vehemently, 'I will not ever, *ever* be told not to do this and not to do that again.' So it hasn't helped my attitude towards authority. But in a way it has made me more tolerant: there were so many acts of kindness that I remember as a child during the war, and without them I would not be here today ...

May Moore (George)

Wartime was a fantastic era to experience. I think the British people, and the humour that came out of the war, will be remembered for ever. You just put up with rationing, darkness, couldn't buy this, couldn't buy that, disasters, heartbreaks. You just put up with it.

Kathleen Schaller

My father died in '46. He never really recovered from the bombing, and the small house we moved into was in an awful area. We never really liked it, and we were very poor. The war did make a big difference to growing up. Without it I think I would have had my parents for longer – my mother and father both died at fifty-four. That's no age, is it?

Iris Hobby (Cutbush)

I was sixteen when war started, twenty-one at the end. Most of my teen years were in the war. I often look back and think how things would have been different without the war. I mean they took all my teenage life. That's why I'm now an 'old-age teenager'! For many of us it took six years of our young lives, and a lot of the boys I was at school with were killed – it was not a good time for anyone of our age group, really. But, then, it depended on what your war experience was: some had satisfaction and recognition if they were in the ATS or the WRNS, but you certainly didn't in the [Women's] Land Army although I don't regret that I was helping to save the country from starving and I know we were all doing a good job.

Carmin Sidonio

All my teenage years were wartime. I became nineteen in the August of 1945. I know 'teenager' wasn't used then, but it was John, my friend in the hostel, who said to me, 'Well, that's the last year you'll be a teen, you'll be twenty next year and you'll be a man.' I realized then that, from the age of thirteen, my experience had been marvellous, really: being a schoolboy evacuee, then taking my first job and learning a bit of a profession. I'd travelled the country from the north of Scotland to London, from London to Sussex and Sussex to Cornwall – which I would never have done previously. And in all that I'd got some education – practical as well as the other. Yes, that was growing up in the war. One person's experience.

Barbara Partridge (Bech)

The war was a funny time. Once it all began, the thing one noticed as a teenager was that there was nobody around who was just that little bit older than yourself, just yourself and then older men, and in between they weren't there, except as figures in uniform buzzing here and there, concerned with things that didn't

413

concern you. I have a very old friend, a year younger than me, and he says, 'Yes, in a curious way we're the lost generation. All we were asked to do was to keep our heads down and not be a nuisance – too young for the war effort and a bit old to be "dear little children".'

I think my wartime experience left me much more able to take any sort of disaster, and I think this is common to an enormous amount of people. A disaster is a disaster, and all you can do about it is just carry on. That was absolutely glued in by the war. Also that you can never take anything except today for granted. I have never believed that life will go on being lovely for ever and ever, because I've known that anything could happen within twenty-four hours, and I think it gives one great strength because you're not thrown out by anything. You can be bereaved, but it doesn't come as such an outrage as it seems to people nowadays. Death is something you live with, it can happen any time. That is what the war taught me.

Jill Monk (Holman)

I think what you've got to realize is that we were really different people from the sixteen-year-olds of today. We didn't have the amusements – the television, the clubbing, all that sort of thing. We made our own amusements and we had respect for our elders and betters. We hadn't the material things and things were very short ... I don't think people today can realize what it was like and what our attitude was. King and country meant a lot to us, in those days. There were none of these snide programmes belittling standards, and there wasn't the out-and-out forefront of sex – that was all very hush-hush. And, quite honestly, I think we were much nicer people. So it seemed quite normal to be doing this [secret Auxiliary work]: it was war work, one was going to help *win* the war.

Peter Smith

A big difference, of course, between war children in Britain and those in the Channel Islands or occupied Europe was that we didn't have enemy troops stationed on our soil. We enjoyed seeing all the Allied troops, but that was a completely different situation from having *enemy* troops to contend with – they were friends, not foe. On the other hand, we knew what it was like to be bombed or even machine-gunned, and we were one of the very few countries to suffer from the V1 and V2 weapons – I think only Belgium was the other country to experience these.

Throughout the war, the propaganda was hugely pro-Soviet and we all admired the heroic stand the Red Army made at Stalingrad, and the population, too, during the siege of Leningrad. But it seemed that once the war ended, the official attitude changed and the propaganda had an anti-Soviet slant and the Cold War developed. At times this flared into hot wars in places like Malaya and Korea. So, instead of this long period of peace we'd all hoped to enjoy, we've had nothing but conflict ever since. Very disappointing. And the terrible revelations of the Holocaust against the Jewish population: there have been similar atrocities in Cambodia, Bosnia, Rwanda and now Darfur. It goes on and on . . .

Jack Keeley

At the time I was disappointed not to go to Canada, but I often wonder now: where were we going? To me then North America was the land of the cowboy, wide open spaces: everyone had a swimming-pool, everyone had cars, everyone was rich in America and Canada. But looking at it today, where exactly *were* we going? . . . I've since heard criticisms of parents sending their children away, but history is made in the circumstances of the time. You can't judge people sixty years later. Look at that man in Brixton! Five children gone, what did *he* feel? He made his decision to send his children overseas based on the circumstances of the time – the Blitz and fears of invasion. Today on the TV you see pictures of cheerful Cockneys laughing at Hitler and all that business-as-usual stuff. But it wasn't exactly like that and we all know it ... And they talk of 'sixty years of peace', but it hasn't been: we've had Korea, the Falklands, Kosovo and now Iraq. I don't think governments *ever* learn.

Suggested Reading

Addison, Paul, *The Road to 1945, British Politics and the Second World War*, Jonathan Cape, London, 1975

Bragg, Melvyn, *Speak for England*, Martin Secker and Warburg, Bury St Edmunds, 1976

Bunting, Madeleine, *The Model Occupation: The Channel Islands under German Rule 1940–1945*, HarperCollins, London, 1996

Calder, Angus, *The People's War*, Jonathan Cape, London, 1995

Fussell, Paul, *Wartime: Understanding and Behaviour in the Second World War*, Oxford University Press, 1989

Gardner, Juliet, *Wartime*, Headline, London, 2004

Gardner, Juliet, *The Children's War*, Piatkus, London, 2005

Goodman, Susan, *Children of War: The Second World War Through the Eyes of a Generation*, John Murray, London, 2005

Lewis, Peter, *A People's War*, Methuen, London, 1986

Mann, Jessica, *Out of Harm's Way, The Wartime Evacuation of Children from Britain*, Headline, London, 2005

Marwick, Arthur, *The Home Front, the British and the Second World War*, Thames and Hudson, London, 1976

Moorhead, Caroline, *Troublesome People: Enemies of War 1916–1986*, Hamish Hamilton, London, 1987

Orwell, Sonia and Angus, Ian (eds), *The Collected Essays, Journalism and Letters of George Orwell*, Volume II: *My Country Right or Left*, 1940–43; Volume III: *As I Please*, 1943–45, Secker and Warburg, London, 1968

Perry, Colin, *Boy in the Blitz, the 1940 Diary of Colin Perry*, Sutton Publishing, Stroud, 2004

Titmuss, Richard M., *Problems of Social Policy*, HMSO, London, 1950

Waller, Maureen, *London 1945*, John Murray, London, 2004

Wicks, Ben, *No Time to Wave Goodbye*, Bloomsbury, London, 1988

Ziegler, Philip, *London at War*, Sinclair-Stevenson, London, 1995

Contributors: Sound Archive

Each contributor's surname is followed by their maiden name
(if appropriate), their date of birth, and the reference number in the
Sound Archive, Imperial War Museum, where their account is kept.

Arrowsmith, Pat, 2/3/30 (12525)
Baker, Reg, 1930 (6498)
Bech, Derek, 29/4/31 (23832)
Bennett, Peter, 7/4/33 (6087)
Biglin, Peter, 23/3/29 (13541)
Bihet (Finigan), Molly, 20/8/31 (12090)
Bond (Cranshaw), Marjorie, 26/9/26 (9978)
Bullman (Tipson), Vera, 3/2/27 (5418)
Carter, John, 16/4/32 (29481)
Collyer (Murden), Myra, 18/6/24 (23845)
Cummings (Walder), Bess, 13/12/24 (20291)
Diamond, Derek, 1933 (18630)
Dumbrell, Noel, 24/12/30 (27236)
Eddington, Paul, 18/6/27 (9328)
Fee (Moss), Evelyn, adult (6236)
Fitzgerald (Stringer), Patricia, 30/5/29 (9829)
Folliott Vaughan (Laver Eriksen), Thurle, Lady, 17/5/30 (19820)
Gibson, John, 26/8/26 (24708)
Giesler, Rodney, 2/2/31 (14822)
Goldthorpe, Keith, 15/1/38 (20290)
Gray, David, 10/10/31 (11733)
Greaves (Catchpool), Jean, 19/9/23 (16835)
Habesch, Geoffrey, 5/4/24 (10304)
Hammon (Cobb), Audrey, 11/4/30 (28744)
Hammon, John, 8/2/28 (28745)
Hancock, Richard, adult (5381)

Hart, Michael, 1/5/28, (21608)

Hartley (Saunders), Doreen, 17/2/25 (23130)

Hayden, Dennis, 11/3/32 (5266)

Hobby (Cutbush), Iris, 30/3/23 (18274)

Houlton, Thomas, 3/2/31 (13141)

Hurford, Ron, 3/8/26 (17520)

Izard, Peter, 17/6/28 (20999)

Keeley, Jack, 27/7/31 (20529)

Kemp, Charles, adult (6120)

Kemp (Drinkwater), Ena, adult (6121)

Knowles (Watkins), June, 24/6/23 (22599)

Lanning (Mundy), Margaret, 'Maggie', 7/12/41 (29072)

Lawrence (Rogers), Joanna, 1929 (6013)

Leopard, John, 30/8/37 (27759)

Leopard (Brownfield), Pamela, 6/1/37 (27760)

Lester, Dorothy, adult (14686)

Maas, James, 22/10/32 (25202)

Martinez, Jesus, 'Cai', 23/2/23 (16488)

Mead (Weller), Irene, 9/4/26 (5343)

Monk (Holman), Jill, 23/3/26 (29234)

Moore, Deryck, 11/10/26 (10884)

Moore (George), May, 19/2/27 (6353)

Morgan (Miller), Millicent, 21/2/28 (5391)

Morrish, David, 17/5/31 (10116)

Mountbatten of Burma, Countess, Lady Brabourne (Patricia
    Mountbatten) 14/2/24 (28632)

Natten (Eames), Paget, 8/4/39 (10691)

Needham, Robert, 7/11/28 (22070)

Nicholson, Michael, 9/1/37 (21537)

Oliver (Adams), Margaret, 'Meg', 2/1/32 (22231)

Owen (Houston-Boswald), Diana, 2/4/25 (8702)

Parker, Tony, 25/6/23 (9233)

Partridge (Bech), Barbara, 15/8/26 (20490)

Patten (Brown), Marguerite, adult (16630)

Reed (Chantrelle), Joan, 16/1/26 (5390)

Reeves (Peace Vaitkus), Joyce, 4/5/26 (9612)

Ryder Richardson, Colin, 19/7/29 (20805)

Sanz, Luis, 1921 (9746)

Schaller, Kathleen, 25/5/28 (16482)

Schaufeld (Löwyová), Vera, 29/1/30 (17469)

Shaw, Geoffrey, 31/1/27 (29232)

Shipton (Attlee), Janet, 25/2/23 (22578)

Sidonio, Carmin, 4/8/26 (15738)

Small (Fabri, née Hadfield), Elisabeth, 14/7/24 (29491)

Smith (England), Maureen, 20/8/33 (15244)

Smith, Peter, 28/8/30 (29071)

Sparks, Kenneth, 29/6/27 (22230)

Stagno, Joseph, 25/2/27 (6203)

Starling, John, 18/2/27 (5420)

Steels, Fred, 22/5/29 (23792)

Stephenson (McManus), Kathleen, 19/12/23 (13371)

Stewart (Watts), Gwendoline, 1925 (5334)

Swann, Donald, 30/9/23 (9133)

Tatum, John, 26/6/23 (28751)

Taylor (Bell), Sylvia, 1935 (5382)

Thornton (Helps), Ann, 26/9/26 (19778)

Tolstoy, Nikolai, Count, 1935 (10721)

Tostevin (Letissier), Marion, 18/7/30 (17517)

Towell (Honnor), Jacqueline, 1933 (23815)

Townson (Limburg), Sylvia, 1935 (5417)

Ward, Colin, 14/8/24 (9327)

Wheeler, John, 26/8/29 (6204)

Whiteman (Walker), Mary, adult (9730)

Whittle (Casselden), Francess, 'Fran', 28/6/44 (29166)

Williams (Bech), Sonia, 7/12/29 (23173)

Winfield (Witcher, née Phillips), Pamela, 14/12/25 (9947)

Woodhead (Butler), Margaret, 9/10/28 (5380)

Wright (Rathbone, née Clough), Beatrice, Lady, adult, (12030)

Contributors: Documents

Each surname is followed by the subject's maiden name (if appropriate), their date of birth, and the reference number in the Documents Department, the Imperial War Museum, where their account is filed.

Alexander, Leslie, 14/12/31 (04/12/1)

Atkey, Molly Walford, (88/26/1)

Barclay (Terry), Ann, 1925 (91/37/1)

Barnett, Guy, 21/8/27 and Tongs, Derek, of similar age (61/19/1)

Bower, Frank, 1/8/26 (96/31/1)

Carter, John, 16/4/32 (KM 14524)

Cooley (Westcott), Sheila, 24/3/29 (92/16/1)

Cox, Peter, 3/8/31 (KM 14606)

Edwards (Huzzard), Dorothy, 1/12/27 (61/75/1)

Greenwood, Mrs (05/15/1)

Grice (Hearn), Elizabeth, 'Bussie', 1926 (91/37/1)

Grimsdale (MacKay), Shiela 10/12/26 (87/23/1)

Hantken (Edwards), Margaret, 'Maggie', 29/10/39 (KM 13975)

Howell, Madge, adult (KM 14318)

Huzzard, Ronald, 'Ronnie', 29/2/20 (61/75/1)

Korybut (Daly), Kathleen, 30/4/30 (61/70/1)

Mingo (Ursell), Marjory, 2/2/28 (96/55/1)

Myatt, Mr and Mrs (05/56/1)

Perry, Colin, 12/2/22, *Boy in the Blitz*, the 1940 diary of Colin Perry, Sutton Publishing

Pritchard, David, 26/6/39 (61/68/1)

Rhodes (Willmot), Lorna 17/9/31 (05/15/1)

Ryland, Brian, 6/12/30 (KM 14595)

Salmon, Andrew, 30/11/30 (KM 14607)

Shaw, Geoffrey, 31/1/27 (97/21/1)

Sutton (Willmot), Charmian 29/6/25 (05/15/1)

Whiteman, George W., adult (86/61/1)
Willmot, Graham, 13/7/28 (05/15/1)
Woods (Cox), Eileen, 6/6/35 (61/66/1)
Wood, Roger, 8/3/34 (MISC 257 (3524))

Index

427